Women in the Chinese Enlightenment

Women in the Chinese Enlightenment

Oral and Textual Histories

WANG ZHENG

University of California Press

BERKELEY   LOS ANGELES   LONDON

University of California Press
Berkeley and Los Angeles, California

University of California Press, Ltd.
London, England

© 1999 by the Regents of the University of California

Library of Congress Cataloging-in-Publication Data

Wang, Zheng.
    Women in the Chinese enlightenment : oral and textual histories /
Wang Zheng.
        p.   cm.
    Includes bibliographical references and index.
    ISBN 0-520-21350-5.—ISBN 0-520-21874-4 (pbk. : alk. paper)
        1. Women—China—Social conditions.   2. China—Feminism.
3. Feminists—China—Interviews.   4. China—History—May
Fourth movement, 1919.   I. Title.
    HQ1767.W39   1999
    305.42'0951—dc21   98-46954
                                        CIP

Manufactured in the United States of America

9 8 7 6 5 4 3 2 1

To Lu Lihua, Zhu Su'e, Wang Yiwei,
Chen Yongsheng, and Huang Dinghui

Contents

Photographs

Acknowledgments

This book is a result of a long intellectual journey that began when I crossed the Pacific Ocean for the first time. I owe many debts to all my teachers, friends, and colleagues who enabled me to reach new vistas.

The book began as a dissertation, and I give special thanks to Susan Mann, Ruth Rosen, and Don Price, the members of my dissertation committee, for their intellectual guidance and encouragement. Susan Mann worked with me from my first interview transcript to the final manuscript for the press; without her unfailing support as I explored themes and formats, this book might not exist. My debts to Ruth Rosen go back to the early days of my graduate school, when she fostered my interest in women's history. The inspiration for this book came from numerous conversations with her and students in her classes on U.S. feminism. Don Price introduced me to the intellectual history of the May Fourth era, which resulted in my fascination with this period. Throughout the project, I benefited greatly from his knowledge of the Republican period. My mentors served as my editors as well. Their grammatical corrections dotted several drafts of the dissertation. The readability of the book owes much to their help.

I am also deeply grateful to two Americanists who had an indirect effect on this book. The late Roland Marchand, with his extraordinary intellectual and moral power, enlightened me on the meanings of being an intellectual and the responsibilities of an academician. It is my great regret that he did not live to see this book. David Brody, who graded my first paper in graduate school, taught me to pursue clarity in thinking and writing. I was privileged to have these two as mentors at the beginning of my career as a historian.

Many friends and colleagues read the entire dissertation and made valuable criticism and comments. Their wisdom, generosity, and encouragement inspired me tremendously and simplified the revision process. I offer deep gratitude to Dorothy Ko, Gail Hershatter, Marilyn Young, Karen Offen, Abigail Stewart, Yi-Tsi Feuerwerker, Cherie Barkey, Jiang Jin, and an anonymous reader for helping me improve this work. Karen Offen also shared with me her work on the history of European feminisms, which provided me with a new comparative perspective. I also thank Rosemary Catacalos and many other scholars at the Stanford Institute for Research on Women and Gender and at the Stanford women's biography seminar for their thoughtful feedback on my readings of individual chapters. I am grateful to Betty Vlack, who helped polish my translation of interviews, Grace Eckert and Fran Brown, who improved the readability of a part of the book, and Robert Borgen and Phyllis Wang, who provided information on some source materials.

The Women's Resources and Research Center at the University of California at Davis granted me a research award when this book was still an embryo. The award encouraged me to develop my ideas and research plan. The Reed-Smith Award and the Research Fellowship from U.C. Davis enabled me to concentrate on writing my dissertation. I obtained these awards with Susan Mann's help.

In China, I have a large support network involved in this project. In order to help me access source materials or meet interviewees, old friends introduced me to new friends. My circle of friends expanded, and so did my debts of gratitude. I give my heartfelt thanks to these friends for their indispensable contributions to my research: Gu Guangqing, Kong Haizhu, Ren Wanxiang, Ren Shunmei, Song Zuanyou, Xiong Yuezhi, Wang Zhousheng, Pan Songde, Shen Zhi, Li Ziyun, Shu Wu, Sun Xiaomei, Du Fangqin, Qu Wen, Liu Bohong, Xu Anqi, Zhan Che, and Zhang Xiaoying. Many women in Shanghai granted me the privilege of interviewing them. Although I do not directly present their stories in this book, much of my understanding of women's lives before 1949 comes from Yang Zhiying, An Zhijie, Li Ziyun, Shao Guanfei, Pang Lian, Xie Zuyi, and the late Chen Junying. I thank them for sharing with me their time and experiences. Liu Guangkun told me of the life of her mother, Liu-Wang Liming, whose story is an important component of this book.

My family members in Shanghai are the other part of this support network. My two sisters, Xiuzhi and Xiujun, took turns caring for my infant daughter and toddler son in the months when my husband had to work in the States. I can never thank them enough for sharing my responsibilities of motherhood so that I need not worry as I engaged in fieldwork. Knowing that I did not have a grant to cover my research in Shanghai, my brother

Xiaoyou lived in a tiny storage room in his office for a year, so that I could use his apartment. I am also grateful to a very special friend, Guo Minjun, who frequently volunteered to watch my children during the day. I could not have conducted my research in Shanghai without the tremendous support in all respects from my family and friends there.

My loving appreciation is to my husband, John, who values my work no less than I do. Trips for research and time for writing were possible because of his financial support and his share of child care and housework. His deep understanding and his infallible support have enabled me to engage in many projects in addition to this one. I wish also to thank my son, Xiayi, and my daughter, Liya, for brightening my days when my mind was preoccupied with grave questions and sad stories.

Finally, I wish to express my deepest gratitude to the women of the May Fourth era who shared their life experiences with me. Lu Lihua, Zhu Su'e, Chen Yongsheng, Wang Yiwei, and Huang Dinghui, to whom this book is dedicated, not only "gave" me this book but also showed me a genealogy from which I can trace my own roots. I hope that Lu Lihua, Chen Yongsheng, and Wang Yiwei, who did not live to see this book, were at peace when they left this world, knowing that their long obscured life stories are cherished by the younger generation.

Chronology

Year	Narrators	General
1895		China is defeated in the Sino-Japanese War.
		The Qing dynasty (1644–1911) continues.
1898		The first Chinese-run girls' school is opened in Shanghai during the "Hundred Days' Reforms."
		Reformers promote women's education and anti-footbinding.
1900	Lu Lihua and Chen Yongsheng are born.	The Boxer Rebellion occurs.
1901	Zhu Su'e is born.	The Qing government agrees to the demands of foreign powers in the Boxer Protocol.
1903		The feminist text *The Women's Bell* is published, ushering in a period of women's publication and activism.
1905	Wang Yiwei is born. Lu Lihua and Chen Yongsheng start school.	The imperial examination system is abolished.

Year	Narrators	General
1907	Huang Dinghui is born.	The Qing government establishes formal education for girls at elementary and secondary normal school levels.
1908	Zhu Su'e starts school.	
1911		The Qing empire is overthrown. Republic begins with warlords competing for the central power.
→1912		The women's suffrage movement emerges and is suppressed in less than one year.
1913	Huang Dinghui starts school.	
1915	Chen Yongsheng leaves Changsha for Shanghai to enter a physical education school.	*The New Youth* is founded, marking the beginning of the New Culture movement and initiating the debate on women's problems.
1916	Lu Lihua leaves Qingpu for Shanghai to enter a physical education school.	
1919	Lu Lihua and Chen Yongsheng participate in the May Fourth movement in Shanghai. Huang Dinghui returns to Wuchang after a half year in Zhounan Girls' School in Changsha. Zhu Su'e leaves Changzhou for Shanghai to enter the Patriotic Girls' School.	The May Fourth movement occurs. Debates on women's problems enter the mainstream media. Male and female mixed student groups are formed in many cities. Women's emancipation becomes the hallmark of the era.

Year	Narrators	General
(1920)	Chen Yongsheng graduates from the YWCA Physical Education Normal School and becomes the chair of the PE department in Beijing National Women's Normal University.	Beijing University becomes the first coeducational university. The Chinese Communist Party is founded.
1921	Wang Yiwei leaves Harbin for Shanghai to enter McTyeire School.	The first plenary meeting of the CCP is held in Shanghai.
1922	Lu Lihua establishes the Liangjiang Women's Physical Education Normal School, joins feminist organizations, and marries.	The Feminist Movement Associations and the Women's Suffrage Associations established nationwide.
1923	Chen Yongsheng enters Baylor College for Women in the United States.	
1924	Wang Yiwei enters Jinshi High School in Beijing.	The first alliance between the CCP and the GMD is formed.
	Lu Lihua participates in the National Assembly Promotion movement.	The women's National Assembly Promotion movement occurs.
	Huang Dinghui marries.	
1925	Lu Lihua divorces and establishes the first Chinese women's basketball team.	The May Thirtieth Massacre occurs. The nationalist movement is on the rise.
1926	Huang Dinghui joins the National Revolution and becomes the director of the Women's Department in Wuhan and a CCP member.	The Northern Expedition begins. The GMD second national congress passes the Resolution on the Women's Movement. The two-party-led women's movement surges.
	Zhu Su'e enters Shanghai Law College.	

Year	Narrators	General
1927	Chen Yongsheng graduates from Baylor College for Women. Huang Dinghui chairs the March 8 celebration in Wuhan, marries Wan Xiyan, and becomes an underground worker in Nanchang after the failure of the CCP-GMD alliance.	The alliance between the GMD and the CCP dissolves. The GMD under Chiang Kai-shek controls most of China. The CCP members become fugitives.
1928	Zhu Su'e joins the GMD. Chen Yongsheng returns to Shanghai. Wang Yiwei enters Fudan University. Huang Dinghui delivers a son, and Wan Xiyan is killed three months later.	
1929	Huang Dinghui is transferred to Shanghai; her son is sent to Wan's family; she marries He Chang, attempts suicide, and is imprisoned for one hundred days. Lu Lihua marries Gu Zhenglai. Chen Yongsheng becomes the first female principal of Shandong Number One Women's Normal School.	The CCP organizes large-scale workers' strikes in Shanghai.

Year	Narrators	General
1930	Zhu Su'e graduates, marries, and establishes a law firm. Huang Dinghui delivers her second son in Hong Kong and is transferred to Tianjin; her son is given away. Lu Lihua works on a new school site.	The Civil Code of the Republican government is passed, stipulating women's equal legal rights.
1931	Lu Lihua leads a women's basketball team to Japan. Huang Dinghui receives a special assignment and separates from He Chang.	Japan invades Manchuria. The national salvation movement spreads nationwide. Women become actively involved.
1932	Wang Yiwei graduates and establishes Nüsheng. Chen Yongsheng teaches at Shanghai Municipal Council Girls' School.	The January 28 Battle takes place in Shanghai: Japanese and Chinese troops exchange fire; the Japanese bombs the northern area of the city.
1935	Wang Yiwei stops Nüsheng. Huang Dinghui marries Chen Zhigao.	
1936	Chen Yongsheng tours Europe after attending the Olympic Games.	
1937	Lu Lihua's school is destroyed in the war Lu Lihua, Huang Dinghui, and Zhu Su'e play leading roles in wartime women's organizations in Shanghai. Wang Yiwei edits Guangdong funü.	Japan attacks China proper. The CCP and GMD form an alliance. The War of Resistance is declared. Women's organizations for war efforts proliferate nationwide.

Year	Narrators	General
1938	Zhu Su'e becomes a member of the Women's Movement Committee of the GMD and editor of *Zhongguo funü*.	
	Lu Lihua opens a school in Chongqing.	
1942	Huang Dinghui is imprisoned; her newborn baby dies.	
1943	Chen Yongsheng leaves the Shanghai Municipal Council Girls' School upon Japanese occupation.	
	Wang Yiwei teaches at McTyeire School.	
1944	Huang Dinghui is released from prison.	
1945	Wang Yiwei reestablishes *Nüsheng*.	The Japanese surrender.
	Zhu Su'e becomes a member of the executive board of the Shanghai Women's Association of the GMD and the principal of Wuguang Girls' School.	
1946	Chen Yongsheng studies at Columbia University.	The CCP and GMD civil war begins.
	Lu Lihua tries to retrieve her school site in Shanghai.	
1947	Chen Yongsheng obtains an M.A. in education.	
	Lu Lihua opens a middle school in Shanghai.	
	Wang Yiwei stops *Nüsheng*.	

Year	Narrators	General
1949	Chen Yongsheng establishes the first school for disabled children in China. Zhu Su'e's school is taken over by the CCP government. Huang Dinghui's party membership is denied.	The CCP takes over most of China. The People's Republic of China is founded. The All-China Women's Federation is founded.
1950	Lu Lihua's school is taken over by the CCP government. Wang Yiwei tutors at home.	China enters the Korean War.
1951	Chen Yongsheng is fired from her own school.	Campaign to "suppress counterrevolutionaries" occurs.
1952	Lu Lihua establishes a knitting co-op.	
1954	Chen Yongsheng teaches at Shanghai Second Military Medical University.	
1955	Chen Yongsheng bears political scrutiny and quits her job. Zhu Su'e is imprisoned. Huang Dinghui is imprisoned.	Campaign to "uncover hidden counterrevolutionaries" occurs.
1957	Zhu Su'e is released from prison on probation. Chen Yongsheng opens a massage clinic.	The Antirightist Campaign takes place.
1958	Lu Lihua's co-op is nationalized; she becomes a factory worker.	Great Leap Forward occurs. Women are mobilized to participate in social production.
1962	Wang Yiwei enters Wenshiguan.	
1963	Huang Dinghui is released from prison with three years' probation.	

Year	Narrators	General
1966	Homes of Huang Dinghui, Zhu Su'e, Chen Yongsheng, and Lu Lihua are ransacked.	The Cultural Revolution begins.
	Huang Dinghui is imprisoned.	
1975	Huang Dinghui is released from prison.	
1976		Mao Zedong dies; a process of reevaluating the Maoist era begins.
1978		The CCP begins the rehabilitation of all those wrongly condemned during the Mao era.
1979	Zhu Su'e is rehabilitated.	
1980	Huang Dinghui and Lu Lihua are rehabilitated.	
	Lu Lihua enters Wenshiguan.	
1981	Huang Dinghui becomes a member of Shanghai Political Consultative Committee.	
1982	Chen Yongsheng enters Wenshiguan.	
	Lu Lihua becomes a member of Shanghai Political Consultative Committee.	
1983	Zhu Su'e enters Wenshiguan.	
1993	Wang Yiwei dies.	
1997	Lu Lihua and Chen Yongsheng die.	

Introduction

ENGENDERING THE MAY FOURTH ERA

"Feminism" (*nüquan zhuyi*) has long been a negative term in the People's Republic of China. In the Communist Party literature, the word "feminism" is always accompanied by the adjective "bourgeois" and often by the qualifier "Western." Not only has exclusion of feminism from the official discourse erased a history of Chinese feminism from the public mind, it has also been integral to the claim that the Chinese Communist Party (CCP) is *the* liberator of Chinese women. The "failure" of feminism is contrasted to the success of the CCP's line on Chinese women's liberation. In the post-Mao era, as part of Chinese intellectuals' challenge to Maoism, efforts to reevaluate Western feminism have appeared.[1] What remains unquestioned, however, is the official presentation of the history of Chinese women's liberation.[2]

In the West, Chinese women's liberation has been a constant theme in

---

1. Since the mid-1980s women from both academia and the official organization known as the Women's Federation have advocated a reevaluation of Western feminism, which suggests Chinese women's growing interest in feminism as a counterdiscourse. See Li Xiaojiang, *Xiawa de tansuo* [The exploration of Eve] (Zhengzhou: Henan renmin chubanshe, 1988), and Shanxi Women's Federation, *Makesizhuyi funüguan gailun* [An introduction to the Marxist theory of women] (Beijing: Zhongguo funü chubanshe, 1991). For studies of post-Mao Chinese feminism, see Wang Zheng, "Research on Women in Contemporary China," in *A Selected Guide to Women's Studies in China*, ed. Gail Hershatter et al. (Berkeley: Center for Chinese Studies, 1998), 1–42; and Zhang Naihua with Wu Xu, "Discovering the Positive within the Negative: The Women's Movement in a Changing China," in *The Challenge of Local Feminists: Women's Movements in Global Perspective*, ed. Amrita Basu, 25–57 (Boulder: Westview Press, 1995).

2. See All-China Women's Federation, *Zhongguo funü yundong shi* [A history of the Chinese women's movement] (Beijing: Chunqiu chubanshe, 1989). Compared

1

works on Chinese women since the early 1970s. Many feminist scholars have focused on the relationship between the Communist revolution and women's liberation.[3] This focus reflects Western feminists' concern over the relationship between socialism and feminism. But, largely because of the inaccessibility of primary source material, the major works in the 1980s drew on the CCP's policy and official documents for an interpretation of Chinese women's recent history.[4] Inevitably, the women in these works do not appear as agents for social change. Readers do not learn how women responded to, coped with, struggled against, or maneuvered to change the circumstances around them, or what role women played in the relations of power in social, political, or domestic arenas. In other words, works based on the CCP's policy tend to reduce Chinese women to obscure entities with little significance in historical processes.

My study grew out of both a political interest in deconstructing the CCP's myth of Chinese women's liberation and an intellectual dissatisfaction with stories about Chinese women that lacked women as protagonists. Refusing to take the party as a heaven-sent savior, we, women scholars from the People's Republic of China, need to examine the historical processes by which the party rose to dominate the women's movement. To shift the focus from the party to women and to look for women's agency, I began by asking questions that did not assume the central role of the party. What, I wondered, were Chinese women doing before the "savior" was born? This question turned my attention to a period of women's activism when political parties had not established their dominance in China: the May Fourth era (1915–1925).

---

to earlier official texts on the Chinese women's movement, this work offers a more sympathetic description of the early feminist movement in China. However, it still presents feminist history as a preliminary bourgeois stage that was bound to be superseded by a higher proletarian women's emancipation led by the CCP. See also Li, *Xiawa de tansuo*.

3. The major works are Elisabeth Croll's *Feminism and Socialism in China* (London: Routledge and Kegan Paul, 1978), Phyllis Andors's *Unfinished Liberation of Chinese Women* (Bloomington: Indiana University Press, 1983), Judith Stacey's *Patriarchy and Socialist Revolution in China* (Berkeley: University of California Press, 1983), and Kay Ann Johnson's *Women, the Family, and Peasant Revolution in China* (Chicago: University of Chicago Press, 1983).

4. In this respect, Christina Kelley Gilmartin's *Engendering the Chinese Revolution: Radical Women, Communist Politics, and Mass Movements in the 1920s* (Berkeley: University of California Press, 1995) represents a breakthrough. The author, who met with a group of Communist women activists, uses interview material to construct a story from the perspective of women activists in the CCP.

Shortly after the 1911 Revolution that toppled the Qing dynasty, the new
Republic of China, which was in a state of political instability, entered a period
of unparalleled intellectual exploration. The intellectual and social ferment—
the May Fourth New Culture movement, as it was later called—created a
wave of feminist agitation and women's activism in China's urban areas.
Male intellectuals began to debate the "woman problem" (*funü wenti*) at
the outset of this New Culture movement and continued to do so throughout the whole May Fourth period.[5] Although the situation of Chinese women
had been a concern of reformers since the late nineteenth century, and although the term "women's rights" (*nüquan*) entered Chinese public discourse at the beginning of the twentieth century, the "woman problem" was
most widely publicized and popularized during the May Fourth era.[6] The
rapidly enhanced public awareness of women's problems was associated with
a dramatic increase in women's participation in the pursuit of women's rights.
Historians in the People's Republic of China call this period the beginning
of a new historical age, arguing that the May Fourth era gave birth to the
CCP. In their view, the May Fourth movement prepared the way for the CCP,
which in turn led women to a higher stage of proletarian women's liberation. Hence Chinese women took the "only correct" route to a bright future. Although I do not adopt this teleological view or endorse the CCP's
leadership as "correct," I agree that the May Fourth era was a unique and
meaningful period for Chinese women. In this volume, I express my perception of what counts as historically significant in the May Fourth era.

Soon after I began my research on women in the May Fourth period, I
noticed a peculiar phenomenon. The May Fourth period has fascinated Chinese and Western scholars, but Western scholarship on the era seldom discusses women, despite the abundance and availability of primary documents

---

5. The Chinese term *funü wenti* was originally a rendition of the English phrase
"the woman question," which had circulated in Europe for centuries. Translating
funü wenti back into English as "the woman problem," I intend to emphasize that
linguistic importation often alters the connotation of a phrase. *Funü wenti*, as it was
used at the turn of the century, suggests not only an awareness that problematized
the women's situation formerly regarded as normal, but also a presumption that
women hindered the nation's ascendance to "modernity."

6. For a discussion of late-Qing reformers' advocacy for women's rights, see Xiong
Yuezhi, *Zhongguo jindai minzhu sixiangshi* [An intellectual history of democracy
in modern China] (Shanghai: Shanghai renmin chubanshe, 1986), chapters 4 and 7.

Jin Yi, *Nüjie zhong* [The women's bell] (Shanghai: Datong shuju, 1903). This pamphlet is the earliest declaration of feminism in China. The author created the slogan
"nüquan wansui" [long live women's rights]. See chapter 1, this volume, for a discussion of *Nüjie zhong.*

about the "woman problem." Over twenty years ago, in a well-researched dissertation, Roxane Witke expressed her amazement at this phenomenon. She suggested that the main reason these scholars did not discuss women was that such work would be categorized as "women's history" and therefore could not rise above "the level of parochial or self-confessed minority history."[7] Now, in the 1990s, when gender has emerged as an analytical category in the study of history, any work on the era that omits discussion of gender is considered parochial and incomplete. The gender issue in the May Fourth period not only demonstrates the cultural and historical specificity of "modernity" in China, but also shapes Chinese society in the twentieth century. By exploring the gender issue, this study attempts to reconfigure a history of the May Fourth era.

The May Fourth era has long been a contested site where scholars express their values and positions. Conservative scholars have held the New Culture movement responsible for the destruction of Chinese tradition. Although cultural conservatives vary in their intellectual pursuits and beliefs, their critique of the era reflects their shared concern to salvage Confucian tradition as a response to the disorientation experienced in a rapidly changing world.[8] Communist scholars, including Mao himself, have defined the May Fourth period as a necessary stage in the world revolution of the proletariat. According to these scholars, the May Fourth movement was a bourgeois revolution led by representatives of the Chinese proletariat. Such a view legitimizes the CCP's leadership in the supposedly inevitable proletarian revolution. Liberal historians in China and the West have called the New Culture movement a "Chinese Enlightenment."[9] In the 1980s,

7. Roxane H. Witke, "Transformation of Attitudes towards Women during the May Fourth Era" (Ph.D. diss., University of California, Berkeley, 1971), 2.

8. Among the conservatives, "New Confucians" emerged as an oppositional force to May Fourth cultural radicals. In the Maoist era, the voices of New Confucians were mainly heard in Taiwan and Hong Kong and among overseas Chinese. In post-Mao China, the New Confucians have gained a larger audience, and open discussion and publication of conservative views have increased in Mainland China. See Luo Yijun, ed., *Ping xinrujia* [On New Confucians] (Shanghai: Shanghai renmin chubanshe, 1989); Charlotte Furth, ed., *The Limits of Change: Essays on Conservative Alternatives in Republic China* (Cambridge: Harvard University Press, 1976); and Wang Hui, "Zhongguo de wusi jiyi" [China's May Fourth memory], *Zhishi Fenzi* [The Chinese intellectual] (spring 1994): 42–56.

9. See Xiong Yuezhi, *Zhongguo jindai minzhu sixiangshi*, and Hu Shengwu, *Cong Xinhai geming dao wusiyundong* [From the Xinhai Revolution to the May Fourth movement] (Changsha: Hunan renmin chubanshe, 1983). See also Vera Schwarcz, *The Chinese Enlightenment* (Berkeley: University of California Press, 1986).

liberal scholars in China began a concerted effort to revitalize the enlightenment legacy of the May Fourth era in order to deconstruct Maoism. "Democracy" and "science" became the only May Fourth themes in prominent male scholars' construction of public memory. In the 1990s, amid rapid economic, social, and cultural transformations in the People's Republic of China, debates about the May Fourth era are a means of self-exploration as well as a strategy to reclaim elite positions for many liberal intellectuals.[10]

My investigation of women in the May Fourth era leads me into these debates. Although my project may seem to be influenced by the Chinese liberal intellectuals' challenge to the Maoist hegemony, my goal to engender the May Fourth era separates me from gender-blind liberal scholars in both China and the West. In fact, contemporary intellectual debates in China about the May Fourth era are largely male-dominated, exclude gender issues, and engage few women readers. I enter the fray, therefore, with my own position, a feminist perspective that holds women as a valid subject in scholarly inquiry and gender as an important dimension in historical processes. In this sense, my study seeks to break male monopoly of the contested site, the May Fourth era.

Just as May Fourth women's activism was stimulated by Western feminist movements of the time, my study of May Fourth feminism is informed by contemporary feminism. The development of Western feminism in the past decade has turned our attention to cultural and historical specificities of gender construction and the diversity of women's experiences. "Universal womanhood" sounds like a naive concept in the 1990s; we need a better understanding of cross-cultural similarities and differences in gender processes. In this book, therefore, May Fourth women are not examined in isolation. Rather, I examine the specific cultural and historical contexts of Chinese women's struggle for liberation by comparing their experiences to those of European and American women in the late nineteenth and early twentieth century.

However, this cannot be a systematic comparative work with a single set of variables applied to each case. The May Fourth women differed so much from Euro-American feminist activists at the turn of the twentieth century that no single set of variables can be identified. Instead, my subject matter

10. The Chinese intellectuals' famous debate on "humanist spirit" began in 1993 and continued through 1995. For details of the debate, see Zhongguo renmin daxue shubao ziliao zhongxin, *Wenyi lilun* [Literary theories], nos. 7–12 (July–December 1995).

requires what Charles Tilly calls a method of individualizing comparison, which reflects the practitioner's concern to "establish exactly what is particular about a particular historical experience."[11] Rather than finding generalization in cross-cultural women's experiences, my goal here is to highlight the unique experience of the May Fourth women and simultaneously illuminate the differences and similarities between Chinese and Euro-American women's struggles for liberation.

The cross-cultural comparison in this case is not at all arbitrary. Euro-American feminism entered China early in the twentieth century. In the May Fourth period, translations of Western feminist texts (many translated from Japanese editions) and discussions of Western women's movements constituted a large part of New Culturalist feminist agitation. Why did Western feminism attract a Chinese audience? What impact did Western feminism have in China? What did feminism mean to Chinese women? How did the fate of Chinese feminism differ from the fate of feminism in Western countries? Following these lines of inquiry, a comparative perspective deepens our understanding of feminism as an international movement.

Finally, this study investigates the construction of a feminist discourse in modern China. I ask the following questions: Who promoted feminism in China? Who was qualified to do so? What was the status of the individuals who had the right to proffer such a discourse? Who derived from it his or her own special quality and prestige? What subject positions were created in the May Fourth intellectuals' discursive practice? What were women's relations to the subject positions created in this period? What were the political consequences for Chinese women who embraced the new subject?[12] Approaching my subject matter with these questions in mind, I illuminate the relationships between the emergence of New Culturalists as a social force and the new subject positions for women created in this period, as well as between modernity and women's liberation in China. Thus this study attempts to demonstrate not only the discursive construction of "new

11. Charles Tilly, *Big Structures, Large Processes, Huge Comparisons* (New York: Russell Sage Foundation, 1984), 88.

12. My conceptualization of the discursive construction of May Fourth women's subjectivity has been shaped and stimulated by reading Chris Weedon, *Feminist Practice and Poststructuralist Theory* (Oxford: Blackwell Publishers, 1987); Judith Butler and Joan W. Scott, eds., *Feminists Theorize the Political* (New York: Routledge, 1992); Irene Diamond and Lee Quinby, eds., *Feminism and Foucault: Reflections on Resistance* (Boston: Northeastern University Press, 1988); Jane Flax, *disputed subjects: essays on psychoanalysis, politics, and philosophy* (New York: Routledge, 1993); Michel Foucault, *The Archaeology of Knowledge* (New York: Pantheon Books, 1972); and Paul Rabinow, ed., *The Foucault Reader* (New York: Pantheon Books, 1984).

women" in the May Fourth era, but also a gendered process of the formation of May Fourth men's discursive power.

My chosen approach is related to the available source material. Texts written by men of the May Fourth era, which I use to examine the formation of May Fourth discourses, are abundant. To supply what these texts do not, I offer the oral histories of May Fourth new women. These oral histories are constructed from interviews that I conducted between 1993 and 1995. Using my interview data, I attempt to analyze phrases and terms that signify the presence of a subjectivity in the May Fourth era and discern which terms and concepts promoted in that era were meaningful to these women. That is, I use women's own words to reconstruct the subject position of the May Fourth new women, rather than merely search texts produced by men to find women's subjectivity. This method allows me to explore the connection between man-made texts and women's consciousness.

In the May Fourth period, the terms *nüzizhuyi* (female-ism), *funüzhuyi* (womanism), *nüquanzhuyi* (the ism of women's rights), and *fuminieshimu* (feminism) were used by various Chinese authors to refer to feminism. The unfixed Chinese terms for "feminism" reflect Chinese intellectuals' efforts to grasp the complexity of Western feminism in that period. Those who insisted on using the terms *nüzizhuyi, funüzhuyi,* and *fuminieshimu* in their translation and writing wanted to call readers' attention to the fact that "feminism" connoted much more than the struggle for women's equal rights. But because the phrase *nüquan* (women's rights) had been used to denote Euro-American women's movements long before the introduction of the term "feminism" into China, because the phrase *nüquanzhuyi* conveys a more concrete and clearer meaning than either *nüzizhuyi, funüzhuyi,* or *fuminieshimu,* and because women's equal rights were the immediate concern of many involved in the Chinese feminist movement, *nüquanzhuyi* was more frequently used than other terms during the republican period. Unlike in Japan, where a transliteration distinguishes "feminism" from the term "women's rights," in China the phonemic transliteration *fuminieshimu* did not circulate beyond texts that introduced feminism. The ideographic character of Chinese writing, which prefers semantic translation to phonemic transliteration, thwarted those who intended to use *fuminieshimu* to convey a more comprehensive and complicated feminism to the Chinese.

In the Mao period, when there was no public forum in which to engage in feminist debate, the CCP had the absolute power to define "feminism." In CCP texts on the women's movement, *nüquanzhuyi* became the only translation of "feminism" that had a fixed meaning. *Nüquanzhuyi* was associated with "bourgeois" and "Western" and was therefore a negative word. In the CCP's definition, *nüquanzhuyi* suggests bourgeois women's narrow pursuit of equal rights without a political or economic revolution—but the Chinese character *quan* can also be understood as "power," and the resulting image of women's power invoked by *nüquanzhuyi* aroused as much, if not more, negative sentiment as the abstract notion of "Western bourgeois" among the Chinese after the Cultural Revolution (1966–1976). The centuries-old fear of women who usurped power seemed to be justified and intensified by the role of Mao's wife, Jiang Qing, in the Cultural Revolution. Against this political background, a new generation of Chinese feminists in the post-Mao era have adopted another term for feminism: *nüxingzhuyi* (feminine-ism). In the dominant gender discourse of femininity in the post-Mao era, the term *nüxingzhuyi* is understood variously as equivalent to "feminism" and as referring to a new study of femininity. Although various translations of this and other feminist neologisms confuse people, the CCP no longer monopolizes the definition of "feminism."[13]

It might seem a simple task to translate these Chinese terms back into English, given that they are all renditions of "feminism." Yet I hesitate when translating *nüquan* into English. Without *zhuyi* (-ism), *nüquan* can mean both "women's rights" and "feminism." In most cases, I use "feminism" for both *nüquanzhuyi* and *nüquan*, because in the May Fourth era these terms were used as equivalent to "feminism." For example, I translate *Nüquan yundong tongmenhui* as the "Feminist Movement Association." But when *nüquan* appears in a text published prior to the introduction of the term "feminism" in China, or when the speaker specifically meant "women's rights," I translate it as "women's rights."[14] In discussing the problems of translation, I hope to call readers' attention not only to the continuous linguistic

13. Scholars in Taiwan have long been using the term *nüxing zhuyi* for feminism, which may be the source of Mainland Chinese scholars' adoption of the term. For a discussion of the discourse of femininity in post-Mao China, see Wang Zheng, "'Nüxing yishi, shehui xingbie yishi bianyi" [An analysis of "female consciousness" and "gender consciousness"], *Funü yanjiu luncong* [Collection of women's studies], no. 1 (1977): 14–20.

14. Karen Offen traces the emergence of the term "feminism" in European feminist history and finds it first used by the French women's suffrage advocate Hubertine Auclert in 1882. It spread to North America and Asia in the early twentieth century. See Karen Offen, *European Feminism(s): 1700–1950* (Stanford: Stanford University Press, forthcoming). The term "feminism" did not appear in Chinese until the May Fourth New Culture period. It came from multiple sources, as New Culturalists translated feminist texts from Europe, the United States, and Japan.

contention in China over the English word "feminism" but also to nuances in the various translations of "feminism." Readers will encounter these varying translations in the written texts as well as in the narrators' accounts. Even the term *nüquanzhuyi* has a variety of nuances, depending on who is using the term. This variety reflects a historical process of discursive negotiation in which various political forces presented their understandings and definitions of "feminism." Examining this process, I attempt to illuminate a paradox in modern China: although the May Fourth feminist agenda has entered the twentieth-century Chinese political mainstream, the term *nüquanzhuyi* has fallen from its May Fourth glory to a debased obscurity in Mao's China.

THE NEW CULTURALISTS AND THE NEW WOMEN

Historians have emphasized various themes in their respective works on the May Fourth movement. Whereas some highlight the patriotic student movement, and some the enlightenment movement led by the New Culture intellectuals, most historians describe the May Fourth movement from a broad historical perspective that includes both cultural critique and students' activism.[15] I am inclined to understand "May Fourth" as a historical period that began with the New Culture movement and ended with the May Thirtieth Incident in 1925.[16] In my view, both the New Culture enlightenment theme and the patriotic theme of student activism were only distinctive in scholarly works. Events and attitudes about the New Culture and student activism were largely blended in the public mind in the years after

15. For discussion of different definitions of the term "May Fourth," see Chow Tse-tsung, *The May Fourth Movement: Intellectual Revolution in Modern China* (Stanford: Stanford University Press, 1960), introduction.

16. In May 1925, a Shanghai worker (a CCP member) was killed by Japanese guards when he and other workers went on strike. The Shanghai CCP branch decided to call for a larger strike and to launch an anti-imperialist movement. On May 30, when thousands of workers and students protested in the Shanghai international settlement, the British inspector in the police station ordered his men to fire at the crowds. Thirteen demonstrators were killed and twenty wounded. The May Thirtieth Massacre shocked and enraged the entire nation. The CCP and the GMD quickly channeled indigenous nationalism into the political goal of the National Revolution. The May Thirtieth Incident made anti-imperialism a more pressing issue than ever. In my view, it was an important event that turned feminist energy into a nationalist drive and made nationalism prevail over other May Fourth themes. For a discussion of May Thirtieth, see Jonathan D. Spence, *The Search for Modern China* (New York: W. W. Norton, 1990), 340–341, and All-China Women's Federation, *Zhongguo funü yundong shi*, 187–210.

the May Fourth Incident in 1919.[17] What affected women of that generation were the events from that entire era. Defining May Fourth as a confluence of intellectual and social trends rather than a single social movement better fits the historical experiences of the May Fourth women. In this study, the term "May Fourth movement" is used narrowly to refer to the high tide of students' activism directly after the May Fourth Incident in 1919. The term "New Culture movement" refers to the new literature and new thought movement that predated the May Fourth Incident. And the term "May Fourth era" or "May Fourth" refers to the entire decade between 1915 and 1925.

Although the major intellectual strands in the New Culture movement had been in existence since the late nineteenth century, the birth of the New Culture movement can be traced to the publication of *New Youth* (originally titled *The Youth Journal*) in 1915. The 1911 Revolution failed to establish a strong modern nation-state. Instead, it ended in a shamble of warlordism. Disillusioned Chinese intellectuals turned to a cultural solution to strengthen and revitalize the nation. They believed that for China to survive as an independent nation, Chinese culture and Chinese national character had to be remolded. *New Youth,* whose creator and editor in chief, Chen Duxiu, would later cofound the CCP, became the first intellectual forum for criticizing the foundations of Chinese cultural hegemony, Confucianism. A group of literary men quickly joined the critique by either contributing to *New Youth* or opening new forums in other periodicals and newspapers.

The New Culturalists, as they were later called, shared striking similarities. Most of them were from declining scholar-official families. All had been educated in the Confucian classics during their childhood. Most had been to "new" schools that followed either Western or Japanese models. Many had been abroad, mostly to Japan. All were conversant with one or more foreign languages. Most had a strong interest in both Chinese and foreign literature. Coming from different areas in China, all ended up in big cities, especially in Beijing and Shanghai, where they found their niche in universities and the press. They represented a new social category emerging in modern China: intellectuals (*zhishi fenzi*). Unlike the traditional Con-

---

17. The May Fourth Incident is a major historical event in modern China. After World War I, the world powers at the Versailles Conference signed a treaty that transferred all of Germany's rights in Shandong to Japan. The news motivated Beijing students and citizens to protest on May 4, 1919, and sparked subsequent mass demonstrations against imperialism nationwide.

fucian scholars, these new scholars were shaped by both Confucian and Western education. Because the connection between education and official-dom had been severed when the civil service examination system was abol-ished in 1905, the new scholars did not belong to the social group that had maintained the Confucian-dominated imperial system. Instead, the dislo-cated new scholars—modern intellectuals—became rebels against the dom-inant culture.[18]

The emergence of New Culturalists was inseparable from China's en-counter with the West. Not only was their education partly Western, but their professions were located in institutions modeled after the West. More important, they found in the West the intellectual weapons that facilitated their challenge to Confucianism. Western ideologies—social Darwinism, lib-eralism, anarchism, socialism, Marxism, and feminism—provided them a position outside of the dominant Confucian framework and enabled them to claim to be the creators of a new culture. Moreover, the power of the West made powerful those who appropriated Western ideologies. At the histor-ical juncture when the demise of the Chinese empire contrasted with the rise of Western imperialist powers, the New Culturalists' promulgation of Western ideologies carried extraordinary weight. This gave them power that marginal groups in other cultural and historical contexts could hardly dream of. Ironically, the unequal power relation between China and the West be-came the source of power for the small group of cultural rebels in early-twentieth-century China.

Adopting a humanist position from Western liberalism, the New Cul-turalists concentrated their critique on the "inhumanness" (*feiren*) of Con-fucianism.[19] The three cardinal principles in Confucianism—ruler guides subject, father guides son, and husband guides wife—were held responsi-ble for making Chinese into slaves. Or even worse, the Confucian ethics that maintained a hierarchical social order were nothing but "eating human

18. For English biographies of leading New Culture men, see Jerome B. Grieder, *Hu Shih and the Chinese Renaissance* (Cambridge: Harvard University Press, 1970) and Lee Feigon, *Chen Duxiu, Founder of the Chinese Communist Party* (Princeton: Princeton University Press, 1983). For autobiographies in Chinese, see Zhou Zuoren, *Zhitang huixianglu* [A memoir of Zhou Zuoren] (Hong Kong: Sanyu tushu wenju gongsi, 1974), and Mao Dun, *Wo zouguo de daolu* [The journey I have made] (Hong Kong: Sanlian shudian, 1981). For a discussion of the new intelligentsia, also see Marie-Claire Bergere, *The Golden Age of the Chinese Bourgeoisie, 1911–1937* (Cambridge: Harvard University Press, 1989), 41–42.

19. The Chinese word *feiren* connotes a life less than human, a life degraded al-most to the level of animals. Here I use "inhumanness," instead of "inhumanity," to convey the original meaning.

beings."[20] If the Chinese ever wanted to establish a modern democratic republic, the New Culturalists argued, they had to replace Confucian principles with freedom, equality, and independence. Liberal individualism was thus used as a subversive and liberating tool to free the subjugated Confucian subject.

The concept of an abstract human being with inalienable rights was alien but powerful because it was advocated as a universal truth. The New Culturalists, with their ready access to Western texts, claimed to have grasped the truth. In an age when evolutionism dominated Chinese intellectual discourse, the "truth" that pointed to a higher stage of human existence was appealing. More important to the New Culturalists, the "truth" exposed the falsehood of Confucianism. In sharp contrast to the autonomous human being, the submissive Confucian subject was described not only as a pitiable figure in the modern world, but also as totally unfit for a new civilization. The self-proclaimed holders of truth would not have been so powerful if they had lacked this claim to universal truth when dismantling the shrine of Confucianism. The shocked reactions and vehement responses they provoked proved that they had chosen an effective tool at that historical moment.

 Attacking Confucianism and advocating a Western liberal concept of human rights at that historical juncture led necessarily to an inclusion of women. One of the three basic principles of Confucian social order is gender hierarchy (husband guides wife). Therefore, a wholesale offensive against Confucianism had to include an attack on gender hierarchy. More important to the New Culturalists, the social institutions based on this principle provided ample evidence of the inhumanness of Confucianism. Footbinding, concubinage, arranged marriage, female chastity, sexual segregation, and so on were cited frequently by New Culturalists to demonstrate what they viewed as the "cruelty, irrationality, backwardness, and stupidity" of the Chinese cultural tradition. Women, therefore, became a quintessential symbol of the Confucian *feiren* (inhuman) system. Moreover, Chinese women were eventually described as having lived an inhuman life (*feiren de shenghuo*) for the past two millennia. Although their ahistorical and generalized portrayal of Chinese woman as victim is problematic, the male New Culturalists loudly identified women's oppression as symptomatic of a Confucian culture built on patriarchy.

20. See Lu Xun, "Kuangren riji" [A madman's diary], in *Lu Xun xuanji* [Selected works of Lu Xun], ed. Wenxue chubanshe (Hong Kong: Wenxue chubanshe, 1956), 53–63.

Because feminist movements, predominantly suffrage movements, were at their peak in the United States and Europe in the early twentieth century, the Western-oriented New Culturalists had one more point of reference when they discussed Chinese women's deplorable situation. The feminist movement was viewed by these men as a necessary stage in the development of human society. It was a sign of *modernity*. Gender equality, therefore, was a principle of modern society that was in direct opposition to the feudal principle of gender hierarchy. If China was to become modern, Chinese women had to be emancipated and to achieve an equal status as human beings. Otherwise, with half of the people enslaved and subjugated, the semiparalyzed nation would never evolve into a modern civilization. The link between women's status and a nation's status in the modern world made women's emancipation, together with human rights and modernization, an integral theme in the symphony of the New Culture.

The New Culturalists' critique of Confucian gender hierarchy and their promotion of women's emancipation generated a feminist upsurge in the May Fourth era. Because these literary men controlled or had access to the press, they could circulate their ideas among readers. Their readership dramatically increased after the May Fourth Incident, when a nationwide student movement came into being. A large student body, including many female students, became followers of New Culture ideas. The New Culture, swept along on the tide of the patriotic student movement, entered the mainstream of Chinese urban society. Identifying with the New Culture became a sign of modern citizenship. Talking about women's emancipation was an easy way to express such an identification. Men who claimed to be progressive all jumped on the bandwagon of women's emancipation. The May Fourth era witnessed unparalleled intellectual agitation for women's emancipation. A Chinese feminist movement emerged as the result of the inclusion of women in men's pursuit of a "Chinese Enlightenment."

In its initial stage, May Fourth women's involvement in social movements was stimulated by nationalism, not feminism. The May Fourth Incident provided young women students the opportunity to cross the gender boundary in the interest of the nation. The May Fourth movement saw the rise of a new social category: female students (*nüxuesheng*). Their patriotic action won them social recognition as a legitimate group in the public realm. Once they became involved in patriotic activism, many female students turned their attention to feminist issues.

In the few years after 1919, the Chinese feminist upsurge blossomed and reached its peak. After a period of men's agitation to make a women's movement in China, a women's movement began to emerge. Not only did women's magazines proliferate—many of them run by women—but also women's organized activities for women's rights appeared nationwide in 1922. The *nüquan yundong* (feminist movement) of the early 1920s was prompted and shaped by the New Culturalists' feminist agitation. Its emergence not only illustrated the discursive power of the New Culturalists but also demonstrated the rapid growth of a new social category: "new women"—that is, educated women who acted from their newly acquired subject position of "being a human."

Born at the turn of the twentieth century, women of the May Fourth generation experienced dramatic institutional changes. The late Qing reformers' campaigns protesting footbinding and promoting women's school education were remarkably successful. Convinced by the argument that a strong nation needed women who were strong, not crippled, upper-class parents let their daughters retain "natural" feet, and the practice gradually spread to other families with access to new ideas. By the time the new republic passed laws banning footbinding, many girls from elite families had already escaped the torture, and many others had unbound their feet. Thus, a large number of women physically capable of an active and mobile life emerged.

A second dramatic change occurred as women's education gained the support of the government in the late Qing dynasty. The 1911 Revolution furthered the development of female education. A version of the American-based "republican motherhood" argument promoting female academies circulated in China even before 1911.[21] By the time female education was institutionalized by the republican government, sending daughters to school had already become a patriotic gesture as well as a desirable status symbol. Public and private schools, together with Western missionary schools, educated a rapidly increasing number of young women in the first two decades of the century. Teaching became an accessible occupation for women who aspired to an independent life.

The location of schools also helped to nurture a group of new women. Because girls' schools above the elementary level were built in either county seats or metropolises, going to a secondary school marked the be-

---

21. "Republican motherhood" in U.S. women's history refers to the promotion of patriotic mothers who raised virtuous sons in the early republican period. See Nancy Woloch, *Women and the American Experience* (New York: McGraw-Hill, 1984), chapter 3. Educating women to be patriotic mothers who would then bring up virtuous republican sons was the major rationale for popularizing women's education in the United States. A similar argument was frequently used when Chinese reformers promoted women's education.

ginning of independence for many teenage girls. In the past, only an arranged marriage would prompt women of the middle or upper class to move so far away from home. Now it was their own choice, in many cases after much hard struggle, to move far away to pursue their dreams. We can imagine that in this situation many a strong-willed girl was drawn to the big city. The May Fourth Incident later drew many young women into social activism from girls' schools in China's metropolises.

In other words, it was crucial to the success of the New Culturalists that at this historical juncture thousands of educated women were already concentrated in big cities where the New Culture publishing activity centered. Without these educated women, the New Culture feminism would have circulated only among men, a prospect some men feared. A few men and women had tried to spread feminist ideas at the end of the Qing dynasty,[22] and their efforts led to the short-lived suffrage agitation after the 1911 Revolution. But they lacked a sufficient number of women readers and thus were unable to gain wide currency for feminist ideas. When the New Culturalists recovered an almost silenced feminist voice several years later, the fate of earlier feminist advocacy was still fresh in their minds.

By contrast, in 1919 the *nüxuesheng* (female students) were a receptive audience for the new ideas. Years of schooling imbued them with nationalism. Expecting to be modern citizens and to make their special contribution to the nation, educated women on the eve of the May Fourth era confronted numerous obstacles. The most serious of these obstacles was the fact that society was still segregated by gender. Especially for women from privileged classes, proprieties prohibited them from mingling with men other than their family members. Except for teaching and nursing, the two recently available "decent" female jobs, few professions were open to women. Even the educational system was gender-segregated: there was no coeducation above the elementary level, and there were only a few women's colleges, which in any case had a different curriculum from that of men's universities. Instead of breaking the gender boundary, nationalism was often used in the public discourse to keep women at home: rearing good republican citizens was seen as a glorious duty for a patriotic woman. Without the means and justification to break into the men's world, the *nüxuesheng*'s future would still culminate in an arranged marriage.

---

22. Peter Zarrow discusses the role that He Zhen—an early feminist—played in popularizing feminism; see *Anarchism and Chinese Political Culture* (New York: Columbia University Press, 1990), chapter 6. For a discussion of early feminist agitation, see also Xiong Yuezhi, *Zhongguo jindai minzhu sixiangshi*, chapter 7.

It is not surprising that the New Culture movement's call for women's emancipation struck such a responsive chord among educated women. The rights of human beings, equality between men and women, independent personhood (*duli renge*), the inhumanness of feudal ethics, and the oppression of women—all these new phrases greatly empowered women in their pursuit of social advancement. The new language enabled them to reexamine their own and other women's lives. What had in the past been considered normal, or "woman's fate," was now labeled "women's oppression." The new language also opened up a vision of a new life, a life beyond the gender boundary. Young women with high aspirations could plan a future that fulfilled their dreams. In these ways, the new language made these educated women the "new women" (*xinnüxing*).

Nationwide discussion of the "woman problem" during the May Fourth period was a discursive practice that raised the consciousness of young women and created a new subjectivity for women in modern China. The "woman problem," which originally emphasized Chinese women's universal subjugation, evolved quickly into "women's problems," a widely extended examination of various women's predicaments (though the Chinese language does not distinguish singular or plural forms).[23] The proposed norms for an emancipated woman—that is, the new woman—were quite specific. The norms included an education that would make her a conscious modern citizen as well as secure her an occupation; an independent personhood, which meant financial self-reliance and autonomy in decisions concerning marriage, career, and so on; a capacity to participate in public life; and a concern for other oppressed women. The description—or rather, the prescription—of the new woman was radically different from that of a filial daughter, good wife, and virtuous mother in the Confucian system.

The liberal feminist prescription of the emancipated new woman was in wide circulation when it came under criticism by the rising Communist Party. The CCP's Marxist analysis pointed to the class bias in the new woman formula and called it a bourgeois feminist fantasy. To date, historians in the People's Republic of China still insist that the failure of "bourgeois feminism" illustrates the correctness of the CCP's Marxist line on women's liberation. However, my interviews with a group of May Fourth women demonstrate that the liberal feminist discourse was successful in constituting a new subjectivity for women in modern China. Far from being a mere

23. For comprehensive entries on the issues discussed nationwide during the May Fourth period, see Mei Sheng, ed., *Zhongguo funü wenti taolunji* [Collected essays on Chinese women's problems] (Shanghai: Xinwenhua chubanshe, 1929).

bourgeois fantasy, the new woman was a feminist social construct and a new social category that contributed greatly to breaking gender boundaries in modern China.

In her influential article "Theorizing Woman," Tani Barlow expounds upon the discursive construction of a new subjectivity for women in modern China.[24] As Barlow says, "Nüxing was a discursive sign and a subject position in the larger, masculinist frame of anti-Confucian discourse."[25] Her insight that the May Fourth discourse made *nüxing* a new category has been important to my conceptualization of this research. However, in her reading of the source material on multiple discourses of the May Fourth era, Barlow emphasizes the importance of a Victorian sex binary in constructing *nüxing*: "Nüxing was one half of the Western, exclusionary, essentialized, male/female binary." She argues that Chinese feminists not only grounded sexual identity in sexual physiology, but also embraced the notions of female inferiority associated with the sex binary. "Thus Chinese women became nüxing Woman only when they became the other of man in the Victorian binary."[26]

This argument gives rise to several questions. Was the critique of Chinese women's lack of personality or human essence merely an attempt to "valorize" notions of female passivity, biological inferiority, intellectual inability, and so on, or was it also a condemnation of Confucian inhumanness and, therefore, an effort to raise women to the position of human being (albeit in the form of man)? If, given their own self-interest, male fiction writers represented woman as the other of man, what was women's interest in circulating the scientific notions of female inferiority in their struggle to move out of an inferior social position? If a new subject position only offered women an identification with a scientifically proved, innate inferiority, how would it have the power to change women's consciousness and to constitute new subjectivity? Was *nüxing*, the new subject position that appeared in the May Fourth era, really constituted by the Victorian binary?

Though I fully recognize the validity in Barlow's argument that the Victorian sex binary was introduced to the Chinese audience during the May Fourth era, I nonetheless maintain that it was far from a dominant discourse. The task of the May Fourth feminists was to discredit the Confucian patriarchal system. What they needed was a theory (or theories) to justify men's

24. Tani E. Barlow, "Theorizing Woman: *Funü, Guojia, Jiating*," in *Body, Subject, and Power in China*, ed. Angela Zito and Tani E. Barlow (Chicago: University of Chicago Press, 1994), 253–289.

25. Ibid., 265.

26. Ibid., 266–267.

and women's escape from the subjection and submission required by that system. The humanist concept of an essential and abstract human being who possesses inalienable rights was in opposition to the Confucian concept of a relational human being who was constituted by hierarchically differential normative obligations. For the May Fourth intellectuals, the essential and abstract human being, when it was held as the universal truth, had the power to pull men and women out of the Confucian web of unequal social relations and set them on an equal footing. That is why they eagerly promulgated liberal humanism and feminism. Against this historical background, the sex binary, which suggested a gender hierarchy, would only do a disservice to their purpose. This was precisely the reason why it was limited in its circulation.

My interviews with a group of May Fourth women have led me to a different understanding of the subjectivity of the new women. Their portraits in this volume show no sign of the presence of a subject position constituted by the Victorian sex binary, even though I asked each woman if she had read any of the famous May Fourth literature that represents woman as the sexed "other." However, the language they use reflects their familiarity with the New Culture feminist texts I examine in chapters 1 and 2. Although none of them could remember the specific article or magazine that provided them with their new language, they articulated New Culture feminist terminology effortlessly. This does not indicate that they never read May Fourth literature based on the Victorian binary. Rather, it demonstrates what, in May Fourth texts, was meaningful to them.

My major argument in this study is that nothing stipulates that the adoption of liberal humanism in China should duplicate the discursive process of differentiation and exclusion by which Western liberal humanism was constructed.[27] Grounded in a very different philosophical, political, and cultural context, the Chinese Enlightenment tells a story of male intellectuals' inclusion of women in their construction of the "modern human being." In this particular context, differentiation and exclusion in the process of establishing new definitions and new identities were practiced by negating the Confucian subject and cultural practices. The inclusion of women, however,

27. Differing from this feminist critique of the Enlightenment legacy, recent studies present a more complex picture of the Enlightenment. They examine women's role in the Enlightenment and analyze mixed messages proffered by Enlightenment thinkers and mixed legacies of the Enlightenment. See Dena Goodman, "Women and the Enlightenment," in *Becoming Visible: Women in European History*, ed. Renete Bridenthal, Susan Mosher Stuard, and Merry E. Wiesner (Boston: Houghton Mifflin Company, 1998), and Offen, *European Feminism(s)*, chapter 2.

did not guarantee a virtual elimination of asymmetrical relations of power, especially when that inclusion was carried out by male intellectuals blind to the masculinist bias in humanism. "To be a human" in the context of the Chinese Enlightenment was to be a man with all the constituting "modern" values. Chinese women, in this sense, were not regulated to become the "other" of man, but rather, were called on to be the same as man.

The May Fourth feminist emphasis on women being "human," rather than on sex difference, took root quickly in China. The power of May Fourth feminism was felt in the following arenas. First, educated women with a new consciousness entered the public space, demanding social, cultural, and political changes. Second, higher education opened up to women. Third, gender segregation in occupations broke down. Finally, equality between men and women as a principle was written into the platform of both the Communist Party and the Nationalist Party (Guomindang, or GMD). Almost a half century later, echoing the May Fourth ideal of humanist inclusion of women, Mao proudly announced, "The times are different. Now men and women are the same. Female comrades can do whatever male comrades can do." However, a women's liberation holding the male-universal as the norm was problematic. In the second half of the century, when this masculinist gender equality became the state hegemony, many Chinese women found it oppressive. Their discontent with the state hegemony led women in post-Mao China to repudiate the notion that they should be "the same as man." The story of Chinese women's revolt against the masculinist Maoist gender equality in the late twentieth century is the topic of another project.[28] The point I want to emphasize here is that the May Fourth feminist discourse, with its hallmark of women being "human," has had an impact on women in China throughout the twentieth century.

My reading of the development of this masculinist discourse on gender equality suggests two main points. First, precisely because the liberal human being is masculine, the subject position created by liberalism in China was a powerful one. When the May Fourth women had access to it, they

28. Chinese women's revolt against a masculinist gender equality in the post-Mao era demonstrates that an empowering and subversive May Fourth discourse has become the state hegemony in the People's Republic of China and that a statist gender equality with an inherent masculine bias can be oppressive to women. Challenging the hegemonic gender equality, Chinese women and men in the post-Mao era have deployed the sex binary found in May Fourth literature. A sexologically oriented and scientifically elaborated femininity has become a new subject position in post-Mao China. It poses a challenge to the masculinist "human" position. The May Fourth legacy is complex. For a discussion of Chinese feminism in the post-Mao era, see Wang Zheng, "Research on Women in Contemporary China."

immediately claimed a share in the power and privileges that had been exclusively men's. Second, to possess this masculine subject position required a denial of female inferiority rather than an embrace of scientifically defined feminine weaknesses, and the May Fourth new women did exactly that.

As rising critical forces in their time, May Fourth humanist liberalism and feminism provided new options for that generation of men and women. To be sure, other competing discourses, old and new, also constituted subject positions for women. The new woman was certainly not the only subject position in the early twentieth century. From the stories of the new women, we learn that there was at least one other new category that the new women did not want to be associated with: *taitai* (wives of officials or bourgeoisie). It is unclear when *taitai* became a special term for wives of upper-class men. But it is certain that in the May Fourth generation, *taitai* included newly educated women and the relatives, friends, or classmates of the new women. Moreover, a *taitai* was associated with modernity, because she could accompany her husband on social occasions. It would be interesting to conduct a comparative study of new women and *taitai*. However, that is beyond the scope of this work. The relevant point here is that, as an educated woman, a new woman could have chosen to be a *taitai*, dependent on her newly rising bourgeois husband for a comfortable and consumerist life. But she opted not to do so. Although a *taitai* could read, dance, play the piano, and have a social life, in essence she did not differ much from the traditional wife insofar as she lacked that quality most essential to the new women: *duli renge* (independent personhood).

The new women, however, were not merely constructed by the New Culture discourse. Ironically, the old culture provided them with a positive subject position as heroines. Traditional Chinese heroines (*jinguo yingxiong*) were women who fulfilled their obligations to the ruler or their kin with remarkable deeds in warfare. The stories of ancient heroic women warriors appeared in both heterodox literature and Confucian orthodox history books. To be a Confucian woman was to fulfill one's obligations as a daughter, wife, mother, and subject. A woman's martial spirit (*shangwu*), demonstrated by fulfilling her obligations, qualified her as a remarkable woman rather than as a masculinized woman or an androgynous woman in the Western sense.[29] By the same logic, to be a Confucian man was to fulfill

29. Du Fangqin, *Nüxing guannian de yanbian* [The transformation of views on women] (Zhengzhou: Henan renmin chubanshe, 1988). It is revealing that Du, a historian of Chinese women's history who does not speak English, never uses femininity and masculinity to describe Chinese ancient heroines. See her discussion of Hua Mulan on page 276.

one's obligations as son, husband, father, and subject. A man's lack of martial spirit (typical among Confucian literati) did not make him feminized. In other words, martial spirit (*wu*) and civility (*wen*) were not gender codes signifying masculinity or femininity. Rather, they were positive qualities that either men or women could acquire.

The Chinese heroine had been a discursive sign produced mainly by men to promulgate among women Confucian ethics such as loyalty and filial piety. Martial heroines in local plays and folk songs reached Chinese women of all classes and localities. Of various martial heroines, the legendary Hua Mulan became the most popular among young women born at the turn of the twentieth century. It is perhaps because they found it easy to identify with this unmarried young woman from a commoner's family, or perhaps because the famous poem "Mulan ci" [Ballad of Mulan] helped circulate Mulan's story among young girls who were able to read. The popularity of Hua Mulan in that period is quite understandable. Replacing her aged father, Mulan disguised herself as a man and joined the army. For twelve years she fought bravely against invaders. When the enemy was defeated, she chose to return home to serve her old parents instead of becoming a high official. Like all the other heroines, Mulan retreated from the men's world once she fulfilled her obligations to her ruler and her country. In addition to being remarkably courageous and skilled in martial arts, Mulan was notably patriotic and filial to her parents. At the turn of the twentieth century, facing the threat from Western imperialists, many men found Mulan and other martial heroines desirable role models for their daughters or female students. Not only did the "Ballad of Mulan" become a popular text for young girls, but many girls were named after Mulan.[30]

The popularization of a traditional heroine was significant to young women born at this time. Embedded in nationalist ideas, young women found in Mulan a subject position that allowed them to envision a life beyond the scope of domesticity and gender boundaries. The welfare of the

30. The references to Mulan appear frequently in women's writings at the beginning of the twentieth century as well as in old women's memoirs in the late twentieth century. Men's eulogies of Mulan and other martial heroines also appeared in newspapers in the late Qing. See Li Yu-ning and Zhang Yufa, eds., *Jindai Zhongguo nüquan yundong shiliao* [Historical source material on the modern Chinese feminist movement] (Taibei: Zhuanji wenxue chubanshe, 1975), 167–172. The legend of Mulan has been passed down mainly through the poem "Mulan ci" [Ballad of Mulan], also called "Mulan shi." It is believed that the poem was written sometime between the fourth and six centuries. See Chinese Department at Jinan University, ed., *Zhongguo lidai shige mingpian shangxi* [A selection of famous poems in Chinese history] (Changsha: Hunan renmin chubanshe, 1983), 180–183. Mulan is familiar

nation required the devotion of China's loyal and filial daughters. Because now the goal was not only to drive away invaders but also to establish a modern nation, the modern Mulan (the young woman who received a nationalist education) was eager to move into the public arena and stay there without being disguised as a man. At this historical juncture, the modern Mulan happily encountered the new ideas of women's rights and equality. Her dream of entering the men's world was legitimized by the language of modernization imported from the West. After all, the image of Mulan was completely compatible with the image of a modern woman enjoying equality with men. That is, in men's armor, a woman could behave just like a man in the men's world. In this sense, the legendary Mulan offered a position from which Chinese women could appropriate the masculine liberal subject position.

The New Culturalists' promotion of women's emancipation may likewise be understood in the light of cultural continuity. Historically, when Chinese literati created signs such as Mulan for women, they played the role of moral guardians. The new intellectuals functioned in exactly that same way in promoting new signs for women. These dislocated intellectuals were greatly empowered by advocating women's emancipation, because in doing so, they assumed the position of liberator as well as leaders of new morality. However, men's role as champions of women's emancipation led to a paradoxical situation: in their effort to dismantle Confucian hierarchical social relations, they nevertheless maintained a gender hierarchy. An examination of the New Culturalists' private lives reveals that these men maintained a social position superior to women (the liberator and the liberated, the enlightener and the enlightened, the instructor and the student). Moreover, their treatment of women in their daily life (and even in their writing) often reflects the old culture rather than the new culture.

Confucian culture continued to exert its power over May Fourth men and women in various ways. Many new women rejected an outright subordinate role, especially to men of the same generation. But when unequal

to American readers of Maxine Hong Kingston's book *Woman Warrior* (New York: Knopf, 1976). Disney's film *Mulan* increases Mulan's popularity in the English-speaking world. However, unlike Disney's representation of Mulan, to the Chinese minds, marriage is irrelevant to the Mulan legend. For many women of the May Fourth generation, to be a "Mulan" meant an alternative choice to entering a marriage. Moreover, the accentuated theme "to be true to oneself" in the Hollywood Mulan expresses well the quintessential American value, but it alters the central moral message in the Chinese Mulan legend, which is "to try one's best to fulfill one's obligations."

gender relations were masked by grand rhetoric such as obligations to the nation, to the people, or to the CCP, young women were often in a dilemma. The Mulan position in their consciousness reminded them of obligations to others, whereas the modern woman position insisted that they had equal rights. For the May Fourth women who joined the CCP, this conflict was most severe because the party demanded total submission of the individual. The solution was to suppress the new woman who had an independent personhood and to draw strength from Mulan, who exhibited strong loyalty and patriotism. It was a painful process, but the revolutionary Mulan could console herself that she joined the CCP not for her father, but for the people. Hence, all her submission and sacrifice acquired new significance.

Educated young men of the May Fourth era—the students of the New Culturalists—are absent from my study, although they are important to the lives of new women. Did educated young men also take gender equality as a principle in life? Did they experience a similar process of consciousness raising? What kind of new subject position was created for them in the May Fourth discourses? How did the subjectivity of men and women differ in the May Fourth era? These questions must be left for a future project. Here I can only suggest that it is not accidental that the era created the term *xinnüxing* (new woman) instead of *xinnanxing* (new man). Though May Fourth feminism changed educated young men's views toward women, it is the new women that emerged as a new social category in modern China. The May Fourth era, in this sense, represents a meaningful breakthrough in the long process of Chinese women's liberation.

May Fourth liberal feminist agitation did not last long. The emergence of feminist advocacies and the flurry of women's organized activities were possible largely because of the unique political situation in the early twentieth century. Between the fall of the Qing dynasty and the rise of a new central political power, Chinese intellectuals and students were able to engage in a cultural revolution on their own initiative. Although prominent New Culturalists soon gained more discursive power than ordinary followers, there was no effective intellectual or political authority to control the expression of different ideas, approaches, solutions, or explorations. Twentieth-century China has never seen a freer intellectual forum than that during the May Fourth period. The National Revolution promoted by the alliance of the GMD and the CCP brought an end to this era of intellectual freedom. Nationalism, promoted as a rallying issue to enhance the political power of the alliance, soon overshadowed other isms after the May Thirtieth Incident in 1925. Although the May Fourth feminist agenda was largely incorporated into the National Revolution, the social space for nonparty feminist activities was reduced drastically.[31]

The failure of the political alliance between the two parties in 1927 resulted in further adversity for feminism in China. Immediately after the dissolution of the alliance, the CCP's fugitive status forced many feminists in the party to either go underground or flee into the mountains. Their immediate concern was shifted from mobilizing women to ensuring their own and the party's survival. At the same time, the GMD's tightening political control further constrained the May Fourth intellectual forum. Although in the GMD-controlled areas, non-Communist feminist organizations were allowed to exist, radical agitation for a feminist revolution disappeared. In a period when the new regime was consolidating, feminism as a subversive ideology was of little use to a ruling class trying to maintain social stability by promoting Confucian norms. Even though both parties claimed to uphold gender equality, and despite the fact that some May Fourth feminist issues continued to be addressed by feminists within each party, women's emancipation did not rank high in either party's plan for achieving political dominance.

Feminist activities and mobilization were subdued in the changed political landscape after the late 1920s. However, the May Fourth feminist discourse, contained and expressed in social categories, institutions, organizations, and legislation, as well as in beliefs and words, had become a part of the twentieth-century process in China. The new subjectivity of women created by this discourse lingered in modern Chinese society. And the new women continued to pursue their feminist goals with whatever means were available to them. These new women, our protagonists in this study, have both testified and contributed to the power of May Fourth feminist discourse. Their solid footprints mark the advancement of Chinese women in the twentieth century.

THE CONSTRUCTION OF ORAL HISTORIES

When I began my research in Shanghai in 1992, I had no idea that I would be able to meet educated women born at the beginning of the twentieth century. But for my project on May Fourth feminism, it was crucial to understand the lives of women of that generation, or, at least, to understand the lives of women activists of that time. So as soon as I landed in Shanghai, I

---

31. For more information on feminism in the National Revolution, see Gilmartin, *Engendering the Chinese Revolution.*

looked for women who had been active in the women's movement during the May Fourth era and for places that might have preserved personal documents of these women.

The first stage of my search was discouraging. None of my friends and relatives knew any women that old, and my acquaintances working in libraries and museums looked baffled when I asked if these institutions had archival collections of diaries, letters, and other personal documents of women; they replied that only a few famous men in the past have been entitled to this kind of attention. I realized then that my search for women's personal writings might be futile. First, the percentage of women who were literate in that generation is very small. Second, even if many educated women had kept diaries and written letters, the chances were slim that these personal documents had survived civil wars and the War of Resistance against Japan. Third, even if some women had been fortunate enough to keep their personal documents intact before 1949, it was still unlikely that those documents would have escaped destruction during the Cultural Revolution. I decided that a more realistic approach would be to locate surviving women.

Given my advantage of being a Shanghai native, I eventually met the women I was looking for through personal connections. I interviewed ten women who were approximately ninety years old and three younger women who told stories of a mother or older sister. Most of the old women who told me their own life stories were members of the Shanghai Research Institute of Culture and History (SRICH), or the Wenshiguan, as the Chinese call it. I, too, will use the term "Wenshiguan," because the English translation conveys a sense of prestige that Wenshiguan does not actually have. The Wenshiguan is an institution that the CCP created nationwide after 1949. Celebrities of different walks of life before 1949, including the last emperor, have been appointed as members of the Wenshiguan by officials from the central committee to local governments. In official parlance, "the Wenshiguan is an honorable institution which the party and government established for the purpose of placing and unifying old intellectuals."[32] The government pays salaries to the members, who are supposed to do research or write historical accounts of past events. But research and publication is not a requirement for maintaining membership. Most members only write

32. Wang Guozhong, introduction to *Shanghai wenshi yanjiuguan guanyuan zhuanlue* [Biographies and autobiographies of members of the Shanghai Wenshiguan], vol. 1 (Shanghai: Shanghai Wenshiguan, 1990). Since 1990, Shanghai Wenshiguan has published four volumes: volume 1 in 1990, volume 2 in 1991, and volumes 3 and 4 in 1993. The publication is classified as *neibu ziliao* (restricted material).

when they have the opportunity to publish—that is, when on special occasions the government or newspapers and periodicals ask them for articles. In short, the Wenshiguan is more a means for old non-Communist celebrities to have a place in socialist China than a genuine research institute. As one of my interviewees poignantly commented, the Wenshiguan "is like a place collecting high-class beggars. . . . All kinds of people are shut up in the Wenshiguan, the ones who had some fame and some followers in the old society. While we are under the surveillance of the cadres sent by the government, the party can show the world that they treasure intellectuals."

Most of the women I interviewed became members of the Shanghai Wenshiguan in the early 1980s. They were recruited into the Wenshiguan for several reasons. The Cultural Revolution had drastically reduced the number of members because the Wenshiguan stopped recruiting. At the same time, many members had died either because of persecution or from natural causes. In 1978 the Wenshiguan began recruiting new members with requirements different from those before the Cultural Revolution. Now, old people with a college degree obtained before 1949 may be accepted as members even if they were not celebrities. Most new members endured exclusion, discrimination, and persecution in the Mao era. In providing them with financial security and social status in their old age, the party seems to be apologizing for its wrongdoings, as well as hoping to use these people's personal networks to reach overseas Chinese, including those in Taiwan. My interviewees see their membership in the Wenshiguan as a compensation for the losses they incurred as a result of actions by the government. Although they appreciate the fact that they are provided for in their old age by the Wenshiguan, they can never be oblivious to their losses—losses for which nothing in the world can compensate.

With a few exceptions, my interviewees are women who received either college or secondary school education in the early twentieth century and established their careers in the 1920s and 1930s. Besides education and career, the women I present here have something else in common: their creative and active lives ended abruptly after 1949. A ninety-three-year-old woman told me shortly after I met her, "In 1949 I was in the prime of my life. I should have been able to do a lot of things. But my life has been wasted since then." The new government not only deprived these women of their cherished careers but also successfully deleted them from history. As a woman born after 1949, I had absolutely no idea before I met these women that such a large number of independent career women existed before liberation. Brought up in the Maoist era, I never questioned the claim that only the Communist Revolution liberated Chinese women. Therefore, facing these witnesses of history and listening to their sagas one after another, I was greatly shocked and deeply touched.

The interviews were often emotional for my interviewees as well. These old women had not expected that someone would value their life stories. They welcomed this stranger warmly, and many poured out their experiences right away (although this was partly because I was introduced to them by someone they knew). They felt quite at ease with this younger Shanghainese woman who spoke their language but came from the United States. Several said that they could tell me a particular story because I was not going to publish it in China. Still, they did not feel entirely unencumbered. They asked me not to tape them whenever they criticized the CCP, even though their criticisms were far milder than those I overheard in the markets, on the buses, and in other public places in China. They did feel free, however, to express their emotions. Along with their stories, they laughed heartily and cried without embarrassment. To some of them, my arrival meant a great deal. An eighty-eight-year-old woman said at the first interview, "My friends have all passed away. I am now very lonely. I can't sleep, always thinking about these things [her past involvement in women's activism]. I won't be able to die with my eyes closed if I do not tell the stories of those sisters." She showed me pictures of her tombstone, which she had made in 1990; the inscribed epitaph mentioned several women who once worked with her. She said, "I has this tombstone done for these people I mentioned here. I was just worried that they would be forgotten. If you had come earlier, I would not have had to make this tombstone. . . . I do not believe in religion. But I think fate may exist. Probably you are sent by God." She died three months after she told me her life story.

In a sense, this book memorializes these women, whose heroic past has long been forgotten. It is a memorial written largely by the women themselves. Their extraordinary accounts of their lives, which were so unexpected to me and so "irrelevant" to my original research design, shaped the reconceptualization of the book and constitute the main story presented here. As a friend to these women, I wish to draw their portraits in the way that they wish to be remembered. Therefore, I have constructed their narratives with their own words from both interviews and their autobiographies. I have made a few minor structural changes from the original material in order to present a chronological story without unnecessary repetition. The tapes from the first round of interviews, conducted between February and July 1993, were transcribed in full length. I then selected information from follow-up interviews conducted between December 1994 and January 1995 to add to the original narratives. The rest of my editing is limited to deleting repetition and removing detailed information on family members.

But as a study of history, this work cannot take the format of a memorial. In my effort to place these isolated stories in historical context, to present a fuller historical drama in which these women played important roles, I, as a historian, must turn these social agents of historical change into objects of scrutiny. Their narratives become in turn the primary source material that I must examine, analyze, and interpret. Rather than being only a record of the women's words, this book expresses my position in relation to my historical subject.

My awareness of the historian's role in presenting history led me to explore a suitable format for this project. Because I strongly wish to let the May Fourth new women speak on their own terms, altering their words as little as possible, I present their narratives in their entirety instead of selecting quotations from their narratives to meet my needs. Accordingly, I have organized chapters around the individual narratives rather than the sequence of historical events. My analyses following each narrative situate the narrator in the specific historical context and present my understanding of the narrative's meanings. Thus, part 1, "The Setting," traces the formation of May Fourth feminism from the written texts produced from late Qing to the May Fourth era and presents a historical setting for the emergence of the new women. Part 2 begins with an introductory chapter that is followed by five chapters, each consisting of a narrative by a new woman and an interpretation by me. I hope that this format allows readers to hear the new women's words directly and to derive their own interpretation of those words.

Because the narratives constitute a major part of this study, I must also address the complexity of doing oral history. Reading the stories of the new women, readers should be aware of certain issues. First, as one scholarly commentator observes about oral history, "The subject's story (the data) is the result of an interaction between two people. The personality and biases of the researcher clearly enter into the process to affect the outcome."[33] Although in my interviews an open-ended question like "How did you get your college education?" or "How did you get involved with the women's movement" often led to a monologue by the narrator—a monologue interrupted only by my requests for clarification—the narratives are never-

---

33. Kathryn Anderson, et. al., "Beginning Where We Are: Feminist Methodology in Oral History," in *Feminist Research Methods*, ed. Joyce McCarl Nielsen (Boulder: Westview Press, 1990), 102.

theless products that reflect a specific set of dynamics between the narrators and I. My manifest interest in women's history and my position as a junior woman scholar from the United States may have encouraged the narrators to glorify their past experiences. American scholars have warned researchers about the superior power position of the interviewer in these situations, noticing as well the narrator's tendency to downplay the significance of their experience.[34] But in my case, the narrators are well-educated women, and many of them have a knowledge of Chinese classics superior to mine. Although their elite status has long been lost, membership in Wenshiguan grants them a respectability expressed by the reverent way they are addressed: the gender-neutral suffix *lao* (senior) is attached to their surnames (for example, Zhulao, Lulao, and so forth). Addressing them in this manner put me, a graduate student researcher, in a reverent position immediately. Even without this *lao* that suggests their respectable social standing, the generational hierarchy in Chinese culture automatically placed these senior women in a position above me. In the interviews, they took obvious pleasure in teaching history to this junior woman by emphasizing their own struggles and achievements in the past.

They generously shared their life experiences with this junior woman because each had her own agenda in the interview. They knew of their deletion from history, and they saw in me, a historian from the United States, one who could give them a voice, or even restore their place in history. The power of the pen and my geographic location contributed to the enthusiasm of my informants. The prospect of having their stories published in the United States may have led them, on the one hand, to express their thoughts freely and, on the other hand, to select stories from their life carefully.

If my junior position was an advantage in inducing senior women to pour out their rich experiences, it was also an obstacle to discussing certain aspects of their life. Sexuality is a topic that educated Chinese are not used to discussing freely. If sexuality is ever discussed, it is usually between friends or relatives of the same generation. It would have been inappropriate for me to probe into a senior woman's sexual life. As a result, this topic was almost untouched in our conversations. But my interviewees' reticence on sexuality should not be interpreted as merely a response to my age. It is also consistent with their view of what made them who they are. Unlike the bour-

34. See Sherna Berger Gluck and Daphne Patai, eds. *Women's Words: The Feminist Practice of Oral History* (New York: Routledge, 1991), and Walerie Raleigh Yow, *Recording Oral History: A Practical Guide for Social Scientists* (Thousand Oaks: Sage, 1994).

geois *taitai*, whose identity was based on her marriage, the new women defined themselves by their career achievements in the public arena rather than by their private lives.

Second, we must consider the effects of these women's unique experience on their oral histories. Their social position has changed dramatically with changing political contexts and discourses. In the 1920s, riding on the tide of feminism and nationalism, they became active social agents. In the 1930s, they reached the position of social elites. After 1949, they were marginalized by Maoism. Finally, in the post-Mao era, they have been rehabilitated, living their old age with social respect but without social power. A keen sense that half of their valuable lives has been wasted may contribute to a stronger nostalgia about the prime of their lives than that possessed by other old people.

Third, because this is a study of the discursive construction of subjectivity, oral history as a method complicates the task of interpretation. For example, there is the important issue of intervening years. These are women in their nineties telling stories of their youth. From the 1920s to 1990s, dominant discourses in China have changed significantly. If language constitutes subjectivity, then how do changing discourses reshape subjectivity? How can I tell if my informants are expressing their subjectivity today, or the subjectivity they constructed in the 1920s? One way I have tried to control the oral history material is by checking the primary texts written in the May Fourth era. Comparing different terminology circulating then and today, I have been able to single out the phrases unique to May Fourth that were used unhesitatingly by these women. Phrases like "independent personhood" (*duli renge*), "promoting feminism" (*shenzhang nüquan*), "the rights of human beings" (*rende quanli*), and so on, were rarely used in the early 1990s' China. But they flowed effortlessly from these old women when they described experiences in their youth, which clearly indicates the presence of a subjectivity constructed by the May Fourth discourse.

In addition to "outdated" vocabulary in these women's speech, the absence of "fashionable" terms demonstrates the persistence of their May Fourth feminist consciousness. In the post-Mao era, "democracy" and "science" have been the two most prominent words in the construction of the May Fourth memory. Intellectual critique of Maoism and the students' democratic movements that peaked in 1979 and 1989, around the sixtieth and seventieth anniversaries of the May Fourth movement, present the goals of the May Fourth movement as being primarily the pursuit of democracy and science. Interestingly, our narrators never use these popular terms to describe their May Fourth goals. When I asked about their experiences during the May Fourth movement, they spoke of patriotic and feminist activities. The absence of popular terms suggests that contemporary intellectual currents have little effect on these old women. Or, even if they have an effect, these women do not conform *their own* May Fourth memories to the public ones so recently constructed. After all, the post-Mao revitalization of the May Fourth era is a maneuver of resistance by intellectuals, rather than a form of dominance by the state.[35]

Fourth, related to the preceding issue is the question: what is the new women's relation to the Maoist discourse? Did they consciously resist that discourse during their long-term marginalization? Or were they, like many other intellectuals, more or less transformed by Maoism? How much of their account is an artifact of Maoism? Does Maoism still serve as a censor, determining what they should or should not say, or what is appropriate to emphasize and what is not? In this regard, the different political identities of these women become highly significant. The one Communist Party member uses much official party language, in stark contrast to the non-Communist women. The sharp differences in these women's speech clearly mark their different positions in the Maoist discourse. Whereas the CCP woman's life has been woven together with the party's history, the other women have no vested interest in Maoism. This factor places them easily in the position of dismantling Maoism in the post-Mao era. However, that is not to say that they have been free of Maoist hegemony. In a very real sense, everyone is still living under the shadow of Mao. Recounting past activities, my interviewees often assumed a defensive tone to argue for their actions. They were not simply responding to my questions. Rather, they were repudiating charges and criticism leveled against them in the Mao era. They relied heavily on the rhetoric of patriotism—*aiguo* (love the country), a positive value in Maoism—to justify and give meaning to their pre-1949 activities. Thus, although their effort to construct their pre-1949 history rejects the CCP

35. In an interview in 1995, Xia Yan, a renowned May Fourth veteran, talks about his recollection of the May Fourth movement. Contrary to the interviewer's emphasis on democracy and science as the most influential issues of the era, Xia stresses that the central themes were anti-imperialism and anti-feudalism. In anti-feudalism, he recalls, "First of all, we emphasized equality between men and women, and freedom of marriage. Female students' participation in the movement embodied the demand of equality between men and women. Then there was the slogan of anti-Confucian ethics, and then we moved to anti-Confucius himself." Xia's talk strikes a rare note amid the dominant construction of the May Fourth memory in contemporary China. See "Cuxi tan Wusi" [A chat about the May Fourth], *Donfang* [The Orient], no. 2 (1995): 24–25.

myth of Chinese women's liberation, the language they often use situates them under Maoist dominance.

Feminist poststructuralism calls our attention to the historically and socially specific discursive production of experience. As Joan Scott puts it, "Experience is at once always already an interpretation *and* is in need of interpretation. What counts as experience is neither self-evident nor straightforward; it is always contested, always therefore political."[36] It is important for us to understand the new women's narratives as discursive products. As such, they inevitably contain conflicting, competing, and shifting meanings. Precisely because the narratives contain multiple meanings, they are valuable for our understanding of the complexity of subjectivity. What is more, the meaning of experience is a crucial site of political struggle. In this sense, these women's effort to give their past experience a legitimized meaning—patriotism—is more a stance of political resistance than proof of acquiescence to hegemonic Maoism. At the same time, using the dominant language to strengthen their historical and social position may also lead to a denial or suppression of subject positions that do not have legitimacy in the dominant discourse. This may explain the obvious lack of self-interest and the prominent fixed subject position of patriot in their stories.

Covering the span of nearly a century, the new women's stories are woven out of the vicissitudes of their individual lives in the social, cultural, and political transformation of twentieth-century China. In the limited space here, I can only sketch five portraits, which hardly does justice to the new women's rich and diversified experiences. Still, these women's own presentations provide important clues to many puzzles about the Chinese women's movement, May Fourth feminism, and Chinese women's liberation. Two decades ago, Marilyn B. Young in her pioneering work *Women in China* asked, "What happened to the urban feminists who did not join the Communists? And what was the fate of those who did?"[37] I hope this work, in the May Fourth women's own words, provides an answer to those questions.

36. Joan W. Scott, "'Experience,'" in *Feminists Theorize the Political,* ed. Judith Butler and Joan W. Scott (New York: Routledge, 1992), 37. See also, Chris Weedon, *Feminist Practice and Poststructuralist Theory.*

37. Marilyn B. Young, ed., *Women in China* (Ann Arbor: Center for Chinese Studies at the University of Michigan, 1973), 2.

PART ONE

THE SETTING

1   Creating a Feminist Discourse

In January 1916, Chen Duxiu published his "1916" in *New Youth*.
He formally proposed that women should rise from the position of
the conquered to the position of conqueror. He formally advocated
that the three principles of Confucianism should be destroyed.
Thus appeared a single spark that would ignite the prairie fire of
a true female revolution.

> Chen Dongyuan, *Zhongguo funü shenhuo shi*
> [A history of the lives of Chinese women], 1928

Of all those self-proclaimed "awakened elements," whether
women or men, there were none who ignored such texts, the so-
called New Culture literature at the time. They also wrote and
talked about it. The number of people who dived into the tide to
swim was so large that it was unprecedented.

> Chen Wangdao, "Chinese Women's Awakening,"
> in *Xinnüxing* [The new woman], 1925

In the mid 1920s, Chinese male intellectuals such as Chen Dongyuan and
Chen Wangdao were still writing on the subject of women. Chen Dongyuan
spent two years writing *A History of the Lives of Chinese Women*. Chen
Wangdao contributed to *The New Woman*, a newly founded women's journal that was entirely staffed by men. The agitation for women's emancipation, which had reached its peak in the early 1920s, was already being overshadowed by a rapidly growing nationalism. But many May Fourth men
had taken to "swimming," and so they kept discussing women's issues even
though the "tide" was on the ebb. As the chapter epigraphs illustrate, May
Fourth men were conscious of their own and other men's roles in advocating women's emancipation.

May Fourth men's attention to the "woman problem" has been largely
overlooked by Western scholars. The only substantial research on the May
Fourth debates on women is Roxane H. Witke's dissertation, completed
in 1971 but never published. In her exhaustive study, she points out that
"most of the May Fourth polemics were carried out by youth in the name

of youth. However, the youth (most often male) talked less about liberating themselves than about liberating women. For a major part of the acting out of their own liberation from the strictures of the old social order was the spectacularly anti-traditional act of championing the cause of women."[1]

The extensive literature on the "woman problem" written by men during the New Culture movement formed a prevailing gender discourse that affected many Chinese women of the twentieth century. This chapter traces the origins and development of gender discourse in early-twentieth-century China. I begin with a review of men's advocacy for women's emancipation in the late Qing period, then focus on the further development of this discourse after the fall of the Qing dynasty in 1911, when Chinese intellectuals advocated women's emancipation as part of their attack on Confucian culture in such publications as *New Youth*, first published in 1915. Examining male intellectuals' role in promoting a feminist discourse, I delineate the process by which ideas about feminism were circulated and embraced by educated women of the May Fourth era (1915–1925). Women's organized activities for women's rights in 1922 and 1923 marked the peak of liberal feminism in China. Meanwhile, parallel to the wave of liberal feminism, a Marxist discourse of women's emancipation, promoted by the newly founded Chinese Communist Party, entered the intellectual contest. The development and interaction of these two competing discourses in the 1920s provided the political and intellectual setting against which our protagonists—the new women—played out their life dramas.

LATE QING PRECEDENTS

The late Qing reformer Kang Youwei should rank at the top of the list of Chinese male champions of women's emancipation, if we judge each by what he advocated. Kang's endorsement of Western liberalism and his pursuit of individual freedom and equality led him to feminism. In *Datong shu* [The book of one world], which he began composing in 1884 and finished in 1902, Kang expressed his own feminist views before Western feminist texts were introduced to China.[2] He not only advocated gender equality, but also placed gender issues at the center of social transformation. His ideas about gender

---

1. Witke, Roxane H., "Transformation of Attitudes towards Women during the May Fourth Era" (Ph.D. diss., University of California, Berkeley, 1971), 331.
2. Kang Youwei's view on gender relations could have been influenced by an American utopian novel *Looking Backward*. The novel, first published in 1888,

equality and independence were the foundation for his design of a one-world utopia, from which all boundaries—such as family, private property, nation, and race— would be abolished, along with the human miseries he believed those boundaries cause. The feminist issues he raised anticipated many issues raised in the Chinese women's movement later on: women's education, women's rights to public office, women's equal legal rights, married women's right to keep their own names, freedom to choose one's spouse, freedom to have a social life, abolition of what Kang called "corporal punishment" (binding feet, piercing ears, wearing girdles, and so on), unisex clothes for men and women, and freedom of marriage. In order to ensure individual freedom and happiness, Kang boldly proposed that marriage should be temporary: men and women should sign marriage contracts that last no longer than one year. For that proposal alone, Kang should be regarded as the most radical Chinese man of his time and the first to articulate the goal of sexual freedom.[3]

An evolutionist, Kang did not expect his vision of "One World of Complete Peace and Equality" to materialize immediately. He cautioned that the process of women's emancipation must go through three stages of social evolution—the Age of Disorder, the Age of Increasing Peace and Equality, and the Age of Complete Peace and Equality—because precipitous change could cause great disorder. For that reason, he did not publish *Datong shu* in his lifetime. Consistent with his view that the first step in women's emancipation was to stop torturing women physically and liberate them from family confinement, Kang organized the first Chinese anti-footbinding society in his hometown in 1883. He continued this effort with his brother and with friends, such as Liang Qichao. Anti-footbinding associations spread nationwide by the end of the nineteenth cen-

---

became a best-seller in the United States. It caught the attention not only of American reformers of the late nineteenth century, but also of Chinese reformers. It was translated into Chinese in the following years. The novel critiques gender relations in nineteenth-century America and expresses familiarity with contemporary feminist ideas in the West. See Edward Bellamy, *Looking Backward* (New York: Penguin Books, 1986), 183–193.

3. Kang Youwei, "Quxingjie Baoduli" [Abolishing sex boundaries and preserving independence], part 5 of *Datong shu* [The book of one world] (Shanghai: Zhonghua Shuju, 1935). In many respects, Kang's feminism anticipated contemporary feminism in the West. For instance, he identified the patriarchal family as the institution responsible for women's subjugation and recognized women's reproductive function as an important factor that made them susceptible to male domination.

tury. In 1898, Kang submitted a memorial on the prohibition of footbinding, which was approved by the emperor as part of the great one hundred days of reform.[4]

Kang's campaign against footbinding had great significance for Chinese women's social advancement. But the social impact of his feminist ideas is far less clear, because *Datong shu* was not published in its entirety until 1935. Although his feminist views anticipated many New Culturalists' ideas about women's emancipation, there is no evidence that the New Culturalists read the draft of Kang's book. There was no such delay in publication of another famous reformer's views on women's issues. In *Ren xue* [The study of *jen*], Tan Sitong, a disciple of Kang, attacked the three principles of Confucianism (*sangang*). Like Kang, Tan also advocated gender equality, freedom to choose one's spouse, and sexual freedom. *Ren xue* was published in 1899, twenty years before the May Fourth movement. However, the feminist ideas of Kang and Tan were apparently unknown to Chen Dongyuan when he wrote *A History of the Lives of Chinese Women*. He merely highlighted Kang's promotion of the anti-footbinding movement and Liang Qichao's advocacy of women's education, calling the period before the 1898 reform movement the "embryonic stage" of the Chinese women's movement.

In Chen's estimation, the most influential publication on women's liberation in the late Qing was *Nüjie zhong* [The women's bell], a pamphlet published in 1903 by Jin Tianhe.[5] Jin Tianhe, whose pen name was Freedom Lover Jin Yi, was a prolific revolutionary writer. In this pamphlet, Jin demonstrated his familiarity with Western liberalism and feminism. He compared Western ideologies to "a ray of sun appearing in a dark China," a ray that had yet to reach Chinese women. Jin tried to ring the "bell" to wake up Chinese women, so that they would join the revolution to overthrow the monarchy. In *Nüjie zhong*, Jin advocated a Western concept of liberal civil rights and women's rights. He believed that "civil rights and women's rights were born together."[6] He stressed that Western scientific

4. Jung-Pang Lo, *Kang You-wei: A Biography and a Symposium* (Tucson: University of Arizona Press, 1967), 38–39. For a discussion of Kang Youwei and *Datong shu* and Kang's role in Chinese women's liberation, see Xiong Yuezhi, *Zhongguo jindai minzhu sixiangshi* [An intellectual history of democracy in modern China] (Shanghai: Shanghai Renmin chubanshe, 1986), 232–242 and 416.

5. Chen Dongyuan, *Zhongguo funü shenghuoshi* [A history of the lives of Chinese Women] (Shanghai: Commercial Press, 1928), 316–329.

6. Jin Yi, *Nüjie zhong* [The women's bell] (Shanghai: Datong shuju, 1903), 3. For a study of Jin Yi, see Li Yu-ning, "Nüjie zhong yu Zhonghua nüxing de xiandai-

research showed no difference in men's and women's intelligence, and he argued that inequality between Chinese men and women "resulted partly from sages' instructions dating from a barbaric age, and partly from the policies of dictatorial monarchs."[7] He believed that the twentieth century was an age of feminist revolution when Chinese women should rise up to recover their rights.

Jin's proposal for women's rights (nüquan) included the right to go to school, the right to make friends, the right to run a business, the right to own property, the right to engage freely in social activities, and the right to choose one's own spouse. He also called for women's political participation, especially participation in revolution and in establishing a republican government. He declared, " If the new government of the new twentieth-century China is not held in women's hands, I will die with my eyes open."[8]

Jin did not merely urge women to leave their conventional confinement to live a new life. He also prescribed new standards for molding new women and proposed eight goals of women's education:

1. Develop noble, pure, and completely natural human beings.
2. Develop free human beings who can eliminate oppression.
3. Develop highly intellectual human beings who possess manly qualities [nanxing].
4. Develop enlightened leaders of women, who can change social mores.
5. Develop physically strong human beings who can raise healthy children.
6. Develop moral human beings who are model citizens.
7. Develop compassionate human beings who are concerned with public affairs.
8. Develop faithful and unyielding human beings who will promote revolution.[9]

Nüjie zhong, then, was more than a "bell" to wake up the oppressed Chinese women. It was a blueprint for making new Chinese women in the twentieth century. The new woman, distinctly different from the traditional

---

hua" [The women's bell and the modernization of Chinese women], in Jinshi jiazu yu zhengzhi bijiaolishi lunwenji [Family process and political process in modern Chinese history], ed. Zhongyang Yanjiuyuan jindaishi yanjiusuo (Taibei: Zhongyang Yanjinyuan jindaishi yanjiusuo, 1992), part 2, pp. 1055–1082.

7. Jin Yi, Nüjie zhong, 48.
8. Ibid., 50–67.
9. Ibid., 45.

woman, should be an independent and active citizen, just as a man should be. It is significant that in his eight points, Jin used the word *ren* (persons, or human beings) rather than *nüzi* (women) to refer to new women. He conceptualized Chinese women in terms of Western individualism. Motherhood was the only traditional role that new women should maintain, and he conceptualized that role in biological terms. Women's other traditional familial obligations as daughters, wives, or daughters-in-law were discarded completely. Therefore, although *Nüjie zhong* took the traditional form of didactic literature for women, it provided a radically new canon for Chinese women to follow.

Published in a time of revolutionary ferment, Jin's pamphlet was enormously popular, especially among anti-Qing revolutionaries. The first printing sold out in a few months. Many newspapers and magazines for women either discussed the ideas in *Nüjie zhong* or directly copied its phrases, and Jin Tianhe was praised as a "Rousseau for Chinese women."[10] With the publication and wide circulation of *Nüjie zhong*, the term *nüquan* (women's rights) entered Chinese social and political discourse. Moreover, it was Jin who first articulated a feminist principle for early-twentieth-century Chinese liberals: natural rights should include women's rights.

Although Jin Tianhe was the most vocal advocate of women's rights in this period, a group of educated women from elite families were also actively spreading feminist ideas. A study of Chinese women's publications between 1897 and 1912 shows that of forty women's periodicals and newspapers published in Shanghai, Beijing, Tokyo (where many Chinese women went for an education), and other cities, the majority were run by women, and only three appeared before 1903. This may indicate that *Nüjie zhong* inspired educated women to take action. The women's periodicals, though mostly short-lived and of limited circulation, promulgated newly introduced Western ideologies with the slogans "natural rights" (*tianfu renquan*), "equality between men and women" (*nannü pingden*), and "recovering women's rights" (*huifu nüquan*). Although influential mainstream newspapers such as *Wanguo gongbao* [Review of the times] and journals such as *Dongfang zazhi* [The eastern miscellany] also printed articles contributed by men and women promoting women's education and covering women's rights issues in Europe and the United States, women's publications stand out in this period because it was the first time in Chinese history that women created

10. For a discussion of the impact of *Nüjie zhong*, see Xiong Yuezhi, *Zhongguo jindai minzhu sixiangshi*, 431–433.

their own newspapers and journals. And they did so with the professed goal of promoting *nüquan*.[11]

This first generation of Chinese feminist activists were highly conscious of their pioneering role in bringing about historical transformations. Like many male reformers and revolutionaries of the time, these educated women used foreign women's social advancement as a reference point to discuss the necessity of reforming social institutions that kept Chinese women subordinate. Articles on women's education, women's political participation, and women's career and occupational opportunities and achievements in Japan, the United States, Great Britain, and other European countries were a prominent feature of Chinese women's journals. Information about ongoing women's movements in Europe and the United States appeared frequently in articles that introduced the foreign women's situations as well as in articles that discussed the Chinese women's situation. Contrasting Western women's progress with Chinese women's sufferings (such as footbinding, illiteracy, gender segregation, arranged marriage, and so on), many women writers urgently called for Chinese women to rise up. In an article titled "The Future of Chinese Women," the author, pen-named "A Hunan Woman," said that Hua Mulan was the only woman who had shone brightly in Chinese history before the nineteenth century. The author deplored the fact that, even given Mulan's great talent and aspiration, she still had to disguise herself as a man to join the army. The author asked rhetorically, "In the long thousands years [of history], except for the fortunate Mulan who became prominent, has there been no one else with unique ideas? It is all because women have been restrained by customs and controlled by the family. Even those with remarkable talent and aspirations have been unable to cross the boundaries to demonstrate their talent and express their aspirations." However, the author argued, this kind of situation would change, and Chinese women would shine brilliantly in the twentieth century:

> Some people may ask, if women in China lived in this way until the
> end of the nineteenth century, how can we expect women in the twen-

11. Shen Zhi, "Xinhai geming qianhou de nüzi baokan" [Women's newspapers and periodicals before and during the Xinhai Revolution] (paper presented at the conference on the Seventieth Anniversary of the Xinhai Revolution, Wuhan, 1981). See also All-China Women's Federation, *Zhongguo funü yundong shi* [A history of the Chinese women's movement] (Beijing: Chunqiu chubanshe, 1989), 37–61. For a discussion of anarchist feminist He Zhen and her newspaper *Tianyibao*, see Peter Zarrow, chapter 6 of *Anarchism and Chinese Political Culture* (New York: Columbia University Press, 1990).

tieth century to develop so fast? I would say, until the nineteenth century, Chinese women had neither historical precedents to invoke nor contemporary examples to emulate. Occasionally, there were women of special quality who thought of doing something. But men rose in flocks to suppress such behavior. Today the whole world is changing. New books and new journals increase in number daily and broaden our scope. Sensible men not only do not prohibit new ideas, but some also advocate women's education. Although their words may not be sincere, we women can use their lip service to pursue our goals. Well! It is wonderful! The current situation that we are in is a state that one could hardly expect to encounter in ten thousand years!

After this shrewd assessment of the changing historical tides, the author called for women's active participation in transforming the world and warned them against being mere onlookers: "If you reduce one point of your responsibility today, you will have ten points less of rights tomorrow." Therefore, women should try their best to promote reform. "Those good at speech should advocate with speech; those good at writing should promote with writing; and those good at doing should do it." The author emphasized vehemently, "We must understand that this is the moment for women to move from the dark to the light. We should not lose this opportunity and sink back to the eighteenth level of hell. It is understandable that women before the nineteenth century did not achieve anything. It would be unforgivable if women after the nineteenth century failed to achieve anything!"[12]

The end of the Qing witnessed the emergence of feminism together with the rise of nationalism. A large number of publications, Nüjie zhong among them, called for Chinese men and women to rise up against the Manchu dictatorship. Many women activists regarded the Qing monarchy as the first obstacle to women's liberation and to the national well-being. Obtaining women's rights became inseparable from an anti-Manchu position. Or rather, participation in anti-Manchu activities meant the beginning of an actual process of achieving women's equal rights. Qiu Jin, the most famous martyr of the 1911 Revolution, exemplified this generation of women activists. A talented woman who was extremely depressed by her unhappy marriage, Qiu divorced her unworthy husband at a time when divorce was unheard of and went to Japan in 1904, where she changed her name to Jinxiong (competing with the male). In 1904, she founded Baihua [Vernacu-

---

12. Chunan Nüzi, "Zhongguo nüzi zhi qiantu" [The future of Chinese women], Nüxuebao (Tokyo), no. 4 (1903), cited from Li Yu-ning and Zhang Yufa, eds., Jindai Zhongguo nüquan yundong shiliao [Historical source material on the modern Chinese feminist movement] (Taibei: Zhuanji wenxue chubanshe, 1975), 393–396.

lar journal], and after she returned to Shanghai in 1906, she founded *Zhongguo nübao* [Chinese women's journal]. She wrote many articles and poems advocating women's rights. While in Japan, she joined the Revolutionary Alliance; she returned to China to participate in anti-Manchu activities and promote women's rights. Qiu firmly believed that to achieve equal rights, women had to shoulder the responsibilities of citizenship. In her poem "Mian nüquan ge" [Promoting women's rights], she wrote, "Equality between men and women is endowed by Heaven. How can we be content to lag behind? . . . Our fair hands are needed in order to recover our rivers and mountains. . . . Taking responsibility on our shoulders, we citizen heroines must never fail to live up to our expectations."[13] Her strong desire to show the world that women could accomplish heroic deeds equal to those of men led to her martyrdom in 1907, when she was twenty-nine years old.[14]

For this generation of women revolutionaries, responsibility to the nation was associated with rights that women deserved. Many female revolutionaries, including Qiu Jin's friends and students, became suffragists soon after the last emperor was dethroned.[15] The short-lived suffrage movement in the early 1910s demonstrated that many women who joined the revolutionary camp had feminist expectations. They had contributed to the birth of the republic, and because they had shared equal responsibility for the

13. Qiu Jin, "Mian nüquan ge" [Promoting women's rights] in *Zhongguo nübao* [Chinese women's periodical], no. 2 (1907), cited from Li Yu-ning and Zhang Yufa, *Jindai Zhongguo nüquan yundong shiliao*, 441. Qiu Jin was one of the few early female members of the Revolutionary Alliance, the anti-Manchu organization created by Sun Yat-sen.

14. Bao Jialin argues convincingly that Qiu Jin had enough time to run away before she was arrested, but she chose not to because she had long wished to be a heroine equal to those anti-Manchu male martyrs. See Bao Jialin, "Qiu Jin yu Qingmo funü yundong" [Qiu Jin and the women's movement in the late Qing], in *Zhongguo funüshi lunji* [Collected essays on Chinese women's history], ed. Bao Jialin (Taibei: Daoxiang chubanshe, 1992). The year of Qiu Jin's birth is unclear. Different historians cite the year of her birth differently. Wang Shilun studied the genealogy that Qiu Jin wrote to her best friend, Wu Zhiying, and decided that the year of her birth was 1877; see Wang Shilun, "Qiu Jin chusheng niandai" [The year of Qiu Jin's birth], *Lishi yanjiu* [Historical studies] 12 (1979): 64–65. In her confession after her arrest, Qiu wrote that she was twenty-nine years old. But Wu Zhiying said that Qiu died when she was thirty-one. The inconsistency could be a result of the difference in Chinese and Western ways of calculating age.

15. If Qiu Jin had not died as a revolutionary martyr, she probably would have become a prominent suffragist like many of her revolutionary friends. For further discussion on the Chinese suffragists in the early 1910s, see chapter 4 and 5 in this volume.

nation, they assumed that the new republic would meet their demand for equal rights. These revolutionaries-turned-suffragists were the first generation of Chinese women who entered the political arena via nationalism. Although the suffragists failed to obtain political rights—a fact often used by the People's Republic of China historians to prove that "bourgeois feminism" is inapplicable to China—the feminist agenda in the first decade of the twentieth century did in fact voice resistance to Chinese political culture. As such, it served as an intellectual precondition for the surge of feminism in the May Fourth New Culture era. Moreover, the first generation of women activists and suffragists set concrete examples for the subsequent generation of May Fourth young women. The narratives of May Fourth new women in part 2 of this study illustrate the important effect of those childhood role models on the May Fourth women's pursuit of a new life. In short, rather than a discrete phenomenon, the surge of feminism in the New Culture era was a continuation and an explosion of a feminist discourse that had existed in China since the late Qing.

PROMINENT CHAMPIONS OF FEMINISM IN THE EARLY NEW CULTURE MOVEMENT (1915–1919)

Only two years after the suppression of China's first women's suffrage movement by the Yuan Shikai government, Chen Duxiu started *New Youth* in 1915.[16] It is not clear if the silencing of women's voices contributed to Chen's aversion to the dark age of Yuan dictatorship. But it is certain that his vision of a new culture for China included women's emancipation. In the first issue of *New Youth*, Chen wrote "To the Youth." Under the subheading "Autonomy, Not Slavery," he stated:

> Given the rise of theories that espouse human rights and equality, courageous and upright people can no longer bear being slaves. Modern European history is called a "history of emancipation." To destroy the power of monarchs is to seek political emancipation. To deny the power of the church is to seek religious emancipation. To promote the theory of equalizing property is to seek economic emancipation. The women's

16. Yuan Shikai (1859–1916) was the leader of the powerful North China army in the late Qing. When the 1911 Revolution broke out, he played an instrumental role in arranging the abdication of the Qing. Because of his power in the military, Sun Yat-sen, the leader of the 1911 Revolution, offered Yuan the presidency of the new republic. The Yuan Shikai government made a series of moves that disillusioned many Chinese who had fought for the republic. Yuan eventually revealed his true political conviction by proclaiming himself emperor in 1915.

suffrage movement seeks emancipation from the power of men. To seek such emancipation is to throw off the yoke of slavery in order to realize an autonomous and free personhood.[17]

At a time when the women's movement was still marginal and encountering many obstacles in the West, Chen viewed it optimistically as a part of the Western history of emancipation from slavery. Moreover, this "history of emancipation," in the opinion of Chen and many New Culturalists, represented the trend of modern civilization and pointed the direction in which Chinese civilization would develop. The goal of this historical trend, as Chen described it, was to pursue "autonomous personhood." This theme of individualistic emancipation would be repeated by other New Culturalists in the following years.

In the next influential article that he wrote, titled "1916," Chen expounded the relevance of individualism to the Chinese people. With a sense of urgency, Chen called upon young men and women to discard the Confucian mentality, to establish independent personhood, and "to conquer but not to be conquered." He argued that individuals in the West cherished autonomy and the rights to equality and freedom; individual power led to national power. By contrast, in China the rule of Confucianism had reduced the Chinese people to a state of slavery.

> The three principles that subordinate the subject to the monarch, son to father, and wife to husband have made the subject, son, and wife appendages to the monarch, father, and husband, lacking their own independent and autonomous personhood. Men and women under heaven are all subjects, sons, and wives, but none is an independent and autonomous person. Beyond that, the three principles have given rise to unchangeable standards of morality. But loyalty, filial piety, and chastity are not at all a master morality that extends standards to others from the self; rather, they are a slavery morality that makes oneself subordinate to others.[18]

This article was regarded by Chen's contemporaries as the first bombshell of the New Culture movement. Chen was "destroying the temple of Confucius and abolishing the worship of him."[19] Tan Sitong had severely

17. Chen Duxiu, "Jinggao qingnian" [To the youth], *Xin qingnian* [New youth] 1, no. 1 (1915): 2.

18. Chen Duxiu, "Yijiuyiliu" [1916], *Xin qingnian* [New youth] 1, no. 5 (1915): 3.

19. Chen's students at Beijing University created this description of Chen's work, which his colleague Zhou Zouren, another famous New Culturalist, thought "very much to the point." See Zhou Zuoren, *Zhitang huixianglu* [A memoir of Zhou Zuoren] (Hong Kong: Sanyu tushu wenju gongsi, 1974), 483.

criticized the Confucian three principles, and Jin Tianhe had vehemently promoted individual freedom and independence, but it was Chen Duxiu who imagined the opposition between Confucianism and individualism as that between slave and master. These images were powerfully persuasive to Chinese people at that time, because China's defeat by the West was fresh in their minds. With the analogy of slave and master, Chen provided an analysis of as well as a solution to China's weakness: China was almost conquered by the West because Confucian culture made Chinese people weak. To rise up from slavery, the Chinese first must acquire a master mentality—namely, the same independence and autonomy that Westerners possessed. And it was the youth—young men and women—who were most likely to become the new citizens who possessed this new mentality. In Chen's opinion at this time, molding new people to create a new culture (or creating a new culture to mold new people) was the only way to move the ancient nation toward modernity.[20]

In "The Way of Confucius and Modern Life," Chen further demonstrated the incompatibility of Confucianism and modern life. Two-thirds of the examples he gave to illustrate the absurdity of Confucianism were rules about women. He contrasted these rules to Western women's activities, which he felt represented the standards of modern civilization. Thus, the women's suffrage movement, as "an example of women's life in modern civilization," was compared with the Confucian teaching that "women's words should not extend outside the home." The pairs of opposites also include Western widow's freedom to remarry versus the Confucian custom of widow's chastity; Western women's free social contact with men versus Confucian gender segregation; Western women's economic independence and employment opportunity versus Confucian women's seclusion and dependence on men; and a Western wife in the nuclear family versus the Confucian ritual obligations of a Chinese wife to her husband's family. In this manner, Chen's professed attack on Confucianism served to expose women's oppression in China. The gender issues he raised in the article would soon be

20. In 1914, Chen Duxiu told his friend, "If I run a periodical for ten years, the whole country's mind will be changed." When he was invited to be the dean of liberal arts at Beijing University in 1916, Chen initially declined the offer because he was running *New Youth*. He accepted the offer only when Cai Yuanpei, the university president, told him to bring the periodical with him to Beijing. Changing people's mind was Chen's and other New Culturalists' goal at this stage. See Tang Baolin and Lin Maoshen, *Chen Duxiu nianpu* [A chronicle of Chen Duxiu's life] (Shanghai: Shanghai renmin chubanshe, 1988), 63–76. See also Lee Feigon, *Chen Duxiu, Founder of the Chinese Communist Party* (Princeton: Princeton University Press, 1983).

developed into a focused, New Culture movement debate on the "woman problem" (*funüwenti*).[21]

As an evolutionist, Chen regarded all the contrasts between Chinese women and Western women as a difference in developmental stages. The way of Confucius represented feudalism, which must be discarded if China wanted to advance toward a higher stage of civilization. Chen contended,

> Confucius lived in the feudal age. The morality he promoted was a morality of a feudal age. The rituals he taught, and the conditions of life surrounding them, were the rituals of a feudal age and the conditions of life of a feudal age. The politics he proposed was the politics of a feudal age. The morality, rituals, life and politics of a feudal age, did not go beyond the scope of the rights and honor of a small number of monarchs and nobility. They had nothing to do with the happiness of the majority of citizens. . . .
>
> I urge the followers of Confucius not to blindly follow, but to wipe your eyes and use your brains. Observe carefully what the way of Confucius was and what the state of modern life is. With your conscience, make a clear judgment about right or wrong, benevolence or evil, evolution or regression.[22]

Chen's equating of Confucian culture and feudalism would become a familiar concept to Chinese men and women of the twentieth century. Women's oppression was, or has been seen as, mainly associated with feudalism. This analytical framework does not explain gender inequality after the stage of feudalism, but Chinese women under socialism today still blame "feudal remnants" as the cause of current women's oppression. In the 1910s, it was a liberating idea that the Confucian "feudal" culture oppressed women and should be abandoned.

If women's lowly status exemplified the backwardness of Confucian culture, Chinese culture must change the status of women in order to evolve and progress. Late Qing reformers such as Kang Youwei and Liang Qichao had made great efforts to change the custom of women's footbinding and to institutionalize women's education, because they believed that the backwardness of Chinese women impeded the evolution of the Chinese nation. Using the same evolutionist logic, New Culturalists turned their attention

21. Chen Duxiu, "Kongzi zhi dao yu xiandai shenghuo" [The way of Confucius and modern life], *Xin qingnian* [New youth] 2, no. 4 (1916); reprint, in *Wusi shiqi funü wenti wenxuan* [Selected articles on women's problems in the May Fourth period], ed. All-China Women's Federation (Beijing: Zhongguo funü chubanshe, 1981), 99–105.

22. All-China Women's Federation, *Wusi shiqi funü wenti wenxuan*, 104–105.

first to the situation of women. But what New Culturalists aimed to redress was more than bound feet and illiteracy. In their view, the submission of women, and the culture that was responsible for making women submissive, should be changed. In other words, without the birth of new women, it could never be said that China had achieved a new culture, a higher stage of civilization. Therefore, New Culturalists such as Chen thought it was urgent to call people's attention to women's issues.

Chen did not wait long before he made a special effort to reach women. In February 1917, *New Youth* began a column on the "woman problem." All authors were said to be women, but at least one article later proved to have been written by a man. The column appeared in four issues over the next five months and altogether printed seven articles on women. One of the seven, "Nüquan pingyi" [On women's rights], was later shown to be the work of the alleged author's husband, Wu Yu.[23] These articles advocated women's equal education and employment, criticized the Confucian concept of women's inferiority, feudal rituals, and the marriage system, and promoted "feminist revolution" (*nüquan geming*). Some authors still argued that the purpose of women's education should be to foster good wives and virtuous mothers. But the most radical article, "Nüquan pingyi," argued that a feminist revolution was necessary. In the article, Wu Yu used citations from Confucian texts to prove that Chinese women had inferior status and lacked equal rights. He described Western women's increasingly public roles and their current struggle for suffrage, which, he emphasized, represented the trends of the world. He called on Chinese women to study and improve their abilities in order to obtain their rights. He hoped that Chinese women would "strive together with men in nationalism, following women in today's Britain and Germany."[24]

The column on the "woman problem" eventually folded either because there were too few women contributors in 1917 or because *New Youth* did not yet have a large female readership. Editorial staff member Liu Bannong wrote, "Our periodical pays great attention to the woman problem. But we

23. After "Nüquan pingyi," Wu Yu published many articles in *New Youth* under his own name. He became a prominent New Culturalist and was famous for denouncing Confucianism.

24. Wu Yu, "Nüquan pingyi" [On women's rights], in All-China Women's Federation, *Wusi shiqi funü wenti wenxuan*, 8–14.
Although "Nüquan pingyi" presented powerful arguments and contained radical ideas, being one of the earliest articles on women's rights in this period, it did not receive the public attention it deserved. Chen Dongyuan did not mention it in his careful study of the influential articles on women's emancipation in *New Youth*. It is possible that the article's classic form of writing impeded popularization. Other

have received very few articles from the outside. After we reporters published our own opinions, no one joined us to discuss them. So this problem has been put aside." Staff member Tao Lügong said, "We seek women contributors who can boldly study and solve the woman problem, analyze woman's true nature, understand woman's true positions, and discuss the close relationships between woman and state and society. But such women are as rare as phoenix feathers and unicorn horns [fengmao linjiao]."[25]

In fact, however, the cold response from women readers did not thwart the men of *New Youth*. Their response might actually have had the opposite effect: the male forerunners of a new culture were more convinced than ever of their responsibility to awaken Chinese women. In "The Woman Problem," published in January 1918, Tao Lügong discussed Western women's pursuit of economic independence and the changing political, economic, and social life of women in the West. Tao emphasized the emergence of Western feminist ideas in the past century, mentioning several female theorists, such as Ellen Key and Jane Addams. Tao believed that social changes gave rise to the emergence of women's problems such as equal opportunity of education and employment in the West and that new ideas made women awaken to address those problems. This Western pattern was relevant to Chinese women. Tao argued,

> The world today is linked by dense networks of transportation and communication. Development in the economy, in occupations, and in ideas reaches everywhere, creating a global trend. What is happening in European societies today will happen in our society tomorrow. Today's women's problems in Europe and America will surely soon appear in this country. There is no doubt. As to how to find solutions, this is a difficult task that no one person can shoulder alone. Solutions depend on today's youth, especially on today's young women.[26]

Tao's article expressed an attitude that was common among the New Culturalists. Their belief in evolutionism and their "eagerness to merge into

---

more influential articles were deliberately written in the vernacular to reach a potential female readership. But insofar as Wu's other articles, which made him famous, were also in the classic form yet written under his own name, one suspects that it was the name that made all the difference. A woman's name, unfortunately, devalued the important article.

25. Beijing Women's Federation, *Beijing funü baokan kao* [A study of Beijing women's newspapers and periodicals] (Beijing: Guangming ribao chubanshe, 1990), 111–117.

26. Tao Lügong, "*Nüzi wenti*" [The woman problem], *Xin qingnian* [New youth] 4, no. 1 (1918): 19.

the major trends of the world" led to their universalistic thinking.[27] The Chinese nation was thought to be at a low stage of development, hindered by Confucianism. To accelerate the process of evolution, Chinese people should consciously remold themselves according to the example of Western culture. Moreover, the rapid changes in Western women's lives constituted an important part of modernity. Logically, only when the same changes occurred in Chinese women's lives could China be regarded as approaching modernity. Therefore, discussing the Chinese woman problem in Western terms was part of the New Culturalists' anxious effort to push China toward modernity.

The renowned "new literature" forerunner Hu Shi also used the Western model to stimulate Chinese women. In "American Women," originally a speech he made at the Beijing Women's Normal School, he argued that American women strove to be free and independent human beings and that Chinese women should emulate American women's self-reliance and get rid of dependency. "At first sight, the spirit of self-reliance seems like extreme individualism. Actually, it is an indispensable condition of a good society."[28]

Hu's promulgation of individualism reached a climax in the publication of Ibsen's play A Doll's House. In 1918 Hu Shi organized a special issue of New Youth on "Ibsenism" [Yibosheng zhuyi]. A Doll's House was translated into Chinese and given the title Nuola [Nora]. Ibsen's critique of the patriarchal European family was used to attack the Chinese family. In opposition to an evil family system, the character Nora symbolized individual resistance. Before she abandoned her family, Nora declared to her husband, "I am a human being, the same as you. No matter what, I will try my best to be a human being." With these words, Nora became the number one Western role model for a generation of Chinese educated women. Nora illustrated what a Chinese new woman should do: courageously rebel against the feudal family and strive to be an independent human being. The image of Nora, associated with the catch word duli renge (independent personhood), spread quickly among urban educated young women, especially after the May Fourth movement. Our aged narrators in part 2 still echo Nora's message.[29]

27. In "More Than Ideological Beings" (Ph.D. diss., University of California, Davis, 1994), Hung-Yok Ip offers a detailed discussion of the May Fourth intellectuals' worldview. She defines the May Fourth intellectuals' cosmopolitanism as "the eagerness to merge into the major trend of the world" (81).

28. Hu Shi, "Meiguo de furen" [American women], Xin qingnian [New youth] 5, no. 3 (1918): 213–224.

29. Hu Shi, "Yibosheng zhuyi" [Ibsenism], Xin qingnian [New youth] 5, no. 6 (1918): 489–507. For a discussion of Nora's impact on Chinese women, see Witke,

In presenting new role models for Chinese women, the New Cultural-ists hoped to destroy the Confucian role models. After the fall of the Qing dynasty, the warlord government retained old legislation that upheld a chastity cult. The government stipulated that three kinds of women should be rewarded and praised: first, *jiefu*, women who were widowed before they turned thirty and remained widows past the age of fifty; second, *lienü* or *liefu*, women who died resisting rape, or who committed suicide after be-ing raped, or who committed suicide after being widowed; third, *zhennü*, women whose fiancés died and who then remained virgins until death. Newspapers in the 1910s often printed stories of *jiefu* and *lienü*. After all the agitation for women's rights during the first decade, and with the emer-gence of many female revolutionaries in the 1911 Revolution, chastity was still officially touted as a supreme virtue in women.[30]

In 1918, as a bold challenge to the prevailing sexual morality, Zhou Zuoren published his translation "On Chastity" in *New Youth*. The provoca-tive article was originally written by contemporary Japanese woman poet Yosano Akiko. She questioned conventional assumptions of chastity and ar-gued that chastity should not be connected with morality. Moreover, she exposed the oppression inherent in traditional sexual morality by analyz-ing double sexual standards in the society. She declared, "If the chastity code did not contradict, but rather benefited the development of human life, then we would welcome it as a new morality. But if only women should keep it, and men can be released from it, then it is contradictory. It is an old moral-ity that makes human life disharmonious and broken. We cannot believe in it."[31] Yosano did not specify the cultural background of the chastity moral-

---

"Transformation of Attitudes," 164–167; All-China Women's Federation, *Zhongguo funü yundong shi*, 69; and Chen Dongyuan, *Zhongguo funü shenghuoshi*, 375–376. For a study of Hu Shi, see Jerome B. Grieder, *Hu Shih and the Chinese Renaissance* (Cambridge: Harvard University Press, 1970). Like all other Western works on Chi-nese May Fourth intellectuals, Grieder's work also overlooks Hu Shih's effort at pro-moting Chinese women's emancipation. The emergence of the "new woman" in China can testify to Hu Shih's and his colleagues' success in spreading Western lib-eralism. Considering the changes in Chinese women's life during the past century, the New Culturalists' endeavor should not be viewed, as Grieder thinks, as a failure.

30. See Hu Shi, "Zhencao wenti" [The chastity problem], *Xin qingnian* [New youth] 5, no. 1 (1918): 5–14.

31. Yosano Akiko, "Zhencao Lun" [On chastity], trans. Zhou Zuoren, *Xin qingn-ian* [New youth] 4, no. 5 (1918): 386–394. For a study of Japanese feminism, see Sharon L. Sievers, *Flowers in Salt: The Beginnings of Feminist Consciousness in Modern Japan* (Stanford: Stanford University Press, 1983). Yosano Akiko's poems have been translated into English. See *Tangled Hair: Love Poems of Yosano Akiko*, trans. Dennis Maloney and Hide Oshiro (Fredonia, N.Y.: White Pine Press, 1987).

ity. To Chinese readers, her powerful argument spoke of a universal truth applicable directly to the Chinese situation.

Zhou Zuoren claimed that he translated this article just for the reference of a few awakened men who were concerned about the woman problem. Hu Shi responded quickly by publishing "The Chastity Problem." He dramatized the absurdity of the coexistence of chastity morality with polygamy and legalized prostitution. Hu openly opposed the government's regulations on *jiefu* and *lienü* and condemned them as "barbaric and cruel laws that should have no place today." He called for the formation of a new public opinion that would regard "anyone encouraging women to be *jiefu* and *lienü* as committing willful murder." With his liberal concept of equality, Hu also promoted one sexual standard for both men and women. He stressed, "Chastity is an attitude with which one 'person' treats another 'person.' Therefore, men should treat women as equals in respect to chastity. If a man cannot reciprocate, then he is not qualified to accept a woman's chastity."[32]

Following Hu Shi, another "awakened" man, Zhou Zuoren's elder brother Lu Xun (Zhou Shuren), launched a bitter attack on chastity morality. In "My Views on *Jielie*," Lu Xun linked the chastity cult with Confucianism and pointed out that whenever the nation was in crisis, Confucians resorted to women's chastity as a means of national salvation. Aiming at the warlord government that promulgated the chastity cult, and with his typical sardonic wit, Lu asked, "How did women without chastity harm the nation? . . . Are polygamous men qualified to reward women's chastity?" He observed, "The more an emperor wanted loyalty from his subordinates, the more men wanted chastity from women." He depicted Chinese men under the dominance of Confucian tradition as despicable cowards. They regarded women as their personal possessions. They seduced and victimized women. And they blamed women for all family failures and for the defeat of the nation. As a fighter for the new culture, Lu Xun expressed his strong wish at the end of the article: "Eliminate the senseless pain in life. Eliminate the stupor and violence of making and enjoying others' pain. We further vow that all humankind should enjoy legitimate happiness."[33]

---

32. Hu Shi, "Zhencao wenti." Hu wrote two more articles attacking the chastity cult: "Lun zhencao wenti" [On chastity] and "Lun nüzi wei qiangbao suowu" [On women who are raped], in *Hu Shi wencun* [An anthology of Hu Shi] (Taibei: Yuandong tushu gongsi, 1968), vol. 1, no. 4.

33. Tang Si (Lu Xun's pen name), "Wozhi jielieguan" [My views on *jielie*], *Xin qingnian* [New youth] 5, no. 2 (1918); reprint, in All-China Women's Federation, *Wusi shiqi funü wenti wenxuan*, 115–123. This article reveals Lu Xun's early con-

The New Culturalists' attack on Confucian sexual morality was extremely radical for their time. Powerfully exposing Chinese women's sufferings, they effectively challenged Confucian ethics. What Chinese men and women had taken for granted for centuries, what had always been a normal way of life, was now revealed to be nothing but a custom that could be summarized in two characters: *chiren* (eat humans).[34] The barbaric inhuman system surely had no reason to persist in the modern world. The few "awakened" men's professed courage and humanity, together with their insight and wit, quickly attracted numerous young followers. In the succeeding years, an explosion of a nationwide discussion on "women's problems" demonstrated the strong impact of these early works. Educated young men and women all over the country began to discuss new sexual morality, marriage, divorce, and so on. As a result, the sexual behavior of the May Fourth men and women changed rapidly. The narratives in part 2 illustrate this point.

Before the May Fourth Incident, an essay in the newly founded *Xin chao* [New wave], an influential New Culture periodical, summarized the New Culturalists' theses on women's emancipation. Stimulated by "several awakened men's talks" on women's problems, Ye Shaojun presented a coherent analysis of "the problem of women's personhood." He defined "personhood" as "a spirit of being an independent and wholesome individual in a big group." Chinese women did not possess personhood, he argued, not only because the sexual division of labor placed women in a dependent position in domestic life, but also because Confucian men denied women's personhood out of their own self-interest. Following New Culturalists' critiques of various aspects of women's oppression in the Confucian culture, Ye listed the many ways in which men trapped women: through women's subordinate normative status (*mingfen*) prescribed in the Confucian principle "husband guides wife"; through the teaching of "virtuous mother and good wife"; through the morality of chastity and *jielie*; and through the treatment of women as sexual and reproductive machines and as appendages. He urged women to acquire a consciousness of being human (*ren*):

---

ception of his famous story "Zhufu" [The new year's sacrifice] (1924), in *Lu Xun xuanji* [Selected works of Lu Xun], ed. Wenxue chubanshe (Hong Kong: Wenxue chubanshe, 1956), 78–94.

34. In his short story "Kuangren riji" [A madman's diary] (1918), Lu Xun first used the metaphor *chiren* to denounce the inhumanness of Confucian rituals. Wu Yu then wrote an essay titled "Chiren yu lijiao" [Eating humans and Confucian ethics]. Both influential works contributed greatly to anti-Confucianist discourse in modern China.

A woman should know that she is a human being. She should fully develop her capacities to do whatever a human being should do. To be a human being one should follow the truth and abandon and destroy the absurd normative status [*mingfen*] and false morality. . . . Men and women should be of one mind on this matter: each human being is a member in the process of evolution; each should reach the state of independence and wholesomeness; and each should enjoy the state of being upright and high-minded, and enjoy the happiness of freedom.[35]

Ye's essay cogently displayed the centrality of women's independent personhood in the "woman problem" as perceived by the New Culturalists in this period. Achieving independent personhood (*duli renge*) was soon to become the hallmark of May Fourth feminism. It also became a goal as well as a behavioral standard for the new women of the May Fourth era.

THE MOTIVATIONS OF MALE CHAMPIONS

The emergence of a group of male champions in early-twentieth-century China is a unique phenomenon with a particular historical context. As I have discussed, a nationalistic concern, an attack on Confucianism, a trust in evolutionism, a faith in liberal humanism, and a belief in universalism combined to facilitate those men's ready acceptance of feminism. The women's suffrage movements in Europe and North America added timely weight to the New Culturalists' belief that the whole world, men and women, would evolve toward equality and freedom. World events in the nineteenth and early twentieth century conveyed a message to New Culturalists that humanism, or "the discovery of the human being," in Zhou Zuoren's words, should include women.[36]

In his study of Zhou Zuoren's ideas about women's emancipation, Chinese scholar Shu Wu comments,

35. Ye Shaojun, "Nüzi renge wenti" [On the problem of women's personhood], *Xinchao* [New tide] 1, no. 2 (1919); cited from All-China Women's Federation, *Wusi shiqi funü wenti wenxuan*, 129–130. The language in Ye's article was typical of the time. Terms like *duli jianquan* (independent and wholesome) and *guangming gaoshang* (upright and high-minded) appeared frequently in many articles written by the New Culturalists and May Fourth students. These terms, signifying an utopian ideal, were deliberately used to mold a new national character. They have become frequently used phrases by educated Chinese in the twentieth century.

36. See Zhou Zuoren, "Ren de wenxue" [Human literature] (1918), in *Nüxing de faxian* [The discovery of women], ed. Shu Wu (Beijing: Wenhua yishu chubanshe, 1990), 3–10. Zhou advocated an individualistic humanism and claimed that, after four thousand years of history, Chinese had not yet discovered the human being.

In the early stages of China's New Culture movement, progressive ideas about women's emancipation and the woman problem in general were all guided by the fundamental idea of "the discovery of the human being." "The discovery of the human being" happened in Europe in the fifteenth and sixteenth centuries. It became an old issue by the beginning of the twentieth century. But it was a fresh issue in China. "The discovery of the human being" in Europe did not, at first, include women. "The discovery of women" only happened two centuries later. But in China, the two discoveries were made simultaneously, which was certainly a more difficult task than that in Europe. The race to catch up by a nation lagging behind necessarily required double effort. However, unlike Europe, which had to experience an interval of two centuries, China accomplished the two discoveries in one battle. If we just talk about speed, we can say the successors surpass the predecessors.[37]

The Chinese enlightenment was perceived as in line with the universal process of evolution—with the difference that the newcomers had the benefit of hindsight in their eventually successful efforts to catch up. European enlightenment began with exclusive male rights, and as a result, the West had to wait another two centuries to make the second discovery—"the discovery of women." The advocates of Chinese enlightenment were fully aware of the limitations of earlier Western models, and in their universalist thinking, China could leap over this long interval if women's emancipation was included in the Chinese enlightenment. Moreover, many New Culturalists observed that Western societies were still male-centered. In achieving women's emancipation, China might "surpass" the West in the process of democratization.[38]

Whereas Shu's observation, substantiated by historical documentation, points to the strands of humanism and universalism in the New Culture, another Chinese scholar, Qian Liqun, emphasizes the importance of cosmopolitanism in the New Culturalists' perception of women's issues. Qian contends that the "awakening of human beings" in the New Culture movement was a simultaneous awakening of the "consciousness of the individual"

37. Ibid., 5–6.
38. For example, Li Dazhao in 1919 called for women's emancipation and criticized the West in this respect: "Democracy in contemporary Europe and America is still not true democracy, because all their movements, legislation, speech and ideas are still male-centered. They have no concern for the interests of the other half, women." Li Dazhao, "Funü jiefang yu democracy" [Women's emancipation and democracy], *Shaonian Zhongguo* [The young China] 1, no. 4 (1919); cited from All-China Women's Federation, *Wusi shiqi funü wenti wenxuan*, 27.

and the "consciousness of humankind." New Culturalists' concern for the development of the individual was linked to their deep concern about the future of humankind. "In the minds of Zhou Zuoren's generation, women's emancipation was closely connected to a holistic development of human nature. Their thinking on the woman problem, in fact, encompassed their thinking on the development of human nature in general."[39]

Hung-Yok Ip, in her study of the May Fourth intellectuals, noticed this same cosmopolitan-internationalist commitment to democracy. Analyzing Chen Duxiu and Li Dazhao, Ip comments,

> To be sure, a nationalistic commitment underlay their wish to construct a "democratic" international relationship, since such a relationship would promote the independence and dignity of the weak nations. Even so, the nationalistic commitment at least did not narrow these two eminent intellectuals' cosmopolitan-internationalist democratic vision to an exclusive concern for the removal of oppression, but inspired them further to appreciate the more positive elements—love, mutual respect and mutual aid—at an international level.[40]

This cosmopolitan-internationalist strand was extant in much of the New Culture works on women. Writers would often discuss women's issues both in the West and in China in the same article, conveying a concern for the entire human race. Li Dazhao wrote "The Woman Problem after the War" to examine Western women's situation and the feminist movement there. The article not only shows Li's familiarity with developments in the West, but also demonstrates his astute understanding of the relationship between gender and class. Such a careful study arose out of his deep concern not only for China but also for world civilization. He ended his article with these words: "I cannot arbitrarily decide if women in China have any interest in women's problems in the world. But I strongly wish that Chinese society was not in 'semiparalysis.' And I strongly hope that China will not be a reason why world civilization in the new century will remain a civilization in 'semiparalysis.'"[41]

---

39. Qian Liqun, Zhou Zuoren lun [On Zhou Zuoren] (Shanghai: Shanghai renmin chubanshe, 1991), 124.

40. Ip, "More Than Ideological Beings," 94.

41. Li Dazhao, "Zhanhou zhi furen wenti" [Women's problems after the war], Xin qingnian [New youth] 6, no. 2 (1919); cited from All-China Women's Federation, Wusi shiqi funü wenti wenxuan, 20. "Semiparalysis" was a metaphor used earlier by Jin Tianhe, the author of Nüjie zhong, when he argued that if women did not have education, the nation would be like a semiparalyzed person. The paralyzed half would eventually affect the other half of the body. Because of the New Culturalists'

Li Dazhao's utopian vision of humanity's future stresses the centrality of gender, an emphasis similar to Kang Youwei's thesis in *Datong shu*. In the high tide of student activism after the May Fourth Incident, Li wrote "Women's Emancipation and Democracy" to instigate a women's liberation movement in China. In that article he argued,

> All classes in the society can be changed. The rich can become poor, and the poor can become rich. Landlords and capitalists can become workers, and workers can become landlords and capitalists. With adequate social transformation, all these classes may disappear. Only the line between man and woman is permanent and unchangeable. Therefore, democracy between the two sexes is more important than anything else. If we want to demand democracy between the two sexes, the women's liberation movement is also more important than anything else.[42]

In later years, in the Communist Party's analysis, a proletarian revolution became more important than anything else, and women's emancipation could only be achieved through women's participation in the revolution, rather than through an independent feminist movement. However, in the first stage of the New Culture movement, male champions—including Li Dazhao and Chen Duxiu, future founders of the Chinese Communist Party—insisted that the gender issue was central. Although they approached the gender issue from a variety of intellectual commitments and concerns, and although many of them changed intellectual ground constantly, the concerted voices of these eminent men nevertheless created a liberal humanist discourse on women's emancipation.

Before we leave these male champions, there is one more question that should be asked. Beyond or beneath their professed intellectual commitment to women's emancipation, is there something at the subconscious level that might explain these men's behavior?

In an interesting study "The Language of Despair: Ideological Representations of the 'New Women' by May Fourth Writers," Ching-kiu Stephen Chan argues that "the modern intellectual wanted desperately to re-present *himself* via a mutation in the crisis of the 'other.'" The May Fourth intellectuals, Chan suggests, not only conveyed to their readers a crit-

---

repeated use, this phrase became well-known in the May Fourth era. Most people used it to connect women's emancipation with the well-being of the nation. But Li Dazhao uses it here to express concerns beyond the nation's interests.

42. Li Dazhao, "Funü jiefang yu democracy"; cited from All-China Women's Federation, *Wusi shiqi funü wenti wenxuan*, 27.

ical sense of unrest and bewilderment, but actually shaped the collective consciousness of historical crisis. Moreover, Chan proposes, "[For] the May Fourth intellectuals (among them iconoclastic writers of all sorts), to capture the historical moments of their time was, in essence, to summon up those experiences of crisis *for* a new mode of representation, and (thus) *as* the question of representation itself." And the act of representation, Chan contends, should be "recognized as an objectifying process of the identity crisis rooted in the collective unconscious of the May Fourth writers."[43] Therefore, the May Fourth men's construction of the images of new women reflected these men's unconscious anxiety over their own identity crisis.

Chan focuses on the representation of women in literary works by May Fourth male writers. His purpose differs from my purpose in this study, which examines the disruption of traditional gender relationships by male champions. His source materials are different from mine, insofar as he does not discuss the nonliterary texts about women written by May Fourth male intellectuals. The messages in their nonliterary texts, such as the debates on the woman problem and agitation for a feminist movement, often differ greatly from those in their literary texts. For example, the representation of new women in literary works, as Chan illustrates, appropriated the sex binary, an intellectual self (male) versus the emotional other (female). But in nonliterary texts, the most prominent theme contradicts the sex binary by appealing to the liberal concept of an ungendered, universal human being. Our previous discussion of male champions' nonliterary works demonstrates that the goal of Chinese women's emancipation, as perceived by those men, was for Chinese women to cross gender boundaries and to become independent *ren* (persons, or human beings). Therefore, the literary representation of new women, though a part of the discourse about new women during the May Fourth era, should be distinguished from the dominant liberal humanist theme in the same discourse. The distinction may help us understand the construction of subjectivity on the part of actual new women, beyond the new women who appear as a trope in male literary representations.

If we keep this distinction in mind, Chan's theory of representation is useful in our examination of male champions' advocacy of women's emancipation. After all, the nonliterary texts by men were but a different form of representation. The critique of women's oppression in Confucian culture

43. Ching-kiu Stephen Chan, "The Language of Despair: Ideological Representations of the 'New Women' by May Fourth Writers," *Modern Chinese Literature* 4, nos. 1 and 2 (1988): 19–38.

and the advocacy of women's emancipation highlighted the point that "the modern intellectual desperately wanted to re-present *himself*" via gender issues. His attack on the gender system in China allowed him to express his alienation from the ancient culture. His embrace of Nora revealed not only his frustration with the Chinese hierarchical and patriarchal family, but also—at a more profound level—his resentment of the burdens and constraints he experienced in a social structure based on networks of hierarchical and differential human relationships and their associated responsibilities and obligations (namely, Confucian ethics). He himself dreamed of being an independent person with individual freedom. Moreover, his fundamental crisis was generated by a painful realization of his peripheral and subaltern position in China's semicolonization by the West. The comforting, centuries-old sense of superiority enjoyed by Chinese male literati was forcefully undermined by the powerful, "superior" West. Taking a leading role in identifying an "oppressed" and "inferior" social group—women— the modern intellectual reaffirmed his own superiority. In short, his outcry for women's emancipation also *represented*, or, gave voice to, his own conscious or unconscious desires, conflicts, and crises.[44]

The modern intellectual's need of representation was psychologically connected to his unconscious identity crisis, a point Chan expounds in his study. Retaining the idea of identity crisis, we may approach the question of male representation from a cultural and social perspective. Why didn't the Western-educated, modern Chinese intellectual simply raise the banner of self-emancipation instead of women's emancipation? What prevented him from openly acting out his own desire to be emancipated? These questions lead us to a point that many Western scholars of May Fourth Chinese intellectuals have made: even the so-called cultural rebels or iconoclasts were severely constrained by the very culture they wanted to remold.[45] In the hegemony of Confucian culture, individual self-interest could not be a professed end of one's action, especially if one desired social prestige. The Confucian maxim *ke ji fu li* (subdue the self and return to the rituals of antiquity) did not grant legitimacy to "being oneself" or "expressing oneself."

---

44. For a comparison of Western and Chinese societies, and a discussion on Chinese moral obligations in the Confucian norms, see Fei Xiaotong's *From the Soil: The Foundations of Chinese Society*, trans. Gary G. Hamilton and Wang Zheng (Berkeley: University of California Press, 1992).

45. For example, Jerome Grieder, *Hu Shih and the Chinese Renaissance*, Lee Feigon, *Chen Duxiu*, and Vera Schwarcz, *The Chinese Enlightenment* (Berkeley: University of California Press, 1986) all noticed the cultural continuity in the New Culturalists.

Instead, the Confucian ethical system "grants each individual a highly personal satisfaction in heeding its standards but directs every person's behavior toward the good of the family and the larger society."[46] To be ethical and moral was to fulfill social obligations to others. Anyone who wanted social standing must display a decent level of social-mindedness. In this cultural context, a demand for self-emancipation would not be seen as legitimate. And anyone who made such a demand could go nowhere beyond being viewed as idiosyncratic. Promoting Western individualism, the New Culturalists nevertheless had to legitimize this effort (either consciously or unconsciously) in terms of national well-being and modernity. Seen in this light, the discovery of women as an oppressed social group by the New Culturalists was indeed fortunate. Representing the oppressed, the modern intellectuals not only were able to express their own alienation and frustration, but, more important, could now also locate their own social positions in a turbulent world. As Zhou Zuoren remarked astutely in 1927, "The masses are still the most fashionable icon now. Whatever oneself wants to do is done in order to fulfill the demand of the masses, just like receiving the mandate from heaven in ancient times."[47]

Chinese women were the first oppressed group that the modern intellectuals chose to represent. Later, under the influence of Marxism and Leninism, intellectuals on the Left would represent workers and peasants, a trend so strong by 1927 that the detached Zhou Zuoren felt he must criticize it.

Representing oppressed women, the modern intellectual achieved several things simultaneously. He satisfied his own culturally implanted need for social responsibility, as well as meeting societal expectations for a scholar. He found a social issue with a potentially large constituency, unlike his effort at "new literature," which could be viewed as merely a fight among literati (wenren) over literary forms. Now, with the new form of literature and vernacular (baihua) to advocate women's emancipation, the modern intellectual found himself moving rapidly away from his former obscurity. The explosion of debate on the woman problem, or by now women's problems, in the May Fourth student movement both testified to the increasing influence of the New Culturalists and helped to extend their influence beyond

46. Frederick W. Mote, *Intellectual Foundations of China* (New York: McGraw-Hill, 1989), 41. In the Confucian concept, a human being is constituted by what he or she is supposed to perform in accordance with Confucian moral codes. For a further discussion of self and society in Confucian culture, see the introduction to Fei, *From the Soil.*

47. Zhou Zuoren, "Beigouyan tongxin" [A correspondence from Beigouyan], in Shu Wu, *Nüxing de faxian,* 12.

literary circles. By the early 1920s, the small number of New Culturalists had established themselves as the guides who would lead youth into a new age. Without understanding the underlying benefits (psychological or social) for male champions of women's emancipation, we could not comprehend why so many educated men followed their trail so quickly during the May Fourth era. It was an exhilarating historical moment, when both educated men and women were empowered by a man-made feminist discourse.

Empowering as it was, the New Culturalists' representation of Chinese women had problems. As Chan points out, in the male literary representation, the new woman spoke what was on men's minds rather than in her own voice. The male representation undermined the initial effort to subvert the dominant discourse on women. In their study of May Fourth literature, Chinese scholars Meng Yue and Dai Jinhua observe that the "oppressed women" and the new women in literary texts were the products of male writers' concepts of women, rather than actual descriptions of the women of that historical time. They find that in the men's discourse, "women were asked simultaneously to wake up and to continue sleeping."[48] In a study of Chinese modern fiction, Yue Ming-bao further criticizes May Fourth male writers' failure to link women's issues to language itself: "[M]any female voices which had historically been silenced by the tools of representation continued to be muffled by the new linguistic tools advocated by the revolutionary intellectuals of the May Fourth period. . . . Even though the writers are sincere in their intentions to defend women, their writing betrays the discursive habits of a patriarchal tradition which excludes women's experiences from its articulation."[49]

When women were inspired by the man-made feminist discourse in the larger social scene rather than in literary images, new dynamics came into play in ways that defied their male champions' imaginations. In women's own organized activities for women's emancipation in the early 1920s, women raised their voices loudly. Encouraged by the new language of women's emancipation, many educated women bravely pursued a life of their own rather than "continue sleeping." As I emphasize throughout this study, women are not passively made by male discourses. The May Fourth new women lived very different lives from the new women images con-

---

48. Meng Yue and Dai Jinhua, *Fuchu lishi dibiao* [Emerging from history] (Zhengzhou: Henan renmin chubanshe, 1989), 43.

49. Yue Ming-bao, "Gendering the Origins of Modern Chinese Fiction," in *Gender and Sexuality in Twentieth-Century Chinese Literature and Society*, ed. Tonglin Lu (Albany: State University of New York Press, 1993), 48, 54.

structed by male writers. Nevertheless, the discursive power of the New Culture elite paradoxically both stimulated a feminist movement and undermined the cause of women's emancipation in China.

With their increasing discursive and political power (especially after the mid 1920s), the New Culturalists defined why they wanted women's emancipation and what constituted women's emancipation. After they rose to the center of intellectual discourse in the early 1920s, the New Culturalists were quite complacent with their new authoritative position in defining women's issues. They could be extremely condescending toward women's own efforts at self-emancipation. Shen Yanbing, the renowned champion of the Chinese feminist movement, revealed his sense of superiority clearly in "On The New Woman," a critique of the newly published women's magazine. In his view, the articles written by women on the subject of women's emancipation only demonstrated the writers' ignorance of Western intellectual and literary theories. Because the articles "simply talk about what every one knows and what you see in every newspaper and periodical," they were devoid of value. Deploring women writers' lack of book knowledge, he admonished them in the voice of the guardian of the New Culture: "I advise the women in The New Woman, when in the future you have read a lot of books and want very much to express your opinions, it will still be better not to publish your own magazine. Because the New Culture movement does not need publications in larger numbers, but publications with higher standards."[50]

The male champions thus simultaneously disrupted and maintained hierarchical gender relationships. It was liberating to many women that the patriarchal power of Confucianism was challenged severely by the New Culturalists. But then women found a new male authority in the New Culture elite. It was reassuring to both men and women that the New Culture elite had assumed the position of moral and intellectual authority, but this authority could undermine the development of an independent women's movement.

The male champions' definition of women's emancipation changed with the changing intellectual and political currents. At the beginning of the New Culture movement, individualism was used to combat the Confucian culture, and women were urged to be independent persons and to revolt against feudalism. After the leftist intellectuals accepted Marxism, the individualistic theme was dropped and replaced by an emphasis on socialist revolu-

50. Pei Wei (Shen Yanbing), "Ping xinfunü" [On the new women], Funü zazhi [The ladies' journal] 6, no. 2 (1920): 1–3.

tion. In a speech to women in 1921, Chen Duxiu stressed that it was erroneous to think that women could achieve independence merely by leaving their natal families, because in capitalism, even if women found employment in society, they were still the slaves of capitalists. Women could only achieve independent personhood in socialism. "Nine-tenths of women's pain derives from economic problems. Socialism can solve not only women's problems but all problems. . . . Therefore, I hope men and women will all strive for socialism."[51] Chen's rudimentary Marxist analysis of women's problems, substantiated by translated European socialist works on women in those years, would develop into a dominant theory on women's emancipation in the CCP. Although the May Fourth intellectuals' endorsement of socialism was driven in part by a search for solutions to women's problems, in Marxist and Leninist analysis, gender issues were soon obscured by class struggle.[52]

Perhaps the most problematic issue in May Fourth men's representations of women is the fact that they viewed women's emancipation as serving larger purposes rather than as being an end in itself. The professed purposes included overthrowing feudalism, advancing the nation toward modernity, overcoming imperialism, and later, saving the nation. Associating women's emancipation with those grand causes helped clear the obstacles for Chinese women's advancement into the public arena, but at the same time, only a women's movement that was appended to a great cause could occupy a legitimate position in the mainstream discourse. The altruistic nature of Chinese women's emancipation eventually made some women feel more used than liberated, a sentiment expressed in the narratives in part 2.

All in all, the role of emancipator allowed May Fourth intellectuals to gloss over the contradictions and conflicts between old and new cultures in the minds of New Culturalists themselves. In naming Confucian culture as the oppressor, the New Culturalists successfully placed themselves in opposition to that oppressor. At the time, no one asked this New Culture elite,

---

51. Chen Duxiu, "Funü wenti yu shehuizhuyi" [The woman problem and socialism] (1921), in All-China Women's Federation, *Wusi shiqi funü wenti wenxuan*, 82–83.

52. Regardless of their different intellectual commitments or political orientations, the majority of May Fourth men who pondered women's emancipation agreed that the abolishing of private ownership was a precondition for women's final emancipation. Socialism, therefore, was embraced by many as the fundamental solution to women's problems. Chen Duxiu expressed this line of thinking in these simple words: "Women and laborers are both weak. If we want to help the weak resist the strong, there is no other way except for socialism" ("Funü wenti yu shehuizhuyi," 82–83).

"To what extent are you yourself a product of the hegemonic Confucian discourse? And what measures are you taking to address the patriarchal assumptions in your own consciousness?" In sharp contrast to the abundant discussion of how women should overcome all kinds of obstacles to achieve emancipation, few examined men's problems in achieving their own emancipation, especially psychological emancipation from the constraints and construction of the patriarchal culture.[53] In other words, raising women's consciousness did not go hand in hand with raising men's consciousness. The position of emancipator seemed to exempt male champions from self-scrutiny. As a result, male-centeredness and patriarchal language were not only present in many New Culturalists' written works but also openly maintained in their private lives.

Lu Xun's life exemplifies this patriarchal recidivism. After a long and unhappy arranged marriage, Lu Xun fell in love with Xu Guangping, a student seventeen years younger than himself. Xu was a new woman who had once been an activist in the May Fourth student movement in Tianjin. Having fully absorbed the May Fourth feminist language, she was ready to break free of the "old ethics" and to pursue her own love: "We believe that nothing should restrain a relationship between two persons of the opposite sex, and only the two involved should decide about their own life. So long as they love each other, respect and trust each other, and treat each other like

---

53. In this respect, Zhou Zuoren was an exception among the New Culturalists. He was consistent in his critique of male-centeredness. In "Beigouyan tongxin," he stressed, "A big error now is that everything still follows men's standards, including the women's movement." In later years, he continued to write short essays expressing his concern over women's fate in a male-centered culture. In many essays he emphasized the necessity and importance of women's own conscious effort at women's emancipation, revealing his distrust of men's activities on women's behalf. However, in the May Fourth era, his focus was on women's sexual freedom instead of men's interest in a male-centered culture. For Zhou Zuoren's discussions on a range of topics relating to women's liberation, see Shu Wu, *Nüxing de faxian*.

An article written in 1920 by Li Renjie touched upon the topic of men's emancipation. The author commented that few people discussed men's emancipation and proceeded to give his view on this issue. He argued that private ownership made men suffer but that a necessary precondition to eliminating private ownership was to allow women independence. Therefore, women's emancipation should come before men's emancipation, and men should help women achieve independence. He urged men to realize their self-interest in women's emancipation, lest men be hypocritical in advocating women's emancipation. He told a story of his friend who gave many lectures calling for women's emancipation, but who kept a concubine and beat his wife. See Li Renjie, "Nannü jiefang" [Men's and women's emancipation], in *Zhongguo funü wenti taolunji* [Collected essays on Chinese women's problems], ed. Mei Sheng (Shanghai: Xinwenhua chubanshe, 1929), 1: 68–88.

comrades, there is no need for any conventional form."[54] Resisting tremendous social pressure, she lived with Lu Xun even though she knew that he would not divorce his legal wife, whom he viewed as "the victim of old customs."[55]

In their ten years together, Xu served as Lu's secretary and homemaker. Many times, this new woman tried to involve herself in public activities or find a career of her own. But each time, Lu Xun vetoed her decision. About her attempt to run a women's periodical, he would say, "What is the point of doing something so inconsequential that it brings no pain, not even a scratch?" About her job opportunities, he would say, "My two articles will bring me the same amount of money that you labor for a month to earn. Plus you have to watch your boss's face. It is better that you stay at home to help me and let me write more."[56] For Lu's sake, Xu forsook her dream of an independent career. The only thing she would not let go of was the three hundred silver dollars that she had saved from her teaching salary before she began to live with Lu Xun. In case she and Lu Xun ever separated, that amount of money would sustain her for a few months until she could find a job.

It was often painful for a new woman like Xu Guangping to consciously sacrifice everything for the sake of the man she loved. As she wrote, "His work is great. But I am just being a housewife!" The thought caused her deep agony but did not change her pattern of self-sacrifice. She knew perfectly well the cause of her internal conflict: "I think I may be a combination of old and new ideas. This combination may be satisfying to some people, such as my spouse. But I am not satisfied; instead, I am often depressed.

54. Xu Guangping's letter to Xu Shoutang, who was writing a chronology of Lu Xun after Lu's death in 1936. The quote is from Zen Zhizhong's *Sanren xing* [A journey of the three] (Beijing: Zhongguo qingnian chubanshe, 1990), 391–392. In this biographical work, Zen uses historical documents to reconstruct Lu Xun's private life and his relationships with his legal wife, Zhu An, and his common-law wife, Xu Guangping.

55. See Tang Si (Lu Xun), "Suiganlu sishi" [Informal essay, no. 40], *Xin qingnian* [New youth] 6, no. 1 (1919); reprint, in All-China Women's Federation, *Wusi shiqi funü wenti wenxuan*, 200–201. Written in 1919, this article expressed Lu Xun's pain in a loveless marriage as well as his moral obligation toward his legal wife. Because she, too, was a victim of the old custom, Lu Xun at that time felt he had to sacrifice his own happiness to accompany her forever. And even after he began to live with Xu Guanping, he continued his financial responsibility to Zhu An. For an understanding of Lu Xun's changing views on pursuing love and of the relationship between Lu and Xu, see also Lu Xun, *Liangdishu* [Letters between two places] (Beijing: Renmin wenxue chubanshe, 1973).

56. Zen Zhizhong, *Sanren xing*, 356–357.

When I am guided by the new ideas, I am discontented with the status quo. When I am restrained by the old morality, I am contented with things as they are."[57]

 It is a telling observation that the combination of old and new in a woman satisfied the needs of men like Lu Xun. Championing the cause of women's emancipation, not all the New Culturalists were ready to give up their male privileges in the patriarchal society, privileges that could only be maintained through women's self-sacrifice. Though new women such as Xu Guangping were inspired by the principle of gender equality, they were at the same time burdened with the Confucian morality deep in their unconscious. As a woman, especially a junior woman, facing the demands of a senior man in a prestigious social position, it would be immoral and selfish for her to assert her equal rights and equal treatment. The "new" principle of equality was in direct conflict with the "old" principle of hierarchical differential social relations and obligations. And the "old" principle, in Xu's case, gained the upper hand in the new woman's personal life. In a sense, the Xu-Lu relationship, the young student and the senior teacher, the emancipated and the emancipator, embodied the relationship between the new women and the male champions of the May Fourth era. The historical burden of the new women was a blessing for the May Fourth men. The male champions' sense of superiority as well as their cultural entitlement to privileges were unchallenged but sustained in an age of unprecedented agitation for women's emancipation.

57. Ibid., 357–358.

2   A Case of Circulating Feminism
The Ladies' Journal

Feminist theorist Chris Weedon has observed that "in order to have a so-cial effect, a discourse must be at least in circulation."[1] What made the New Culturalists' efforts at women's emancipation decisively different from Kang Youwei's effort was not that the ideas of New Culturalists were more rad-ical, but that their ideas were *circulated* much more widely than Kang's. Rapidly expanding women's education in the early twentieth century pre-pared a growing number of female recipients for new ideas. The May Fourth student movement further turned many female students into active pro-mulgators of New Culture ideas. With both men's and women's involve-ment, women's magazines and women's columns or forums in newspapers sprang up like mushrooms after the May Fourth Incident in 1919. *The Ladies' Journal* [*Funü zazhi*] was the most influential and had the widest circulation, the most subscribers, and the longest life of the mainstream women's magazine that followed the New Culture fad. As such, it best il-lustrates the process of popularizing the New Culture feminism.

THEMES BEFORE THE MAY FOURTH INCIDENT IN 1919

The Commercial Press in Shanghai published *The Ladies' Journal* in Janu-ary 1915, the same year that Chen Duxiu started *New Youth*. As the most successful publishing house in China, the Commercial Press had bookstores in twenty-eight Chinese cities, as well as in Hong Kong, Macao, and Sin-gapore. *The Ladies' Journal* was thus able to reach women across a wide geographical area, unlike most women's magazines, whose influence was

1. Chris Weedon, *Feminist Practice and Poststructuralist Theory* (Oxford: Black-well Publishers, 1987), 110.

limited by constraints in distribution and finance. And because women's literacy was still a status symbol in the 1910s, the journal naturally targeted women of the middle and upper classes. Female teachers and students contributed to its forums and columns. But most of the articles were written by men, including the editor in chief, Wang Yunzhang, and many of its readers were men.[2]

From the beginning, *The Ladies' Journal* emphasized the importance of women's education. In the opening issue, several teachers (male and female) offered their views on Chinese women's education and the role *The Ladies' Journal* could play in promoting this process. The contributors believed that *The Ladies' Journal* should facilitate the exchange of knowledge between women and that such education would teach women to be virtuous mothers and good wives for the sake of the nation. As one woman contributor wrote, "Is it not a woman's greatest duty to help her husband and to teach her son? Is it not the intention of the journal to respect this duty and make the majority of women good wives and virtuous mothers for the nation?"[3]

The effort to make women virtuous mothers and good wives by educating them was inspired or legitimized by Western examples. Contributors frequently referred to Western models in emphasizing the importance of women's education. American women's domesticity was praised and romanticized in a contributor's argument for using education to maintain Chinese women's domesticity. "In the country with the most extensive women's rights, women regard helping their husbands as the basic duty."[4] This male writer used American "true womanhood" defensively to fend off opposition to Chinese women's traditional role, whereas a woman contributor positively linked women's domestic role to nationhood, using Western models:

> In the last two decades, communication between China and the outside has vastly increased. We have begun to see our own inadequacy. We realize that what made Europe and America powerful in the world is not merely their strong ships and formidable guns. It is their educated virtuous mothers, good wives, and ladies who became the backbone

2. For a discussion of the background of *The Ladies' Journal*, see Jacqueline Nivard, "Women and the Women's Press," in *Republican China* 10, no. 1b (November 1984): 37–55. For more information on the Commercial Press in Shanghai in the May Fourth era, see also Mao Dun, *Wo zouguode daolu* [The journey I have made] (Hong Kong: Sanlian shudian, 1981), vol. 1, chapters 4 and 6.

3. Liang Lingxian, "Jingshu wujia jiude wei funüzazhi shi" [Presenting my family morality to *The Ladies' Journal*], *Funü zazhi* [The ladies' journal] 1, no. 1 (1915): 6.

4. Yu Tiansui, "Yuzhi nüzi jiaoyuguan" [My view on women's education], *Funü zazhi* [The ladies' journal] 1, no. 1 (1915): 1.

of the citizenry as domestic managers. . . . We women are benevolent by nature and our love for kindness is better than others. With the resources of two hundred million women in our country, with *The Ladies' Journal* as a forum for exchanging ideas on moral and intellectual education, we will work to benefit our country.[5]

The connection between women's education and national well-being had first been made by Liang Qichao in the late Qing.[6] Liang used examples of advanced women's education in the West and in Japan to argue that a strong nation and an intelligent people all begin with women's education. In his influential advocacy for women's education, women's traditional role of mother and wife acquired political significance. Women's ability to play that role intelligently determined whether the Chinese nation would survive in the modern world. In Liang's analysis, the dual goals of strengthening the nation and preserving the race depended entirely on educated mothers and wives. Liang's advocacy, together with his and other reformers' efforts to establish girls' schools, caused women's educational opportunities to expand steadily from the beginning of the twentieth century. Along with the development of women's school education, the theory emphasizing the sociopolitical significance of the virtuous mother and good wife entered the mainstream. In 1915 the educated ladies were still repeating the theme Liang had expounded seventeen years earlier.[7]

The Chinese theory of the virtuous mother and good wife in the early twentieth century bore a close resemblance to republican motherhood in the early years of the United States. As the United States moved toward becoming a modern nation, American women in the late eighteenth century were extolled as custodians of values, and women's education was seen as the key to prepare a woman for the glorious role of wife and mother. "Our ladies should be qualified to a certain degree, by a peculiar and suitable education, to concur in instructing their sons in the principles of liberty and government."[8] The nation's success depended to a large extent on how mothers shaped the values of their sons, who would become republican citizens.

Compare to US women

5. Liu Sheng, "Fakanci" [Opening remarks], *Funü zazhi* [The ladies' journal] 1, no. 1 (1915): 2–4.

6. For further discussion of Liang Qichao's role in promoting women's education, see chapter 4.

7. See Liang Qichao, "Bianfatongyi" [General ideas on reform], in *Zhongguo funü shenghuoshi* [A history of the lives of Chinese Women], by Chen Dongyuan (Shanghai: Commercial Press, 1928), 321–324.

8. Benjamin Rush, "Thoughts on Female Education," quoted in Nancy Woloch, *Women and the American Experience* (New York: McGraw-Hill, 1984), 91.

The republican mother, a well-educated woman, would imbue her daughters and sons with virtue, piety, and patriotism.

Just as republican motherhood legitimized women's education in the United States, Europe, and Japan, Liang Qichao's elaboration on the sociopolitical function of mother and wife legitimized women's education in China. The needs of the nation provided women with the initial opportunity of institutionalized education, an opportunity that would eventually cause many changes in women's lives. Although educated women were still excluded from public life, the role of republican mother or of the virtuous mother and good wife moved them halfway toward full citizenship. In other words, national debate on women's role in the new nation announced women's entrance into the nation's political life, even though they still occupied only a peripheral position in political discourse.

Although the emergence of women's education in China sounds like a familiar story repeated in many countries, the different historical and political contexts in which women's education was proposed laid the ground for different dynamics. For instance, when Chinese advocacy of women's education began, women's education was already well established in Japan, the United States, and many European countries. The sharp contrast between China and other countries in this respect—a contrast frequently pointed out in numerous texts—made the Chinese eager to catch up. Moreover, China was experiencing a period of national defeat by the West and Japan, and its scholars proposed women's education as a solution to the national crisis.

In the United States, women's education had spread during a time of national victory and growth. At the beginning of the nineteenth century, rapid social, economic, political, and geographical development in the United States gave rise to a profound yearning for stability. American men living in this turbulent world sought peace and security at home. Home was an "oasis in the desert," a "sanctuary" where "sympathy, honor, [and] virtue are assembled." It was a refuge "from the vexations and embarrassments of business." Men's need for a haven encouraged the cult of "true womanhood" and the ideology of domesticity. The newly emerged middle-class wives were put on a pedestal as keepers of the haven and guardians of values. Thus glorified, American women's traditional domestic role was sustained in a rapidly changing world.[9]

In contrast, Chinese men who brought women into the national politi-

---

9. See Nancy F. Cott, *The Bonds of Womanhood* (New Haven: Yale University Press, 1977), introduction and chapter 2. Also see Woloch, *Women and the American Experience*, chapter 6.

cal discourse were not seeking stability in the home. Rather, they called for changes in family and nation that would make China competitive in the modern world. Women were seen as half of China's human resources waiting to be developed. In many reform-minded men's analyses, China had fallen behind the West largely because half its population was backward, and women's education must transform this backward half, keeping in mind the model of the Western housekeeper. In consequence, the pre-1919 literature on Chinese women's education in *The Ladies' Journal* developed two parallel themes: one stressed the importance of women to the nation, and the other deplored the "poor quality" of Chinese women. Elaborating on the first theme, writings borrowed from the West the concept of women's benevolent nature and virtues. But the second theme was more often voiced: contributors discussed Chinese women's weaknesses and the ways to correct them for the sake of the nation. Some of the male contributors' comments amounted to an attack on womanhood. One male contributor listed eight main shortcomings of Chinese women: self-indulgence, laziness, licentiousness, bias, stupidity, narrow-mindedness, jealousy, and viciousness. After his misogynist remarks, the writer admonished, "Women's lack of morality is summarized briefly by these eight points. I hope that women educators will reform these evil habits and nurture an upright bearing in women."[10]

Men's admonitions also emerged in short stories. In one story, titled "The Enemy of Republican Citizens," the author described witnessing a mother beat her son to make him study. The story concludes with a vehement pronouncement:

> China will never perish in the hands of warlords but will perish in the hands of women. Unlike Western women, Chinese women cannot make men into brave good citizens like those in the European war. Rather, they hurt them and ruin them, making them idiots, unhealthy citizens who lack the strength to do things. A woman of this kind is not the mother of republican citizens, but the enemy of republican citizens.[11]

It is not clear how female readers responded to those harsh accusations. But the editor apparently regarded it as his duty to correct women's weaknesses. And the journal published articles written by women on the same

10. Ding Fengjia, "Nüjie zhenyan" [Admonishing women], *Funü zazhi* [The ladies' journal] 4 (1918), no. 2: 5–6 and no. 3: 1–4, quote in no. 3: 4.
11. Huang Yi'nong, "Guomin zhi di" [The enemy of republican citizens], *Funü zazhi* [The ladies' journal] 5, no. 9 (1919): 6.

topic. In the column for female students' essays, one student gave new meaning to the word *fu* (woman). The Chinese character *fu* is composed of two parts, *nü* (female) and *zhou* (broom). She argued that the ancient sages meant it was women's duty to keep the household clean. Without women's professional management, a home would run down. But women's broom should also sweep away another kind of dust: "Women have lived in darkness for two thousand years. Dependency has become their nature; jealousy, partiality, and superstition have become their natural habits, which are hard to break. They are all like dust in the heart. Only learning can correct the mistakes. Learning is like a broom that will sweep away all the dust in the heart."[12]

Whereas this woman contributor was concerned about "old" habits, another writer attacked the "new" habits of some women. An editorial titled "The Ideal Female Students" criticized female students' "disgusting behavior." The writer argued that although many female students were possessed of remarkable learning and morality, a few "black sheep" gave them all a bad name, so that the term "female student" (*nüxuesheng*) aroused fear and disgust in most Chinese people. What did those black sheep do?

> Opening their mouths, they talk about freedom and equality, equality between men and women, and political participation. In practice, they depend on others for their living. As soon as one becomes a student, she ceases to cook and do laundry. She becomes a good-for-nothing. Before, people said that female students dressed plainly, not like other women. But now this is not so. After they learn just a few English words, they try to write love letters in English so their parents cannot read them. Some master the Chinese language, but they often use it for the wrong purposes. No wonder those who insist that "ignorance in women is a virtue" now argue eloquently against sending daughters to school.[13]

At the end of the editorial, the writer reminded female students of their important duty: "Female students are today's students and tomorrow's virtuous mothers and good wives. You are closely connected to your family's prosperity and failure." Such attacks on female students' "disgusting behavior" reveal anxiety about the consequences of modern education. The task of reforming Chinese women was apparently a difficult one. Whether they were ignorant or learned, one had constantly to beware of their various shortcomings.

12. Chen Shizhen, "Shenfucong nüzhou zhiyi" [On the definitions of "woman"], *Funü zazhi* [The ladies' journal] 2, no. 4 (1916): 12.

13. Piao Ping Nüshi, "Lixiang zhi nüxuesheng" [The ideal female students], *Funü zazhi* [The ladies' journal] 1, no. 3 (1915): 1.

A more positive approach to molding Chinese women into virtuous mothers and good wives was to promote Western models of domesticity for Chinese women to emulate. Even reformers of this period who were viewed by the New Culturalists as conservatives looked to the West for inspiration. They were inspired by the ideology of domesticity and by the material existence of the middle-class nuclear family, especially in the United States. In their opinion, the American emphasis on domesticity was close to the Confucian teaching that asserted, "Cultivating oneself, one can manage the family; managing the family well, one can rule the country." What the ancient Chinese family needed was modern American management. *The Ladies' Journal* was full of translations from U.S. publications such as *Ladies' Home Journal* and *Mother's Magazine*. The contents ranged from personal hygiene to the Parent-Teacher Association and home economics. The scientific management of the modern home, the democratic spirit in child education, the companionship that the American wife provided to her husband, and the beautification of the home—all were emphasized as indispensable ingredients in modern civilization. The editor in chief hoped that by publishing accessible and interesting articles that taught modern, scientific homemaking, the journal would "cause the reform of housekeeping, increase the desire for learning, and turn the old family into the new family."[14]

Promulgating an American ideology of domesticity as a means of Chinese family reform, *The Ladies' Journal* also printed articles on world events. The column "Jishumen" [Reporting column] presented information on women around the world, including reports on European women's entrance into the labor force as a result of World War I. Accompanying photographs showed a Belgian female miner, a British milkmaid, female butcher, driver and porter, and a German female factory worker and mail carrier. Other

14. Xi Shen (Wang Yunzhang), "Tongxing wenda" [Correspondence with readers], *Funü zazhi* [The ladies' journal] 3, no. 7 (1917): 15. Editor Zhu-Hu Binxia, a woman who had been to Japan and the United States, offered a vivid and romantic description of the middle-class American family; in "Meiguo jiating" [The American family], she portrayed a happy and efficient American housekeeper who regarded her family as the sphere of her intellectual development. Zhu-hu also commented that American women's domesticity exemplified the Confucian teaching on family and nation. In *Funü zazhi* [The ladies' journal] 2, no. 2 (1916): 1–8. Such depictions, which advocate an American ideology of domesticity, may reflect the needs of the budding bourgeois class in Chinese metropolises. Located mostly in port cities where Western influence was strongest, bourgeois families often consciously imitated Western style as a way of self-identification. In a sense, *The Ladies' Journal* contributed to the shaping of the Westernized upper-class *taitai* (Mrs.) in China.

articles described Harriet Beecher Stowe's contribution to the abolition of slavery, British female students' organized activities, the Swedish women's movement, Japanese women's occupational opportunities, Philippine women's freedom in social activities and their high domestic and social status, and so on. Information conveyed by this column seemingly contradicted the dominant theme of domesticity. But it was a logical part of the editor's effort to broaden Chinese housekeepers' minds and to keep them updated on world events and developments.[15]

The journal also provided a forum for conflicting ideologies at home, mostly through the column "Guowen fanzuo" [Selected essays by female students]. Targeting female students as the main readership, the column invited them to contribute essays that they wrote in school. The published essays demonstrated the liveliness of female students' thought as well as the impact various ideologies had on them. In an essay analyzing the meaning of the word *fu* (woman), student Lu Zhenquan expressed an entirely different opinion from the one discussed previously. She argued that the combination of the symbol for "female" with the symbol for "broom" showed ancient people's contempt for women.

> The word *fu* means that a woman should hold a broom to clean. In the meaning of the ancient term "broom-woman," women were regarded as men's servants. The character for "slave servant"—*bi*—also has a female component, which is another proof of the contempt toward women. That is a great inequality in humanity. Every day, the world comes closer to civilization, and the human race is moving toward equality. We, the ones who unfortunately have female bodies, should reconsider the meaning of the word, respect and treasure ourselves, follow Confucian ethics, and protect our chastity in order to realize women's sacred values.[16]

In this contradictory passage, student Lu expresses indignation against "great inequality" but also readiness to follow conventional norms.

Another female student acknowledged the role of the virtuous mother but insisted that women be autonomous. In her call for organizing an autonomous students' union, Yin Tongwei argued, "It is very important for the citizens of the republic to have autonomy. Since women are the mothers of republican citizens, women's school education must make its high-

---

15. See "Jishumen" [Reporting column], *Funü zazhi* [The ladies' journal] 2, no. 3 (1916), 3, nos. 3, 5, and 10 (1917), and 5, no. 5 (1919).

16. Lu Zhenquan, "Fu cong nüzhou shi" [Defining "woman"], *Funü zazhi* [The ladies' journal] 2, no. 5 (1916): 2–3.

est priority the fostering of women's autonomous ability."[17] Student Sun Xiyu suggested that women achieve self-cultivation and moral refinement so that they could better shoulder the task of managing the family.[18] But student Ma Renchang was concerned with "what one can do to achieve independence":

> People without an occupation cannot make a living, let alone be independent. Dependency has serious consequences. Not only will the dependent person be impeded, but also the society and the nation will be affected. Nearly everything in the world begins with the individual, then extends from the individual to society, and from society to the nation. The individual is very important to the nation. Common people without talent or knowledge have to rely on others for a living. Such people, having to bear contempt and bullying by others, are most pitiable. Therefore, independence is the foundation of social existence.[19]

In her essay, Ma totally ignored the role of mother and wife, and she did not mention the importance of family either. She openly advocated an independent career. The centrality of individual independence in her argument is reminiscent of those famous essays by the New Culturalists before 1919, and it is likely that the teachers of these female students were exposed to New Culture literature. Whatever access these students had to New Culture ideas, their essays show that terms such as "equality," "freedom," "autonomy," and "independence" circulated among students before the May Fourth student movement in 1919.

Not only do the student essays reflect strands of the era's intellectual discourse, but the editorials also reveal the editor in chief's awareness of issues raised in the New Culturalist agitation for women's emancipation. As a matter of fact, in confronting the force of the New Culture movement, *The Ladies' Journal* took a conservative stance by publishing editorials that repudiated New Culture ideas. For example, the editorial in the May 1918 issue opposed coeducation in universities. The author insisted that China had different ethics from those of foreign countries. Chinese men and women should be separated to avoid intimacy. Universities should not break the ritual codes for the sake of female students. Moreover, the author argued, the

17. Yin Tongwei, "Nibenxiao xuesheng zizhihui zhengji huiyuanqi" [A notice calling for an autonomous student union in the school], *Funü zazhi* [The ladies' journal] 4, no. 1 (1918): 2.

18. Sun Xiyu, "Nüxuesheng zhi zeren" [The duties of female students], *Funü zazhi* [The ladies' journal] 4, no. 11 (1918): 3–4.

19. Ma Renchang, "Ren bi ruhe er houneng duli lun" [On what one can do to achieve independence], *Funü zazhi* [The ladies' journal] 4, no. 4 (1918): 2.

few occupations suitable for women did not require those women to possess the profound knowledge that universities provided.[20]

Although the journal was open-minded enough to publish letters from readers who disagreed with the editors' opinions, most of the editorials had a negative tone. In the August 1918 issue, an editorial titled "Nüquan pingyi" [On women's rights or power] warned its readers against the dangers that would come if women held rights or power. Because the Chinese word *quan* can mean both "rights" and "power," *nüquan* has often been understood as "women's power." Using this understanding of the term, the author listed all the cases in Chinese history in which "women usurped power." He contended that whenever an empress grabbed power or interfered with the rule of the emperor, the result was either domestic turmoil, or the fall of a dynasty. He suggested that officials in the republic should channel their wives' ambitions into safe avenues, allowing them to be principals or teachers in a girls' school. But "never let them meddle in finance, law, taxation, or other matters relating to the public interest," he warned. *Nüquan* would not only threaten the interest of the nation but also lead to women's dissolute social behavior and cause conflicts in the family. The author of the editorial emphasized that Chinese women should not imitate Western women in all ways, because "there are differences between Chinese and Western customs and habits. And in terms of women's autonomous ability and women's self-respect, China is far behind Euro-America." The author warned women readers that, for the sake of the republican nation, republican society, and republican family, they should not abuse women's power.[21]

As late as May 1919, an editorial was still harping on the theme of educating virtuous mothers and good wives. But now the argument took on a defensive tone, struggling against the widespread advocacy of women's vocational education. Again the author used the example of American women to illustrate his point. But this time the image of American women was negative: "It cannot be denied that twentieth-century American women have a very advanced intellectual education. But American women are selfish and love to dream, which is the result of their advanced education. . . . Seeking a career, American women grow tired of family life. More and more separate from their husbands and live independently. As a result, America's pro-

20. See Wang Zhuomin, "Lunwoguo daxue shangbuyi nannü tongxue" [On the inappropriateness of coeducation in China], *Funü zazhi* [The ladies' journal] 4, no. 5 (1918): 1–8.

21. Jiang Xuehui, "Nüquan pingyi" [On women's power], *Funü zazhi* [The ladies' journal] 4, no. 8 (1918): 4–7.

ductivity is reduced and population growth is low."[22] Because American women's vocational education led to such disaster, the author was adamant that China should reject the American model. Instead, because men and women had different normative statuses and different obligations, education should be differential, too. "A man and a woman should each do what is appropriate to his or her role and never meddle in the affairs of the opposite sex." The author expressed a strong wish to maintain gender boundaries, and his language was utterly unlike the ongoing discourse of gender equality. This editorial and others cited previously show that *The Ladies' Journal* held fast to its opposition to the New Culture.

In May 1919, the influential New Culture journal *Xin Chao* [The new wave] published an article by Luo Jialun criticizing all the journals published by the Commercial Press. Luo condemned *The Ladies' Journal* for "only telling women to be slaves of men." This "is a real crime against the human race. I have even heard that in quite a few schools students are only allowed to read that kind of journal! . . . If these journals are not reformed thoroughly, there should be no place for them in society."[23] This direct attack by the New Culturalists combined with the May Fourth student movement to create powerful support for discarding the old ideas, old language, and old culture. *The Ladies' Journal* was pressured to change.

The New Culture did not break into the conservative journal right away. From May to October 1919, there was little change in *The Ladies' Journal*. The clamor of the students' demonstrations, petitions, and public talks seemed to be taking place in another world. The journal continued to publish articles that taught readers how to manage a modern home—with one exception: a report on Deng Chunlan's call to abolish the gender barrier in universities. Living in the remote province of Gansu and encouraged by the tide of gender equality, a young woman named Deng requested enrollment in Beijing University. When the school did not reply, she published announcements in national newspapers, calling on like-minded women to form a female student group that would petition in Beijing to allow women to enroll in universities. She also appealed to all the men in the nation who were "patriotic, humanistic, and lovers of the Chinese race" to support the cause. Deng's actions encouraged numerous others to demand women's equal ed-

22. Song Guoshu translated and commented on Zhang Dengren's "Shuo nüzijiaoyu" [On women's education], *Funü zazhi* [The ladies' journal] 5, no. 5 (1919): 8. Both Song and Zhang were university students.

23. Luo Jialun, "Jinri Zhongguo zhi zazhijie" [Magazines in contemporary China], in *Zhongguo xiandai chuban shiliao* [Historical materials on publishing in modern China], ed. Zhang Jinglu (Beijing: Zhonghua shuju, 1954), 83.

ucation in China. The September issue of *The Ladies' Journal* printed her announcements and her original letter to Cai Yuanpei, the president of Beijing University, but made no comment on her efforts. This curious gesture of the journal, letting in a little bit of news of the new wave but showing no intention to follow the new wave, reveals the editor's ambivalence. It was too difficult for the leading women's journal not to respond to the women's big event of the day. However, the editor in chief was not ready to give in to the new tide. It is also possible that all the conservative articles printed in the issues after the May Fourth student movement had been solicited long ago, and the editor in chief had no intention of disrupting his routine management of the journal, even though he felt the pressure to do so.[24]

Then, all of a sudden, the journal printed a November editorial boldly titled "Emancipated Women and Women's Emancipation," written by "Pei Wei," a pen name for Shen Yanbing. Unlike the previous essays, it was published in the vernacular and repeated the New Culturalists' major points on women's emancipation. The editorial was a declaration that the New Culture had successfully invaded hitherto conservative territory. The author, Shen Yanbing, was a translator of textbooks at the Commercial Press and a rising New Culture star at the time. Decades later, he recalled the situation. Under the influence of *New Youth*, Shen began his new literary activities. He translated Western and Russian literature into Chinese and wrote literary critiques as sideline work. He was a prolific writer, and by the end of 1919 his name had appeared in many New Culture journals and newspaper columns. One day he was approached by Wang Yunzhang, who was the editor in chief of both *The Ladies' Journal* and *The Short Stories Monthly*. Wang asked Shen to be the editor of a new *Short Stories Monthly* column devoted to new literature. Wang also asked Shen to write articles "discussing issues like women's emancipation" for *The Ladies' Journal*. Later Shen found out that the top executives of the Commercial Press had decided to follow the new wave. Shen was given a mandate to present reformed journalism to the Press's readers.[25]

Shen did not waste any time. He spent most of his energy reforming *The Short Stories Monthly*, but he also wrote and translated eight articles on

24. The editor in chief, Wang Yunzhang, was also in charge of *Xiaoshuo Yuebao* [The short stories monthly]. According to Shen Yanbing, who succeeded Wang as the editor in chief of *Xiaoshuo Yuebao*, Wang had enough submissions stockpiled to fill an entire year of issues. Shen had to discard all those articles Wang had paid for in order to start a reformed monthly with New Culture themes. See Mao Dun, *Wo zouguo de daolu*, 140.

25. Ibid., 134–135.

women. "Emancipated Women and Women's Emancipation" was the first to appear in *The Ladies' Journal*. The others were printed in the first issue of 1920, making the obvious statement that the journal was now in "new" hands. Articles on home economics, cooking, and making clothes and toys were replaced by discussions of women's emancipation. Shen observed victoriously, "This meant *The Ladies' Journal*, which had promoted good-wife-and-virtuous-mother-ism for five years, was forced to change with the powerful current of the times."[26] The respectable journal's endorsement of New Culture indicated that New Culture was no longer a radical fringe. Rather, it had exploded into Chinese mainstream intellectual, social, and political discourse, and the topics of New Culture feminist agitation became legitimate issues for "decent" women to talk about. In this sense, taking over the mainstream fortress *The Ladies' Journal* greatly enhanced the discursive power of New Culture feminism.

THE DEBATE ON WOMEN'S EMANCIPATION

Unlike the early stage of the New Culture movement, when male champions focused on exposing women's oppression, during the May Fourth student movement men's attention shifted to women's emancipation. When *The Ladies' Journal* first responded to the rising New Culture feminism, women's emancipation was a popular yet unclear concept. The slogan of women's emancipation was raised as a revolt against the old culture and old society that oppressed women. But what was the goal and the content of women's emancipation? And in what way could women's emancipation be achieved in China? These were unsettled, even unsettling, questions. In the reformed *Ladies' Journal*, a number of articles explored these questions from various perspectives. The December 1919 editorial warned readers that stirring a woman's heart with emotional words, without a sober assessment of women's capability, would surely lead to trouble and failure. The result would be harmful to women and society. This editorial, most likely written by the conservative editor in chief, expressed the misgivings many people had about women's emancipation.[27]

The concern over women's capacity for emancipation was common even among those who advocated women's emancipation. This concern was related to their view of the goal of women's emancipation. For many advo-

26. Ibid., 136.
27. See Ji Zhe, "Benzazhi jinhou zhi fangzhen" [The future policy of our journal], *Funü zazhi* [The ladies' journal] 5, no. 12 (1919): 1–3.

cates, women's emancipation had a functional goal: to improve society at large. Shen Yanbing stated the point plainly,

> Why should we promote women's emancipation? For the sake of being humanitarian? No. To release women's anger? Certainly not. I dare say that the goal of our promoting women's emancipation is for the sake of social evolution. Because we take social evolution as a fundamental concept, we try to raise the level of women's personhood and ability, *making them the same as men.* We also try to make future generations better than we. Because we want to raise the level of women's personhood and ability, we will first discard all kinds of bondage over women—which is a means rather than an end.[28]

The emancipated women, in Shen's opinion, were the ones who could both enjoy human rights and fulfill human duty. Duty here was to shoulder half the responsibility of reforming society. "Women should be prepared and develop the ability to carry this load. That is true emancipation."[29] After all, Shen contended, women's emancipation depended on emancipated women rather than on men. For the sake of social evolution, men should no longer carry the entire load of social responsibility. But this reasoning led Shen and other male writers to see women themselves as a great obstacle to women's emancipation: in the writers' opinion, Chinese women were largely unprepared or even unqualified for emancipation. As a male writer put it, "We think women should have the same position as men in reform. But in our country the majority of women themselves have not reformed. How can they reform other things? Women in our country can be said to be totally lacking in the ability to reform the country, because they have none of the qualifications required for reforming the country."[30]

Because women's emancipation was essential to social evolution but women were not yet qualified for this emancipation, male reformers had no choice but to try their best to make women qualified. Thus "women's emancipation" became the "reform of women." Ironically, like the pre-reform *Ladies' Journal*'s goal of turning women into modern housekeepers, many male contributors to the journal were once again trying to reform women— albeit with a different goal in mind. As a result, despite their new language,

28. Pei Wei, "Funü jiefang wenti de jianshe fangmian" [Constructing women's emancipation], *Funü zazhi* [The ladies' journal] 6, no. 1 (1920): 2; emphasis added.

29. Pei Wei, "Jiefang de funü yu funu de jiefang" [Emancipated women and women's emancipation], *Funü zazhi* [The ladies' journal] 5, no. 11 (1919): 2.

30. Yun Fang, "Gaizao shidai de funü yingjuyou shemo zige?" [What qualifications should women in the age of reform have?], *Funü zazhi* [The ladies' journal] 6, no. 6 (1920): 2.

many articles took the form of didactic literature, either criticizing women's weaknesses or setting up new standards for women to attain.

Shen Yanbing had four admonitions for educated women. First, seek self-emancipation: establish a noble personality and ideals that are higher than the existing norms and do not be disturbed by the suggestions of the ignorant masses. Second, understand the true meaning of new intellectual waves: emancipation is mental emancipation requiring a strong will; human life should be based on mutual help, not merely on making demands and vying with one another. Third, women should try their best to improve their abilities and help their poor and ignorant sisters rather than waste time vying with men for rights. Fourth, women's activities should not exceed the scope that current social life allowed.[31]

Although these admonitions placed limits on women's emancipation, they were nevertheless embraced to different degrees by many men and women. Articles by men had titles like "A Point Today's Chinese Women Should Be Conscious Of—Self Responsibility," and "Several Deep-Rooted Bad Habits that the New Woman Should Eradicate." Stressing the theme that women should improve themselves in order to shoulder the responsibility of social reform, the authors' tones varied from encouraging to condemning. A warm appeal from Peng Ji'nen said,

> Female compatriots! You should be aware that you are in danger—under men's oppression and social bondage. Escape from this danger requires much energy. You should raise and store your energy. All I have said is either to urge most women to abandon that kind of inhuman life and to live a rational "human" life, or to help you rise up to shoulder responsibility and to pursue happiness for humankind. I hope our contemporary female compatriots will not confine yourselves in boudoirs any more.[32]

A discussion of women's personhood by Wang Pingling blamed women for the rise of male-centered culture and the low level of China's social evolution. "What prevented Chinese society from evolving is women's loss of personhood and their relinquishing of natural duty. With men alone managing affairs in society, there was certainly little progress." Women themselves were responsible for what they had become. Wang argued that women had let their abilities degenerate and given up their rights, willingly

31. Pei Wei, "Jiefang de funü yu funü de jiefang," 1–6.
32. Peng Ji'neng, "Jinri Zhongguo nüzi yingjuewu de yidian—zijide zeren" [A point today's Chinese women should be conscious of—self-responsibility], *Funü zazhi* [The ladies' journal] 6, no. 6 (1920): 4.

living a life "in hell." "I am sure this is not a result of men's deliberate oppression and abuse. To be honest, it happened because women themselves had no ability." Because women had only themselves to blame, Wang asserted that they should focus on self-emancipation: "In today's high wave of promoting emancipation, what we hear women saying is either how men have bullied them or how men have abused them. In my view, these words should be saved for a while. You should first reform yourselves. Senseless outcries rather than eager self-reform will be ineffective. Women's emancipation should start with women's self-emancipation."[33]

The authors who emphasized women's self-reform listed what they saw as women's many weaknesses: dependency, vanity, narrow-mindedness, incorrigibility, superstition, conservatism, lack of judgment, and lack of the concept of nation. In fact, when it came to negative or contemptuous views toward women, there was little difference between conservative men and New Culture men. It is likely that some advocated women's emancipation precisely because they had negative views toward women and were eager to reform them. What is apparent in this practice of reforming women is the obvious sense of superiority expressed by those male authors. Chinese women, it seems, became the most convenient medium for Chinese male intellectuals to reclaim or maintain their sense of superiority at a time when their nation's status in the world was declining rapidly.

Besides critiques of women's old mentality and bad habits, many authors suggested new qualities that women should have: independence, a sense of duty to society, a reform mentality, a critical mind, a spirit of mutual help, a spirit of public service, a love for learning, an open and upright manner, and a healthy body. Some requirements were highly idealistic. One author exhorted the new women, saying, "From now on, you should have the mind of a philosopher, the attitude of a writer, the perception of a scientist, and the body and hands of a worker, in order to become a wholesome element in the social reform movement and to build the permanent and universal happiness of humankind."[34] Articles presenting an idealistic portrait of the new women's requisite attributes reveal the utopian notions of the May Fourth generation. In order to achieve the "wholesome" (*jianquande*) society envisioned by male intellectuals, the shaping of "wholesome" new

33. Wang Pingling, "Xinfunü de renge wenti" [The new women's problem of personhood], *Funü zazhi* [The ladies' journal] 7, no. 10 (1921): 11.

34. Ibid., 13–14. See also, Peng Ji'nen, "Jinri Zhongguo nüzi yingjuewu de yidian," Yun Fang, "Gaizao shidai de funü yingjuyou shemo zige?" and Huang Heji, "Xinfunü yingyou de juewu" [The consciousness that the new women should have], *Funü zazhi* [The ladies' journal] 6, no. 10 (1920): 18–20.

women was urgently required, because the backwardness of women obstructed the progress of society.

In the few essays by female authors, there was consensus that new women should improve themselves quickly in order to meet the demands of social reform. But the focus of women writers was usually on the new possibilities opening up to them. Xu Shiheng named several goals for new women to reach. First, eradicate bad habits such as binding the chest, piercing the ears, wearing makeup and luxurious ornaments, and keeping the hair long.[35] Second, make an independent living by work rather than rely on men. Third, participate in public affairs to shoulder women's social responsibility. Fourth, begin a mass movement by women to promote social evolution. Fifth, pursue autonomy in decisions about marriage. Those who were not betrothed should actively pursue their own will. Those who were betrothed should break the engagement if it was made against their own will. Widows should decide their own future without the bondage of old ethics. Marriage should be an alliance of man and woman made of their own wills, based on love, knowledge, morality, and common interests.[36]

In response to contemptuous views toward women in society, women writers often stressed qualities that would gain respectability for new women. Li Peilan suggested that emancipated women should have a natural and graceful manner, open and upright behavior, and a persistent will. "If we cultivate our personality and do not leave room for others to gossip, we will surely win people's respect."[37] Miao-Cheng Shuyi cautioned that new women should pay special attention to morality. She warned those who chose to attend the newly opened coeducational universities that "they have to be very careful in every respect. If a rumor ever started, it would give others a weapon against women. The woman involved would not be able to wash away her shame, even with all the water from the Yellow River, and the hope for equal education would be stifled for other women."[38] Paradoxically, in

---

35. In the early twentieth century, upper-class women considered it fashionable to bind their chests, because a big bust was associated with lower-class women who engaged in physical labor. Cutting long hair was a hot issue in the May Fourth era because long hair was seen as unhygenic and time-consuming. The bob cut, which resembled the hair style of American flappers in the 1920s, soon became associated with Chinese new women.

36. Xu Shiheng, "Jinhou funü yingyou de jingshen" [The spirit women should have from now on], Funü zazhi [The ladies' journal] 6, no. 8 (1920): 12–18.

37. Li Peilan, "Jiefanghou de funü rengeguan" [The emancipated women's view of personhood], Funü zazhi [The ladies' journal] 6, no. 5 (1920): 4.

38. Miao-Cheng Shuyi, "Xiang yu funü" [Scent and women], Funü zazhi [The ladies' journal] 6, no. 3 (1920): 5.

order to gain social respect, emancipated women had to exercise even more self-restraint in following conventional norms.

This male-run women's magazine devoted much attention to reforming women, but the journal also echoed a major theme in the wave of women's emancipation by pointing to problems that blocked women's social advancement. In fact, the national debate on women's problems led by New Culture journals found an influential forum in *The Ladies' Journal*. Various issues related to women were discussed in the journal throughout 1920. Women's education, women's careers, women's economic independence, free social interaction between men and women (to break gender segregation), freedom of marriage (autonomy in choosing one's spouse), freedom to love, freedom to divorce, new sexual morality, family reform, emancipation of slave maids, abolishing the "little-daughter-in-law" system, abolishing prostitution, the problem of chastity, contraception, birth control, women's hairstyle and clothing, women's physical training, and so on. All these issues were first raised by men. Naming women's problems became such a vogue that Shen Yanbing could not help commenting sarcastically, "In China the easiest thing to talk about is the woman problem because every aspect of it can be attacked. Casually picking a topic, such as marriage, family system, women's personhood, concubinage, and endless others, you can make it into a big long article just by pouring out a stream of curses. Spirited young men and women readers will clap their hands, cheering, 'Great, great!'"[39]

Discussing women's problems obviously attracted a large readership. For this reason, the top executives of the Commercial Press opted for an editor in chief who was able to follow the new wave more closely.[40] In January 1921, Zhang Xichen replaced Wang Yunzhang to begin a new stage of *The Ladies' Journal*. Zhang had been an editor of *Dongfang zazhi* [The eastern miscellany], an influential journal of the Commercial Press. An obscure New Culturalist, Zhang rose to fame after 1921 because of his reform of *The*

39. Yanbing, "Du *Shaonian Zhongguo funühao*" [Reading *The Young China* issue on women], *Funü zazhi* [The ladies' journal] 6, no. 1 (1920): 1. The six-volume *Zhongguo funü wenti taolunji* [Collected essays on Chinese women's problems], ed. Mei Sheng (Shanghai: Xinwenhua chubanshe, 1929), presents the fullest coverage of the debate on women problems. For a detailed discussion of the May Fourth debate on women, see Roxane H. Witke, "Transformation of Attitudes towards Women during the May Fourth Era" (Ph.D. diss., University of California, Berkeley, 1971).

40. Shen Yanbing was their first choice for the position. Although Shen had contributed to every issue of *The Ladies' Journal* since the end of 1919, he chose to be the editor in chief of *The Short Stories Monthly*. See Mao Dun, *Wo zouguo de daolu*, 140.

Ladies' Journal. He read extensively on the subject of feminism, including many Japanese sources in his reading, and believed that to "construct a new culture, the foundation should be the 'mental revolution' of men and women."[41] Bringing in Lu Xun's youngest brother, Zhou Jianren, as his collaborator, Zhang changed both the content and format of the journal to promote a feminist mental revolution.[42] The typeface became smaller, to make the journal more compact. Essays addressing key issues became more theoretical. Scholarly surveys appeared, tracing local customs related to women's life. More room was given to readers to express their views on women's emancipation and related issues. Prominent New Culturalists such as Zhou Zuoren and Lu Xun were solicited for contributions. And translations of works on feminism and women's issues by Western and Japanese authors occupied a large portion of each issue (Zhang translated many of the Japanese works), giving guidance and legitimacy to the debate on Chinese women's emancipation. The change was a great success. In June 1921, the editor told readers that a second edition of previously sold-out issues was being printed to meet the demands of readers all over the country. Circulation reached ten thousand, three times more than the early stage of the journal. This reformed *Ladies' Journal* was praised by Mei Sheng, a New Culture editor who compiled several volumes of essays on women in the 1920s, as "number one among the current publications on women in China."[43]

41. See Zhang Xichen, preface to *Funü wenti shijiang* [Ten lectures on the women's problem], by Hisao Honma, trans. Zhang Xichen, vol. 1 in *Funü wenti congshu* [The series on women's problems], ed. The Women's Studies Association (Shanghai: The Women's Studies Association, 1924).

Hisao Honma (1886–1981) was a professor at the Waseda University in Tokyo, specializing in English literature and Japanese literature. Between 1918 and 1927, he was editor in chief of *The Waseda Literature*. In his original ten-chapter book, *Ten Lectures on the Women's Problem*, only one chapter discusses the Japanese women's movement; the rest are devoted to introducing feminist works and issues current in Europe and the United States. To the Chinese version, Zhang Xichen added a chapter on the Chinese women's movement.

42. Zhang Xichen was born in 1889. A native of Shaoxing, Zhejiang province, he and Lu Xun became friends when Zhang was a student in the Shanhui Normal School, where Lu taught for a while. When Zhang became editor in chief of *The Ladies' Journal*, Lu Xun recommended his youngest brother, Zhou Jianren, to Zhang. In October 1921, *The Ladies' Journal* hired Zhou as an assistant editor. Zhou and Zhang shared the same views on women's emancipation and sexual morality. For Zhou Jianren's views on women, see Xie Dexian, *Zhou Jianren zhuan* [A biography of Zhou Jianren] (Chongqing: Chongqing chubanshe, 1991), 84–99.

43. See "Bianji yulu" [Editor's words], *Funü zazhi* [The ladies' journal] 7, no. 7 (1921): 116. Mei Sheng edited *Funü nianjian* [An almanac of women] in 1924, *Zhongguo funüwenti taolunji* [Collected essays on Chinese women's problems] in 1926, and *Nüxing wenti yanjiuji* [Collected studies of women's problems] in 1928.

In the reformed journal, women's voices were much louder. The editor in chief made several calls for women's contributions. Although the major essays were still written by men, new columns like "Readers' Club" and "Correspondence" provided a space for informal discussions that women were more likely to join. Zhang also organized several special issues soliciting readers' views on different topics. Women readers responded warmly to those efforts. Interestingly, although women answered the call of this male editor to contribute, they often openly expressed their distrust of men. Lao Qiuying wrote, "I think women's emancipation is women's own matter. It should be solved by women themselves. Men's words on women's emancipation are absolutely unreliable. We can only rely on women's own consciousness."[44] Writing on the topic "My Hopes for Men," Xin Zhu cited cases in which men in the new wave treated women as sex objects. She complained,

> The topic of the essay is "My Hopes for Men." But the more I write, the more strongly I feel that for contemporary men, no matter of the new school or the old school, I have no hope. Oh! The traditional contempt toward women has lasted thousands of years and is deeply rooted in people's minds. We hope to reform, but it is not easy. To be frank, women dare not have any hope for men. We cannot hope. We need not hope. It has been so many years. What is the use of talking about it?[45]

But, she went on, because this discussion was intended to break the barrier between men and women and to enhance understanding of each other, she felt obliged to express a little hope, even though she knew that the hope was unrealizable any time soon. What she hoped was that men would treat women as human beings instead of as objects, a hope expressed by all other women contributors. Other women also listed "be faithful to women," "respect women," "help but do not harm women," and "be open and upright in your attitudes toward women" as their hopes for men. The sentiment in these discussions expressed explicitly a gender conflict that was muted in

---

All three were published by Shanghai New Culture Press (Shanghai xin wenhua shushe). In order to promote studies of women's problems, in 1922 Zhang Xichen organized a Women's Studies Association, most of whose members were frequent contributors to the journal.

44. Lao Qiuying, "Duiyu disan jieji funü de xiwang" [Hopes for women of the "number three class"], *Funü zazhi* [The ladies' journal] 7, no. 10 (1921): 110.

45. Xin Zhu, "Wosuo xiwangyu nanzizhe" [My hopes for men], *Funü zazhi* [The ladies' journal] 10, no. 10 (1924): 1519.

much of men's "objective" study of women's problems. Some men warned against the "tendency" to see women's emancipation as "a fight between men and women" and insisted that in discussing all kinds of problems, "we should stand beyond the limits of sex, concentrating on our study, rather than belittle or attack the opposite sex on the basis of preconceived opinions."[46]

In 1922, Zhang Xichen started to organize special issues, each focusing on a single problem. These special issues not only revealed his concerns but also highlighted key issues for readers to follow. The special issues were on divorce, birth control and Margaret Sanger, love and marriage, celibacy, political participation, chastity, the women's movement, spouse selection, women's careers, men and women's mutual understanding, and the new sexual morality. Zhang's view of women's emancipation was based on a combination of evolutionism, liberal individualism, sexology, and a feminism represented by Ellen Key. He wrote several major articles to introduce Western concepts of sexuality and love, particularly Ellen Key's ideas on love and maternity. Zhang was one of a few men of the time who believed that sexual liberation was the core of women's emancipation, and he used *The Ladies' Journal* to promulgate his ideas.[47]

Answering readers' criticism that *The Ladies' Journal* paid too much attention to love and ignored more important issues relating to women's interests, Zhang explained his position in the following way. First, most Chinese readers misunderstood the word "love," because, until recently, there had been no word for love in the Chinese language. To most Chinese, even the newly coined term *lian'ai* (love) was associated with "lasciviousness" (*jianyin*). Second, the major difference between *lian'ai* and *jianyin* was that love was a union of two people, whereas lasciviousness was one person's satisfaction of possessive desire. Love acknowledged individual personhood and equality; love was a lofty unity of spirituality and sexuality. Third, the

---

46. Another major discussion that reflected the gender gap in opinion arose over a man's account of his marriage. Most men expressed their sympathy to the man, who was unhappy in his relationship with his wife. But some women expressed strong sympathy toward the man's wife and criticized the man's condescending attitude and self-centeredness. See Lian Shi, "Funü de feiren shidai" [The inhuman age of women], *Funü zazhi* [The ladies' journal] 9, no. 4 (1923): 44–46. Some male readers criticized the women's supposed readiness to pick a fight between men and women. See "Duqianhao" [Comments on the previous issue], *Funü zazhi* [The ladies' journal] 9, no. 6 (1923):121–123.

47. Se Lu (Zhang Xichen), "Jindai sixiangjia de xingyuguan yu lian'aiguan" [An introduction to modern thinkers' concepts of sexuality and love], *Funü zazhi* [The ladies' journal] 6, no. 10 (1920): 1–8, and "Ailunkai nüshi yu qisixiang" [Madam Ellen Key and her ideas], *Funü zazhi* [The ladies' journal] 7, no. 2 (1921): 21–27.

fundamental solution to women's problems was love, because women's problems were, after all, the problems of two sexes. Human society was based on the union of two sexes. If the union was bound by power and money, the society would be predatory. The only way to change such a society was through the union of two sexes by love. If men acknowledged women's freedom to love, they would not treat women as objects that could be robbed, sold, and used, and equality between two sexes would be achieved. Zhang explained his objections to socialist views on women's emancipation:

> Socialist advocates think that so long as private ownership is eliminated, there will be no more problems. This would certainly destroy the foundation of men possessing women and parents possessing children. But I think it is equally or more important that women and children assert to men and parents, respectively, their individual personhood and free will. . . .
>
> The human race has two basic desires, for food and for sexuality. The two desires are at the center of all social customs, norms, morality, law, and institutions. . . . Therefore, hunger and love are the basis of all social problems. All entangled struggles in society originated in these basic desires. Socialism is a fundamental solution to the hunger problem; and "freedom-to-loveism" is a fundamental solution to the love problem. . . . "Freedom to love is a start in solving women's problems as well as an end in solving women's problems."[48]

Promoting "freedom to love" (*lian'ai ziyou*), Zhang continued the attack on Chinese traditional sexual morality begun by Zhou Zuoren, Hu Shi, and Lu Xun. The focus now shifted from condemning forced chastity to advocating a sexual relationship based on the new concept of love. Love was now regarded as the only basis for a moral marriage. Love was added to autonomy as a basic principle in May Fourth youths' resistance to arranged marriage. Unions based on love were legitimate without legal procedures. The slogan "freedom to love" became one of the loudest in the May Fourth era. Although stories in *The Ladies' Journal* often depicted bewilderment among both young men and women about the new sexual norms, love, as defined by advocates such as Zhang Xichen, became an ideal that the May Fourth youth were eager to pursue.[49]

48. Zhang Xichen, "Lian'ai wenti de taolun" [Discussions on the love problem], *Funü zazhi* [The ladies' journal] 8 (1922), no. 9: 121–123 and no. 10: 120–121.

49. In "Liuge nantongxue geiwodexing" [Letters from six male classmates], *Funü zazhi* [The ladies' journal] 9, no. 7 (1923): 41–44, He He, a female student, described the norms of freedom to love in her school. But she was upset by love letters from her male classmates. She did not want to abuse the freedom to love because "love"

With his emphasis on sexual emancipation and his conviction about individual rights, Zhang made *The Ladies' Journal* an influential forum for promoting a feminist discourse. He agreed with Ellen Key that the goal of a feminist movement should not be to turn women into men, because he believed that "in the human race there is only sex difference between men and women, but no superiority and inferiority between them."[50] He often warned against an understanding of equality as women's imitation of men. Combining a positive recognition of human sexuality theorized by Havelock Ellis and a romanticized view of the "sacredness of motherhood" expounded by Ellen Key, Zhang argued that women's sexual consciousness and society's protection of sacred motherhood were higher goals of women's emancipation. Nevertheless, he insisted that women's equal rights and freedom to love were a precondition to the rise of "sexual consciousness" in women. Based on this understanding, *The Ladies' Journal* did not merely emphasize the love problem, but also devoted much space to exploring ways to achieve women's equal rights. In doing so, it both reflected and contributed to the development of a liberal feminist discourse.[51]

PROMOTING A CHINESE WOMEN'S MOVEMENT

In late 1919, during what contemporaries called the high "sound wave" (*shenglang*) of women's emancipation, agitation for a Chinese women's movement appeared in New Culture periodicals. New Culturalists began to talk about the significance of women's movements in world development and why China needed to follow world trends. These men usually were familiar with women's movements in Europe and the United States. For them, the emergence of a feminist movement was a necessary stage of social evolution, and the birth of a Chinese women's movement would mark China's

---

was a sacred word in her mind. Readers' responses show that it was common for female students to be swamped with love letters. M. Y. H., a young man who did not wish to reveal his name, complained that he rejected his parents' arrangement for a marriage under the influence of the new wave. But now who was he going to marry? The number of female students in his school was small, and he did not dare approach them for fear that they would think him a hooligan or that his love letters would be published in magazines and newspapers. See, M. Y. H., "Qingnian qiouai wenti" [The problem of courtship among youth], *Funü zazhi* [The ladies' journal] 9, no. 9 (1923): 124–125.

50. Se Lu (Zhang Xichen), "Dao funü jiefang de tujing" [The way to women's emancipation], *Funü zazhi* [The ladies' journal] 7, no. 1 (1921): 2. See also, Se Lu, "Ailunkai nüshi yu qisixiang."

51. Se Lu, "Funü yundong de xinqingxiang" [New tendencies of the women's movement], *Funü zazhi* [The ladies' journal] 9, no. 1 (1923): 2–7.

advancement toward modernity. Understandably, their visions of a Chinese women's movement were modeled after women's movements in the West.[52]

In *The Ladies' Journal*, early articles on a women's movement were written by Shen Yanbing. In "The Definition and Demands of the Women's Movement" published in August 1920, Shen Yanbing reminded his readers that people had been talking about women's problems for over a year and what was needed now was to do things rather than merely to talk: "The doing is called a 'movement.'" How to start the movement? Shen devoted his entire essay to an introduction of Western feminist movements, in order to give readers a comprehensive understanding of the definition and issues of the "women's movement." He told readers that a women's movement was not just for suffrage, but also to express demands in education, economic life, marriage and family, and public life in society and nation. He emphasized, "If we want to actively promote a women's movement, we cannot but follow the most contemporary and most comprehensive definition."[53] It is interesting that just a few months before, in another essay titled "How Should We Be Prepared to Talk about Women's Emancipation?" Shen criticized people who advocated the concept of women's suffrage without considering "if it is what this society needs or if it is what our current society is able to accept." He insisted that, besides learning the history of Western feminism, people should learn about Chinese social reality in order to find solutions to women's problems. He emphasized that to learn social reality one "cannot merely rely on reading a few books." And he admitted apologetically, "We ourselves often do not follow our own advice."[54] Now, introducing a "comprehensive" Western feminism to China, he seemed to suggest that a fuller knowledge of feminism was what Chinese society needed and could accept.

Like other major advocates, Shen merely translated feminist texts from the West rather than followed his own advice about studying Chinese social reality. His perception of social needs was necessarily partial. The feminist demands he introduced certainly did not reflect the needs of most women

52. The newly published periodical *Shaonian Zhongguo* [The young China] ran a special issue on women in October 1919. Li Dazhao, Tian Han, and Huang Rikui wrote on the subject of the women's movement. In *Jiefang yu gaizao* [Emancipation and reform] 1, no. 3 (October 1919), Li Da published "Funü jiefanglun" [On women's emancipation], which promoted the women's movement in China.

53. Yanbing, "Funü yundong de yiyi he yaoqiu" [The definition and demands of the women's movement], *Funü zazhi* [The ladies' journal] 6, no. 8 (1920): 6.

54. Yanbing, "Women gaizenyang yubeile qutan funü jiefang wenti" [How should we be prepared to talk about women's emancipation?], *Funü zazhi* [The ladies' journal] 6, no. 3 (1920): 5.

in the agrarian Chinese society of the early twentieth century, a point proved later by the CCP's experience in rural areas. However, his and other New Culturalists' perception of a feminist need helped create a new social reality. Because many articles used the framework of Western feminism to discuss the Chinese women's movement, and because many others directly translated Western feminist texts, the issues raised by Western feminists formed the male advocates' notion of a proper agenda for the Chinese women's movement. Women's equal opportunity in education and employment, political participation, and love and family—issues stressed by women's rights groups, suffragists, and free love or sacred motherhood advocates, respectively, in Europe and the United States—were accepted as one "comprehensive" package that the Chinese women's movement should embrace.[55]

This wholesale endorsement of Western feminist issues was based on the needs of urban educated Chinese men and women at that particular historical moment. Therefore, when those issues were discussed in the Chinese context, they necessarily acquired culturally and socially specific meanings. For instance, education was unanimously viewed as the most important issue in the Chinese women's movement, but discussions of the need for women's education revealed a wide range of purposes. Coeducation in higher learning was first proposed by three male students at Beijing University before the rise of student movement. Xu Yanzhi, one of the three pioneers, gave the following account of how this action began:

> Last year about this time—ten days after spring vacation—my friend Wang Ruoyu came to chat with me. But we both felt bored. So we went to look for Kang Baiqing at No. 10 Yizihutong on the north riverbank. It was getting dark. We turned on the light and sat facing one another in a triangle. We were eating turnips and sugar cane and chatting a lot. But we still felt unsatisfied. Then we suddenly realized, it was because no women were present! If we wanted to enjoy socializing between men and women, we had to first generate some public opinion. So we three each decided to write one article advocating coeducation within one week and send them all to *Chenbao* [The morning news].[56]

55. The CCP had to drop the feminist agenda they inherited from the May Fourth era when they tried to consolidate their power in rural base areas. On this topic, see Kay Ann Johnson, *Women, the Family, and Peasant Revolution in China* (Chicago: University of Chicago Press, 1983), and Judith Stacey, *Patriarchy and Socialist Revolution in China* (Berkeley: University of California Press, 1983).

56. Xu Yanzhi, "Beijing daxue nannü gongxiao ji" [A record of coeducation at Beijing University], *Shaonian Shijie* 1, no. 7 (1920). In *Wusi shiqi funü wenti wenxuan* [Selected articles on women's problems in the May Fourth period], ed. All-China Women's Federation (Beijing: Zhongguo funü chubanshe, 1981), 264.

Xu's article to *Chenbao* stressed his painful personal experiences of gender segregation in Chinese society and cited an American woman's lecture that emphasized the psychological benefits of coeducation for both sexes. He also condemned deprivation of women's equal educational opportunity. He reasoned that "one big cause of pain in life is bad marriage. The solution to this problem is free marriage [freedom to choose one's spouse]. If we want to have free marriage, open socializing between men and women is a must. And coeducation is the best way to encourage open socializing between men and women."[57]

Coeducation as a way to encourage open socializing between men and women was warmly embraced by many male students. For them, eliminating gender segregation was a precondition for "free marriage" rather than a step toward gender equality. Fighting the arranged marriage system required not only that one challenge parental authority and claim autonomy but also that one had opportunities to meet women (educated, "decent" women instead of courtesans) in order to choose one's spouse. In this sense, for the May Fourth young men who were inspired by Western concepts of love and marriage, the goals of women's emancipation—coeducation, open socializing, freedom to marry, and freedom to love—were goals they, too, shared. After all, modern Chinese educated men's emotional fulfillment or fantasies, which were more or less shaped by Western romantic literature, could only be realized through new women who were able to share with them intellectual and social experiences as well as an understanding of love. This may in part explain why so many young men eagerly jumped on the bandwagon of women's emancipation.

The debate over coeducation at the university was heated but short. May Fourth female students such as Deng Chunlan rose to demand equal opportunity in higher learning. Since the early 1920s, and starting at Beijing University, public universities had begun, one after another, to enroll women. Xu Yanzhi said proudly a year later, "Although at that time we three were minors whose words did not carry much weight, what we said was like candlelight before the sun and moon appear. In my recollection, we never dared to dream that, in only one year, we would achieve the situation we have today."[58]

But there was more to the issue of women's education in China than

57. Xu Yanzhi, "Nannü jiaoji wenti zagan" [Thoughts on socializing between men and women], *Chenbao*, May 4, 1919. In All-China Women's Federation, *Wusi shiqi funü wenti wenxuan*, 179.

58. Xu Yanzhi, "Beijing daxue nannü gongxiao ji," 264.

higher education. In the view of many advocates, China lacked a women's movement because few women received an adequate education of any kind. The keys to promoting a women's movement were universal education at the primary level and education that enabled women to be independent and free in society. As one author asked rhetorically, "Without educational opportunity, women are still in a deep sleep, lacking a basic social consciousness. How can we expect them to stand up and solve their own problems?"[59] In those male advocates' minds, women's educational opportunity became a precondition of raising women's social consciousness in China.

Others who emphasized education often linked it with another major issue, women's economic independence. Because the focus of attention was women in the urban middle or upper classes, women were often described as dependent, a burden on men, or even parasitic. The only way to remove women from such dependency was to foster careers that guaranteed women's independence. Education had to be the foundation of this economic independence. In this context, women's vocational education became an especially lively topic. Chen Wentao, in "Promoting Independent Women's Careers," drew a distinction between women's work and women's independent careers. He argued that what most women did was work—housework and family labor—that could not gain them independence. Factory workers had a little independence because of their low pay, but businesswomen and teachers could be regarded as having an independent career. He criticized those who limited women's vocational education to traditional women's work and emphasized instead that a woman should be treated as a vital individual, not a mother and wife. "What we need today, in short, are 'women's independent careers.' People who promote women's careers and women's vocational education should never ever forget this point. . . . All careers in society, except for one or two special men's careers that women's physiology prevents them from doing, are women's occupational fields, including officialdom and congress."[60]

To prepare women for careers equal to men's, education had to be equal too. Most articles on the Chinese women's movement advocated education and career as the basic solution to numerous women's problems, as well as a way to ensure social evolution. Hu Shi, the prominent New Culturalist,

59. Lao Zeren, "Zhongguo funü yundong de jianglai" [The future of the Chinese women's movement], *Funü zazhi* [The ladies' journal] 7, no. 9 (1921): 10.

60. Chen Wentao, "Tichang dulixingde nüzi zhiye" [Promoting independent women's careers], *Funü zazhi* [The ladies' journal] 7, no. 8 (1921), 10.

joined others in popularizing women's education and career by making speeches to female students. He argued that women's economic independence was the basis of the women's movement, and that without it, equality, freedom, and independence would all be false. "If women could have economic independence and knowledge, other social or political problems would be easy to solve."[61] Although the issues of equal rights to education and career had been copied from the Western feminist movement, by now they did not sound foreign to Chinese audiences. Rather, as Chinese advocates centered on the connection between these issues and the fostering of Chinese women's independence, education and career were increasingly seen as the most urgent problems in the Chinese women's movement. In a sense, the debate on women's education and career illustrates that the process of adopting Western liberal feminism was a process of transforming or tailoring it according to the interests of various social groups in China. New Culture feminism was charged with a culturally specific content. It was not merely an imitation of Western feminism.

Although liberal feminist issues constituted the major part of *The Ladies' Journal*, the liberal feminist theme of the Chinese women's movement was contested soon after May Fourth 1919. The 1917 Russian Revolution aroused great interest in socialism among Chinese intellectuals. Socialist literature, translated from Japanese, English, German, French, and Russian, found increasing readership among educated Chinese youth. As some of the leading New Culturalists turned to socialism, a socialist analysis of women's problems emerged. Copying from Japanese socialist analyses, Chinese socialists categorized the world women's movement according to a crude Marxist terminology of class. According to Tian Han, the female rulers in Chinese or Western histories represented a "number one class" women's movement; the female nobility of the Middle Ages who controlled power belonged to the "number two class" women's movement; feminist movement in nineteenth-century capitalist countries was the "number three class" women's movement; and the "number four class" women's movement was launched by working-class women in the industrialized capitalist countries. The concept of the "number three class" and "number four class" women's movements, soon applied to the Chinese scene, was later

61. Zhao Jingshen recorded Hu Shi's speech to the feminist branch of Tianjin Students Comrade Association. Hu Shizhi (Hu Shi), "Nüzi wentide kaiduan" [The beginning of the women's problem], *Funü zazhi* [The ladies' journal] 8, no. 10 (1922): 127.

changed to adopt CCP terminology, becoming "bourgeois" class and "proletarian" class movements.[62]

Writing in *The Ladies' Journal* in 1921, Zhang Xichen used this terminology to call people's attention to Chinese working-class women. He accepted the socialist critique that the Western women's movement cared little for a women's labor movement because the former was dominated by the "bourgeois number three class," whereas the latter was led by the "number four class." However, unlike socialists who believed that the "number four class" women should be the main force of the Chinese women's movement, Zhang saw that in China neither women nor labor had any powerful organized movement. At the same time, the "number three class" women in China were developing a social consciousness, and a "number three class" women's movement was emerging. So he reminded the rising Chinese "number three class" women not to ignore working-class women, as had the Western women's movement. He hoped that "the existing and not yet existing women's organizations and women in the 'number three class' will pay close attention to the 'number four class' working women and not be restricted to the 'number three class' women's rights issues. This is truly a new policy for the future women's movement."[63]

Having learned from the lesson of the Western women's movement, and influenced by socialism, Zhang and others who promoted a feminist movement in China were consciously aware of the class issue in the would-be Chinese women's movement. As an ideal solution to the gap between women of the different classes, they tried to enhance middle-class women's awareness of the problems of the working class and of other oppressed women so that lower-class women would be included in the Chinese feminist movement. As an expression of the editor in chief's class consciousness and socialist orientation, *The Ladies' Journal* printed translations of socialist analyses of the woman problem, including sections from August Bebel's *Women and Socialism* and Japanese socialist author Yamakawa Kikue's *Women's Victory*, and an introduction to women's liberation in Soviet Russia.[64]

62. Tian Han, "Disi jieji furen yundong" [The "number four class" women's movement], *Shaonian Zhongguo* [The young China] 1, no. 4 (1919). In All-China Women's Federation, *Wusi shiqi funü wenti wenxuan*, 32–34.

63. Se Lu (Zhang Xichen), "Guoji funü laodonghui yu Zhongguo Funü" [The international women's labor conference and Chinese women], *Funü zazhi* [The ladies' journal] 7, no. 11 (1921): 5.

64. Contributions from readers also reflected awareness of lower-class women's problems and pains. See "Duzhe julebu" [Readers' club], *Funü zazhi* [The ladies' journal] 7, no. 5 (1921): 104–106.

Still, the term "women's movement" was not clearly defined. Authors simultaneously deplored the absence of a women's movement in China and criticized the weaknesses of the Chinese women's movement. Confusion resulted in part from the awkward role of male advocates. They were promoting a Chinese women's movement using the concept of Western feminism, and they tended to regard themselves as the ones who were making that movement. But Western women's movements were made mainly by women, and they were marked by organized activities with specific goals. In China, it seemed, there were only men talking about a women's movement—men who believed that their talk was essential. As Zhang Xichen said, "To reach educated women who lack a developed consciousness, there is an urgent need for advocacy with words. We may say that [a populist-style] 'to-the-people' movement is the basis of the women's movement, and further, that advocacy is the precondition of the 'to-the-people' movement in today's China."[65]

Some women even thought that male advocacy *was* the women's movement. A woman author analyzed the pre-1923 situation this way: "Those actually engaged in the women's movement were only two kinds: students, and some working in the field of education. Students constituted the majority, and most of them were men. So the central elements of the women's movement, in a narrow sense, were male students."[66]

But in many men's minds, males' talk was not a women's movement. By 1922, increasing numbers of male advocates felt that talk was not enough—that it was time for action. Yun Daiying encouraged his friend in these words, "Be more practical, work harder, move forward more bravely. One down-to-earth movement activist is better for the society than a hundred flighty people with lofty ideals."[67] However, no male advocate became such an activist for the women's movement; none would engage in organizing the movement, because they felt that men could not replace women when it came to accomplishing that task. The major goal of the Chinese women's movement was to promote Chinese women's independent personhood. Only

---

65. "Bianji yulu," *Funü zazhi* 7, no. 7 (1921):116. By "to the people," Zhang meant the nineteenth-century Russian reformers' efforts to reach the lower classes. He encouraged male advocates to learn from those Russians and to raise educated Chinese women's consciousness with their advocacy.

66. Fang Minyun, "Woguo muqian funü yundong yingqu de fangzhen" [Policies that the Chinese women's movement should adopt], *Funü zazhi* [The ladies' journal] 9, no. 1 (1923): 111.

67. In Zhang Youluan, "Jinhou gengyao qieshixie" [Be more practical], *Funü zazhi* [The ladies' journal] 8, no. 1 (1922): 28.

women's conscious action on their own behalf would mark the advancement of the Chinese race. Men's responsibility was to awaken women to action. Men had talked enough, and it was time for women to rise up. The tone of male authors became urgent. One insisted:

New women, even if not for your own sake, for the sake of saving the masses, you should make up your mind to shoulder this great task. Quickly rise up to carry out all kinds of women's movements to solve all kinds of problems. You see, talk about women's problems in China has been going on for a few years. But its achievements are limited to speeches by a few new figures. It has not solved any problem. . . . It is time for a women's movement in China to proceed! You should not hesitate anymore! As soon as you raise your arms, intellectual men will surely answer your call.[68]

Another author tried to inspire women by a trumpet call:

Dear sisters, have you seen the men's Renaissance in Europe from the Middle Ages to modern times? Now it is time for your renaissance. . . . Young sisters, strive, strive! Quickly stoke your fires of enthusiasm and shine your lights of wisdom. Join this heroic and moving great cause!
    Dear sisters, you should realize, the previous culture has been men's culture; the future culture will be men's and women's equally shared culture, or, maybe, a women-centered culture. . . . Don't you rise up yet? Respectable young women, strive and strive! A glorious throne is waiting for you![69]

Actually, many female students had taken action soon after the May Fourth Incident. They not only participated bravely in the patriotic movement against international imperialism and the weak response of the Chinese government, but also worked for women's emancipation. Deng Yingchao, one of the early feminist activists, recalled,

Along with the May Fourth patriotic movement, a women's emancipation movement occurred that played a major part in the May Fourth democratic movement. It raised issues like "equality between men and women," "opposition to arranged marriage," "open socializing," "freedom to love," "freedom to marry," "coeducation in universities," "all institutions open to female employment," and so on. In Tianjin, the first thing we did was to combine previously separate

68. C. K. "Funü wenti yu Zhongguo funü yundong" [Women problems and the Chinese women's movement], Funü zazhi [The ladies' journal] 8, no. 11 (1922): 56.
69. Tang Jinggao, "Wosuo xiwangyu nüqingnian" [What I expect of young women], Funü zazhi [The ladies' journal] 8, no. 1 (1922): 14.

organizations of male and female students into one and work together.[70]

The May Fourth female activists' new manner was vividly described by Dora Black, a Cambridge University graduate in sociology, who arrived in China in November 1920 in the company of her lover, Bertrand Russell. Having visited Shanghai, Hangzhou, Nanjing, Hankou, Changsha, and Beijing, she found the intellectual atmosphere in China free and lively. She met many female students, whose questions often surprised her. They would, without any hesitation, ask her questions about love and motherhood through male interpreters. Their radical pursuit of individual freedom and social reform, in Black's view, surpassed that of the most progressive European women, who were moderate and cautious in their efforts for women's liberation. European women who believed in Oriental women's submissiveness, Black commented, would be shocked to hear Chinese young women's bold, frank, and radical talk. She astutely observed a militant streak in those young women and linked it to the female warrior prototype in traditional Chinese drama. "In contemporary China, this kind of female warrior is appearing everywhere." After describing young women's simple dress, lack of feminine ornament, and natural manner in public, she said, "I feel Chinese women all have a boyish liveliness. That is the special character of the Chinese female."[71] Black's positive image of China's new women is largely missing from descriptions by male emancipators at the time.

According to Black, feminist issues were embraced by female students all over the country. But most of the issues, such as love and marriage, were better subjects for advocacy than for organized activities, because they addressed individual consciousness and individual autonomy in personal life. Female students and teachers began their own publications to advocate new ideas, but women's publishing activities were often deemed of low value by the men who ran influential publications. A few other activities organized by women

70. Deng Yingchao, "Wusi yundong de huiyi" [Recollections of the May Fourth Movement], in All-China Women's Federation, *Wusi shiqi funü wenti wenxuan*, 5.
71. Madam Russell (Dora Black), "Zhongguo de nüquanzhuyi yu nüxing gaizao yundong" [Chinese feminism and the female reform movement], trans. Yun He, *Funü zazhi* [The ladies' journal] 9, no. 1 (1923): 51. The article first appeared in a Japanese women's journal. Dora Black and Bertrand Russell got married after they returned to England from China. The article in *The Ladies' Journal* is accompanied by a picture of Dora Russell with her newborn baby, which suggests that in 1923 many readers in China were still interested in the famous couple's whereabouts. For Dora Russell's recollections of the visit to China, see her autobiography, *The Tamarisk Tree: My Quest for Liberty and Love* (London: Elek-Pemberton, 1975), chapter 7.

took place. For example, female students in Beijing and Tianjin petitioned to the Department of Education for equal educational opportunities for students in girls' schools. However, because such activities occurred only sporadically, they seemed unlike the Western experience, where women organized nationally or internationally to fight for certain causes over a long period.[72]

Nevertheless, something resembling a Western women's movement eventually emerged: the nationwide suffrage movement, or, more exactly the political participation movement (*canzheng yundong*). It began in 1921, when provincial warlord governments promoted autonomous rule, and women in Hunan, Guangdong, Sichuan, Jiangxi, and Zhejiang used the opportunity to push for women's constitutional rights. These organized activities at the provincial level achieved moderate success. Women's equal political rights were written into the constitutions of Hunan, Guangdong, and Sichuan, and a few women were even elected to provincial and county legislatures. In 1922, when President Li Yuanhong ordered the parliament to prepare for a national constitution, a new wave of this women's *canzheng* movement swept the nation.[73]

Female students in Beijing initiated these nationwide organizational activities. In July 1922, female student representatives from three schools in Beijing met to plan a *canzheng* movement. As a result of the different goals of the organizers, two organizations were formed. A Women's Suffrage Association (Nüzi Canzheng Xiejinhui) declared a focused goal of obtaining women's equal political, economic, and educational rights. The Feminist Movement Association (Nüquan Yundong Tongmenhui) embraced a much broader platform. In a blend of feminist and socialist language, it declared:

> The distinctions between all social classes are easy to eradicate. Only the natural difference between the two sexes is permanent. If we do not eradicate the class distinction growing out of this permanent natural difference, class oppression will persist in the form of a permanent natural difference. Therefore, our demand for democracy between the two sexes is stronger than anything else, and our responsibility for a democratic revolution between the two sexes is greater than anything else. . . .

72. "Funü xinxiaoxi" [Women's news], *Funü zazhi* [The ladies' journal], reported female students' activities in Hunan, Beijing, Tianjing, and Shanghai in issues throughout 1920. The column also reported international women's activities.

73. Yan Shi, "Zuijin de nüquan yundong" [The recent feminist movement], *Funü zazhi* [The ladies' journal] 8, no. 10 (1920): 61–63. See also, All-China Women's Federation, *Zhongguo funü yundong shi* [A history of the Chinese women's movement] (Beijing: Chunqiu chubanshe, 1989), 124–131.

Our procedure is as follows: first, unite revolutionary democrats to resist feudal warlords; second, unite revolutionary socialists to resist imperialist capitalism. At the same time, we want men and women in general to pay attention to, understand, and respect our position in politics and in society. That is our sole mission.[74]

The Feminist Movement Association (FMA) demanded women's equal rights in all aspects and stressed in particular the importance of equal educational and career opportunities. It also made special efforts to include lower-class women by demanding equal pay and protective legislation for female factory workers, and prohibition of the sale of slave maids and of footbinding. This inclusive feminist agenda, copied later by the alliance of the GMD and CCP in the National Revolution, certainly demonstrated May Fourth feminists' awareness of the class dimensions of gender as well as their intention to unite women of different classes. In short, although it was the product of years of liberal feminist agitation, the emerging *canzheng* movement was also informed by an increasingly influential socialism.[75]

After July 1922, branches of the FMA and the Women's Suffrage Association were quickly established in major cities all over China. Declarations of establishment and petitions by women's organizations frequently appeared in *The Ladies' Journal*. Writing at the end of 1922, the editor in chief made no secret of his excitement over the rapid development of a feminist movement: "This year is the most optimistic period for women in our country. Like flowers and plants in early spring, the feminist movement in different places is flourishing. Women confined to the family for thousands of years have either broken or are going to break their chains and rush out into society."[76] In order to guide and further advocate the growing women's movement, Zhang organized a special issue on the movement in January 1923.

74. "Nüquan Yundong Tongmenhui xuanyan" [A declaration of the Feminist Movement Association], *Funü zazhi* [The ladies' journal] 8, no. 9 (1922): 126–127. For a detailed quote of its agenda, see chapter 6 in this volume.

75. A study of Miao Boying, an early female Communist Party member, reveals that Miao followed the party's instruction to be involved in establishing the Feminist Movement Association. Though there is no further evidence to connect the newly founded CCP and the Feminist Movement Association, it is highly possible that the Beijing founders of the FMA were familiar with socialist ideas circulated by the CCP. See Zeng Changqiu and Zhou Jianchun, "Zhongguo diyige nü Gongchandangyuan Miao Boying" [The first female communist in China: Miao Boying], *Renmin ribao* [People's daily], June 8, 1987. Dora Russell, in "Zhongguo de nüquanzhuyi yu nüxing gaizao yundong," also comments that the new women she met were all socialists.

76. "Bianji yulu" [Editor's words], *Funü zazhi* [The ladies' journal] 8, no. 12 (1922): 124.

The special issue on the women's movement laid out the major debates on "the policies that the current Chinese women's movement should adopt." Concerned male and female readers freely expressed diversified views. Zhang Xichen, in a major essay, elaborated his theory of two-stage emancipation. He welcomed the rising women's movement, which followed the path of Anglo-American individualistic feminism. However, he warned Chinese women against the conflict between "femininity and individuality" that he perceived in the Anglo-American women's movement. He argued that, although it was necessary for Chinese women to reach the first stage of awakening as a human being, they must prepare themselves simultaneously for the second stage of awakening as a sexual being. For him, the women's rights movement was a step toward the goal of the motherhood rights movement. The ultimate goal of the women's movement, however, was not merely to serve the individual interests of men and women, but to further the evolution of the race and the advancement of humankind. This depended on the fulfillment of love and women's "sacred motherhood" (*shensheng de muxing*).[77]

Most authors showed little concern about women's ultimate sexual freedom. Rather, they concentrated on other priorities. The majority agreed upon the primacy of education and career, which promised women's independence. Many had doubts about the effectiveness of the *canzheng* movement. Chinese politics was so dirty, they argued, that women's participation might only result in their own contamination. However, most believed the movement itself was a process in which women could improve their ability and raise their consciousness. Quite a few contributors addressed the class issue in the women's movement. A recent strike by women workers in Shanghai filatures had accentuated the gaps between working-class and educated women. Although some authors called for an alliance between the two classes, a few argued that only a proletarian women's movement could be the major force in a society polarized by class. The debate suggests widespread popular acceptance of a feminist agenda as presented in the declaration of the FMA, but it also reveals the increasingly loud voice of a Marxist class analysis.[78]

---

77. Se Lu, "Funü yundong de xinqingxiang," 2–7. In this and other essays on love, the connection between love and racial evolution is based on the theory that children born to parents united by love are more intelligent and healthier than those born otherwise.

78. See Fang Minyun, Zhang Youren, Zi Yaohua, Shang Yi, Lu Ziran, Zhang Youhe, and Huang Heji, "Woguo muqian funü yundong yinque de fangzhen" [Politics that the Chinese women's movement should adopt], *Funü zazhi* [The ladies' journal] 9, no. 1 (1923): 87–127.

Much to the editor in chief's disappointment, the *canzheng* movement did not gain momentum despite the full press it received in *The Ladies' Journal*. In less than a year, women's nationwide organized activism faded away. A few months after the special issue on the women's movement appeared, criticism of the women's movement began. Yan Shi, for example, alleged that upon their establishment, many women's organizations would hold one or two grand parties, make a few exciting statements or declarations, hold news conferences, invite celebrities to give speeches, and do a few practical things. But, he complained, "Such actions, after all, are like a firecracker: when it is just lit, it makes a loud bang and shoots high into the sky. It is awesome to people watching. But in a while, there are just a few pieces of broken paper scattering on the ground. Although day and night we expect a women's organized movement, we cannot but oppose strongly such superficial organizations."[79]

Yan Shi criticized many women for joining organizations out of vanity rather than necessity. Yan did not realize that the feminist movement had become such a modern vogue in May Fourth China that it attracted both men and women who lacked serious commitment. Yan and a few other authors also pointed out that a lack of strong and committed leadership was a major reason that organized activities were haphazard. Gao Shan presented his assessment of the problem:

> Leaders must be experienced and mature women who regard the cause as a lifelong career. Therefore, those who can shoulder this task must have leisure, financial resources, and a stable environment. Women in school are unsuited to leading an organized movement because they are limited by time and financial ability, not to mention the fact that once they marry and their environment changes, their ability to continue the movement becomes still more problematic.[80]

Although these analyses of the fledgling feminist movement put it on shaky ground, they nevertheless held out hope for its future development. Because these writers had a "comprehensive" model of a Euro-American feminist movement, they disagreed with the criticism that the Chinese women's suffrage movement was unrealistic or senseless. People with a New

79. Yan Shi, "Funü tuanti yundongli de weiruo" [The weakness of women's organized movement], *Funü zazhi* [The ladies' journal] 9, no. 6 (1923): 17. Yan Shi was a pen name. Judging from the content and frequency of his essays, he might have been an editorial-board member.

80. Gao Shan, "Jianglai de nüquan yundong" [The future feminist movement], *Funü zazhi* [The ladies' journal] 9, no. 12 (1923): 15.

Culturalist distaste for dirty politics believed that current Chinese politics was too messy for women to get involved in and that it would be more productive for women to concentrate on education and career movements. Editor in Chief Zhang agreed with the emphasis on education and career. However, he contended that women's political participation was a major world trend and that Chinese women should not only strive for suffrage but also engage in political reform. Moreover, whereas education and career promoted women's individual advancement in different fields, the suffrage movement united all women under one simple goal. Women pursuing equality in education and career could thus support suffrage without any conflict. The success of suffrage, Zhang predicted, based on his knowledge of the Euro-American experience, would immediately raise women's political and legal status.[81]

Consistently endorsing a comprehensive program for a Chinese women's movement, Zhang also insisted upon the centrality of sexual revolution. In an editorial for the January 1924 issue, he stated again that differential treatment of men and women in society was an enormous human mistake—a mistake that was based on misconceptions about sex. He argued:

> All the misunderstandings between men and women originate in misconceptions about sex. The most fundamental is a misconception of sexuality. So long as human beings regard sexual behavior, demands, and desires as low and dirty, women will be forever placed in an inferior position, and there will never be any hope of solving women's problems. That is what we dare to predict.
>
> We often hear those who have contempt for the female say that women are just reproductive machines. This statement certainly overlooks women's other abilities. But even if it were true, females should not be looked down upon. Those who utter that statement in contempt for women do not know the lofty value of reproduction. Women certainly shoulder a greater task than men in reproduction. If the human race recognizes that reproduction is the most sacred act of human beings, there will be no contempt toward women. So in our view, changing the concept of sex is the sole important and urgent task today, as well as the primary approach to solving women's problems.[82]

This editorial, however, only expressed the concern of Zhang and a few of his colleagues. Other articles revealed different emphases.

81. Ji Zhe (Zhang Xichen), "Women jinhou de taidu" [Our views of the future], *Funü zazhi* [The ladies' journal] 10, no. 1 (1924): 2–7.
82. Ibid.

Within liberal feminist views, there were at least two major distinctive, but not necessarily exclusive, schools. We may categorize Zhang and his colleagues as liberal cultural feminists in their emphasis on changing the mentality of male-centeredness and associated cultural values. The other major view can be categorized as liberal socialist feminism. Analyzing the weakness of the women's *canzheng* movement, many writers demonstrated an awareness of class bias in the demands for equal rights. They pointed out that opening up more coeducational universities would only serve the interests of a small group of women from well-off families. Although it was important to let that small group of women have equal education and awaken first, it was also urgent to extend educational opportunity to women of poorer classes and to provide them with needed services. Wei Chuan argued that a large-scale women's movement would be possible only when nine out of ten women received an education and made an independent living. So he called on the few awakened and educated women to shoulder the responsibility of educating women throughout the country. He suggested that these women run voluntary schools for women who otherwise were unable to attend school. Vocational schools were needed in order for poor women to have skills and economic independence. Such liberal socialist feminists focused on practical services for the majority of lower-class women, and they were concerned with improving the lives of lower-class women.[83]

Feminists with a socialist orientation were not the only ones to pay attention to the welfare of lower-class women. According to Xiang Jingyu, who conducted a survey of the Chinese women's movement in 1923, the Shanghai Feminist Movement Association and Christian women's organizations such as the YWCA and the Women's Christian Temperance Union (WCTU) made efforts to improve the condition of women factory workers. Christian women's organizations, Xiang remarked, "pay special attention to women factory workers, who are in general looked down upon by educated women," and "they claim they will try their best to help women factory workers."[84] Because of their affiliation with international Christian orga-

83. Wei Chuan, "Duiyu funüjie de xiwang" [Expectations of women], *Funü zazhi* [The ladies' journal] 10, no. 1 (1924): 73–77. He Jueyu, "Funü yundong de cuolu yu zhenggui" [The right and wrong routes of the women's movement], *Funü zazhi* [The ladies' journal] 10, no. 4 (1924): 591–593. Similar views were also expressed in discussions in the special issue, *Funü zazhi* 9, no. 1 (1923).

84. Xiang Jingyu, "Zhongguo zuijin funü yundong" [The recent Chinese women's movement] (1923), in *Zhongguo funü yundong lishi ziliao* [Historical source materials of the Chinese women's movement], ed. All-China Women's Federation (Beijing: Renmin chubanshe, 1986), 90.

nizations, those women's organizations had the resources as well as the institutional stability necessary to run projects for poor women's welfare. By comparison, newly established feminist organizations had good intentions but limited resources and little organizational experience. The discussions in *The Ladies' Journal,* in a sense, reflected the reality that feminist organizations had not had much success in reaching out to lower-class women.

In sharp contrast to liberal feminism, which aimed at women's political, legal, social, economic, and sexual equality as well as a new consciousness, the newly established Communist Party specified a different approach. Taking Soviet Russia as its model, this Marxist approach stressed the economic system as the basis of women's emancipation and called for eradication of the capitalist system as the way to achieve women's freedom and equality. Shang Yi wrote in 1923,

> In the contemporary social order, to demand women's emancipation is like demanding labor's emancipation within capitalist society. The goal will be difficult to achieve. Universal suffrage cannot buy labor's freedom. Likewise, women's suffrage will not buy women's freedom. The women's movement and the labor movement have one thing in common—namely, both have to look to a new social order. A real women's movement has to be a proletarian women's movement and a women's movement within the proletarian movement.
>
> The goal of the women's movement is to replace today's social order with a new social order. In order to succeed, the women's movement has to go hand in hand with a proletarian mass movement.[85]

Open to different views of women's emancipation, the editors of *The Ladies' Journal* were initially unaware of the emergence of a competing discourse. In the next couple of years, however, the CCP's discourse on the women's movement threatened to overshadow liberal feminism. In 1923, when the CCP decided to launch a national revolution movement jointly with the GMD, the Marxist theoretical debate on the women's movement was turned into a CCP political tactic for mobilizing women. The Third National Congress of the CCP passed a resolution on the women's movement, instructing female CCP members to guide the feminist movement into the national revolution movement. After the resolution passed, Xiang Jingyu, the chief female CCP leader of the women's movement, analyzed the "mistakes" of the feminist suffrage movement in her survey of the Chinese

85. Shang Yi, "Funü yundong yu xinshehui de jianshe" [The women's movement and the construction of a new society], *Funü zazhi* [The ladies' journal] 9, no. 1 (1923): 31–33.

women's movement and urged educated women to participate in the national revolution movement. In the article, she criticized the editor in chief of *The Ladies' Journal* for his support of a moderate suffrage movement, and she offered her own severe critique of the suffrage movement.

> They do not understand China's situation. They do not understand that current Chinese politics are run by separatist warlord regimes and that the true people's politics is still in a process of revolutionary reform. They just blindly bump into political reality. As for the genuine political movement—the national revolutionary movement, which is the precondition of a feminist suffrage movement—they lack the courage to join. And yet they are quite obedient and stoop to compromise with the warlord power that impedes feminism and women's suffrage and is opposed by all the awakened people in the country.[86]

This severe criticism might not have been heard by many people, because it was published in an obscure CCP publication. In order to address a larger audience, Xiang contributed to the discussion on the future of the women's movement in *The Ladies' Journal*. In her long essay "The Future Chinese Women's National Revolutionary Movement," she presented a CCP analysis of the current political and economic situation. China was a colony of imperialist powers. The Chinese people, who were enduring the double oppression of foreign imperialism and domestic warlordism, had never tasted human or civil rights. Against this background, she argued, it would be erroneous for Chinese women to follow the "old format" of the Euro-American feminist movement in the eighteenth century. If Chinese women only pursued the status of Chinese men, Xiang predicted, the result would be a disaster:

> If the suffrage movement succeeds, a group of sly women could use the opportunity to rush into the pigsty of Beijing or other provinces, collaborating with those male pigs to bring calamity to the country and the people. If the career movement succeeds, and women leave their protected position to seek an independent life in society, they will be robbed by foreign imperialists and Beiyang warlords at any time and in any place. In short, before the Republic of China achieves independence, freedom, peace, and unification, it is impossible to achieve the goals realized by Euro-American women in the eighteenth century, let alone women's true emancipation.[87]

86. Xiang Jingyu, "Zhongguo zuijing funü yundong," 92.
87. Xiang Jingyu, "Jinhou Zhongguo funü de guomin geming yundong" [The future Chinese women's national revolution movement], *Funü zazhi* [The ladies' journal] 10, no. 1 (1924): 29.

Then what was the correct route to Chinese women's emancipation? Placing Chinese women in the global imperialist system, Xiang called on women to join the national revolutionary movement to overthrow British and American imperialist powers and the Chinese warlords supported by those powers. How was this nationalist movement connected to women's emancipation? Xiang argued that, because China was an oppressed nation resisting imperialism, the Chinese national revolution must join the Western workers' revolution to form a world revolution. The success of this world revolution would eventually emancipate labor. Because women and labor were reduced to slaves by a private-ownership economic system, the emancipation of labor from this economic system would emancipate women as well.

As the chief voice of CCP nationalism against the power of liberal feminism, Xiang's essay deserves a further look. Interestingly, her critique of Western feminism, though laden with nationalist sentiment, was not from a nativist position. Rather, it was based on a Marxist and Leninist analysis of the world situation. At the most basic level, she did not differ much from the ones she criticized. In fact, she applied the European socialist line to Chinese women's emancipation more rigidly than those who promoted feminism, because the CCP was not merely related to Marxism intellectually but organizationally attached to the Third International of the Communist Party.[88] By and large, both radical and moderate modern Chinese intellectuals who agitated to change China all looked to foreign ideologies for inspiration and analytical frameworks. What I want to emphasize here is that nationalism did not make the CCP less Western-oriented. Appropriating, assimilating, and interacting with Western discourses (dominant or marginal, complementary or conflicting) has been a major historical process of modern China, a process in which different political forces and social interests have come into play.

When Marxism-Leninism was held out as the truth, it had the exclusive quality exemplified in Xiang Jingyu's essay. Xiang emphasized more than the political necessity for Chinese women to join the national revolution. She was also pointing out what she saw as the only true path to women's

---

88. The Third International of the Communist Party (the Comintern) was established by Lenin in 1919, and shortly after that he sent two agents to China. The Comintern agents helped set up the Chinese Communist Party and passed the Comintern programs to the CCP. For an in-depth study of the conflict between European socialism and feminism and of the impact of the Soviet Revolution on feminism, see Karen Offen, *European Feminism(s): 1700–1950* (Stanford: Stanford University Press, forthcoming).

emancipation. Significantly, she mentioned twice the "old format of Euro-American feminist movement in the eighteenth century" as a contrast with the true path, which was labor emancipation in the twentieth century. Deliberately or unconsciously, in her need to present an evolutionary truth, she depicted Western feminism as an outdated artifice of the "eighteenth century" bourgeois revolution, whereas Marxism represented the rising proletarian revolution of twentieth century. In her words, "the Chinese women's movement has entered the period of labor emancipation and humankind's historical transformation in the twentieth century. The evolution of history has already shown the world's women the route to women's final emancipation."[89]

Xiang's "truth" obviously did not convince the editors of *The Ladies' Journal*. Publishing Xiang's and other's tracts on national revolution might express the editors' support of the political movement. But it did not mean that they accepted a Marxist analysis of women's problems. Nor did it mean that they agreed that their feminist agenda should be replaced by a nationalist agenda. As a matter of fact, the men running *The Ladies' Journal* were unmoved and untouched by the nationalist Marxist rhetoric.[90]

In late 1924, a second wave of organized activity occurred when Sun Yat-sen called for a national assembly. But women again failed to achieve their goal of suffrage when the Duan Qirui warlord government denied women's rights to political participation in the assembly. Analyzing the lessons from the failure of the recent National Assembly Promotion movement (*guomin huiyi cujin yundong*), Zhang Xichen suggested that women should pay more attention to promulgating feminism rather than campaigning for suffrage. Feminism was to fundamentally change the mentality of men and women. Without this mental revolution, Zhang emphasized, the Chinese women's movement would be ineffective. Significantly, to convey the idea of a feminist transformation of mentality, Zhang used the term *fuminieshimu*—a phonemic transliteration for "feminism" introduced to China from Japanese works on feminism—rather than *nüquanzhuyi*, a semantic loanword connoting "women's rights." Reflecting his knowledge of feminism through his reading and translating of Japanese works on feminism, Zhang's choice of this word underscored his intention to draw Chinese readers' attention to a feminist revolution at the cultural and psychological level. It also showed

89. Xiang Jingyu, "Jinhou Zhongguo funü de guomin geming yundong," 32.
90. In the same issue, a few other essays mention the national revolution movement. See Xie Yuanding, "Cu funü chedi de juewu" [Stimulating women's thorough awakening], *Funü zazhi* [The ladies' journal] 10, no. 1 (1924).

his discontent and impatience with the "first stage" of the women's movement that focused on women's rights.[91]

Thus, Zhang in 1925 continued his advocacy of feminism. But the Chinese social and political scene had changed drastically since Zhang began writing on the subject in 1920. Many New Culturalists had changed from alienated cultural critics to dedicated political activists. The two political parties were now making a concerted effort to launch a national revolution, which elevated nationalism to a dominant theme in the political discourse. Understandably, Zhang's call for a feminist revolution in consciousness sounded conspicuously dissonant, particularly to those promoting a nationalist movement. An article in the CCP's newly published periodical *Zhongguo funü* [Chinese women] openly challenged Zhang's theory of mental revolution. The author, Qi Wen, contended that Zhang's revolution in consciousness was just "a reform of prejudice against women in social customs and morality." This "revolution" was unable to change women's oppressed economic and political status. Qi Wen predicted that this "revolution" could only come after the condition of production and economics was changed. Therefore, she argued, "Mr. Zhang Xichen's so-called 'mental revolution' does not occupy an important position in women's emancipation. What women's emancipation should do is, first, the comparatively easy step, abolish inequality between men and women in the legal system; then the second step, which is more difficult, abolish private ownership. That is to say, true women's emancipation must come *after* the success of proletarian revolution and the abolition of private ownership."[92]

---

91. Zhang Xichen, "Zuijin funü yundong de shibai he jinhou yingqu de fangzhen" [The recent failure of the women's movement and policies we should adopt in the future], *Funü zazhi* [The ladies' journal] 11, no. 7 (1925): 1120–1124. The term *fuminieshimu* as a translation of "feminism" appeared earlier in the journal. Introducing feminism to the Chinese audience, Wei Xin translated Japanese author Harada Minoru's work on feminism. Harada addressed the problem of translation at the beginning of the article and pointed out that the word *nüquanzhuyi* was too narrow to convey the meanings of "feminism," whereas *nüzizhuyi* or *funüzhuyi* were too abstract. He suggested using *fuminieshimu* instead. See "Fuminieshimu gaishuo" [On feminism], *Funü zazhi* [The ladies' journal] 8, no. 5 (1922): 64–71. In Zhang Xichen's translation of Japanese author Hisao Honma's *Ten Lectures on the Women Problem*, Zhang also used the word *fuminieshimu*.

Harada Minoru (1890–1975) was a professor of education who translated Western works into Japanese. One of the works he translated was *Love and Marriage* by Ellen Key, which stimulated lively debates in May Fourth China.

92. Qi Wen, "Zhenshi de funü jiefang zai nazhong tiaojianxia caineng shixian?" [Under what conditions would a true women's emancipation be realized?], *Zhongguo funü* [Chinese women], no. 2 (January 1926): 4–5.

Qi's article showed the CCP's conscious effort at "guiding" feminism toward the national revolution. It also revealed the CCP's awareness of the importance of *The Ladies' Journal* and the function of its own new journal *Chinese Women*. Actually, published as it was after the National Assembly Promotion movement in which the CCP had attempted to exert its influence, *Chinese Women* [*Zhongguo funü*] was an effort by the CCP to promulgate its definition of a women's movement and to channel urban feminist energy into the national revolution movement. This goal required a challenge to the ongoing liberal feminist discourse. Zhang Xichen, a prominent advocate of feminism and editor of an influential journal, inadvertently became the major rival to the rising nationalist Marxist discourse of women's emancipation.

Significantly, the women who ran *Chinese Women* were new women who had emerged in the May Fourth era. Yang Zhihua, Xiang Jingyu, Zhang Qinqiu, and so on were all female students who experienced the May Fourth student movement and activities for women's emancipation. However, instead of becoming professional feminist movement leaders like Madam Stanton and Madam Mott in America, whom Zhang Xichen highlighted in his analysis of the weaknesses of the Chinese women's movement, these new women were led by their pursuit of women's emancipation to embrace a proletarian revolution. In this sense, the emergence of a new political discourse and political activism embodied by the CCP diverted much feminist energy from an independent women's movement, a point the editor in chief and his colleagues seem to have overlooked.[93]

In summary, in 1925 the definition of the women's movement by the editors of *The Ladies' Journal* was seriously challenged by the nationalist Marxist line of the CCP. An organized feminist movement that centered on women's political, legal, and economic rights existed at the national level only for a short period of time in late 1922 and early 1923. The second wave of women's organized activism that accompanied the National Assembly Promotion movement in late 1924 marked the beginning of the two political parties' conscious efforts to co-opt the feminist movement. With effective maneuvers for adherents by both the CCP and the GMD, the party-led

---

93. For information on these female communists' activities, see Shanghai Women's Federation, *Shanghai funü yundong shi* [A history of the Shanghai women's movement] (Shanghai: Shanghai renmin chubanshe, 1990). Their active role in channeling women's suffrage activism toward a women's national revolution movement is also discussed in All-China Women's Federation, *Zhongguo funü yundong shi*. See also Yang Zhihua, *Funü yundong gailun* [A brief history of the women's movement] (Shanghai: Dongya tushuguan, 1927).

women's national revolutionary movement gained discursive power, whereas the liberal feminist discourse, much of which had been assimilated into the agenda of a nationalist women's movement, dwindled in its power to compete for followers.

THE FALL OF A FEMINIST FORTRESS

The Ladies' Journal did not play the role of liberal feminist fortress for very long. Its owner, the Commercial Press, had no particular interest other than targeting a large market. The executives of the press supported the editors when their novel feminist agitation dramatically increased the journal's circulation. But in a new climate, when the public responded negatively to the editors' "heresy," it was time for the press to dump those editors.[94]

Zhang Xichen's persistent efforts to promote sexual liberation eventually brought about his downfall. In January 1925, Zhang and his collaborator Zhou Jianren published a special issue on the new sexual morality. In two major essays, Zhang and Zhou discussed the relativity of morals and advocated a new sexual morality that was based on whether one's behavior violated others' freedom and interests. Zhang argued that, because sexuality was a natural desire of human beings, it should not be seen as dirty. Moreover, men should pay attention to and satisfy women's sexual needs. Both essays were full of novel ideas intended to open up the minds of the public and to address the current sexual morality's injustice toward women. However, their advocacy of sexual freedom beyond the restraints of traditional morality drew a severe attack from a professor in Beijing University, Chen Bainian, who accused them of trying to restore polygamy. The attack by a professor from a prestigious university caused an uproar, and the chief executives of *The Ladies' Journal* removed Zhang and Zhou from their positions. They were not even given a chance to defend themselves in *The Ladies' Journal*.[95]

94. Nivard argues that conservative forces were on the rise in those years as a reaction to the radical social changes caused by the May Fourth ideologies. It's not clear if conservative forces caused sales of the journal to drop, but the press's decision to remove its daring editors might have been based on concerns about the journal's reputation rather than its circulation figures.

95. Zhang Xichen, "Xin xingdaode shi shemo" [What is the new sexual morality?], *Funü zazhi* [The ladies' journal] 11, no. 1 (1925): 2–7; Zhou Jianren, "Xingdaode zhi kexue de biaozhun" [The scientific standard of sexual morality], *Funü zazhi* [The ladies' journal] 11, no. 1 (1925): 8–12; and Chen Bainian, "Yifuduoqi de xinhufu" [A new amulet of polygamy], *Xiandai Pinglun* [Modern reviews], no. 14 (1925): 6–8. Zhang Xichen eventually published *Xin xingdaode taolun ji* [A collection of debate on the new sexual morality] (Shanghai: Kaiming shudian, 1929).

Starting in September 1925, *The Ladies' Journal* was in entirely new hands. Discussions on love, marriage, divorce, and sexuality disappeared. Translations of feminist texts and Western stories vanished. The new editor in chief was a man concerned about fostering women's artistic taste. He quickly published a special issue on art. Even the readership seemed to change rapidly. Now the readers no longer asked questions about love, courtship, marriage, or the women's movement, but about photography and health. Although many articles in the journal discussed topics of women's education and women's professional training, *The Ladies' Journal* was no longer a voice of feminism.

In hindsight, this marked the end of an era of radical cultural transformation. The radical New Culturalists lost an important front to continue their offense, and their tone became defensive and resigned. When Lu Xun published Zhang Xichen's defense against Chen Bainian's charge—a defense that no one wanted to print at the time—he commented sarcastically, "I think it is too early for Mr. Zhang and Mr. Zhou to publicize those comments in China—although these have been old words abroad. Abroad is abroad."[96] Lu Xun was suggesting that even after so much talk about love and new sexual morality during the whole May Fourth era, the public was far from ready for sexual emancipation. Zhou Zuoren in 1927 expressed a similar opinion. When he was asked to write something on the woman problem, he said, "After all, women's problems include only two things: economic emancipation and sexual emancipation. But now there is no way to talk about this. It is not just that there is no way to practice it. There is simply nothing to say. If you talk, you cannot avoid offending others."[97] Although he kept writing about sexuality and women's predicament under the old sexual morality, now the once avant-garde New Culturalist's words had a weary tone.

But New Culture was not defeated in one battle. Those New Culturalists who truly believed in their vision of a new culture continued to fight. Zhang Xichen was one of those. Soon after he was removed from *The Ladies' Journal,* he and Zhou Jianren resigned from the Commercial Press and began a new journal of their own. In January 1926, *Xin Nüxing* [The new woman] was published as a sequel to *The Ladies' Journal.* Old friends who previously contributed to *The Ladies' Journal* now wrote for *The New*

96. Lu Xun, "Bianwan xieqi" [Afterword], in Zhang Xichen, *Xin xindaode taolun ji,* 98.

97. Zhou Zuoren, "Beigouyan tongxing" [A correspondence from Beigouyan], in *Nüxing de faxian* [The discovery of women], ed. Shu Wu (Beijing: Wenhua yishu chubanshe, 1990), 11.

Woman. Love, marriage, sexuality, and so on were constantly discussed in this new journal.

Interestingly, in the opening issue, Zhou Jianren published a major essay on "The Double Standard of Morality." Ten years before that, his brother Zhou Zuoren had risen to fame by publishing a translation titled "On Chastity" in *New Youth.* Whereas "On Chastity" used modest language and logical argument to challenge the double sexual standard, "The Double Standard of Morality" used the language of science to depict explicitly the female reproductive system in order to explicate the roots of the double sexual standard. Zhou Jianren's matter-of-fact analysis of women's menstrual blood and pregnancy in relation to his critique of the concept of female pollution in different cultures or religions would have been unimaginable for his elder brother. Zhou Jianren's views on the dialectical relationship between culture and economic life also demonstrated his sophisticated intellectual inquiry into the question of women's oppression. Pointing out socially constructed differences between men and women, Zhou emphasized the malleability of culturally formed concepts, especially those concepts relating to sexuality. If Zhou Zuoren's translation ushered in an age of scrutiny on sexual morality, Zhou Jianren's essay represented the culmination of ten years of intellectual pursuit. However, Zhou Jianren did not make a splash with his essay as his brother had ten years ago. Very likely, the self-selected audience for such literature, educated young men and women, had become too familiar with the language to be excited by it any more.[98]

To some extent, it was the success of feminist discourse that reduced the discursive power of publications like *The New Woman.* Chen Wangdao lamented the silencing of the women's movement in 1926, complaining, "Most of the truly awakened women have buried themselves in professional studies."[99] But Chen was referring only to the liberal feminist movement. In fact, the women's movement in the nationalist revolution was on the rise at the time, along with the Northern Expedition, in many parts of the country. Chen's observation reflected the irony that when educated women were actually pursuing economic independence and establishing their individual careers, fulfilling the liberal feminists' widely publicized goal of emancipation, a liberal feminist magazine like *The New Woman* no longer appealed to them. The male advocates of feminism fully recognized this irony. When they

---

98. Zhou Jianren, "Erchong daode" [The double standard of morality], *Xinnüxing* [The new woman] 1, no. 1 (1926): 1–11.

99. Chen Wangdao, "Zhongguo nüzi de juexing" [The awakening of Chinese women], *Xinnüxing* [The new woman] 1, no. 9 (1926): 641.

finally closed *The New Woman* in 1929, the editors congratulated their own success rather deploringly.

> The reason for stopping the journal is simple: the times no longer need us. The times are like a tyrant with absolute power. Shocking heresies five or six years ago have become bland words to everyone today. Terms such as "women's emancipation" and "women's movement" were discussed and promulgated excitedly by everyone in the intellectual class after the May Fourth movement, and they were simultaneously opposed and cursed by a group of people with backward ideas. But now they have become clichés, like eating when you are hungry and putting on clothes when you are cold. Of course, whether one has food and clothes or not remains a problem.[100]

The editors' emphasis was not on how the May Fourth liberal feminist discourse decisively made "women's emancipation" a positive term in Chinese vocabulary, a feat for which they could claim some credit. Instead, they stressed the fact that the actual realization of women's emancipation was a long way from the professed oral support of women's emancipation by people of various political orientations. In the end, they gave up their advocacy, but not because they had already achieved a complete victory. On the contrary, it was because in the late 1920s the space for free debate and agitation was much narrower than it had been in the May Fourth era. The split between the Nationalist Party and the Communist Party in 1927, and the Nationalist Party's power in most of China, made leftists and leftist ideologies illegitimate. Intellectual debates now unavoidably carried political implications and were therefore risky. The editors saw their dilemma clearly. Admitting their discontent with their own "empty talk," they complained, "But which direction to turn? Toward the Left? In a party-ruled country where the party's power is absolute, we may be regarded as red and may have our heads chopped off."[101] The political environment had deteriorated to such an extent that a free exploration of the paths to women's emancipation was no longer possible. By comparison, ironically, the warlord age marked by disintegration of political power had been a rare golden age for the growth of feminism in China.[102]

The final fall of the feminist fortress *The New Woman* symbolized the

---

100. "Feikanci" [Abandoning the journal address], *Xinnüxing* [The new woman] 4, no. 48 (1929).

101. Ibid.

102. For a discussion of the fate of feminists in the national revolution movement during the period of white terror, see Elisabeth Croll, *Feminism and Socialism in China* (London: Routledge and Kegan Paul, 1978), 148–152.

decline of May Fourth feminism in the late 1920s. But in the process of male feminist agitation and female feminist activities during that decade, urban Chinese society witnessed irreversible changes in women's lives. The two most obvious changes were the replacement of gender segregation with co-education from secondary school up, and women's advancement in society with increasing career opportunities and political participation.

Another profound change has not often been recorded: a new female subjectivity emerged with the popularization of May Fourth feminism. In 1924, Zhang Xichen gave an account of this change:

> In the past ten years, there is something most powerful that is developing most rapidly—that is, a shapeless reform in consciousness. This reform is what is called women's awakening as "human beings." Ten years ago, although there was a brave movement demanding suffrage, the goal of the participants was just political equality between men and women. But since the New Culture movement, the notion of women's emancipation has been transformed. Ordinary women have begun to question the customs, habits, rules, and superstitions that have been passed down since antiquity. Women who have had some contact with new thought all have the consciousness that *"a woman is a human being, too."* The books which have been regarded as women's bibles, such as *Nüjie, Neixun, Nülunyu,* and *Nüfan,* have all been trampled under the feet of new women.[103]

Zhang's observation captured the central theme of May Fourth liberal feminism. The New Culturalists could claim a great accomplishment: new women demanding independence, autonomy, and gender equality had emerged on the tide of May Fourth feminism. There was a direct connection between New Culturalist advocacy of women's emancipation and Chinese women's new consciousness, as this chapter documents. Nevertheless, the emergence of new women during the May Fourth era was also part of a long-term response to a nationalistic discourse about women that had begun in the late Qing dynasty. Improving the race and strengthening the nation had provided the rationale for abolishing footbinding and popularizing women's education. Women's wholesome bodies and women's education in turn provided a physical precondition as well as an institutional base for new women's social advancement.

---

103. Se Lu, "Zuijin shiniannei funüjie de huigu" [A review of women in the past ten years], *Funü zazhi* [The ladies' journal] 10, no. 1 (1924): 21–22; emphasis added. *Nüjie* [Precepts for women], *Neixun* [Exemplars in the female quarters], *Nülunyu* [Analects for women], and *Nüfan* [Female exemplars] are texts that teach Confucian moral codes and behavioral standards relating to women.

As beneficiaries of this nationalistic discourse about women, the new women were deeply influenced by nationalism. At first, there seemed to be no conflict between the discourses of nationalism and liberal feminism, because in the New Culturalist argument that centered on cultural transformation, the ancient nation would progress toward modernity by making Chinese women independent individuals who enjoyed equal rights. The two discourses became competing and contradictory only after the birth of the CCP. Combining Marxism and nationalism, the CCP discourse called on women to reject the pursuit of equal rights under the existing political and economic systems. It urged women to join a revolution that would ensure an independent and unified nation first and overthrow private ownership eventually. Aided by the power of its coalition with the GMD, the CCP's nationalist discourse gained weight in the second half of the 1920s. However, as this chapter illustrates, liberal feminism was overshadowed but did not disappear. In fact, since the May Fourth feminist wave, "women's emancipation" and the "women's movement" have become lasting signs of modernity in Chinese political culture, even though the definitions of those terms have shifted frequently to meet political needs in various historical settings. Part 2 demonstrates how feminism and nationalism shaped women of the May Fourth generation, and how these women rose as a major force for rapid social change in early-twentieth-century China.

—> nationalist feminism vs liberal feminism

PART TWO

PORTRAITS

3 · Forgotten Heroines
An Introduction to the Narrators

The May Fourth period was marked with newly popularized phrases such as "women's emancipation," "equality between men and women," "women's rights," and "women's independent personhood." The new language centering on the woman problem (*funü wenti*) became the main signifier of the New Culture. But what did these new phrases mean to women of the time? How did *they* respond to the contemporary intellectual currents? Acknowledging May Fourth men's role in making feminism a positive and desirable ideology in the early-twentieth-century discourse of Chinese modernity makes us wonder how individual women acted upon or reacted to May Fourth feminism. Only historical women, rather than female images in male literary representation, can tell us what changes took place in their consciousness as a result of the period's cultural transformations. Consequently, we turn to May Fourth women's own words for an understanding of the impact of May Fourth feminism in twentieth-century China.

Before presenting the May Fourth women's life stories to readers, I must discuss two separate but related issues involved in reading the following narratives. One is the historical context of producing these life stories. The narrators in this book told their stories against a specific social and political setting as well as in response to my questions. Presenting their narratives also has much to do with my own interest and preoccupation as a historian at this particular historical moment. In order to prepare readers for a contextualized reading, I must foreground some of the hidden agendas (of both the narrators and myself) and implications in the following narratives. Thus, this introduction to our subjects begins with a discussion of the contemporary context in which specific meanings of their narratives have been formed.

The other issue is the complicated historical background against which the narrators wove their life experiences, which cover the span of almost a century. The interpretation after each narrative attempts to unpack the life stories and put individual women actors back into the historical drama. But because this part of the book is structured around each woman's life and thus does not present a history of the May Fourth women chronologically, the lack of temporal coherence between the chapters may confuse readers. This chapter thus offers thematic links for the chapters that follow; at the same time it situates major issues raised by the narratives in a broad historical context.

THE CONSTRUCTION OF PUBLIC MEMORY

After the founding of the People's Republic of China in 1949, the Chinese Communist Party created three models of pre-1949 women in the public memory: women who had joined the Communist revolution and who, therefore, rose to the status of heroines; women who had been oppressed by feudalism, imperialism, and capitalism and thus were victims to be liberated by the party; and bourgeois wives (*taitai*) who depended on their husbands and therefore were the embodiment of a decadent, parasitic, and exploitative class to be eliminated in the revolution.[1] In numerous literary texts, including novels, biographies, movies, plays, and operas produced during the Mao era (1949–1976), the transformation of women victims into revolutionary heroines was a prominent and popular theme, whereas the third model appeared only occasionally, as a background prop. The construction of Communist heroines in CCP political discourse is a fascinating subject that is beyond the scope of this study. However, because the implications of these models are closely related to the context of the production of the life stories in this book, a few relevant points should be examined here.

Functioning mainly to illustrate the glorious history of the CCP, the construction of Communist heroines served both to celebrate and obliterate women's contribution in history. The key issue here is not whether women get to be remembered, but rather, *which* women get to be remembered. The heroines celebrated in CCP discourse were first and foremost Communists. The constructed stories about these heroines never failed to harp on the themes of their loyalty to the party and the revolutionary cause as well as the glory of the party, the liberator that transformed a victim into a hero-

1. The model of oppressed women was also a May Fourth heritage. For a discussion of the May Fourth male literary representation of oppressed women, see Yue Ming-bao, "Gendering the Origins of Modern Chinese Fiction," in *Gender and Sexuality in Twentieth-Century Chinese Literature and Society*, ed. Tonglin Lu (Albany: State University of New York Press, 1993), 47–65.

ine. The Communist heroines, therefore, were exemplary models of Chinese women who lived a meaningful life by identifying with the party and devoting themselves to the revolutionary cause.

This exclusive construction of women's experience has its positive implications. The large numbers and frequent appearance of Communist heroines in CCP-sponsored literature can be read as the CCP's acknowledgment of women's agency in the history of Chinese revolution. Although in most Communist heroine stories there was a male figure who embodied the party and pointed the road to liberation or fostered the growth of heroines, the heroic female protagonists who demonstrated extraordinary qualities usually left a deeper impression, especially in young girls' minds. For Chinese women born after 1949, myself included, the literary images of Communist heroines provided empowering role models and self-esteem.

Rather than manifesting a revolutionary break from the conventional treatment of women in Chinese history, the representation of Communist heroines is in line with traditional Chinese historiography, which, since antiquity, had selected and represented exemplary women to serve as didactic role models for other women. If the representation of exemplary women in Chinese history served to formulate or maintain gender norms, the construction of Communist heroines also helped demarcate gender roles and promote state-endorsed virtues for women to follow. Indeed, many virtues of Chinese women promoted by old dynastic regimes were confirmed and celebrated in the Communist literature. However, there is a crucial difference between an imperial exemplary woman and a Communist heroine. The ancient woman's extraordinary accomplishments were usually a form of fulfilling her duty to her family, whereas the Communist woman's heroic deeds demonstrated her exclusive devotion to the party and the nation, often at the expense of her family. This highly politicized image of nationalist-minded Communist heroines undoubtedly reflects the legacy of May Fourth feminism, which held the incorporation of women into all social domains as the precondition for Chinese modernity. In redirecting women's virtues of loyalty and devotion away from the family and toward the nation and the party, the image of Communist heroines further consolidated the legitimacy of the integration of women into the men's world. This was no small feat in a culture with centuries-old institutions of gender segregation.[2]

---

2. The term "gender segregation" does not refer to "the separate spheres of public and private." "Gender segregation" operated more like racial segregation, maintaining a social order in which interactions between men and women were restricted. In social, economic, and religious activities, men and women were designated to

Arguably, the production of Communist heroines empowered women and involved many female Communists. Communist martyr Xiang Jingyu, for example, became the preeminent national heroine in the 1950s through the concerted efforts of many of her surviving female comrades. *The Journal of Chinese Women*, which was run by the All-China Women's Federation, printed many articles about Xiang in 1958 on the thirtieth anniversary of her death. In that same year, the journal reprinted some of the articles in a pamphlet. Of the eight people who contributed to the pamphlet, seven were Xiang's female comrades.[3] These senior Communist women's promotion of Xiang could be read as their conscious effort to reclaim women's agency in the revolution—in other words, as a form of negotiation with the party for recognition and power.

Yet the promotion of Communist heroines often consisted of more complicated dynamics. Meanings other than a general celebration of women's contributions were attached to particular heroines. Xiang Jingyu, for example, was eulogized not only for her devotion to the revolution but also for her leading role in conceptualizing a CCP-led women's movement. Confirming Xiang's contribution was thus tightly linked to the project of proclaiming the success of the CCP's route to women's liberation and "failure" of the "other, erroneous" women's movement—namely, the feminist movement. Each heroine was made to transmit a specific political message for the party, and together they formed a public memory that retained no trace of non-Communist women's activism. The celebration of Communist heroines, therefore, went hand in hand with the obliteration of non-Communist women's agency. This simultaneous celebration and obliteration helped to form a master narrative that created and maintained the legitimacy of CCP dominance.

The narrators in this book fall, in one way or another, into the category of women omitted from the CCP's master narrative. Before 1949 Lu Lihua, Zhu Su'e, Wang Yiwei, and Chen Yongsheng were non-Communist independent career women, a social category that defies not only the image of deplorable victims and the model of Communist heroines, but also the classification of bourgeois *taitai*. More significant, these women's accom-

---

different zones. Male zones were often where formal powers were exercised. For example, although many elite women received an education from private tutors, the institution of formal education, which had been connected to civil service in the imperial system, was a male zone.

3. See Zhongguo funü zazhishe, *Lieshi Xiang Jingyu* [Martyr Xiang Jingyu] (Beijing: Zhongguo funü zazhishe, 1958).

plishments before 1949 were totally unrelated to the CCP's line about women's liberation in China. Before I met them, I was ignorant of the achievements of such career women and unaware they had been erased from the public memory. Although I was unable to grasp fully the meanings of their life stories at the time I conducted my interviews, I felt the shock immediately. Many evenings, riding my bike through Shanghai streets as I returned after an interview, I was filled with mixed emotions of excitement, indignation, and sadness. The triumphs and tragedies in these women's long lives not only touched me but also changed my perceptions profoundly, disrupting many of my long-held notions about women before 1949 and about the liberator role of the CCP. Challenging the CCP's master narrative of Chinese women's liberation soon became a conscious and inseparable agenda from my desire to write these women back into history.

As for the narrators, they themselves have endured marginalization for almost a half century. When we first met in 1993, these women had received gestures of apology from the government for injustice done to them during the Mao era. But the apologies did not change their powerless and voiceless situation. When they saw me, a historian who was interested in their past experiences, they knew this was their opportunity to present history in the way that *they* remembered it. Although they could not know how I would ultimately conceptualize their oral histories, telling their stories was their conscious effort to reclaim their contribution to history and to reconstruct the public memory. In that respect, the narrator's agenda and my own agenda coincide.

At the same time, my selection of these particular narrators was determined by their eagerness to participate in history-writing. The interviewees who have their own agenda are the ones most ready to give a detailed account of their past experiences. It is no coincidence that a general question from me would induce a stream of narrative from these women. After I completed my first round of interviews, having talked to thirteen women, I saw a clear pattern. The richest and most colorful stories were told by those who had many accomplishments before 1949 but were reduced to marginal positions in the Mao era. Apparently, they have a stake in presenting their history. Even the daughters and sisters of such women were eager to tell stories they remembered. From this category of women, I chose narratives in the first person by women born in the first decade of the century.[4]

4. Though I emphasize these narrators' active participation in history-writing, I caution readers of the inherent bias in my presenting these narratives. As a social category, career women before 1949 were erased from the public memory in the Mao era, but not all individual career women experienced the exclusion, marginalization,

RECLAIMING WOMEN'S AGENCY IN CHINA'S "MODERNITY"

Because women's emancipation has long been an integral theme in the discourse of Chinese modernity, male and female scholars in the People's Republic of China tend to include the subject in their presentation of China's modernization process—a distinctly different treatment of that subject than offered in similar works by Western scholars. The long-established Maoist master narrative dwells at length on women's emancipation led exclusively by the CCP. In recent years, scholarly efforts to document women's own struggle for emancipation have appeared in China. Although the CCP line on women's liberation is still asserted to be the correct one, many vivid stories of various women's persevering battles against cultural and social bondage challenge the prevailing myth that Chinese women were granted liberation by the CCP before women themselves were awakened.[5] My study not only places women in the center of historical transformations, but also examines the relationship between the changing gender discourse and competing intellectual and sociopolitical forces. The narrators' oral histories help us see how gender has been central in China's modernity, how feminism mingled with nationalism and made rapid inroads into cultural and social conventions, and how women played the decisive role in bringing about significant social changes in the twentieth century. The emergence of the social category "career women" in the early twentieth century epitomizes all these themes.

At the turn of the twentieth century, the dominant cultural norms in China specified a woman's role as mother, daughter, and wife and regulated her behavior strictly in a gender-segregated world. Although women from lower classes had always been engaged in economic activities in or outside

---

and persecution experienced after 1949 by the narrators in this book. A *Chinese Women's Who's Who*, published in 1988, lists 102 non-Communist career women born in the first decade of the century who stayed in mainland China after 1949. Their accomplishments before 1949 are mentioned, and 76 of the women seem to have held a position or title after 1949. Because the *Who's Who* says erroneously that Lu Lihua, one of our narrators, held her school principal position without interruption after 1949, the accuracy of the book's accounts is in question. Still, it is obvious from the dates of publications mentioned there that some women were able to continue their careers after 1949, especially those in medicine and science. *Zhongguo funü mingren lu* [Chinese women's who's who], ed. Xue Weiwei (Xian: Shaanxi renmin chubanshe, 1988).

5. A recent study with a women-centered approach is Luo Suwen's *Nüxing yu jindai Zhongguo shehui* [Women and modern Chinese society] (Shanghai: Shanghai renmin chubanshe, 1996).

their households, and women in elite families had often been involved in literary creativity, gender operated as an organizational principle in such a way that interaction between men and women was restricted and many institutions were exclusively male zones.[6] Formal school education, which had been central to maintaining the civil service system in imperial China, was one such male zone. The male monopoly on formal education was challenged when a few Western missionary schools offered education to poor Chinese girls in the mid-nineteenth century. But school education for women was still rare. It was not until after China's defeat by Japan in the Sino-Japanese War in 1895 that women's education became a prominent issue on the late Qing reformers' agenda. The Qing government accepted women's education as a necessary measure to strengthen the nation and improve the race, as long as that education did not subvert gender norms. This thorny problem—that women had to be brought into national politics yet restricted to female roles and behaviors—was resolved by women's own choice and efforts.

Although the dominant rationale for women's education was to prepare patriotic and virtuous mothers who would rear healthy and talented sons, many women were attracted to the rising advocacy for women's equal rights that accompanied the spread of women's education. For many women, an education was a step into the men's world and a qualification for citizenship, rather than merely a means to become a virtuous mother of good citizens. Women wove the two lines of argument—national strengthening and equal rights—into a single thread: national strengthening required women's equal participation in all spheres. Among those who took the initial step toward this goal were the first groups of Chinese women who went to study in Japan in the late Qing.

After 1894–1895, when Japan defeated China in a decisive war over influence in Korea, Japan became simultaneously an emblem of China's humiliation and a model of Asian modernity. Geographically and culturally closer than the United States and Europe, Japan was an attractive destination for Chinese who wanted to explore the means to revitalize China or to learn new skills to establish themselves in a changing Chinese society. Thousands of men from elite families landed in Japan in the first decade of the twentieth century, studying politics, military affairs, economics, medicine,

---

6. Chinese families vary in size from one conjugal unit to several generations with several conjugal units. Women's work varies because of differences in the household size as well as differences in geography. The Chinese character *jia* (family) can also be used to refer to the whole clan. In the period under discussion, families in most of China, especially the rural areas, were patrilineal and patrilocal.

science, literature, and so on. Initially, a few Chinese women went to Japan with their husbands and fathers; later, the number of independent women students increased. The Japanese made special efforts to accommodate Chinese women students. The renowned female educator Shimoda Utako founded the Practical Women's School for Chinese women students in 1901. Promoting women's education "as the basis of education for males," Shimoda held a version of "republican motherhood" that was similar to the views held by the Chinese reformers who advocated women's education. She believed that educated good wives and virtuous mothers would strengthen Asian nations in the competition with the "white race."[7] This model of women's education appealed to the Qing government, which had insisted that women's education should follow the tradition of women's learning to "teach women the ways of being a wife and mother."[8] With a practical goal of training teachers for girls' schools in China, provincial governments in the Qing began to send women students to Japan in 1905. By the end of the Qing dynasty in 1911, about two hundred Chinese women had studied in Japan.[9]

Despite the aims of both their Japanese educators and the Qing government, many of the Chinese women students became social activists and revolutionaries rather than guardians of domesticity. They seemed to be informed less by a curriculum emphasizing sewing skills and home economics than by the stimulating environment in Japan, where Western works on liberalism, socialism, anarchism, and feminism were translated and circulated among Chinese student groups.[10] The Chinese students in Japan were, to some extent, a self-selected group. The motivation to study there was in many cases born of a deepening sense of national crisis after China's military defeats and territory concessions to foreign powers, especially after the Qing government signed the humiliating Boxer Protocol with foreign powers in

7. See Joan Judge, "Knowledge for the Nation or of the Nation: Meiji Japan and the Changing Meaning of Female Literacy in the Late Qing" (paper delivered at a workshop on "New Perspectives on the Qing Dynasty" held at the Center for Chinese Studies, University of California, Los Angeles, October 4, 1997), 7.

8. Luo Suwen, *Nüxing yu Zhongguo jindai shehui*, 131.

9. Various studies on the subject of Chinese women students in Japan present conflicting figures. Xie Changfa lists 180 women students by name from 1902 to 1911 in "Qingmo de liuri nüxuesheng jiqi huodong yu yingxiang" [Late Qing women students in Japan and their activities and influence], *Jindai Zhongguo funüshi yanjiu* [Research on women in modern Chinese history], no. 4 (August 1996). Joan Judge in her unpublished paper presents a number much higher.

10. For an analysis of Japan's role in Chinese acquaintance with Western knowledge, see Lydia H. Liu, *Translingual Practice: Literature, National Culture, and Translated Modernity—China, 1900–1937* (Stanford: Stanford University Press, 1995).

1901.[11] The students' tenacious search for paths to national salvation was expressed in a wide range of activism, from disseminating new ideas through translation and publication (mostly retranslating Japanese versions of Western works into Chinese), to joining secret societies dedicated to anti-Manchu activities. Women students, though a small minority, contributed conspicuously to this lively scene. Between 1903 to 1911, women students in Japan founded a number of organizations and at least nine journals to promote women's equal rights and women's education, denounce the Chinese family system and arranged marriage, and advocate anti-footbinding. Although these women's journals were short-lived, lasting for only one issue or up to two years, they were both informed by and contributed to the emerging women's rights movement in China. Instead of being a cradle of motherhood, Japan—especially Tokyo, where these journals were published—became an important base for Chinese feminist activism before the 1911 Revolution.

These early feminists envisioned a women's education that was different from that practiced in Japan. In fact, a strong critique of Japanese women's education appeared in *The Women's Journal* [*Nübao*] in 1909. Declaring that the goal of the journal was to "promote women's education in China and to foster women's rights [*nüquan*] in East Asia," an editorial criticized women's education in Japan for enslaving women. "It is a pity that all the journals on women's education in Japan do not promote women's rights. . . . Because Japanese and Chinese people are of the same race and use the same written language, we cannot bear to see Japanese women forever endure a suppression that amounts to imprisonment by men. Therefore we will add essays in Japanese in order to awaken them."[12] The editor in chief, Chen Yiyi, in her essay "Men Are Superior, Women Are Inferior and Virtuous Mothers and Good Wives," pointed out that different curricula for men and women in Japan reflected a deeply rooted fallacy that "men are superior and women are inferior." She evoked stories of Chinese heroines such as Hua Mulan and Liang Hongyu to argue that women were capable of great achievements by themselves but that Japan's educational sys-

---

11. After an anti-Christian, antiforeign peasant uprising in northern China (the "Boxer Rebellion" in 1900) was suppressed by a combined Western military expedition, the Qing government agreed to the demands of foreign powers to compensate for the loss of foreign lives and property in that uprising. The Boxer Protocol in 1901 included the payment of an indemnity of 450 million taels (approximately 333 million dollars at the time), equal to almost half of the Qing annual budget.

12. "Buke budu benbao" [One has to read this journal], *Nübao* [The women's journal], no. 2 (1909).

tem only used women to help men achieve.[13] Chen's critique of the "virtuous mother and good wife" goal of women's education anticipated a major theme of the May Fourth era:

> A virtuous mother and a good wife are both for men, being his mother and his wife. The terms sound beautiful, but such women are actually men's high-class slaves. Women's education in Japan is thus criticized as the education of high-class maids. . . . Why should women's education be established for men's sake? . . . Sages and mediocre thinkers are products of different educations. One reaps what one sows. Given the goal of bringing up virtuous mothers and good wives, women will certainly become virtuous mothers and good wives. This is what I feel extremely sorry about. Educators should expect the educated to be sages not to be mediocre thinkers. . . . I would like to call on the field of women's education: NEVER MAINTAIN THE "VIRTUOUS MOTHER AND GOOD WIFE" PRINCIPLE; PURSUE THE FUNDAMENTAL GOAL OF FOSTERING HEROINES. JAPAN'S PERNICIOUS INFLUENCE HAS TO BE LIQUIDATED. . . . GIVING WOMEN AN EDUCATION EQUAL TO THAT OF MEN IS TO GIVE WOMEN RIGHTS EQUAL TO THOSE OF MEN.[14]

The influence of these women students in early-twentieth-century China was not limited to the effect of their publications. Many of them became prominent figures once they returned home. Qiu Jin, for example, became the primary role model for Chinese women in the twentieth century as a result of her heroic devotion to the anti-Manchu revolution. As Qiu's example illustrates, for that generation of women who were still living in a gender-segregated society, to be included in the national struggle along with men was an extremely important equal rights issue. Qiu Jin's contemporaries saw her as a woman who entered the men's world without disguising herself as a man and accomplished heroic deeds far beyond the reach of most men. Numerous heroines from China's long history inspired Qiu. Indeed, Qiu and her contemporaries saw her as being in the same category as those ancient heroines (*nüxia*). However, this twentieth-century *nüxia* expressed her desire to cross the gender boundary in nationalist and feminist neologism, which established her as the first *modern* heroine. Individual heroines had appeared sporadically throughout Chinese history, but Qiu Jin signaled a historical period in which heroines emerged in large groups

13. Liang Hongyu was the wife of a famous general, Han Shizhong, in the Southern Song dynasty. In 1130 she joined her husband on the battlefield to resist Jin invaders. Liang's courageous involvement in warfare has been popularized through stories and plays.

14. Chen Yiyi, "Nanzhun nübei yu xianmu liangqi" [Men are superior, women are inferior and virtuous mothers and good wives], *Nübao* [The women's journal], no. 2 (1909): 5–7. The large print is in the original text.

in response to changing political and intellectual currents. The rising nationalism provided legitimacy for many Chinese women's transgression into male territory—a transgression for which they now had a new term: the pursuit of women's equal rights (*shenzhang nüquan*). Consciously or unconsciously, women often hinged their pursuit of equal rights on the nationalist cause. This entanglement of nationalist devotion with self-emancipation was a distinctive feature of the process of Chinese women's emancipation, a feature rooted in the national crises during the first half of the twentieth century. The wide circulation of Qiu Jin's story also strongly shaped the next generation of women's dual vision of nationalism and emancipation, as the narrators illustrate.

Qiu Jin's image as a steadfast anti-Manchu revolutionary overshadowed the underlying feminist goals of the late Qing women's movement until after the Qing dynasty was toppled. Once the Republican government was established, however, many women who had participated in the 1911 Revolution began a militant women's suffrage movement. A group of students who had returned from Japan played a leading role in this suffrage campaign. Among them, Tang Qunying, a classmate of Qiu Jin's at the Practical Women's School and an early female member of the Revolutionary Alliance, became the most prominent leader. But even while Tang and many other women revolutionaries were forming various women's organizations to pursue women's equality in the new republic, the provisional national council refused to include equal rights for men and women in the provisional constitution. Greatly disappointed by this refusal, Tang, chair of the newly formed Women's Suffrage Alliance (Nüzi Canzheng Tongmenghui, or WSA), led a group of suffragists to petition the national council in March 1912. When they were denied access to the council, the furious suffragists broke the windows of the meeting chamber, kicked down the guard who tried to stop them, and threatened that they would "appeal to force if their demands were rejected." In August 1912 the Revolutionary Alliance, of which many of the suffragists were members, deleted equal rights for men and women from the platform of the reorganized Nationalist Party (GMD). Outraged by this betrayal, Tang and Wang Changguo, vice-chair of the WSA and also educated in Japan, on two different occasions slapped Song Jiaoren, the leader of the GMD who drafted the new platform, to "release the anger of two hundred million women compatriots."[15] Their militancy did not help them win women's suffrage in 1912, but it sent a clear message to the pub-

15. See Wang Jiajian, "Minchu de nüzi canzheng yundong" [The women's suffrage movement in the early republic], in *Zhongguo funüshi lunwenji* [Collection of essays on Chinese women's history], ed. Li Yu-ning and Zhang Yu-fa, vol. 2 (Taibei:

lic that women would not only fulfill their duties as citizens but also fight for the rights of citizenship. The thwarted suffragist leaders Tang Qunying and Wang Changguo continued their efforts at the local level and made a successful recovery during the heyday of May Fourth feminist activism. In 1921, Wang Changguo became one of the first two elected women members of the provincial council in Hunan.[16]

Women educated in Japan also became the earliest career women in China.[17] Some engaged in publishing, some in business enterprises, and most either opened girls' schools in their hometowns or became teachers in girls' schools to pursue their original goal of promoting women's education in China. A few of our narrators first learned the phrase "equality between men and women" from these teachers. Moreover, rather than becoming good wives and virtuous mothers, some of these women who had studied in Japan rejected marriage and remained single. Newly created careers in teaching made it possible for these educated women to make unconventional choices. By the time our May Fourth protagonists came of age, it was commonly accepted for educated women to become independent single career women. Their teachers had already demonstrated to them the feasibility of such a life. The link between the late Qing women activists and May Fourth women was tangible.

May Fourth women, however, found themselves in a quite different historical setting. A few years after the suppression of the first suffrage movement, women's issues reappeared with even greater force in China. Promoted by the rising New Culturalists, women's emancipation issues reached an unprecedented scope and depth by the end of the second decade. Owing much to the rapid development of girls' schools in the first decade of the republic,[18]

Taibei Commercial Press, 1988): 577–608. Also see Luo Liuzhi, "Nüquan yundong lingxiu Tang Qunying" [Tang Qunying: A leader of the feminist movement], in *Funü* [Women], no. 3 (1983). Reports of suffragists' militant actions in the contemporary newspapers are collected in *Zhongguo funü yundong lishi ziliao, 1840–1918* [Historical source materials of the Chinese women's movement, 1840–1918], ed. All-China Women's Federation (Beijing: Zhongguo funü chubanshe, 1991), 592–595.

16. All-China Women's Federation, *Zhongguo funü yundong shi* [A history of the Chinese women's movement] (Beijing: Chunqiu chubanshe, 1989), 126.

17. Other career women emerged in the late Qing with an education either from Western missionary schools in China or from the United States.

18. Combining nationwide enrollment in four-year primary schools and three-year high-primary schools, there were 1,761 female students in 1905, 20,557 in 1908, and 215,626 in 1919. See Luo Suwen, *Nüxing yu jindai Zhongguo jindai shehui,* 137 and 156.

female students became a significant new social category and receptive readers of the New Culture messages during the May Fourth era. Significant change was not only revealed in the number of women students, but also demonstrated in the rationale for women's education. The dominant model of the good wife and virtuous mother that was challenged by Qiu Jin's generation was targeted during the May Fourth period as an example of the old culture and deserted resolutely by the independent, self-sufficient, public-minded new women. According to May Fourth feminists, the pursuit of women's equal rights and equal participation in all spheres of social life was itself a sign of modernity and the key to a strong and independent nation. The nation's well-being was still the ultimate goal. Yet, instead of calling for women's sacrifice to reach that goal, the New Culture nationalism premised a strong China based upon women's self-fulfillment. Nationalism had never before and has never since blended so well with a feminist agenda.

Not surprisingly, the May Fourth era became a watershed in modern Chinese history. The new consciousness generated by May Fourth feminism motivated numerous educated women to pursue a human life unrestricted by centuries-old gender norms. Gender segregation was broken in China's urban areas as a result of educated women's conscious effort to move into all the previously forbidden territories. Urbanization and professionalization were stamped with women's increasing participation in social, political, and public life. The landscape of Chinese urban society was transformed rapidly by the rise of the May Fourth new women. Even the growing consumer culture in urban China targeted the emerging new women to make its appeal. Historian Luo Suwen in her recent study of women in modern China observes,

> In the second part of 1919, female images in advertisement increased. . . .
> Between 1921 and 1925, images of beauty were used widely by newspaper advertisers, presenting women as the symbol of civilization and vanguard of stylish consumption. . . . In the 1930s, the images of modern women were not simply of beauties wrapped in luxury; they had to be educated and physically strong and enjoy all the new achievements of urban civilization, including sharing enjoyment with men in entertainments and at leisure. Urban women in 1930s' China became the embodiment of modernity.[19]

This commodification of May Fourth feminist themes testifies to the profound social changes caused by the rise of new women. Since the admission of women to higher education in 1920, women's career options had broad-

19. Ibid., 434 and 436.

ened.[20] This in turn gave rise to the formation of career women as a new elite social group in the 1930s urban setting. This group's social influence was augmented by a wave of new women literature, new women movies, new women fashions, and new women advertisements. The 1930s urban Chinese understood that the emergence of new women was a dramatic social change that served as the best index of China's modernity.

The narratives by the May Fourth new women in this book are not intended to be a medium for representing "modernity."[21] Instead, my goal is to enable the readers to hear and understand the new women's own voices, voices that have long been silenced. Through the new women's narratives, I trace the formation of their new consciousness in the currents of May Fourth feminism and nationalism and document the actions derived from their new subject positions. I try to understand the relationships between feminism and nationalism, and between dominant discourse and women's agency. I reflect upon the triumphs and tragedies in their long lives to learn lessons for the present. Listening to and understanding the voices of May Fourth new women is, for me, not only a crucial way to achieve a better understanding of twentieth-century China, but also a profound process of understanding my own history. They have enabled me to identify many legacies of May Fourth feminism and May Fourth new women in the society in which I grew up—legacies that inevitably shaped who I am today. I believe that different readers will find in the narratives various meanings other than those articulated in this book.

20. By 1922, there were already 669 women in colleges, not including those in missionary colleges and abroad. Ibid., 352.

21. Although my project focuses on women, not the nation, the women and men I study were constructed by and contributed to the dominant discourse of nationalism in twentieth-century China. In *Rescuing History from the Nation: Questioning Narratives of Modern China* (Chicago: University of Chicago Press, 1995), Prasenjit Duara criticizes the dominance of nationalist history that has followed a linear, evolutionary history of the Enlightenment and colonial model:

> The first lesson we learn is that the history of China we confront has already been narrativized in the Enlightenment mode—and not simply by the Asian historical scholarship we read or through which we read our sources. From the first years of the twentieth century, many of the historical actors we study themselves sought to narrate their history in the linear, teleological mode and thus performatively propel Chinese history into the progress of universal History. (26)

The pervasiveness of this dominant nationalist history can be seen clearly in the narratives in this study. By exploring the gender dimension of this history, I try to understand how and why a dominant nationalist discourse has been maintained and reproduced throughout the twentieth century.

THE FEMINIST MOVEMENT REVISITED

Since the late Qing, women's rights had been included in the advocacy of human rights by cultural radicals and revolutionaries. During the May Fourth era, feminism, as one of the "isms" from the West, was further promoted by New Culturalists, who saw it not only as the most effective weapon to attack the old Confucian culture, but also as a key to modern civilization. When May Fourth new women embraced the feminist agenda, feminism changed from phrases and concepts into practices that transformed individual women's lives along with the structure of social institutions. The power of feminist discourse was further expressed and enhanced when the principle of gender equality was endorsed by both rising political parties, the Communist Party in 1920 and the Nationalist Party in 1924. Paradoxically, whereas social changes brought by feminism were hailed in the political mainstream as proof of China's progress, the term "feminism" (*nüquan zhuyi*) acquired a derogatory meaning. Why and when did this happen? How did this affect the feminist movement in China? These questions lead us into a deeper examination of the historical process in which feminism was simultaneously transforming and reinventing even as it was appropriated, twisted, defined, and redefined.

In her study of European feminisms, historian Karen Offen observes a pattern: competing for clientele, socialist parties adopted the strategy of calling feminism "bourgeois" and denigrating feminist efforts as "narrow" while appropriating the feminist agenda into their own programs.[22] This pattern applies equally well to the history of Chinese feminism. Even the negative terms were duplicated: the phrases "narrow feminism" and "bourgeois feminism" were used by the Chinese Communist Party shortly after it was founded. The only difference is that the CCP added the adjective "Western." The fledgling feminist movement in May Fourth China was first rivaled by the newly born Communist Party and then co-opted by the alliance of the GMD and the CCP in the National Revolution between 1924 and 1927. When the National Revolution's feminist agenda attracted many feminists to its camp, the partisan monopoly of the Chinese women's movement began to take shape. CCP feminists used the phrase "women's emancipation movement" (*funü jiefang yundong*) to demarcate their difference from the "feminist movement" (*nüquan yundong*), asserting that the former correctly identified radical revolution as the precondition of

---

22. Karen Offen, *European Feminism(s): 1700–1950* (Stanford: Stanford University Press, forthcoming).

women's emancipation, whereas the latter incorrectly pursued women's political and legal rights without regard for the evils of the existing economic and political systems. The ability of the CCP to propagate this reductionist definition of feminism correlated with its fluctuating political power in the first half of the century. In other words, before the CCP established its political dominance in China, the party's definition of feminism by no means monopolized understandings of feminism. In their accounts of life before 1949, our narrators use various terms when referring to "feminism"—terms such as *nüquan zhuyi* and *funü zhuyi*, with or without the adjective "narrow"; the terms used not only reflect these women's different political orientations, but also reveal the complicated contestation among competing discourses.

The five portraits in this book may be considered representative of urban educated women's positions in the intense political struggles of the first half of the century. Lu Lihua, Wang Yiwei, and Cheng Yongsheng are nonpartisan women with different political orientations; Zhu Su'e is a Nationalist Party member; and Huang Dinghui is a Communist Party member. Pursuing their self-emancipation, these women made various political choices under different circumstances. Readers will notice that despite their different political views, these women all worked to improve women's situation. The narratives make it evident that the feminist agenda, though sometimes relabeled the agenda of "the women's emancipation movement," was pursued by women of diverse political backgrounds. The lines between the nonpartisan feminist movement and the party-led women's emancipation movement were sometimes blurred, especially in the periods when the CCP was seeking political alliances. In that sense, the narratives that follow highlight my view that feminist pursuit in China was not restricted by political boundaries, which precisely testifies to the power of the May Fourth feminist discourse in China.

These diverse narratives also enable us to explore the relationship between feminist groups and other political forces in China. The so-called narrow feminist movement—the nonpartisan independent feminist movement that maneuvered to create its own social space in republican China—is the focus of my investigation. Who were the women who made up that movement? How did they perceive the meanings of their own activities? What sustained their efforts? And what limited their influence? What was the fate of nonpartisan feminists when the feminist movement was marginalized and excluded during the Mao era? The narratives shed light on these questions. To illustrate, I present a brief biography of Liu-Wang Liming, a feminist leader in China whose endeavor intersected with our narrators' feminist efforts. Her life displays the complicated historical process in which non-partisan feminists fought against great odds to maintain an independent feminist agenda. This biography, which is based on my interview with her daughter and other written documents, reflects the historical milieu in which our heroines played out their drama.

The Story of Liu-Wang Liming

Liu-Wang was born in 1897 in Taihu county, Anhui province. Her original name was Wang Liming. Liu was her husband's name. Her father was a doctor of Chinese medicine and died when she was nine years old. The family had to depend on her mother's needlework for a living. In 1907, an American missionary school run by Chinese was opened in the county. The school originally took only poor boys who could not afford old-style private schools. Wang Liming and several other girls pleaded with the principal, who eventually let the girls enroll in the school. Educational opportunity profoundly changed Wang's life, as it did the lives of many women at that time.

With talent and hard work, Wang Liming quickly became a prominent student. She ranked number one in each year's examinations. Schooling for her did not merely mean academic work. She was also quick to pick up new ideas circulating at the time. At twelve, she became the first girl in the county to unbind her feet, disregarding her mother's opposition and others' mockery. After Wang Liming finished grade school, the principal sent her to Jiujiang Ruli Academy, the only girls' middle school in the area bordering Anhui, Jiangxi, and Hubei. She excelled there as well, and upon graduation she became a teacher in the middle school.

In 1915 when she was still a middle-school student, she joined the Chinese branch of the Women's Christian Temperance Union (WCTU), which was first established in Zhenjiang in 1904 and then spread to Shanghai, Nanjing, Jiujiang, and Hankou. In 1916 she received a scholarship from the WCTU to study biology at Northwestern University in Illinois. A few years later at the University of Chicago, she met Liu Zhan'en, a young man she had known in Jiujiang. Liu had also lost his father as a child and was a Christian. Like Wang Liming, Liu was an excellent student and had received a graduate scholarship to study in the University of Chicago. They fell in love and married when Wang Liming graduated in 1920. Like thousands of Chinese students abroad in the early twentieth century, the young couple regarded an education in the United States as a means to the goal of strengthening China. Liu-Wang returned to China right after her graduation, and her husband returned in 1922 after earning a Ph.D. in education from Columbia University.[23]

Although many returning students pursued professional careers in urban China, Liu-Wang chose to be a social activist. She soon rose to prominence in Shanghai's lively social scene of the early 1920s. In the Introduction to her book *The Chinese Women's Movement*, she recounts, "In the early summer of 1920, I returned to Shanghai from the United States. Because of my friends' encouragement, and because of my own wishes since childhood, as well as because of what I saw abroad while I was studying there—especially feminist demands—I unhesitatingly joined all kinds of Chinese women's movements. Since then, part of my life has been closely connected to these movements, and most of my mind has been occupied by them."[24]

In 1922, in the second upsurge of the suffrage movement in China, she was a founder of the Shanghai Women's Suffrage Association and the chair of the organization. She was also among the leading activists in the Shanghai Committee to Promote the National Assembly in 1924, demanding women's equal rights and women's participation in the national assembly. In 1927, after the Northern Expedition reached Shanghai, the GMD government appointed Liu-Wang to its committee on the women's movement. In the 1930s, Liu-Wang was still the main leader of the Shanghai Women's Suffrage Association, which changed its name to the Chinese Women's Movement Association after the republican government passed the new civil code in 1930 that granted equal rights to women.

But Liu-Wang Liming's name was most closely associated with the Chinese WCTU, the Zhonghua Funü Jiezhihui. She became the general secretary of that organization in 1926 and retained her position until the mid 1950s. By the early 1930s, the Chinese WCTU had branches in fifteen provinces and had ten thousand members. Its headquarters were in Shanghai, and it established several facilities there for women: the Shanghai Settlement House—the only welfare institution for women in China, which

23. To people in the English world, Liu was known as Herman Chan-En Liu, and Wang was Mrs. Herman C. E. Liu. Before she got married, Wang's English name was Frances Wong. The compound last name in Chinese she adopted after she married Liu was a sign of her progressive stance. It was a popular practice at the time. In addition, as the following narratives illustrate, many women simply retained their own names after marriage, which has become the only practice in the People's Republic of China.

24. Liu-Wang Liming, *Zhongguo funü yundong* [The Chinese women's movement] (Shanghai: Commercial Press, 1933), 1. Hereafter, this work is cited parenthetically.

provided welfare to beggars, slave girls, and deserted women; the Women's Vocational School, which trained women for new employment opportunities; the Shanghai Women's Apartment for single career women, where one of our narrators, Wang Yiwei, once lived; and *The Women's Voice*, with Wang Yiwei as its editor in chief. Around this periodical they formed the Society of the Women's Voice, composed of scores of women scholars and writers who often contributed to *The Women's Voice*. As a nonpartisan women's organization, the Chinese WCTU's influence and achievements were second only to those of the Chinese YWCA. And with financial support from the WCTU in the United States and her husband's income to support their family, Liu-Wang was one of the few voluntary professional woman activists in China. She never worked as a biologist.

In 1933, when Liu-Wang published *The Chinese Women's Movement*, she wrote that she "felt sad that the Chinese women's movement was too naive and lacked sound plans, leadership, and organization" (4). She thought that knowledge of the women's movement must be increased to address those weaknesses, and so the book not only summarizes her views on the development of the Chinese feminist movement, but also issues directives for the ongoing feminist movement. It asserts that New Culture feminist goals are the objectives of the Chinese women's movement and emphasizes women's political participation, economic independence, educational opportunity, freedom to marry and divorce, and new sexual morality (eliminating the double standard and encouraging marriage based on love). Because Chinese women had recently obtained legal equal rights, the book focuses on how to effectively use those legal rights. At the beginning of the book, Liu-Wang offers a distinctive May Fourth feminist definition of the women's movement: "The women's movement means women's revolution. The Chinese women's movement is Chinese women rising to make revolution. The scope of our revolution is very broad. We hope to move on many fronts to eliminate the old *inhuman* ways of life and reconstruct new ones" (2; emphasis added).

How to reach the goals of women's revolution? Liu-Wang's approach reflects May Fourth feminism informed by socialism. She proposed a socialist economic system that would eliminate class polarization and injustice. She believed that this system would offer women equal employment opportunity, and consequently, women would have economic independence and independent personhood. But she opposed Marxist class struggle as a means to achieve the goal of socialism. She condemned the Communist Party's cruelty and dictatorship. And she advocated a democratic socialism through parliamentarianism. In all these goals, women's political participation was extremely important. Holding maternity to be a sacred state that endowed women with compassion and kindness, Liu-Wang believed that women's political participation would lead to much better results than men could achieve on their own (172–173). Liu-Wang hoped that women would use their votes to produce a more humane and just socialist system.

Liu-Wang was certainly aware of the CCP's critique of the feminist movement. In her book she argued:

> Many critics say that the women's movement has failed because it is a movement of a small number of women of the intellectual class, instead of a mass-based [women's] movement. This is only partly correct. Is it not the hope of the women in the movement that women in the entire country will unite and strive together? The common goal of activists in the women's movement is to relieve the pains of the majority of women. However, a movement with permanent value must begin with a small number of people's consciousness, which eventually will become the public's consciousness, and a small number of people's beliefs, which eventually will become the public's beliefs. Although the movement is still young, we firmly believe that it will have a lasting, significant impact. (2–3)

Because of these strong convictions, in the early 1930s Liu-Wang continued her efforts to promote a feminist movement that had begun a decade before. In her view, the women's movement was hindered by domestic turmoil and foreign invasion, not by its being advocated by a small number of intellectual women activists. She was prepared for a long process in which the consciousness of a few elite women would slowly become the consciousness of the majority of women, and a young, weak feminist movement would develop into a mature, strong movement. To that end, she created a new women's magazine, *The Women's Voice*, that would express women's voices independently.

Liu-Wang was still concentrating on promoting a feminist movement when the Japanese military occupied Manchuria in 1931. For Liu-Wang, China's resulting sense of national crisis intensified rather than reduced the need to pursue women's emancipation. She maintained that China would remain a semiparalyzed weak nation (a metaphor popularized by the New Culturalists) if women's situation were not improved. She insisted, "Our movement is the first to seek women's own emancipation by sweeping away all the customs and practices that have humiliated and abused women. Then we will engage in moving the Chinese nation and the human race toward a bright new century" (19). Women's emancipation remained her priority, and she was unswayed by either the intensified nationalism or the CCP's line about the women's movement.

Despite the CCP's disparaging assertion that prioritizing women's emancipation was "narrow feminism," Liu-Wang did not see women's emancipation as the only goal, nor lack concern for national interests. Rather, "narrow feminists" such as Liu-Wang insisted that even during a national crisis, women's rights and women's suffering should not be forgotten. Their ongoing concern for the nation is demonstrated in their campaigns calling on women to make donations and offer services for the national salvation. In September 1931, after the Japanese occupied Manchuria, Liu-Wang chaired the founding meeting of the Shanghai Women's National Salvation Alliance and called for women's resistance to Japanese goods and women's support for the Chinese army.[25] In September 1937, when the Shanghai Women's Consolation Society called on women to make donations for the War of Resistance, Liu-Wang donated her gold bracelet and diamond ring.[26] And the Chinese WCTU was an active participant in the umbrella women's organizations for national salvation. Even so, Liu-Wang is remembered by both Wang Yiwei and Zhu Su'e, two of our narrators, as a leader who occupied herself exclusively with the women's movement and had no involvement with the national salvation movement promoted by both the CCP and GMD. It seems that when the national salvation movement became a contested sphere for the two parties in the early 1930s, Liu-Wang tried not to be involved. She maintained her independent feminist stance while expressing her patriotic concerns.

Liu-Wang's negative view toward the CCP changed during the War of Resistance. Her husband, Liu Zhan'en, was a famous intellectual patriot and president of the University of Shanghai [Hujiang daxue]. When the War of Resistance began after the Japanese troops attacked northern China in 1937, he became the chair of the Shanghai National Salvation Association. When the Japanese puppet government in Nanjing tried to make him minister of education, Liu refused; he continued his resistance activities in Shanghai even after it was occupied by the Japanese. On April 7, 1938, Liu was assassinated by Chinese secret agents working for the Japanese. Liu-Wang took her three children to Chongqing, the wartime capital of the republican government, where she became more actively involved in resistance activities. She was one of the few female councilors to the National Political Council

25. Shanghai Women's Federation, *Shanghai funü yundong shi* [A history of the Shanghai women's movement] (Shanghai: Shanghai renmin chubanshe, 1990), 143.
26. Ibid., 143 and 181.

formed by the GMD in the war years. Because she dared to criticize the GMD's corruption openly, and because she was a celebrity—especially after Liu Zhan'en's death—Liu-Wang was approached by the CCP while she was in Chongqing. The Communist leader Zhou Enlai and his wife Deng Yingchao became Liu-Wang's acquaintances. Liu-Wang showed her support for the CCP's resistance position by sending her eldest son to the CCP-run military college in Yan'an, the base area of the CCP. Meanwhile she sent her younger son to a GMD-run military school. Fighting the Japanese invaders was her most urgent concern during this period, a state of mind shared by millions of Chinese whose lives and livelihood were endangered by the Japanese invasion.

In addition to her high-profile political activities in Chongqing, Liu-Wang continued her role as a leading activist on women's behalf. She established the Zhan'en Institute for Refugee Children, which raised hundreds of orphans during the war. She opened a round-the-clock nursery to care for the children of career women. She was the president of the Sichuan Yibing Institute for Refugee Children, and the principal of the West China Women's Vocational School. Meanwhile, she was still chairing the Chinese WCTU, which was involved in the resistance effort. With other women activists, she organized the Chinese Women's Friendship Association to mobilize women in the GMD-controlled areas to participate in the resistance. The national crisis and her husband's assassination seemed to push her toward the CCP line of mobilizing women for the resistance effort.

After the CCP and the GMD formed the second United Front in 1937, both parties called for women's participation in the war effort. Women's activism in urban areas soared as a result of this unanimous goal to resist Japanese invasion. The CCP's political influence increased rapidly, because the United Front allowed Communists to play an active role in mobilizing resistance in the GMD-controlled areas. The women's movement, promoted by the United Front, was now defined as women's equal participation in resisting the Japanese. Although the wartime women's movement called for women's contribution to the war rather than emphasized gender issues, many women activists experienced empowerment in their expanding public activities. Career women played a central role in urban women's mobilization. Women's organizations mushroomed and partisan lines blurred. After the fall of eastern China, many women activists fled the Japanese-occupied areas and ended up in the CCP base area in northwestern China. The ongoing war pushed the May Fourth feminist agenda aside but brought many women into political and military participation.

Throughout the war Liu-Wang held a firm nonpartisan position. When the second United Front was broken, and the CCP and the GMD began to fight against each other, she called her two sons back home because they were going to be sent into battle to kill their own compatriots. Like many Western-educated Chinese intellectuals at the end of World War II, she dreamed of a democratic coalition government. Because she believed in the importance of women's political participation, she joined the Chinese Democratic League (CDL) in 1944 and was elected a member of its central committee.

After the war she returned to Shanghai in 1945 and revived the activities of the Chinese WCTU in eastern China. She worked with Wang Yiwei again on the revived *Women's Voice*. But she played a more prominent role in the Chinese Democratic League, and most of her energy was devoted to opposing the impending civil war. In 1947 the GMD government declared that the CDL was illegal and ordered it disbanded. Liu-Wang escaped from Shanghai to Hong Kong. There she attended the congress of the central committee of the CDL, which resolved to continue in defiance of the GMD order. Liu-Wang was elected director of the financial committee of the CDL. After declaring its open opposition to the GMD, the CDL endorsed cooperation with the CCP.

In early 1949, after Beijing was taken over by the CCP, Mao Zedong invited major nonpartisan organizations, including the CDL, to attend the preparatory meetings of the Chinese People's Political Consultative Conference (CPPCC) in Beijing. Liu-Wang went to Beijing as the representative of the CDL and became its official representative in the first congress of the CPPCC. In March 1949, the All-China Women's Federation was established and the Chinese WCTU became one of its group members. Liu-Wang was elected a standing member of the executive committee of the federation, which reflects the CCP's recognition of Liu-Wang's influence as a prominent feminist leader. In this beginning stage of the CCP's rule, its United Front policy worked well to gain the support of progressive forces in China. By granting official titles to leaders of nonpartisan organizations, the CCP created an image of broadly based democratic participation.

After 1949 Liu-Wang held positions in the All-China Women's Federation, the Chinese People's Political Consultative Committee, and the Political and Legal Committee of the Government Administration Council. These positions were more honorary than powerful, lacking specific responsibilities. However, in these early years of the CCP rule, she was able to continue her work in the Chinese WCTU. In 1956 she headed a four-member delegation to West Germany to attend the tenth conference of the International WCTU, where she was elected vice-chair of the organization. Because of her defense of new China's achievements and her major role in eliminating the Taiwan delegation from the conference, she was praised by Zhou Enlai publicly for her patriotism. That praise, however, served as an ending note to the glorious chapters of Liu-Wang's life.

In 1957 when the anti-rightist campaign began, Liu-Wang was labeled a rightist of the ninth grade because she refused to inform against the two political targets of Mao Zedong; as a result, she lost all her titles and honorary positions. The independent status of the Chinese WCTU was also lost. In line with tightening CCP control, the All-China Women's Federation, originally formed as a United Front strategy to gain support from different women's organizations, became an organ of the party and channeled women's activism toward the interests of the party-state. From 1957 on, member groups such as the Chinese WCTU could no longer maintain their independent constitutions.[27] In a sense, Liu-Wang's downfall signified the official closure of social space for women's spontaneous activism.

On September 1, 1966, at the beginning of the Cultural Revolution, Liu-Wang was arrested on charges that she was a secret agent of the U.S. CIA. The evidence of her crime found in her daughter's home was a small suitcase full of her manuscripts, including the poems she wrote to her rightist son in the labor camp, and a typewriter thought to be a transmitter. As Liu-Wang was led away, she uttered a sentence in English that her daughter had heard once before when Liu-Wang was labeled a rightist: "I am carrying the cross of Jesus Christ." With that, she was gone. Her family never saw her again.

Liu-Wang died in a Shanghai prison on April 15, 1970. She insisted on her innocence till the end of her life. Her daughter and son brought her case to the central government after the Cultural Revolution, and Liu-Wang was posthumously rehabilitated in 1980. In 1981 the Political Consultative Committee, the Chinese Democratic League, and the All-China Women's Federation jointly held a memorial service for Liu-Wang Liming.[28] At the

27. For a detailed study of the All-China Women's Federation, see Zhang Naihua, "The All-China Women's Federation, Chinese Women, and the Women's Movement: 1949–1993" (Ph. D. diss., Michigan State University, 1996). Zhang emphasizes that the All-China Women's Federation's monopoly of women's organizations did not begin until 1957. Liu-Wang's experience as an independent feminist leader of one of the largest women's organizations fits well with Zhang's periodization of the federation's history. However, the following narratives also show that at the local level some urban feminists were deprived of their capacity for activism soon after the liberation.

28. See "Liu-Wang Liming zhuidaohui zaijing juxing" [Liu-Wang Liming's memorial service held in Beijing], Renmin ribao [People's daily], March 19, 1981.

memorial, Liu-Wang was officially honored as a patriot, the only laudable title for non-Communists in the CCP's language. As befit her titles before she was labeled a rightist, she was given a tomb in the Babao Cemetery in Beijing, which is reserved for high officials. Because all of Liu-Wang's belongings had been confiscated and even her ashes had not been returned to her family, all that her daughter could put in the tomb was a comb that Liu-Wang had left behind.

A devoted feminist leader, Liu-Wang Liming accomplished much in her pursuit of women's emancipation before the Japanese occupation. Even during the war, she was able to continue her efforts, endeavoring to relieve women's wartime sufferings. But in the Mao era, this star of feminist activism was eclipsed—a pattern that is repeated in the following narratives. The establishment of the All-China Women's Federation by the CCP fulfilled the dreams of many early Communist feminists to unify the women's movement. It signaled the successful conclusion of the CCP's institutionalization of that movement. When class struggle and proletarian dictatorship intensified in the succeeding years, social space for women's spontaneous activism soon disappeared in Mao's China. A feminist movement did not "fail" in China because of its "erroneous" line or its Western origin. It was the CCP's hegemonic social reorganization that made Liu-Wang, many other feminist activists, and their feminist movement fade away in the People's Republic of China.

4   Lu Lihua (1900–1997): School Principal

Lu Lihua, 1936   Lu Lihua, 1995

When I entered Lu Lihua's apartment for the first interview, she was sur-
rounded by a group of old women, chatting loudly. Before Lu had time to
introduce these women to me, they spoke simultaneously, explaining that
they were Principal Lu's former students, they were now in their late sev-
enties or eighties, and they were retired physical education teachers. Lu,
ninety-three years old, seemed quite happy among her loving students.
While her students had kept fit, presumably through physical exercise, Lu
was heavy and no longer agile. It seemed that she had been away from phys-
ical education for a long time. Yet her mind was clear and her voice loud,
partly because she had hearing problems. After her students left, she ami-
ably began her recollections.[1]

---

1. The following narrative is constructed from three separate interviews, conducted in March 1993, December 1994, and January 1995.

NARRATIVE

My father ran the largest grocery store in a town in Qingpu [miles from Shanghai].[2] The store had been passed down to him by his forefathers. He had taken an exam for an officer's position in the military, but he failed and came back to run the store. He read books. In the small, isolated town where we lived, few people read books. Even boys did not read. I was the second child—I had an older sister—and the second child was the least fortunate. I was born in 1900. At that time, the country was overthrowing the Qing dynasty and establishing a republic, struggling between two different eras. The old society was at its worst. People believed that a girl would bring the family misfortune. My father was unhappy, saying, "I have lost face because my second child is also a girl." That is why he became cold toward my mother.

My mother was illiterate and had bound feet. When I was six, she began to bind my feet, too. But I cut the wrapping cloth off at night. I usually obeyed my parents, but not with this footbinding. I was afraid of the pain and did not like bound feet. With bound feet, a girl could be distinguished as a girl. I wanted to be the same as boys—without distinction. They said, "You will harm yourself by having big feet in the future. You will not be able to marry into a good family." I said, "Let me harm myself. I cannot take this pain." Blood oozed from my feet, and I showed this to my mother: "Mom, look, how can I bear this?" She said, "There's no other way. You have to bear the pain." With those words, she continued binding my feet. I quietly resisted. She bound my feet during the day; at night I went to my grandma, who lived just across a bridge, and cut the wrapping cloth off. Mother said, "If I fail to bind your feet, how can I be a mother? Won't you blame me in the future?" I said, "No, I won't blame you. Let me have my big feet so long as I can walk." Three times I cut the wrapping cloth off. She said, "I don't believe that I cannot make you do this. You cut it off, but I will wrap your feet up anyway!" I thought to myself, "You wrap them up, but I will cut it off anyway!" Finally my mother gave up. That is why my feet do not look very good, because they were already bound a little. Following my example, other girls in our town also refused to have their feet bound.

My mother did not think it was wrong to have two girls. But my father looked down upon her because she had us. Father was depressed and did

2. In the early 1900s, Qingpu county belonged to Jiangsu province. Later, it belonged to Shanghai.

not want to do anything. He even smoked opium. Our family business declined. My mother knew that she could neither depend on the grocery store nor on my father. Therefore, she and two of my father's unmarried sisters farmed some land. They grew soybeans and cotton to support the family. At five or six years of age, I already understood many things. I saw that my mother's life was too hard, and I tried to comfort her. I told her, "Mom, don't worry. When I grow up, I will be like a boy. Whatever boys can do, I will do, too." My mother loved me very much. But she had to hide her affection because others would say, "Why cherish a girl so much? When she marries, she will belong to someone else's family, even if she lives to be one hundred years old."

I always admired Mulan, who had gone into the army, and other ancient heroines in the military. I read about them from the time I was a child. I went to school when I was six, disguised as a boy. At first my father would not let me attend school. There was a little story about it. Once my mother was sick. She said she wanted to have rice porridge. I was very filial to my mother, so the next morning I went early to the river to wash rice. There was a boat at the water's edge, and as I tried to push it aside, I fell into the river. My feet caught in between the stakes on the riverbank. I was only six years old. Now I think God saved my life. Someone came to fetch water, and their bucket pulled me out of the river. I looked like I was dead. More people arrived to see what was happening. Someone said, "Let's see if we can save this dead horse." They laid me face down on a big stone. Water ran out of my mouth, and I cried loudly. My heart was not dead. The people all scolded me: "Little girl, can't you play somewhere else? Why play at the river so early?" Crying, I said, "No, I was not playing. I came to wash rice for my mother. She is sick and wants porridge." The town's people were of two minds. One said, "It would be better for the little girl to die. What's the point in saving a little girl?" At that time, baby girls were often abandoned, thrown into the garbage dump. I was the second girl, my mother was sick, and my father disliked me. Everyone looked down upon me. But someone else said, "The little girl is alive again because she is filial. That is why she did not die when she should have." After this incident, my father changed his mind about me; he decided that I was good, and so he sent me to school.

Another thing I remember. My great-grandfather, then ninety years old, was respected by townsfolk. He knew that my father sighed all the time and was unhappy because he lacked a son. One night he called all his descendants into his room, and I heard him say to my father, his eldest grandson: "Junren, why are you sighing all the time? Is it because you have only girls and no boys? Let me tell you tonight, you shouldn't behave this way. Boys and girls are the same. In our family, we have six women and three men. More women than men. If we only had three men, would we truly be a family? A family needs both men and women. And a country is the same: it needs both men and women. Without men it wouldn't be a country, and without women it wouldn't be a family. You are wrong to act this way." My father admitted his mistake, saying, "I thought because I have no sons, no offspring, I had lost face." Great-grandpa asked, "Now have you thought it through?" Father said, "Our second girl is quite good, quite filial. From now on, I will raise her as a boy." After that he sent me to a *sishu* [old-style private school]. He let me wear a boy's *changpao magua* [long gown and mandarin jacket] and disguised me as a boy. I was the first girl to attend school in our town.

The teacher was a relative of mine. Because I studied hard and learned texts by heart faster than the other kids, he liked me very much. But some boys would tease me, calling me names such as *nübannanzhuang* [cross-dresser]. I ignored them. Some of our relatives were just as sarcastic. Because there was no boy in my family, those relatives would eventually inherit our family property and felt free to say things such as, "A woman has no use. She will belong to someone else's family, even if she lives to be one hundred years old," and "Cross dressing, what terrible manners!" My father was very upset by those remarks, but they did not affect me. So long as I was doing well in my studies and my father loved me, I did not care about others' remarks.

In that private school, we studied the *sishu wujing* [Four Books and Five Classics].[3] After three years, I was able to read all kinds of books. Then the revolutionary new wave came, and I learned about Qiu Jin.[4] I read the newspaper because my father, who was quite progressive, was the first and only one in town to subscribe to the *Shenbao* [Shanghai news], the only newspaper available in the town. I grabbed the newspaper every morning when I was about eight or nine years old. At first I just looked at pictures of those revolutionaries, Sun Zhongshan and Huang Xing, and some women revo-

---

3. The Four Books are *The Great Learning, The Doctrine of the Mean, The Analects of Confucius,* and *Mencius.* The Five Classics are *The Book of Songs, The Book of History, The Book of Changes, The Book of Rites,* and *The Spring and Autumn Annals.* These were the standard textbooks in the imperial system.

4. Qiu Jin was a famous female revolutionary who was killed by the Qing government in 1907. Her martyrdom made her the first Chinese heroine of the twentieth century. See chapters 1 and 3. Also See Elisabeth Croll, *Feminism and Socialism in China* (London: Routledge and Kegan Paul, 1978), 65–69.

lutionaries.[5] I clipped out the pictures and posted them on the wall because I admired those people. Sun Zhongshan said that in the future women could go to school and could be teachers and that men and women were equal. I admired him. I thought that when I grew up, I would join Mr. Sun Zhongshan's revolution. That was the period when my mind changed.

When I was nine years old, I left school. I felt bad being disguised as a boy among the boys, and I began to wear girl's clothes. For the next three years I was an apprentice in my father's store. I thought that if I could not continue in school, I should take care of the store. I learned how to use the abacus, how to distinguish silver dollars, and how to manage the store. My mother gave birth to another girl, who died in infancy, and lost a boy in a miscarriage. So my father prepared me to succeed him at the store. I thought, "What will I do—commercial business?" People said that all merchants were dishonest. I did not want to be in that trade. My father had not wanted to be a merchant, and neither did I. I wanted to leave town to go to school. In our home town there was only an old-style private elementary school. But after the Xinhai Revolution [the 1911 Revolution], a girls' primary school was established in a nearby town, and I heard of that and wanted to go. It was three *li* away.[6] My parents thought that because I was only twelve, I was too young to go that far. But I decided to go anyway.

When I entered the Shuaiying Girls' School, all the other students were younger than I was. The teachers asked me to read the textbooks for first and second grade, and I did so without difficulty, because I had already studied for three years. They promptly put me in the third grade. After one year, I graduated and went to the girls' higher primary school in the county, starting with the second grade there. After I graduated from that school, I took the exams for the Women's Normal School in Hangzhou. At that time I very much wanted to be a teacher. When I was in the girls' higher primary school, a kindergarten teacher was often sick, and I offered to substitute for her. The kids liked me a lot, and I loved to be with them. The experience made me want to be a kindergarten teacher. But in the end, I did not go to the Normal School. A physical education teacher liked me and suggested I go to the school that she had graduated from. That is how I came to the Chinese Women's Gymnastics School in Shanghai.

I was seventeen years old when I came to Shanghai. Our family business

5. In the narratives, I use the name Sun Zhongshan, instead of Sun Yat-sen, to conform to the narrators' usage. Huang Xing (1874–1916) was the commander-in-chief during the 1911 Revolution.

6. Three *li* is equal to approximately one mile.

had declined. I took my savings, and my mother and grandma gave me their savings, and my parents accompanied me to the school. At that time, few girls went to physical education schools; there were just over thirty students in my school. My teacher told me that the graduates would all teach in normal schools, even at the provincial level, and I thought that teaching in a provincial school would be like going to heaven. But not long after I entered the school, my mother died. She died of anguish and fatigue. My father treated her unkindly because she had not given him a son, and she had to work in the fields and at home to support a family of nine people. I had always felt sorry for my mother and had been determined to make her proud of me. But now she was dead. It was such a heavy blow that I totally lost my drive. Because our family was having financial problems, I decided to quit school. I went back to the school to get my luggage.

As a student I had offered to help with the administrative work in the school, and the principal liked me a lot. When he learned what had happened to me, he said, "It is not right for you to leave school. I understand you are filial to your mother. I understand your current pain, but you should continue to study. You don't have the money for fees—I can give you a waiver. You'll just pay for your own meals." I was very moved, thinking what a kindhearted person he was! I followed his advice. He asked me to help with some school chores and told me that I could remain at the school after I graduated. Suddenly I was happy, all because of this old principal. After I graduated, he did indeed ask me to remain at the school as a teacher. I was so happy because I could continue to study. I didn't have to go to strange places to look for a job, and I could stay in Shanghai to join the students' movement.

The year I graduated was the same year that the May Fourth movement happened. I was like a fish in water. I joined all kinds of activities and made speeches at schools in Suzhou, Wuxi, Hangzhou, and Shanghai. People said I was brave. I shouted slogans in public: " Love our country! Down with imperialism! Overthrow feudalism!" Once, a newspaper reported that some students had been killed in a demonstration—among them, a student called Lu Lihua—and my family rushed to Shanghai, thinking that I was dead. I actually just got hit by a policeman's club and felt a little dizzy; no guns had been fired in the conflict. Thus I became famous. I joined the students' union, Huanqiu xueshenghui [the Global Students' Union], in Shanghai. I was the representative from my school. The students' organizations were formed all across the country. Beijing delegates came to Shanghai first, then Shanghai students followed their example to organize and to hold demonstrations. Then Guangdong, Guangxi, and all the other provinces responded by setting up organizations of their own. As we can now see, the May Fourth movement was the turning point of the revolutionary movement. It was a mass movement, and many young people joined. Quite a lot of them were female students. But the ones I knew then have now all passed away.

Although I was young, I was active in all kinds of things. I got to know more and more people. Huang Yanpei, Cai Yuanpei, Ma Xiangbo, and other old teachers came to the students' union to give speeches, and I received them and saw them off.[7] Sun Zhongshan also came from Guangdong. In their speeches, they emphasized that Chinese people should organize themselves and be patriotic in order to overthrow feudalism, Japanese imperialism, and Chinese warlords. At the same time, they promoted the new culture and new intellectual waves and said that education, industrial enterprises, and physical education were three main things needed to strengthen China. Of all the speakers, Ma Xiangbo made the deepest impression on me. He was about eighty years old at the time. He had sold his family property to build Zhendan University, and when Zhendan University was taken over by the French, he built Fudan University, meaning to recover Zhendan University. He was famous for his speeches. He appealed loudly to the audience, saying, "Revolution is made of hardships. We should never content ourselves with five minutes of enthusiasm. At the moment, China urgently needs three important things: (1) because 95 percent of Chinese are illiterate, we must promote education; (2) to be rich, we must promote industrial enterprises; and (3) to be strong, we must promote physical education." Hearing those words, I thought to myself, "Zhang Jian has established industrial enterprises to make the nation rich, and Cai Yuanpei is leading education.[8] I am unable to do those things, but what can I do? I have studied physical edu-

7. Huang Yanpei (1878–1965) was the director of the Education Department of Jiangsu province after the 1911 Revolution. He created the China Vocational Education Society in Shanghai in 1917. After 1949, he held several prominent positions in the central government of the People's Republic of China, including the deputy chair of the Standing Committee of the National Congress. See Cihai Compiling Committee, ed., *Cihai* (Shanghai: Cishu chubanshe, 1980), 2056.

Cai Yuanpei (1868–1940) was an educator who created the Patriot Girls' School in Shanghai in 1902. He was the minister of the Education Department of the provisional government in 1912 and the president of Beijing University in 1917. He supported the New Culture activities fermented in Beijing University and encouraged coeducation in universities. See ibid., 610.

Ma Xiangbo (1840–1939) established Zhendan College in Shanghai in 1903 and Fudan University in 1905. See ibid., 1132.

8. Zhang Jian (1853–1926) was an entrepreneur who created many enterprises around the turn of the century and was appointed the director of enterprises in the provisional government after the 1911 Revolution. See ibid., 1086.

cation, so I should do physical education. We want our nation to be prosperous and our people to be strong, but only if we have strong people first will our nation become prosperous."

How to make people strong? I was a young teacher, so I had a developmental perspective. I decided we should train teachers, women physical education teachers. Because one physical education teacher taught an entire school, if I trained one hundred teachers a year, then one hundred schools would have physical education teachers. At the time, physical education teachers were in short supply.

After I heard Ma Xiangbo's talk, I began to visit him. I admired him a lot. He lived in an orphanage in Tushanwan, which today is called Xujiahui. He had sold all his land and donated all his money for the school. Now in his old age he lived alone in the orphanage. He literally destroyed his home to further education in China. I told him of my dream of opening a school. There was another reason for my decision. I had been in poor health in my childhood, but after I entered the girls' school and took physical education classes, I came to love physical exercise, and my sickness disappeared, so that I felt physical education was really able to strengthen one's health. Moreover, at Ma's place, I met his student Yu Youren, a famous calligrapher,[9] and I thought to myself, "Old Mr. Ma has such a great student who makes his life happy in old age. If I ran a school, I would have students in my old age." I liked to emulate anything good. Ma Xiangbo asked me, "Lihua, do you really want to open a school?" I said, "Yes. But I am such a young person. Would you please serve as chairman of the school board?" Regulations at the time required that you have a school board before you could open a school, and because I was young, people would not believe in me. Therefore I wanted to invite Ma Xiangbo and other prominent people to be on the school board.

Ma Xiangbo agreed to be the chairman. He also introduced me to Wang Zhenting and Gu Weijun, both of whom were once ministers of foreign affairs. Ma told me, "Lihua, you should have people on the school board who can truly help you. These diplomats have all experienced the pain of being a diplomat for a weak nation. They are humiliated by the fact that China

9. Yu Youren (1879–1964) was an early member of the Revolutionary Alliance. After the republican government was established in January 1912, he was appointed the deputy minister of transportation. In 1922 he established Shanghai University with other GMD members and became the president of the university. He was elected a member of the executive committee of the Central Committee of the GMD in 1924. In 1947 he became the head of the Procuratorate. Yu enjoyed fame as a good calligrapher. But in mentioning Yu only as a calligrapher, Lu reveals here her reluctance to acknowledge her ties to prominent GMD members.

lacks physical education and sports, and they want China to have physical education and sports. They will surely help you in your effort." With Ma's name on the invitation, those diplomats agreed right away. I also invited several other famous people, including Zhang Bolin, the president of Nankai University in Tianjin, whom I had met at national education conferences. With such a strong school board, I got the school registered right way. Normally, board members would give money to the school, but I did not ask our board members to share the expense, fearing that if I did so, they would refuse to be on the board. Besides, a man like Ma Xiangbo was penniless. In 1922, three years after my graduation, I established my own school— Liangjiang Women's Physical Education Normal School.

When the school opened, we had only eighteen students. It was hard to survive. But gradually, students came from several provinces—Guangdong, Sichuan, Hunan, and Manchuria. In two or three years our school was enrolling more than one hundred students each year. I had to learn all kinds of local dialects. I had originally thought the school would be just for students from Jiangsu and Zhejiang, two provinces near Shanghai; that is why it was called Liangjiang. I thought I would be happy if all the physical education teachers in the two provinces were from my school. I didn't expect that students would come from all over the country. Why did so many students come? They all had the same idea as I did: women have to be strong. In their admission interview I asked, "Why do you want to go to a physical education normal school?" They answered, "We want our country to be strong and people to be healthy." I said, "That's a good wish." There were women with bound feet whom I turned away. But they argued with me, saying, "We were born in the era when parents bound our feet. Why can't we teach physical education?" I told them, "In teaching physical education, you have to demonstrate physical movements; with your bound feet, it would be difficult to do so." We did admit one student with bound feet who is now eighty-eight. She once led a team to participate in the East Asian Games in Japan, and she taught in Shenyang Women's Normal School [in Manchuria].

Now, looking back, I feel like it was a miracle that I was able to open that school. After my graduation, I taught in five schools and earned one hundred silver dollars a month, twenty silver dollars per school. It was a lot at the time.[10] I was very frugal, reluctant to spend even three cents for a trolley car. Because I taught in my old school, it provided me with room and

10. Shen Yanbing, in his autobiography, gave an account of his salary during the May Fourth movement. In 1916 he entered the Shanghai Commercial Press as a new translator. He made twenty-four silver dollars a month as a beginner. Five

board, and because I did not spend any money and only sent a little to my family to support them, I could save most of my salary in order to open the school. Quickly, in two and a half years, I saved three thousand silver dollars. I thought it was a lot of money and that I could establish a school. I could buy facilities and rent a place for five or six hundred silver dollars. But I didn't realize how much the daily maintenance would cost. The first eighteen students' fees ran out quickly, so I had to use my own reputation as credit to borrow money from my friends. I also borrowed money from schools who were on good terms with me because I had some fame in Shanghai at the time. In this way, I survived the first school year. The second year, we had over thirty students, but it was still difficult. In the third and fourth year, we enrolled over one hundred students and finally became independent. I had a tough time because of poverty. I remember once on the Eve of the Chinese Spring Festival, I had no money to pay a driver at our school. It was the Spring Festival, and he and his family needed the money, so I took off my woolen skirt and sent it to a pawn shop to get the extra cash. Another time, I couldn't pay the electricity bills for the school, and our electricity was cut off. But I persevered. Without perseverance, one cannot achieve anything.

Even when the financial pressures disappeared, there were social pressures. "How can you run a school so well?" In our society there was a lot of jealousy of those who accomplished something, especially women. "Where did you get the money?" many people asked, thinking I had some rich backers. Though my school board members and teachers all had high social status, they did not help me financially. I was responsible for all the financing. Especially as a woman, I didn't want to beg others for money or to ask for donations. I didn't want to ask for money; I didn't want to beg from others; but I was willing to take out loans because I could pay them back. Other schools would run for half a year or at most three or four years, then they would close. Not my school. My school stayed open, so I had credit,

---

months later, his pay was raised to thirty silver dollars. After a year's work, he had savings of over two hundred dollars. In 1919, because of his productivity, his salary was raised to fifty silver dollars a month, whereas other employees had to work for ten years to reach that level. Shen also made forty silver dollars in extra income by contributing to several periodicals and newspapers every month. So as a college graduate and an increasingly prominent writer, Shen made about ninety dollars a month. At the same time, as a young woman physical training teacher, Lu made one hundred silver dollars a month. This was, indeed, a lot of money. See Mao Dun, *Wo zouguo de daolu* [The journey I have made] (Hong Kong: Sanlian shudian, 1981), 100 and 129.

especially after ten years, and could ask for loans from banks. The largest loan I got was thirty thousand silver dollars, with which I bought land and built buildings. The Educational Bureau had ruled that physical education schools had to have their own buildings, which scared other people so much that they closed their schools. I couldn't close mine, because having the school was my goal in life. If I closed the school, I would lose face. I had to hang on. After we'd built only three floors of our new building, money ran out. We had to stop construction for a year because I could not find any money. Why couldn't I get another loan then? Because I didn't want to build the school in the foreign concessions.[11] I hated the concessions most. I wanted to build in the Chinese part of the city to win honor for Chinese, but I suffered for doing this. The banks told me that property on Chinese land was not secure, so even if your assessed value was a hundred thousand silver dollars, you could not get a loan of ten thousand silver dollars. If you built in the concessions, an assessed value of ten thousand silver dollars would get you a loan of ten thousand silver dollars. I was furious. What?! I am suffering for being patriotic? I was mad at the Chinese people! Why do they have no pride? Why do Chinese look down upon Chinese? I refused to change my mind: I built my school in the southern district, three stories at first, and one more floor when I had more money. All the other physical education schools closed, and only mine persevered. In the end, people recognized that I had devoted all my life to the school, and so I was given credit. Later, some bankers said to me, "Principal Lu, if you have something you need to have done, just let us know." I invited several bankers to be our school board members. Thus I was able to get loans.

After my school building was completed in the southern district, the city's Educational Bureau revealed its intention to use it as their office building. I thought it would be insecure to run a school there, so in 1931 I bought land and houses in Jiangwan to build a new school. When the new school was just about finished, the battle of January 28 destroyed everything.[12] But I began rebuilding the school soon after the war and designed the layout of

---

11. After the defeat in the Opium War, besides the colonization of Hong Kong, the Qing government was forced to open five cities including Shanghai to residence by British subjects and their families. In subsequent years, the United States, France, and other foreign powers also claimed their rights in the five treaty port cities and established their respective or joint settlements there. Foreigners were granted extraterritoriality in China.

12. The Japanese troops attacked the northern area of Shanghai on January 28, 1932. The Chinese Nineteenth Army stationed in Shanghai resisted for over one month.

the school myself. We remodeled forty classrooms, built new dorms, and bought twelve pianos for gymnastics dances. We also built a gymnasium with a full set of facilities, a canal for boating, and a swimming pool. Between 1932 and 1937 was the prime time for Liangjiang: we attracted more and more students from all over China, and overseas Chinese in Japan and Southeast Asia sent their daughters to our school. It was famous as the "best physical education school in the Far East."

When I was a student in the Chinese Women's Gymnastics School, the sports outfit we wore was an imitation of outfits worn in the Western YWCA, which ran a women's physical education school and shared some teachers with us. At that time we wore a top with the collar up and sleeves that reached to the elbows, a belt that tied at the waist, *denglong ku* [bloomers] that came down to the knees, and cotton stockings that covered the legs. But at Liangjiang, from the beginning, my students wore shorts and shirts with short sleeves, just like the outfits foreigners in the Western YWCA wore, because our team had to compete with them at games. How could you have worn trousers to the games? We wore whatever they wore and had our outfits tailor-made: very pretty white shirts and bright red shorts. But people cursed our new style. They called the turndown collar *tanxiong* [exposing the chest]. They called short sleeves *loubi* [baring arms]. They called shorts *loudatui* [exposing thighs]. This language appeared in newspapers. Everybody laughed at us. When our basketball team traveled to Beijing, even people who had studied sports abroad were surprised to see our women players wearing red shorts, and they felt uncomfortable. Actually, they were behind the times.

I just wanted to learn from those who were more advanced. Whatever foreign countries have, we should have, too, and we should learn good things from foreign countries—that's what I was thinking. Foreign countries had dancing on stage, so I organized our students to dance on stage. I organized basketball and volleyball games, and I had a swimming pool built in my school. All these were new things at the time. Some people said, "She goes to see a dance performance one day, and the next day her students give the same performance." Later, public opinion changed; people got used to it. I said to newspaper reporters and editors, "You have the power to make public opinion. I don't blame you for writing what you did, but you just haven't seen enough of the world." What I really meant was they were too short-sighted. I said, "I think China should have this aspiration: whatever foreigners have, we should have too. Only that way will we be able to compete internationally."

In 1925 I established the first women's basketball team in China. In April

1931, I led our Liangjiang women's basketball team to Japan. It was the first time a Chinese women's sports team went abroad. The event received a lot of public attention. At the time there were already signs of a Japanese invasion of China. Sports in Japan had developed quickly, and the Japanese did well at the Olympics. But most people thought there were no sports at all in China. When I said our team would go to Japan, people were surprised. "Liangjiang is so bold in daring to compete with the Japanese. It will be like going to your death. You will be beaten in competition and lose face." I replied that it might not turn out that way. But they said, "Go ahead and try. You may lose all face and have to jump into the Eastern Sea." I was very angry. Why do we Chinese have no will to win honor? Are we Chinese really good for nothing? I had my own estimation of our team: we had practiced hard and competed with teams all over the country, as well as with foreign teams. Because we always won, I had confidence that we would put on a good show in Japan. Yet I dared not discuss the issue with any one, nor did I dare ask for donations for the trip. I just kept this idea to myself and saved money for the trip, making a budget and calculating all the expenses. I even prepared for the likelihood that the Japanese would not compete with us and thus we would earn no income from the games. In that case, I planned so that we would still have enough money to pay for our expenses and treat the trip as a study and travel tour. In any case, we would not borrow one cent from others.

We had a hard time. We were in the fourth-class cabin on the ship to Japan. When we arrived in Japan, each player got one more egg each day as extra nutrition. We rented rooms in private homes and did everything for ourselves, independently. I did not care about all those nasty things people said. I did not tell the media until we were aboard the ship.

Once we were in Japan, the Japanese not only wanted to compete with us but also wanted to win every game. They tried to make conditions unfavorable for us—by using their own balls, arranging games close to one another to wear us out, and so on. But out of ten games in Japan, we won six. One game ended in a tie, and one game they won by cheating. Anyway, they lost six games out of ten. They had never expected to lose to us. In fact, at first, even the Chinese diplomats in Japan did not attend because they were afraid we would be defeated and they would lose face. After we won three games in a row, the diplomats asked us for tickets and threw a party for us, saying that we had earned glory for our country. In the end, the Japanese players became good friends with us, and both sides shed many tears when we left. Then the Koreans invited us to compete in their country, and we won all the games there.

We worked really hard for those victories. The Japanese tried to make us use their balls, sing their national anthem, and raise their national flag. But we insisted on using each other's ball for half of a game—China did not make basketballs then; we used balls made in America. We also insisted on singing our own national anthem and raising our own flag. We failed to change only one thing: the busy schedule for all the games. We had only ten players; even though I had budgeted for twelve, one got sick before we left China, and the other was pregnant. The remaining ten students were only twenty-one or twenty-two years old. They were all petite but agile. Although they were exhausted, they really surprised people. Japanese newspapers said the whole country was shocked by the victories of the Chinese Liangjiang women's basketball team. Even the Japanese royal family came to see our games, invited us to a party, and gave us presents. One thing I liked is something that happened long after we returned to China. Once our team was on a train that stopped at a station in northern China, and a group of Japanese college students were on another train at the same station. When they heard that we were there, they came to see us. The trip to Japan was a success. And later we also won many victories on a trip to Southeast Asia. The Liangjiang women's basketball team was finally regarded as the Chinese women's national team. That was not my original goal; I just wanted to promote women's sports, which we eventually did. But the trips abroad also won glory for our country. The young players are now in their late eighties, and they still tell me that the trip to Japan is the one unforgettable event in their lives.

When the War of Resistance began, Japanese invaders bombed the outskirts of Shanghai in their offensive against the city.[13] Our school in Jiangwan was right on the front line, and everything was destroyed in the gunfire. Then the Japanese troops turned the school site into a military camp and used the swimming pool as a horse manure pit. Liangjiang was forced to close. After that, I threw myself entirely into the national salvation movement. I organized Shanghai funü yundong cujinhui [the Shanghai Women's Movement Association]. Over one thousand women joined the organization—most were students, some housewives. We collected over eighty thousand dollars for the War of Resistance. Women in our organization also cooked meals to send to the wounded soldiers in hospitals. We rented two office rooms in a big office building downtown to run all those activities. As the

---

13. On July 7, 1937, Japanese troops attacked areas close to Beijing and began a large-scale invasion. The GMD and the CCP formed the second united front to begin China's resistance.

chair of our association, I became one of the seven board members of Weilaohui [the Women's Consolation Society].[14]

After the war, the school site in Jiangwan was occupied by the Nationalist military headquarters. It took me two years of running back and forth
between Shanghai and Nanjing to obtain official approval in order to get
my school back. I negotiated hard with the Nationalist government to get
the necessary certificate for returning my property. But when I finally gave
the certificate to the military in Jiangwan, it was no use. They said, "We
got the property from the Japanese, not from you." I was really mad to hear
that. The Guomindang was losing the civil war, everything had broken down,
and the government was really corrupt. I plucked up my courage and told
the military that I built the school myself, yet I now had no place to live
and had to stay in a hotel. Thus they had to agree to let me have one room,
and then another room. In this way I gradually got back most of my school
building. It was impossible to run a physical education school without facilities, so I ran a middle school there. Later, when I got back my building
in the southern district, I opened a branch of Liangjiang Middle School. All
together, there were over four hundred students in the two branches. I ran
the school for two years. Then came the liberation.[15] Since the liberation, I
have not been in education. I became a factory worker.

Even before the Cultural Revolution, there was a period when I was questioned by the Communist Party: "How come you did not have a relationship with the Guomindang? That would be a miracle. Impossible." I felt
wronged because I really had nothing to do with the Guomindang. I was
just working in education. Anyone who had progressive ideas would feel
uncomfortable with the Guomindang. "But you ran a school for decades,"
they said. "How could they let you run it if you were not a Guomindang
member?" I replied, "I knew a lot of Guomindang members. I knew many
of the relatives of Jiang Jieshi and Song Meiling, but I did not have a party

14. The Women's Consolation Society was an umbrella organization of Shanghai women during the war, responsible for mobilizing women of all strata to become involved in fundraising, nursing, sending consolation to the soldiers at the
front, and so on. Both the GMD and the CCP, now in alliance for the second time,
were involved in the organization. Song Meiling (Madam Chiang Kai-shek) was the
chair of the national Women's Consolation Society. The first chair of the Shanghai
branch was He Xiangning, then Shi Liang. Lu Lihua was in charge of fundraising
and donations.

15. In 1949 the CCP took over mainland China and founded the People's Republic of China. The Chinese in mainland China usually refer to the event as "liberation," the period before 1949 as "pre-liberation," and the period after 1949 as
"after liberation."

relationship with the Guomindang."[16] Still, they did not believe me. They said, "The Nationalist government treated you very well, gave you enough awards to fill two rooms. You did not have a relationship with them? If so, why didn't you get involved with the Communist Party when they contacted you?" In those years I knew it was good to be progressive, but I had a firm conviction that I should be nonpartisan—because if you let the progressive party come to a school, the Guomindang would surely come, too, and make trouble and arrest students. Why should I put my students through that hardship? I would rather not have any party organizations in my school. Plus I was scared.

The Communist Party contacted me mostly through Sister Deng [Deng Yingchao]. We were really like sisters. She came to Shanghai in the 1920s, and during the War of Resistance we worked together. She contacted me because my school was successful. I liked social activities, and women's organizations, and so I joined the Feminist Movement Association, which was organized by some rich women, such as the wife of the ambassador to the Soviet Union, and by some principals of progressive schools such as Shenzhou Girls' School. The Feminist Movement Association was formed after the May Fourth students' movement. At the time, there were over ten women's organizations in Shanghai, and I joined them all. The purpose of all these women's organizations was to advocate women's rights, *nüquan yundong* [feminist movement]. I joined the Women's Temperance Union, the YWCA, and so on. I also joined the ones organized by the Guomindang, because they asked me to join. So long as you were for women's interests, I would join your organization. But I did not like to be in any organization that fought against another organization. I wanted women to join together to work for the women's movement. That is why the Communists said that my political ideas were unclear. But I had no choice, because I ran a school. My main goal was to run the school.

Deng Yingchao contacted me during the War of Resistance. She came to Shanghai with the mission to invite Madame Sun to the north, but she claimed publicly that she came to Shanghai for medical treatment.[17] I attended the meetings held for her. We knew that she was a Communist, and we had heard of Zhou Enlai, too. In the Communists' eyes I was respected

16. Jiang Jieshi (Chiang Kai-shek) was the president of the Republic of China; Song Meiling was Madam Chiang Kai-shek.

17. Lu's memory is inaccurate here. Deng Yingchao came to Shanghai to invite Madame Sun to Beijing in June 1949 instead of during the War of Resistance. But prior to that trip, Deng had been to Shanghai many times. In 1949 Deng came to

because I was serious about my work, my school. Women's organizations wanted to expand, because the more members they had, the more social support they would receive. As far as I was concerned, so long as an organization pursued women's rights, I was willing to join it. After liberation, when they investigated my history, they said to me [Lu imitates the dialect of the Communist cadres from the North], "You said you have no relationship with the Guomindang. But how could they let your school exist for decades? It is impossible! Only a Nationalist could be a school principal." I replied, "I don't know. I really had no relationship with them." Actually, because the Guomindang saw that I was devoted to my school and did not make alliances with either the Right or the Left, they didn't bother me. See, my sandwiched position caused many grievances.

In 1938 I left Shanghai for Chongqing. There I met many young student refugees. When they learned that I was the principal of Liangjiang, they asked me for help, so I went to the War Relief Committee, which suggested that I run a free school. But I lacked funds to do that. I had heard people talking about Shanbei Gongxue [a school run by the Communist Party in Yan'an] when I was in Hong Kong. Some people who had visited Shanbei told me that students there needed to be self-reliant in supporting themselves and the school. I thought it was a good idea and decided that I could run a school like that, too. The only thing I needed was land. Fortunately, one of my former students in Chongqing donated two hundred *mu* [about thirty acres]. I asked Sister Deng for more information about Shangbei Gongxue. Deng knew I would not join the Communist Party, but she supported my idea for the school and gave me a pamphlet, "The Organization of Shanbei Gongxue," which described courses and methods of organization of the school. She said to me, "Sister Lihua, I know you are well-intentioned. But let me warn you, you may come to grief because of this." She knew what was going to happen.

On the donated land, I opened a Chongqing Branch of Liangjiang Women's Physical Education School. I initially planned to have three hundred students, but so many homeless young women pled to be accepted that in the end the total enrollment reached five hundred. We built simple houses for classrooms and dorms. Room and board were free. Students worked in

---

Shanghai as a high official in the CCP and wife of the famous leader Zhou Enlai. She met with prominent women activists and celebrities in Shanghai. In a sense, attending those meetings with Deng was a claim of high social status. Thus in 1949 Lu still belonged to the circle of elite women.

the fields to produce vegetables and grains, or in workshops to do sewing. We had to support ourselves. Once the students came, they were like my children. I had to provide for them and raise them. With no funds, I had to adopt this self-reliant method. Because physical labor was the major part of the curriculum, our students wore straw shoes, straw hats, and green overalls. Thus we attracted the Guomindang's attention. They thought we were running a Communist school. They came and asked me, "What kind of school are you running?" I said, "A working school. This is wartime, and because we lack funds, we must work to support ourselves; it is impossible to wear gowns and sit in the classroom anymore." They said, "To be very blunt, you are a peripheral organization of the Communist Party!" They told me to switch back to the curriculum regulated by the Department of Education of the Guomindang. I said, "Fine, you take the school over and give us money." Then they threatened to ban our school if I did not change the curriculum. In less than two years, the Chongqing school was closed. I was exhausted. There were so many students, and I had to worry about their meals, beds, quilts, and so on. It was too much for me. After that, I just organized students who did not want to leave the school and set up a handicraft cooperative. In this way we supported ourselves during the war years.

I married when I was about twenty-three years old. I had just started my school and was terribly busy. I got to know him [his name was Wu Jian-luan] when he worked for a dental organization. We became friends. Because he intended to pursue me, he was very nice to my father, and my father said to me, "You are too busy. Wu can help you in school." I thought Wu wrote well, so I asked him to be the secretary of our school. My father told me to marry him. Because my friends all knew he was my boyfriend, I thought I had to marry him. Moreover, I felt I needed someone to help me with my school. But I was not content with him. We had different personalities. He played with students as well as quarreled with them, and instead of helping me, he often caused trouble for me, which made me very upset. He wanted me to give him a higher position and more power. Of course, he could not be the principal of a girls' school, but he wanted more power. Yet I did not want to give him that because he lacked the ability. Therefore, he became very resentful.

Once I broke my arm and was hospitalized for a month. For the entire month, he never visited me. Other teachers told me that he took a trip to Suzhou with some students. The girl students were young and he was a teacher! So I told him that this was a girls' school and I would keep running it. I said that I could no longer tolerate his behavior and I had to sacrifice family. He was so mad to hear those words that he left me right away. He went to Suzhou and married a woman there before getting a divorce from me.

After two years, he came back to me. I said, "I have heard of your marriage. It's fine with me. But we need a formal divorce." In the old society, divorced women had been looked down upon, and divorce was still a heavy blow to women. Tabloids loved to print stories about people's marriages, and I was a school principal, so I did not want stories printed about me. I told Wu that I would like to go through legal procedures, but I did not want to make a public statement in the newspaper. He agreed, but a few weeks after our divorce, he published a statement in a newspaper. In the divorce statement he accused me of being fickle. I was deeply hurt, and my contempt for him increased. He used to take his sister and nephew to my school to steal because he wanted his family members to take over the school, but I did not expose any of those mean things. I really hated the marriage and did not want to even mention it. That is why I did not tell you about this marriage the first time we talked: the marriage and divorce caused so much pain in me. I endured a lot of social pressure at the time. But only some people knew about this part of my life because serious newspapers did not print stories like that. It was a difficult time for me, and I was greatly hurt by this matter.

I got married again when I was thirty. My new husband, Gu Zhenglai, was working with the Boy Scouts, as he had done all his life. He was a teacher, and I was a teacher. Cai Yuanpei and Tao Xingzhi had created a nationwide Education Improvement Society, which all principals and heads of educational bureaus joined. Every year there was an annual conference in a province. My husband and I first met at those conferences. We both liked what the other had to say, so we grew closer. He had been in Jimei [a city in the south] as the head teacher. Then he came to Shanghai to run the Chinese Physical Education School, and I helped him. He was forty and I was thirty when we married.

Before I married him, I had had many friends [boyfriends], but I was devoted to my career. He had a similar career, so we had things in common to talk about. We understood the hardship and pain in each other's life. He was older than I, but I thought he was quite good, so we married. In 1931 we went to Japan together. He went on a study and survey tour, and I led the women's basketball team of my school to compete with Japanese teams. After we returned, my husband died in 1932. We had been married only for a little over one year. He died in the January 28 battle, commanding the Southern District Protection League. He was sick because of exhaustion and mal-nutrition, and even though I got the best doctors for him, it was in vain. To put it in a simple way, I lived the life of an unmarried person.[18]

Later in the War of Resistance, when I was in Chongqing, I lived with a man whom I had known in Shanghai. He worked in an insurance company. In Chongqing he often came to see me in my school. He told me that he had carried a torch for me before. Because we had known each other for a long time and could take care of each other in Chongqing, we lived together for about two or three years. After the war he returned to his wife in Shang-hai, and I began to live my own life in Shanghai.[19] Not long after we re-turned to Shanghai he got sick and died. My fate was such . . . [she laughs]. Well, a person devoted to a career could not properly care for a family. I would rather be busy outside of the family than have the comfort of a family life. I was unafraid of hardship in my career, and I took little joy in family life. Even with Gu Zhenglai, who was a decent and honorable man—we did not spend much time together. I was a school principal, and he was a school prin-cipal, too. After a busy day's work, he sometimes came to my school to see me, and I sometimes went to his school to see him. We took only one trip—the trip to Japan—together.

I do not have any children of my own. My elder sister had eight. When she had four or five, she asked me to take two to Shanghai, a boy and a girl. I am not the kind of old-fashioned person who has to go through adopting the children and changing their names. I was not selfish enough to claim them as my own. Instead, I agreed to let the two kids come here, thinking that they would add fun to my life and could receive a good education. When the January 28 battle began, the two children—already fourteen and fifteen years old—wanted to go home; they hoped to return to me after the battle ended. No one expected that both would fall ill as soon as they got home, but they did: one contracted tuberculosis, and the other diphtheria. They both died in the countryside. Then my sister bore more children, and she sent the sixth and eighth to me. I declined at first, saying that my *ming* [fate] was too hard and that two children had already died. But my sister did not listen to this, and another boy and girl came to live with me when I estab-

18. By this, Lu means she had little sex life.

19. The relationship Lu describes here was not uncommon during the War of Resistance. Having left their hometowns, men and women gathering in other cities cohabited with or without a legal marriage. The special term for women in this kind of relationship was *kangzhan furen* (wives of the War of Resistance). The relation-ship often involved a married man and a single woman. See chapter 6 for further discussion.

lished a middle school after the War of Resistance. They have done well in Shanghai, and now often come to take care of me. My sister died when she was seventy-five. She was five years older than I, born in a different era. She grew up before the Xinhai Revolution, therefore her ideas were kind of old-fashioned. She had bound feet and no schooling, because school for girls was not popular in her day. She later blamed my parents for not letting her attend school. My parents said, "At the time, nobody went to school, so how could we let you go to school?" All her life was a hardship, with too many children.

When the children lived with me, I hired a helper to do housework. Except for the years in Chongqing, when I cooked for myself, I had meals in school with my students. Otherwise, how could I know if they had decent food? I spent time with them from morning till night. That is why my students have been so good to me. Once, when a student needed surgery, I accompanied her to hospital. She told me, "Principal Lu, please don't leave me. I want to see your face when I open my eyes after my operation." I stayed with her in the hospital. Another time, a student caught typhoid and fell unconscious. I sent her to hospital, holding her in my arms during the journey in the pedicab. When we arrived at the hospital, the nurse meeting us was shocked to see me holding the student. She said, "My goodness! You have to be sterilized right away! She has no hope." But the student was eventually saved. After she recovered, she gave me ginseng as thanks for saving her life.

Many of my students remained *laoxiaojie* [old maids]. They were devoted to their careers and worked all their lives. Some of my friends never married, or married very late in life. The manly types of women usually focused on their careers. I was kind of like a boy, too. I did not fear dealing with men. Zhang Xiangwen was a manly type and married very late.

After the Communist Party came to Shanghai, I was fired and became jobless. The reason for this is that one of my former students wanted my position. She was Zhou Gucheng's wife, and her husband talked to the officials in charge of education.[20] Another student of mine told me the inside story. In 1950, soon after Shanghai was taken by the Communist Party, the people from the Educational Bureau came to my school and declared that the government would take over the school. They made Zhou's wife the acting principal and said I was a VIP of the Nationalist government because Shanghai newspapers had printed pictures of me with some Guo-

20. Zhou held a high position in the National People's Congress.

mindang officials and because Pan Gongzhan [the director of Shanghai Guomindang headquarters] was the chair of our school board. Thus I was driven out of my school and had nothing left. All my blood and sweat had been
poured into my school. Other than my school, I had not an inch of land under my feet nor a piece of tile over my head.

But I was not afraid. I organized two other women to open a new style
knitting shop on Nanjing Road. It quickly became prosperous. But six years
later, the government started nationalization, and our small cooperative was
nationalized. They paid us a few hundred yuan for our property, and we were
assigned to different factories. We had no choice. One had to eat. It was good
that I could make a living by my own labor. I never wanted to rely on anyone, not even on my children. I was a worker in the Fifth Woolen Sweater
Factory, where I made forty-five yuan a month until I retired at age sixty-
two. I worked as a quality-control inspector, a pretty good job. I was soon
used to being a worker and earning food with my own hands: nothing bad
about that. I said jokingly, "Before, I commanded others; now, I receive com-
mands." When I was running the knitting shop, people passing by whis-
pered to each other, "Look, that is Lu Lihua, the principal of Liangjiang. Now
she is just working with the yarns." I thought, what's wrong with that? I
relied on my own labor. I am the type of person who tries to follow current
ideas. Otherwise, one could get too angry. Other big capitalists sank, too.

My school property was all taken away by the government, and I and
my two children had to live in a room that measured seven square meters
[about seventy square feet]. The room faced north, which was hot in summer and cold in winter. During the Cultural Revolution, my little room was
searched because people thought I had valuable things from the past. I told
them that all my assets were in my school, which had been taken over by
the government. I only had 360 yuan savings in a case under my bed. They
found the case, but did not take my savings. My retirement pension was
twenty-seven yuan, and the food subsidy at the time was five yuan. I lived
on thirty-two yuan a month through all those years.[21] The government did
not rehabilitate me until 1980. I was assigned a bigger apartment, recruited
into Wenshiguan, and became a member of Shanghai People's Political Consultative Conference. But the government has still not told me anything
about my school property. I did not look for Sister Deng after 1949. She was

---

21. During the same period, the author worked on a state-owned farm, living
independently on a monthly salary of twenty-four yuan. With low prices and few
consumer goods available during the Cultural Revolution, Lu's income would have
been enough to support herself.

in the Communist Party, and if I complained about anything that the government had done to me, I would be complaining about her party. I was treated this way, and I did not know what she thought of me. Of course, she knew what happened to me. But I am a person with dignity and pride; I did not want to ask anybody for help. I believed that things would eventually be cleared up. So I told them to check all the Guomindang's files and if they found anything relating to me, I was willing to receive punishment. But I should say, throughout all my life, I have not done anything bad to the Communist Party or to the people.

When I was young, in my twenties, I saw that Christians love to help others. I had good opinions about religion. Especially during the May Fourth movement, I went to Christian schools to advocate revolution and national salvation. But students there advocated belief in Christianity to me. They sold me a Bible, asking me to be a Christian. Before I read the Bible, I felt OK about Christianity. After I read it, I was turned away from it. God created the world in six days! How could that be humanly possible? But actually, my attitude was wrong. God's ways cannot be explained in human terms; I understand that now. But at the time, I simply set the Bible aside. Although I often went to church on Sundays, I did not take what was said into my heart. Not until 1950 did I realize my mistake: I need to care for my soul. After so much hardship, pressure, poverty, and injustice, I am tired.

All my life shows that if I had been a man I would not be in this shape; if I had had some support in high places, I would not have fallen into this bad situation! As soon as I started my school, I realized it was hard to be a woman. There was all kinds of gossip about me: "She is capable, and she knows a lot of people who will help her," which implies that I had a [sexual] relationship with them. This is all because I am a woman. Otherwise, there wouldn't be this kind of gossip. And what is more, when my school ended up like this, who spoke for me? No one. They knew I was a woman all alone. Whenever I think of this, I feel how miserable Chinese women are! I wasn't the only one; many women friends of mine had similar experiences. They had to endure the loss of their reputations and were oppressed by that loss to such an extent that they gave up their careers and failed. Chinese women are more miserable than foreign women in this sense. As I said before, we have to pursue *nüquan* [women's rights]; it won't do to let injustice continue. Contempt toward women has been passed down through history. For example, if a woman divorced once and wanted to marry again, it was a big deal and she was heavily criticized. But a man could have three or four wives. I used to ask myself why women were abused like this. But to whom could I speak? All we could do was organize societies, and it was good even just to advocate ideas. So we had Nüquan Yundong Tongmenhui [the Feminist Movement Association], which was led by a school principal, and Nüzi Canzhenghui [the Women's Suffrage Association], which was led by Liu-Wang Liming.[22] I joined all of them.

I participated in these activities all the time. Everything I did was for women's rights and physical education. I was part of the Shanghai women's movement. I knew the earliest woman activists: Kang Tongbi, who was Kang Youwei's daughter, and Zhang Zhujun, who ran a hospital.[23] There were a few *gao nüquan de* [feminists] at the time of the Xinhai Revolution. I think they should be praised in historical writing. I learned of them in the newspaper when I was little and admired their efforts against footbinding. I thought I would visit them if I went to Shanghai. When I came to Shanghai, I visited Kang and Zhang at their Tianzuhui [Natural Feet Society]. I told them that, after reading the story of their anti-footbinding activities, I asked girls in my hometown to unbind their feet. Hearing my story, they called me "little commander." Later, when I became the school principal, they invited me to join their activities. What we did was to advocate women's rights, hold meetings, and make speeches—no real actions. Most participants were doctors, school principals, and teachers. We were few in number— sometimes we had a meeting of twenty, sometimes forty people. The only action at the time was when we mobilized for a new constitution. Women's organizations united to form the Shanghai Women's Association, and I went with a group of women to Nanjing to petition the Nationalist government. Our slogan then was "Down with the warlords and up with equality between men and women."[24]

In the May Fourth students' movement, students formed all kinds of or-

22. The two feminist organizations in Shanghai in the early 1920s were mainly led by women who received an education in the United States or Japan and had a career in Shanghai. Several of these women were involved with the YWCA and the WCTU. In contrast, the two organizations in Beijing were led by college students.

23. Kang Tongbi (1889–1969) was one of the women editors of and major contributors to the first women's journal in China, *Nüxuebao* [Women's education], founded in 1898. Because of its close association with the late Qing leading reformers, as a result of the suppression of the "Hundred Days' reform" *Nüxuebao* did not last long. Kang remained active in various women's organizations in Shanghai.

Zhang Zhujun (1879–?) was a renowned female doctor who graduated from a mission school in Guangzhou. She established two hospitals and a women's school in Guangzhou. In 1904 she went to Shanghai, where she established several hospitals in the following years. She organized a Red Cross team during the 1911 Revolution to provide medical treatment to wounded soldiers.

24. Lu here refers to the National Assembly Promotion movement in late 1924 and early 1925.

ganizations. Men and women in these organizations contacted one another freely. We heard of freedom to love. And many young men and women began to *lian'ai* [love], and eventually married pairs appeared, one after another. So conservative people said, "What are students organizations? Just organizations for *lian'ai*." We thought it was natural for men and women to fall in love. But as for myself, I was conservative in my behavior. I received love letters from male students, but I did not dare answer those letters. Because I was a student known to many people, I did not want to attract gossip.

I seldom read novels or stories. They made me dispirited. In *The Dream of the Red Chamber*, the women suffered a lot and had no status at all. I did not like it. I read a little new literature, such as Hu Shi's vernacular works, and Western stories. But I did not read much because I was always busy doing things. I learned the word *nüquan* [feminism or women's rights] from newspapers and from those women who were promoting *nüquan*.

What most irritated me was hearing about cases of abused women. Why is life this way?! In a women's organization, there was a Zhang Xiangwen whom I really respected. She was truly devoted to her career. She also suffered the loss of her reputation. Many women gossiped about her, saying that she was indecent and always meeting the head of some bureau. In fact, she and the man had become friends while both were studying in America, and later they got married. Then there was no more gossip about her. But she didn't marry until she was more than fifty years old, because the ex-wife of her husband had not yet died. Until then, she didn't dare marry him. She was the principal of a school and president of a hospital. Her three sisters were all doctors who ran hospitals. Her elder sister, Zhang Zhujun, ran a hospital in Shanghai during the Xinhai Revolution. When I came to Shanghai, I heard everyone constantly gossiping about her relationship with so-and-so. It was very ugly to hear. This was abuse of women. Now it is different because all women work. Then, only a few women worked outside the home, because women did not dare do things. You were fine if you did not do any work. Once you did work, you were regarded as bad. People said that the more things you achieved, the worse you were. So women were unwilling to work outside the home. That is why a lot of career women quit in the middle of their careers. Many schools just closed down. What a pity! They were just unable to hang on. A bad reputation was the heaviest blow. Moreover, your parents would complain, "What is the point of doing work and being attacked by others?" People exhorted me, too, saying, "What is the point? Why are you doing this? You are almost worn out by the school, plus you have to bear so much criticism." I replied that I wanted the nation to be strong and people to be healthy. I said this, and I had to stick to it. Let people gossip. I have been slandered so much that I forget a lot.

Let me give an example: Yang Xiuqong was a young swimmer whom I knew. She was sent to the Olympic Games in Germany. Her mother wanted to accompany her but did not have enough money. They came to see me. At the time, I was sick, staying in a hospital. When they told me of the situation, I suggested that Yang could give a swimming performance in Shanghai and use the ticket income to pay her mother's way. They liked the idea, and I helped arrange Yang's performance in Shanghai. But Shanghai newspapers said that I was using Yang to achieve fame for myself and for my school. Yang Xiuqong and her mother felt very sorry for this and asked me what they could do to clear my name. I said, "You may just tell the truth to the audience before the performance." They did, but the next day the newspapers did not mention it at all! This kind of thing I had to bear. To whom could I speak? If I did not have religion, I would be terribly upset by things like this. Anyway, I knew in my own heart that I did not do bad things. One had to look at the bright side of things to have a peaceful mind.

One thing in my life that makes me happy is that my students are all very good to me. They treat me better than they treat their own mothers. They often come to see me. Some still call me Mom even though they are over seventy years old. I have students in Shanghai and all over the world. Every month I receive many letters. I also write letters to them. I can write eight letters a day.

Chinese women are still not truly liberated. Parents still prefer boys to girls, just as when I was a child. Women's education is still insufficient. Without women's education, we won't be able to achieve women's self-respect and self-strength.[25]

I have been thinking of writing an article, "The Twentieth Century and I." I feel the twentieth century is my time. I often think of how a poor girl in a rural town has become a woman like me today. The change has been tremendous. In the late Qing, young girls had to endure footbinding. Today, women are half of the sky.[26] Comparing women's activities in my youth to the present, I think the Women's Federation is an organization belong-

25. Women's self-respect, independence, self-confidence, and self-strengthening are requirements proposed by the Women's Federation for all Chinese women. Lu is obviously familiar with the current slogan of the Women's Federation and is subtly criticizing the official organization's agenda.
26. "Women can hold up half of the sky" is a phrase that has been popularized in China since the Mao era. In contemporary Chinese language, "half of the sky" is often used to refer to women.

ing to the state. Although everything is done in the name of democracy, it is difficult for women to organize by themselves. People think that everything is already run by the state and thus it is unnecessary for us to run anything. For example, in the past there was no *tiyu* [sports or physical education] in China, so we organized sports teams and held games everywhere. Now the state is running it. You either join the district team or the municipal team, and facilities are provided by the state. Thus you would think, "Well, the state is running it, no need for us to bother." In the past people had initiative. Now people are passive. We no longer possess the ability to show initiative and think hard to achieve difficult things on our own. We have no place to direct our energy and initiative, such as in my private school that was taken over. Well, no need for me to strive anymore.

If you asked me to organize a women's association today, I would not do it. People would think, "What is your intention? Do you want to oppose the Women's Federation?" The Women's Federation is not an organization you can join freely. Membership requires certain qualifications and has to be approved by different levels of authorities. In the end, you do not have initiative anymore. Sometimes I wonder, what is the best form of a state—one that can both reflect people's minds and the government's needs? When the government does too much, people's initiative is destroyed. Nowadays, women are just working at their different posts, but there are no more activities in society. Only when people can use their initiative will they be able to achieve a lot, such as when I strove hard to run my school and it finally reached an enrollment of three hundred students. Although there was jealousy and gossip, I did not care; I felt very happy about my achievements. With all the restrictions nowadays, you have energy but nowhere to direct it. Well, I am a nonpartisan person, so I can speak the facts.

In my youth, we thought of ourselves as new women who dared to rush forward and break old conventions. You know, in 1954 when the Shanghai government took over the private schools, over half of the more than four hundred private schools were run by women. Women mostly ran elementary schools. It was the head of the Educational Bureau of Shanghai who told me this after I was rehabilitated. He meant that I was not singled out for that treatment because the government actually took over more than four hundred private schools. But my school was taken over in 1950, a fact for which he had no explanation. After my school was taken over, I lost interest in many things. What hurt me greatly was the thought that the graduates of my school would suffer fewer promotions and flagging careers. People would think there was something wrong with my school. Fortunately, my students all understood my situation and treated me very well. To tell you the truth, my students treat me better than my own daughter. That is my greatest consolation.

INTERPRETATION: WOMEN'S EDUCATION
AND THE RISE OF THE MAY FOURTH WOMEN

When she comments that her sister, who was five years older than she, was born in a different era, Lu Lihua presents a meaningful periodization of Chinese women's history. Her own life differed dramatically from her sister's because her "era" gave her what previously had been available only to women from elite families: the opportunity to have an education. Throughout China's long history, elite women had access to tutors, but formal schooling was not available for girls until 1844, when a British female missionary opened the first girls' school in Ningbo. After that, missionary schools were established by Westerners in all the major cities along the coast.[27] By 1902, there were 251 missionary schools nationwide, with a total of 10,158 students, of which 4,373 were female. Missionary schools offered limited educational opportunity for Chinese girls from different family backgrounds. More important, they set examples for the Chinese to follow.[28]

On June 1, 1898, reform-minded gentry-official Jing Yuanshan, with the support of famous reformers such as Kang Youwei and Liang Qichao, opened the first Chinese girls' school in Shanghai. The event was reported in major Shanghai newspapers and the *Hunan News* [*Xiangbao*]. It attracted public attention because the school was supported by scholar reformers, the business elite, and officials. Before the school opened, Liang Qichao had published two articles advocating girls' schools and asserting that women's education was a means to achieve national strength. He argued that because Chinese women were not allowed to have education and were confined to the women's quarters and restricted by custom, they had become "as lazy as vagabonds and as stupid as barbarians." He asked rhetorically, "With two hundred million vagabonds and barbarians, how can our country not be harmed? . . . With men's and women's equal rights, the United States has become powerful; with women's education spreading, Japan has become

27. All-China Women's Federation, *Zhongguo funü yundong shi* [A history of the Chinese women's movement] (Beijing: Chunqiu chubanshe, 1989), 34.
28. Shen Zhi, *Funü jiefangshi wenda* [Questions and answers on the history of women's liberation] (Hangzhou: Zhejiang renmin chubanshe, 1986), 28.

strong; to build a prosperous nation and an intelligent people, we have to start with women's education."[29]

Liang's articles marked the beginning of a nationalist discourse that legitimized women's education in one generation's struggle to strengthen the Chinese race and defend the nation (*qiangzhong baoguo*). When Jing sought funding from people in business and government, he used the slogan *qiangzhong baoguo* to touch donors' hearts. The historical significance of the opening of the girls' school by Chinese themselves was quickly recognized by contemporaries. The first girls' school only lasted for two years, because Jing was implicated and fled to Macao when Kang and Liang's reform movement failed. However, the idea of girls' schools entered the nationalist discourse and remained a respected and progressive cause that all enlightened people endorsed. Many more girls' schools were opened by the Chinese nationwide, and by 1907, there were 428 girls' schools at different levels in twenty-two provinces, with a total enrollment of 15,496 students.[30]

It was not until 1907 that the Qing government itself responded to the new trend in women's school education. The government issued two decrees on March 8, 1907, calling on local governments to open girls' elementary schools and secondary normal schools. The decrees embraced the new ideas that had been circulating in society for some time. They claimed that the goal of elementary schools was to "foster women's virtue and necessary knowledge and skills, as well as to pay attention to women's physical development."[31] However, the major concern of the Qing government was to preserve Chinese women's "traditional virtues" in the face of Western influence. The decrees stipulated that promoting knowledge and preserving Confucian ethics should not interfere with each other and that "all the talk of indulging freedom, such as ending differentiation between men and women, granting freedom to choose one's mate, and allowing women to speak in political gatherings, should be strictly banned in order to maintain correct morals and manners."[32] Yet no matter how conservative the guidelines for women's education were, the girls' schools endorsed and established by the government

---

29. Liang Qichao, "Changyi sheli nüxuetang qi" [A suggestion to establish girls' schools], *Shiwubao* 44 (1898); reprint, in *Jindai Zhongguo nüquan yundong shiliao* [Historical source material on the modern Chinese feminist movement], ed. Li Yu-ning and Zhang Yufa (Taibei: Zhuanji wenxue chubanshe, 1975), 997.

30. Luo Suwen, "Zhongguo diyisuo ziban nüxiao" [The first girls' school established by the Chinese], *Shehui Kexue* (Shanghai), no. 2 (1988): 144–146. Shen Zhi, *Funü jiefangshi wenda*, 28–31.

31. Li You-ning and Zhang Yufa, 982.

32. Ibid., 976–977.

were new and progressive institutions that the later republican government inherited and expanded. In 1909, there were 308 girls' elementary schools nationwide, with 14,054 students. Five years after the fall of Qing dynasty, the number of female students in elementary schools reached 160,000, and the number in secondary schools reached 8,000 in 1916.[33]

The establishment of the republican government after 1911 greatly stimulated women's school education. A girls' school was even established in a rural town near Lu's home in 1912, and a year later she moved from that school to the girls' school run by the county government (*xianli nüxiao*). At the age of twelve, Lu was older than the other students in the elementary school. Certainly, it would have been unlikely for her parents to think of sending her seventeen-year-old sister, a girl of marriageable age, to school. Thus her sister missed the opportunity to live an entirely different life.

One point should be made clear: formal schooling for women did not begin with Lu Lihua's generation. Rather, what was new in this generation was the opportunity for a girl like Lu, who was from a small business family in a rural area, to go to a girls' school. In other words, in the early twentieth century, education was no longer a luxury that only women born in elite families could enjoy. More significantly, public, private, and missionary schools became institutions that were taken for granted. Other narratives in this book also testify to drastic change around the turn of the century, from the opening of the first Chinese girls' school to the time when formal schooling for girls became a must for all wealthy or comfortable families. This rapid, smooth change in social norms was possible because the expansion of women's education was associated with modern nation building and with the creation of a nationalist discourse. In a sense, nationalism became the vehicle that carried women out of their traditional domestic confinement into the public arena. Without this vehicle, it would be hard to imagine any other sanction that would permit Chinese women from "decent" families to "expose their heads and faces in public" (*paotou loumian*).

If the male-created nationalist discourse benefited Chinese women by offering them formal schooling in the first decade of the twentieth century, by the end of the second decade, many young women themselves had embraced nationalism heartily because they found it empowering. In Lu's case, her parents were not motivated by nationalism when they decided to send her to school. She was given the opportunity because her family lacked a male heir. And Lu did not embrace nationalism at the time she chose the women's physical education school. What attracted her was the prospect of

33. All-China Women's Federation, *Zhongguo funü yundong shi*, 36–39.

getting a job in a provincial-level school. The huge demand for physical education teachers at all levels of girls' schools was itself an example of how nationalism created social space for women. But Lu was not consciously aware of nationalism and its possibilities until the May Fourth movement. Only after hearing Ma Xiangbo's speech did it dawn on her that to serve the country better, she could do something more than get a job in a provincial school. The needs of the nation and her personal ambition found a perfect solution in the opening of a women's physical education normal school. By the time young women enrolled in her school, they were familiar with nationalist rhetoric: as they said to Lu, "We want our country to be strong and our people to be healthy." Nationalism certainly motivated their choice of the school because physical education was seen as a key element in strengthening the Chinese race and defending the nation. At the same time, these young women must have been aware of the job opportunities created by nationalism. Even women with bound feet aspired to the modern career of being a physical education teacher. Nationalism promoted and legitimized their strong desire to live a new and rewarding life despite their crippled bodies.

At nineteen, Lu was excited to see the rise of the May Fourth movement. Since childhood, she had admired heroines, and her formative years were filled with the stories of revolutionaries. But then she had been in her family-run grocery store in a small town, far away from the revolutionary currents in which quite a few young women became well-known for their heroic deeds. Now as a student in a Shanghai women's physical education school, she suddenly found herself at the center of a historic event. The student movement swelling in the nation made her feel "like a fish in water." She was energized by her involvement in all kinds of social activities: petitions, demonstrations, public speeches, meetings, and so on. Once she disguised herself as a housemaid and went with other female students disguised as rich women to Shanghai's largest department stores, asking the managers to sign an agreement for a general strike.[34] Chinese were unaccustomed to see women doing these things in public; therefore, people said she was bold. No matter what people might have meant by this, Lu was undaunted. She continued to shout slogans in public: "Love our country! Down with imperialism! Overthrow feudalism!" She knew her bold, unconventional behavior was sanctioned by the nationalist cause.

The May Fourth Incident offered a timely opportunity for educated Chinese women to break the strictures of gender segregation and create more

---

34. Shanghai Women's Federation, *Shanghai funü yundong shi* [A history of the Shanghai women's movement] (Shanghai: Shanghai renmin chubanshe, 1990), 51.

social space. Up to the eve of May 4, 1919, schools above the primary level were gender segregated, and female students lived in seclusion. When male student representatives from Beijing University went to Beijing Women's Normal School to contact female students in order to jointly launch the May Fourth demonstration, the administrators of the Women's Normal School still clung to the ancient norm that "man and woman should not be in intimate contact" (*nannü shoushou buqin*). They put male and female student representatives at opposite corners of the auditorium and sent a student supervisor back and forth to pass information between them. Because the students could not discuss the issue freely, female students from the Women's Normal School did not participate in the May Fourth demonstration. But that was the end of the seclusion of female students. On the night of May Fourth, students of the Women's Normal School ran to the Beiyang warlord government offices, demanding to be thrown in jail along with the male students who had been arrested during the day. From then on, female students in Beijing, and soon throughout the country, strode out of the seclusion of their schools to join the May Fourth movement. This was the beginning of educated Chinese women's social freedom to work shoulder to shoulder with men.[35]

For the female students in Shanghai, China's first open-port city, it was comparatively easy to break gender segregation. They joined the student movement at once, without any social pressure. When the Shanghai Students' Union was formed, twelve girls' schools joined, and three female teachers and eight female students worked with some men as leaders of the union. As Lu told us, while working in the students' union she was entrusted with highly visible jobs, including receiving prominent speakers. Contemporaries applauded gender integration in the student movement. An essay in the Shanghai newspaper *Shibao* [Eastern times] enthused:

> Since the beginning of the Shanghai Students' Union, men and women have worked together. They are efficient at organizing meetings, and outsiders have nothing to gossip about. This shows there is only benefit, and no disadvantage, when educated men and women work together. Now there are many things to be done, some of which men can do well and some of which women can do well. At this moment, men should not look down upon women, and women should not be too polite. If the boundary between men and women gradually disappears, each can fulfill his or her duty. This is progress for our country.[36]

35. All-China Women's Federation, *Zhongguo funü yundong shi*, 71–72.
36. *Shibao*, October 14, 1919.

Female students in the movement were conscious of the gender dimension of their patriotic activities. For them, participation in the movement meant not only saving the nation but also claiming equal status for women. Therefore, they insisted on doing everything that male students did, including being beaten up by the police and arrested. When students went to petition the Beiyang warlord government in October 1919, four female student representatives from Tianjin were captured by the police. The police decided to let the women go. But the four women followed them to the police station, declaring that they wanted to stay with male students who had also been captured and wait for the verdict.[37] In another case, when Tianjin female representative Liu Qingyang was arrested, a director of the police station wanted to release her right away because he and Liu were both ethnic Hui. But she declined, saying, "Men and women are both citizens. [Women] should endure what men must endure. I would be willing to die in the police station." When the director asked Liu's brother to persuade her to go home, she replied, "This is the first time we women have worked for society. [We] should never walk a step behind men. Even if it means death, we should be included. We representatives must set an example for the women of our country so that we will not be looked down upon by men in the future. Brother, I don't think you would like to see me become a sinful person in the eyes of ten thousand generations of women in order to seek temporary comfort."[38]

The May Fourth women's gender awareness had been heightened by the New Culture feminist agitation that preceded the May Fourth Incident, and it was carried to a new height in the May Fourth student movement. Lu Lihua, like many students of that generation, became aware of the New Culture wave during the May Fourth movement. She learned the term *nüquan* (feminism, or women's rights) when she joined two feminist organizations, the Feminist Movement Association and the Women's Suffrage Association, both of which were established in October 1922. The establishment of these feminist organizations in many big cities marked the peak of New Cultural feminism.

But the large-scale organized feminist movement of the early 1920s did not last long, and most people thought that the movement was of little consequence. As discussed in chapter 2, male advocates of feminism thought

37. *Yishibao*, October 4, 1919.
38. *Yishibao*, August 29, 1919. For more on Liu Qingyang's life, see Vera Schwarcz, *Time for Telling Truth Is Running Out* (New Haven: Yale University Press, 1992).

the women's movement had merely made loud noises without achieving solid goals. Lu's account confirms the point that women's organized activities at the time were mostly limited to making speeches and holding meetings. However, as Lu's story tells us, those activities were meaningful to women such as Lu. It is significant that Lu mentioned her feminist activities when she was recalling the oppression and injustice she had experienced in her youth. She said with indignation, "I used to ask myself why women were abused like this. But to whom could I speak? All we could do was organize societies, and it was good even just to advocate ideas." Making speeches and declarations was important to these women. They felt that society was unjust to women and that it needed to be educated about new ideas. Holding meetings was a method of empowerment. Women who fought hard battles alone in society felt inspired and encouraged by those meetings, which reiterated feminist ideas as well as gathering like-minded women. Thus, in circulating feminist ideas by women and for women, the women's organizations of the early 1920s provided emotional and psychological support to women like Lu. That is why Lu joined all kinds of women's organizations in Shanghai.

Certainly, Lu joined women's organizations not just for psychological consolation. She was also consciously pursuing women's equal rights. She herself had keenly experienced and witnessed women's oppression. In her own words, "What most irritated me was hearing about cases of abused women." She emphasized that what she did all her life was for women's rights and physical education. She was careful not to become involved with either the GMD or the CCP. But she was willing to join any organization that worked for women. Although she does not use the term to identify herself, it seems quite appropriate to say that Lu is a feminist, *nüquanzhuyizhe*, a woman who pursued women's rights.

As a matter of fact, Lu fits quite well the model of emancipated women created by the New Culture liberal feminist discourse. She received a secondary education, had a career, lived independently, was free to choose a spouse and free to divorce, and participated in social activities. She was certainly a new woman of early-twentieth-century China. It is important to note that in 1919, when she designed her future career in the new cultural and intellectual waves, she was not at all inhibited by the fact that she was a woman. Knowing that male leaders like Zhang Jian and Cai Yuanpei were taking the lead in industrial enterprise and education—two of the three important things for China—Lu decided that she would focus on the third thing, physical education. She made the decision with great ease and, of course, excitement. And she threw herself into the cause right away.

Her remarkable confidence calls for close examination. Her blindness to gender barriers can be explained in two ways. First, the social environment at the time encouraged young women to establish their own careers, as rapid social, cultural, and economic transformations opened up new horizons. Second, Lu had always thought, or at least hoped, that she could achieve as much as men did because her earliest role models were Hua Mulan and other martial heroines.

Lu's narrative and several other women's narratives have a common and telling point: in recalling significant episodes in their lives, they all stress that they admired Hua Mulan when they were young. Obviously, this role model influenced their personal development. In other words, Lu and other new women of twentieth-century China were inspired initially by ancient legendary figures that had been popularized in Chinese culture for centuries. The cultural tradition, after all, was not entirely negative in its influence on women. Heroines like Hua Mulan were eulogized in both elite and folk literature. Although these eulogies emphasized loyalty and filial piety (Mulan joined the army so that her aged father did not have to go), no one could overlook the obvious gender implications—women were capable of achieving great military deeds, just like men. Moreover, when these heroines clad in men's armor performed martial arts even better than men, their manly behavior was not feared but admired by everyone, including men. When it came to serving the country or fulfilling one's filial duty, the gender boundary was blurred. In a sense, the category of *nüyingxiong* (heroines) in Chinese culture constituted a special position that allowed women to cross the gender boundary. Or, to put it the other way around, women who wanted to cross the gender boundary could aspire to become heroines. Not every woman throughout Chinese history had the opportunity to become a heroine, even if she had the aspiration. But the 1911 Revolution and the May Fourth movement offered many early-twentieth-century women the opportunity to become heroines by fighting for their country. Qiu Jin, whom Lu also admired, became the number one heroine in this way. When May Fourth came, Lu knew that this was her moment. Thus, ancient heroines provided a cultural precondition for the rise of the new women of the twentieth century.

However, these new women could not be the same as the ancient heroines they admired. Ancient heroines had crossed the gender boundary to fulfill their duty to their parents or to their families. They did not attempt to enter political and social life as women, but instead played men's roles temporarily, out of necessity. Once they accomplished their task, they resumed their former domestic roles. As the "Ballad of Mulan" shows, Mu-

lan declined the high court position offered by the emperor (who was unaware of Mulan's true sex) and returned home to live a woman's life.
Significantly, once Mulan entered the domestic setting of her home, she
changed into female clothes. Created as she was by pens of literary men,
this heroine had a fine sense of propriety. She knew she could not appear in
the emperor's court as a woman. There was no permanent place for heroines in the ancient men's world, though women's heroic deeds were highly
praised by men. Fulfilling a man's duties did not help women gain equal
rights with men; equal rights was a concept unknown to ancient heroines.

The new women of the twentieth century were also invited to cross the
gender boundary in performing patriotic deeds. But they were far less eager to cross back. These new women were acquainted with Western liberalism and feminism, and they found in the concepts of human rights and
gender equality a new justification to remain in the public arena. Or, to be
more exact, women of the early twentieth century joined the nationalist
cause in order to break the gender boundary. They saw their ability to fight
alongside men as proof of their qualifications to be citizens of the modern
nation. This point was stressed repeatedly by women activists from Qiu Jin
on. Logically, once they had accomplished their patriotic tasks, they expected
to be treated as full citizens.

The story of women's participation in the 1911 Revolution and the formation of women's suffrage organizations right after the fall of the Qing
dynasty demonstrates the emergence of modern Chinese heroines.[39] But
modern heroines' new vision of women's rights clashed with the traditional
gender expectation held even by many male revolutionary leaders. In January 1912, the revolutionary army headquarters issued a decree to disband
the women's military fighting corps all over the country. Seeing that their
military contribution was no longer needed, women warriors and rescuers
turned to suffrage. On February 20, 1912, five women's organizations
formed the Women's Suffrage Alliance in Nanjing, with a membership of
about two hundred. But one frustration after another awaited them. The
provisional constitution issued on March 11 failed to mention women's suffrage. In August the bill on congressional elections issued by the Yuan Shikai
government did not give women the right to vote or to be elected. In the
same month, the newly formed Nationalist Party (GMD) deleted the phrase

---

39. According to a survey, in the 1911 Revolution there were more than 380
women activists recorded by name, including the ones fighting for women's suffrage after 1911. See *Jinian Xinhai geming qishi zhounian xueshu taolunhui lunwenji* [Papers from the conference on the seventeenth anniversary of the Xinhai Rev-
olution] (Beijing: Zhonghua shuju, 1983), 2019.

"gender equality" from the party program, a regression from the program of the Revolutionary Alliance. The Women's Suffrage Alliance fought hard, but against heavy odds. Finally, in January 1913, the Department of Internal Affairs of the Yuan Shikai government ordered it to be dissolved.[40]

The short-lived suffrage movement illustrates several interesting points. First, revolution gives rise to high expectations. The women who joined the 1911 Revolution believed that the fall of the Qing dynasty would move the nation and women into an age of democracy. Before she died in 1907, Qiu Jin had a vision of gender equality, although she offered no concrete plans for women's rights. But by the end of 1911, many women revolutionaries seized on suffrage as the first step to achieving gender equality. The impact of revolution was inflated in the eyes of those whose lives had been changed by it.

Second, the Chinese women's suffrage movement was a part of the international suffrage movements in the sense that the former was stimulated and shaped by the latter. Chinese suffragists were not only familiar with the development of the international suffrage movements but also had direct contact with them. The Women's Social and Political Union, which led a militant campaign for women's votes in England, sent a telegraph to the Chinese Women's Suffrage Alliance in March 1912. The English suffragists were excited by the Chinese suffragists' actions, and they encouraged the Chinese suffragists to "create a new century for women all over the world as well as a paradigm for all the civilized nations."[41] Carrie Chapman Catt, president of the International Woman Suffrage Association (IWSA), and two other members of that association visited Shanghai, Nanjing, Tianjin, and Beijing in September 1912, giving speeches at every stop. The one-month visit was publicized by newspapers in China, and these international suffragists were reportedly "welcomed widely by Chinese women."[42] Because Chinese women knew of the long struggle for women's suffrage in Western democratic countries, and because they were impressed

40. All-China Women's Federation, *Zhongguo funü yundong shi*, 54–58. Shanghai Women's Federation, *Shanghai funü yundong shi*, 31. Croll, *Feminism and Socialism in China*, chapter 3.

41. Wang Jiajian, "Minchu de nüzi canzheng yundong" [The women's suffrage movement in the early republic], in *Zhongguo funüshi lunwenji* [Collection of essays on Chinese women's history], ed. Li Yu-ning and Zhang Yufa, vol. 2 (Taibei: Taiwan Commercial Press, 1988), 590.

42. Ibid., 598. The meeting of the leading international suffragists and Chinese suffragists was also recorded in a group portrait. The Chinese suffragists' involvement in the international suffrage movement continued even after the movement was suppressed at home. A picture of the 1913 IWSA Congress at Budapest shows

by the examples of daring and persistent international suffragists, Chinese modern heroines dared to demand equal political rights as soon as the republic was founded. Many Chinese militant suffragists saw it a necessary and urgent strategy to press the National Council to accept women's suffrage while the new constitution was being written. And yet, despite being informed by the experiences of international suffrage movements, the Chinese suffrage movement could not move beyond its own sociopolitical context. The intense power struggles after the collapse of the empire resulted in the rise of the warlord power and realignment of political forces. Perhaps nothing could be further removed from the concerns of those who were shuffling the political cards than women's right to vote. When feminism was still on the fringe of intellectual and political discourse in China, the small number of suffragists faced too many powerful adversaries to make much progress toward their goal.

Third, although they did not achieve their goal, the suffragists signaled the emergence of the new women—modern heroines who demanded a legitimate place in the public arena. In order to achieve independence, many suffragists became seriously engaged in their careers, running a school, a hospital, or a company, and their struggle to challenge the gender barriers continued even after suffrage failed. The effort and example of this first generation of modern heroines made it possible for young women such as Lu Lihua to confidently anticipate a career. In Lu's narrative, it is clear that she was very conscious of the contribution these early feminists made. "They should be praised in historical writing," she emphasized. Those women had served as her early role models.

In sharp contrast to the weak voice of suffragists in 1912, the New Culture feminist discourse reached a much larger audience—the rapidly growing female student body—and women's rights became the hot issue of the day. The upsurge of the feminist movement, like the heyday of the suffrage movement, was short-lived. This time, women's collective efforts to remove gender barriers were not suppressed by the warlord government but co-opted by a rising political power—the alliance of the GMD and the newly founded CCP. Even after women's feminist concerns were diverted to the nationalist cause, many feminist activists continued their struggle, as Lu Li-

---

a banner with Chinese characters on the stage where Carries Chapman Catt was presiding. The Chinese characters read, *"Tongxin gongji"* (Sharing our common experience in unity). Both pictures are printed in Adele Schreiber and Margaret Mathieson, *Journey Towards Freedom: Written for the Golden Jubilee of the International Alliance of Women* (Copenhagen: International Alliance of Women, 1955).

hua's case shows. Lu summarizes her life this way: "Everything I did was for women's rights and physical education." Because she was only briefly involved in the organized feminist movement of the 1920s, she does not see her fight for women's rights as limited to that short period of nationwide activity. As a matter of fact, her life illustrates the point that women like Lu pursued the feminist cause by devoting themselves to their individual careers rather than to an organized women's movement. Lu's devotion to women's physical education epitomizes the new women's struggle to break gender barriers in society by means of individual effort. In other words, the New Culture liberal feminist discourse constructed a new female subjectivity that continued its vitality even when an organized feminist movement dwindled in the altered political environment.

Even so, the new women's individual struggle against gender oppression was difficult and often painful. As Lu emphasizes, "As soon as I started my school, I realized it was hard to be a woman." The agony Lu experienced shows vividly the dilemma of the new women. They wanted to be independent, but they faced a cultural norm that was unprepared to accept independent women in public. Moreover, they entered a men's world and had to enlist support from men in powerful positions in order to get things done. As a result, any woman with a successful career exposed herself to slander by people who charged that she achieved her goals because she gave sexual favors to men. Being accused of such loose sexual behavior was the worst attack that any Chinese woman could endure. Even the new women were far from being sexually liberated in this respect. As Lu says, "A bad reputation was the heaviest blow." In my interviews, Lu did not use explicit language to describe those sexual charges against her. Over half a century later it was still too painful to mention them. But another interviewee told me of the gossip she heard about Lu in the 1920s and 1930s. Rumor was that Lu danced with men in order to get funding for her school, that she slept with two other men before her marriage, and that her relationship with other men before her marriage caused such distress to her husband that he died not long after they married.

This gossip, and Lu's attitudes toward the gossip as well toward her own sexual life, are telling comments on the sexual norms in Shanghai in the 1920s and 1930s. Given the New Culturalists' concerted attack on the traditional sexual morality and their efforts to promote new concepts of freedom to love, marry, and divorce, women of Lu's generation obviously had more freedom in socializing with men, choosing their own spouses, and getting a divorce. By her own account, Lu had sexual relationships with three men at different periods of her life. But the gossip about her shows that even though women could divorce, doing so was perceived negatively by the public. A sexual relationship outside marriage was also perceived negatively. Lu herself internalized those negative views even though she was oppressed by them. In the first interview, she only mentioned her second marriage. In the follow-up interview, when she began to talk about the other two men in her life, she nevertheless remarked, "Those were not good things in people's eyes."

Apparently, the sexual double standard was far from being destroyed by the New Culturalists. As Lu said indignantly, "If a woman divorced once and wanted to marry again, it was a big deal and she was heavily criticized. But a man could have three or four wives." The traditional concept of chastity was still embraced as a key virtue in women and posed a serious obstacle to new women's social advancement. Career women had to live in the public eye, which scrutinized them constantly. Informed by the New Culture feminism, new women believed that they should have the freedom to divorce and the freedom to pursue love. But once they exercised those freedoms, public opinion accused them of being immoral. In other words, new women were still measured against the traditional sexual morality. If they failed to reach the standards set for virtuous women, their reputations suffered, which eventually hurt their careers. According to Lu, many women quit their careers because they were unable to endure this "heaviest blow" of all. Understandably, the conflict between the new vision of gender equality in all aspects of life and the old reality of sexual oppression created tremendous tension in the lives of new women.

Although the road into the men's world was full of hidden mines because a career woman's relationship with men could easily explode into a scandal in public, Lu persevered in her career. She became a prominent career woman in Shanghai, which means she dealt with men quite successfully. Without powerful social connections, anyone—woman or man—would find it almost impossible to achieve what she did. In fact, the board of her school was packed with powerful and wealthy men: Pan Gongzhan, the director of GMD headquarters in Shanghai, and Zhang Gongquan, Qian Xingzhi, and Chen Guangfu, three rich bankers in Shanghai.[43] Those connections made her suspect to the Communists after 1949. But her ability to

43. The three bankers are mentioned in her autobiography in *Shanghai wenshi yanjiuguan guanyuan zhuanlue* [Biographies and autobiographies of members of the Shanghai Wenshiguan] (Shanghai: Shanghai Wenshiguan, 1990), 2: 144. Pan Gongzhan was mentioned by her nephew who was present at one interview. Because Pan was a GMD leader, Lu apparently did not want to mention him in her autobiography.

use powerful social connections did not mean that she herself was in a powerful position. After the Communist Party drove her out of her own school, she came to the painful realization that she was a woman all alone. Certainly, her ties to the GMD worked to her disadvantage in the changed political environment. But even with ties in the Communist Party (such as she had through people like Deng Yingchao), it is doubtful that she would have been able to keep her school. The woman who replaced her as principal was the wife of a big shot in the National People's Congress. That is why Lu said poignantly, "If I had had support in high places, I would not have fallen into this bad situation!" She lacked a powerful husband or a powerful father, which means she had no access to the male-dominated power structure that could have eased her situation.

Nevertheless, a career woman like Lu played an important role in the social transformation in the years before 1949. She founded a women's basketball team and led the team to Japan and Southeast Asia; she collected funds to build a women's physical education school that was regarded as "the best physical education school in the Far East;" and she changed Chinese women's sports outfits from long-sleeved shirts and "bloomers" to short-sleeved shirts with turndown collars and shorts, which consequently changed public attitudes toward "immodest" clothing for women. She stresses that it was always her conviction that "whatever foreigners have, we should have too." This phrase sounds very much like the rhetoric of the 1990s, and her pride in her quick adaptation to Western things reflects attitudes widespread in China during the 1990s, but her experience as a women's physical education promoter was indeed full of episodes in which she consciously emulated Western models. After all, making physical education a requirement in girls' schools and allowing women to participate in Western sports were regarded as modern phenomena that followed Western patterns. Therefore, Lu's life story is inseparable from the story of modernity in China. She presents a picture in which women like herself took the lead in changing Chinese women's behavioral norms and articulating visions of modernity in their social practices. Emulating the Western models, Lu and other career women achieved more than fulfilling the nationalist expectation of strengthening the nation. They created new niches for other women as well as for themselves in the rapidly changing urban society, and they strengthened their own elite position in the Westernizing metropolis.

Lu's role in the national salvation movement of the 1930s also illustrates another role played by the career women of her generation. In Shanghai and other big cities, many career women organized on their own for national salvation. The active and important role they took in mobilizing resources for the War of Resistance demonstrated that career women had become a prominent social group in the 1930s. In addition to expressing their patriotic sentiments, the scope of their efforts and achievements revealed their confidence in their own ability as well as in their social position.

Ironically, an accomplished and capable woman like Lu found no place under Communist rule, despite the government's claims that Chinese women have been liberated since 1949. In the republic, educated women of Lu's generation encountered powerful conservative forces that hindered their advancement, but they were nonetheless able to create social space for themselves. By contrast, in the Mao era, women had much easier access to equal education and career opportunities, but they also had much less freedom to take the initiative in activities supporting women's interests. Lu's comment at the end of her narrative is very significant. This ninety-four-year-old woman, an activist in her youth, sees clearly that although "women are half of the sky" (a famous Maoist phrase that suggests women's public role is equally important to men's), there was nevertheless little room in Mao's China for women's spontaneous activism. After the establishment of the Women's Federation as the official representative of women's interests, women in the Mao era had no means to raise issues beyond those already on the agenda of the Women's Federation. The only choice for women who wanted to be active was to identify with the official line. Lu's experience helps us to see the paradox of Chinese women's liberation under the CCP. Women in the People's Republic of China successfully moved into the public arena and achieved economic independence with the enforcement of the CCP Marxist line about women's emancipation. Although the state policy of gender equality (which reflected much of the May Fourth feminist agenda) enhanced women's—especially urban women's—social and economic status, women nevertheless gained less autonomy and freedom than Lu's generation to develop their own pursuits and raise their own voices. According to CCP theory, women's interests were supposed to be represented by the socialist state. But it is more accurate to say that women's interests were *defined* by the party-state, a role that the CCP assumed when it was born. The omnipresent state control limited both women's and men's initiative. It was that kind of initiative that enabled May Fourth women like Lu to play a dynamic role in the first half of the twentieth century. In that sense, the early Chinese women's movement owes much to the weakness of the republican state.

5   Zhu Su'e (1901–): Attorney

Zhu Su'e, 1933   Zhu Su'e, 1995

*Zhu Su'e welcomes me to her comfortable apartment, where she has lived
for sixty years. She is small in stature but has a big voice. Even at ninety-
four, she speaks distinctively and eloquently. Her mind is still quick and pre-
cise. She must have been a competent attorney in her prime. Beyond these
remarkable qualities, she amazes me with her resilience. She is a woman
who can laugh hard at the absurdities that made her life miserable.[1]*

NARRATIVE

I was not from a scholarly family. My father was a manager of a bank in
the city now called Changzhou, and my mother knew a few Chinese characters. My teacher was a *juren*.[2] My father was very open-minded, think-

---

1. The following narrative is constructed from interviews conducted on February 19, 1993, March 5, 1993, December 22, 1994, and January 7, 1995.
2. *Juren* refers to a successful candidate in the imperial examinations at the
provincial level in the Ming and Qing dynasties.

ing both girls and boys should get an education. I am the third child, born in 1901, and have seven siblings. My two elder sisters were both educated, but I was the only girl in the family to attend a university. One younger sister and one younger brother went to Indonesia in the 1930s to open schools there, and another younger brother studied in the United States and now lives there. My second sister, who is two years older than I, graduated from Changzhou Women's Normal School. My mother bound my sisters' feet—and mine, too—when we were young. But I refused to let mine stay bound. She bound them in the morning, and I took the wrapping off in the evening. That is why my feet are not small. I remember when I was about thirteen, my mother complained, "You don't want to wrap your feet. I just let you have your way. You can never be married out in the future!" I replied, "Fine! If I can't be married out, that will be fine. I will not eat your meals. I will support myself!"[3]

My father graduated from law school, so he was open-minded. When we were little, he sent my second sister, two younger brothers, and me to an old-style private school that was run in the *juren*'s own house. I was about seven or eight years old. Two servants accompanied us on the first day, bringing a pot of brown sugar tea and a red rug. We knelt on the red rug and kowtowed to the picture of Confucius and then to both the teacher and his wife. After that we served sugar tea to our classmates so that we would be harmonious and not quarrel. We read the Four Books and Five Classics alongside the boys. After one year, a spinster opened a girls' school, and my father sent us girls there. Our teacher was over thirty years old. Sometime after that—maybe it was already in the republican period—the government-run Women's Normal School of Wujing county was established. Other families were feudal and refused to send their children to a *yang xuetang* [Western-style school] because they feared children would learn bad things. But my father was open-minded, and he quickly sent my sister and me to that public school. The school system was like this: four years of primary school, three years of higher primary school, one year of preparatory courses, and four years of normal school. We had to take an examination when we entered the Women's Normal School. It was a fill-in-the-blank exam: we had to supply two characters that had been omitted from a four-

3. The Chinese exogamous marriage system gave rise to gender differentiated words for "marry." When a woman marries a man, this is called *jia* (marrying out), which connotes that a woman leaves her natal home to move into her husband's home. When a man marries a woman, this is called *qu* (marrying in), which connotes that a man takes a woman into his home.

character phrase. After the exam, my sister and I were placed in the second grade. In third grade we began to take English, which was taught by a foreign woman who might have been a missionary. At that time there were a lot of missionaries. My uncle's whole family were taken to the United States by some ministers. A woman taught us Chinese. She was knowledgeable but fierce. Her fiancé had died, but she still had to marry into his family. She had actually married with a tablet that represented her husband.[4] That is why she developed a very odd temperament.

The students were all from scholarly or official families. Friends played at each other's homes and many of them had huge houses, some with thirteen gates, and pavilions in the big garden. Changzhou had numerous *jinshi* and *juren* and some *zhuangyuan*, too. It was no big deal to be a *xiucai*.[5] My schoolmates were all from scholarly families. Many of the children from scholarly families either joined the Communist Party or the Guomindang. Qu Qiubai's younger sister used to be my classmate.[6] It was because of my father's openness that I was able to go to school with girls from those kinds of families. My mother was very virtuous, and she took care of the household. Father made the decisions about our education.

My sister graduated from that normal school. She had twelve years of education, equal to a high school education. I didn't graduate from that school because my mother became ill. I was her favorite, so I dropped out of school for a few years to keep her company. It is not always good to be a favorite. After staying at home for a few years, I was unhappy. During that time I read father's books, which had to be dried in the sun during summer. He didn't allow us to read these books, so I stole them and read secretly in my mosquito net at night. Between thirteen and fourteen years old, I read all the old novels: *The Dream of the Red Chamber, The Water Margins, The Flowers in the Mirror, A Journey to the West, The Scholars,* and so on. My tears wet the pillow as I read. Father had very few Western novels; in those days, translated books were rare in the inland region.

I was not happy to stay at home while my sister continued at school. Once my teacher sent a letter to my parents, asking why I was still absent after

4. In other words, this was a proxy marriage. On proxy marriage, see Arthur P. Wolf, "Gods, Ghosts, and Ancestors," in *Religion in Chinese Society,* ed. A. P. Arthur (Stanford: Stanford University Press, 1974), 150–152.

5. *Jinshi* refers to a successful candidate in the highest imperial examinations. *Zhuangyuan* is a title conferred on the one who placed first in this highest imperial exam. *Xiucai* is a title for scholars who studied in schools at county or prefecture levels. The lowly *xiucai* occupies the bottom of the degree hierarchy.

6. Qu Qiubai (1899–1935) is one of the early CCP leaders.

all this time. My mother and sister tried to hide that letter from me, but I found it. After reading it, I cried. One year later, the student movement came along, and I decided to leave home. After the May Fourth movement and influenced by the New Culture, I thought I would not read these old books at home anymore. I wanted to leave town to study. I was kind of revolting against my family. I thought, "My sister is continuing her school and I am younger, so why should I accompany mother?" I did not think this was right. I decided to go to Shanghai to study in a boarding school. So I came to Shanghai and entered Aiguo nüzhong [the Patriotic Girls' School]. My sister graduated from the normal school and became a teacher there and then became a principal of a school. Later, in the War of Resistance against Japan, our whole family moved to Shanghai.

I am different from others in a way. I am quite stubborn. I saw in my relatives' families that all the men were oppressing women: oppressing their wives, pulling their hair, beating them, looking for other women on the side, staying out at night, and gambling or smoking opium. I have two aunts, my mother's younger sisters. Both married into good families whose houses had four big leaf-doors with a stone lion at the front gate. A *zhuangyuan*'s house could have a stone lion. *Bangyan* and *tanhua* had no lion but a stone of round shape, and those just below that rank had a rectangular stone.[7] There were three kinds of stones to mark the different ranks. Although my aunts' husbands were from prestigious families, they gambled, smoked opium, and fooled around with other women. The two aunts often came to my mother to cry. My mother had my father, who was an honest and upright man. For example, when we finished dinner, we were supposed to put our stools back under the table. If a stool was not put in its correct position, he would fix it himself. I saw him do so. My father always disciplined my brothers, but he was lenient to us girls. He said that, without discipline, a child would not become an upright person. When I saw my aunts' troubles, I could not help wondering why women should be oppressed and abused. Weren't they human beings, too? The Qing feudal system continued, and women were still oppressed. After crying, I said to myself, "No, that is not right. Why should women be bullied?" That is why I chose to study law. What is the use of law? To protect *nüquan* [women's rights]; *shenzhang nüquan* [to promote women's rights].

In the May Fourth period I did not know much yet. My sister and Shi

---

7. *Bangyan* and *tanhua* are titles conferred on the ones who ranked second and third places in the highest imperial examination.

Liang were one grade higher than I was.[8] I remember they stood on benches and gave speeches. At that time in our city, only students gave speeches in the streets. There were no other activities. After the May Fourth movement, the New Culture was the most important. It reformed Chinese written language and criticized feudalism. I learned the word *nüquan* from reading new magazines after the May Fourth movement. I don't remember the names of those magazines. I think that after the May Fourth movement, there was mainly the New Cultural Movement, and not a women's movement. When I learned about the new ideas, I wanted others to stop controlling my life. Mother was keeping me at home: my sister had already graduated from the normal school, yet I had only finished higher primary school. After so many years of fulfilling my duty, I did not want to stay at home anymore. I decided to leave home to study, so nobody could control me. That is how I came to Shanghai in the fall of 1919—all because those magazines made me feel Changzhou was a small place, and I wanted to see the big world.

My parents supported me financially. My mother loved me. I remember I took two hundred silver dollars with me to Shanghai and stayed at a cousin's home for a few days while I took the entrance exams. When I was accepted by the Patriotic Girls' School, I went home to get my luggage. I remember having my quilt in one bundle and other things in a string bag as I boarded the train back to school. At that time porters would help you put your luggage away. When I got to Shanghai, I took a pedicab directly to the school. Each term I paid about one hundred silver dollars for all the expenses. The school provided room and board. After graduating from the Patriotic Girls' School, I attended an art school in Suzhou for a year. I loved calligraphy and painting. But then I saw that artists were all poor, so I decided I should not choose that as my career, because if I did, I would never achieve economic independence and would always have to rely on others. At the time I did not think I would get married; I just wanted to be independent. So in order to achieve that independence, I chose a career in law.

Then I entered university, Shanghai Law College. I studied there for four years. There were only a few female students at the time. One of my female classmates was the daughter of my professor Peng who taught bankruptcy law. Her name is Peng Qingxiu. Another was the daughter of the owner of a big pharmacy called Shanghai East and West Pharmacy. Her name was Zhou Wenji. Another student was called Yin Jin; another was Du Yuying.

8. Shi Liang was a famous lawyer and a leading figure in the National Salvation Association, which called for a united front to resist the Japanese invasion. She became the first minister of justice in the People's Republic of China.

Including me, there were five female students in our class—more than other classes, which had only one or two.

There were some female law students who had graduated earlier than I did. One who graduated two years earlier than I did became a big shot later, Shi Liang. Qian Jianqiu also graduated earlier.[9] Later she worked in the women's movement with me. I was among the third or forth group of female graduates. I might be in the second generation of female lawyers. I thought studying law was always right. Law is to protect *renquan* [human rights]. I saw too many men oppress women, which provoked me. I thought that the feudal oppression should be overthrown. I had no way to overthrow a state and a government. But to achieve men's and women's equal rights in the family, that was feasible. Back then I just had this little idea, no big ideas yet. I just hoped to become a lawyer. If anyone violated women's rights, I could debate against him. When men oppress women, we women should stand up to say something for women. That was what I thought.

I read a lot. In my high school we had many books and magazines. My papers were often posted on the wall—few students got their papers selected for the wall. I made a mistake to study law as my career; I should have become a writer. That way, after 1949 I could have stayed at home and written novels. I would have published several books. I chose the wrong major for myself. I just thought that if I was a lawyer, I could protect women's rights. I did not know my career would end in 1949. It was too short.

I graduated in 1930 and began to practice law. Of my female classmates, Zhou went to Hangzhou to become a judge, and Ying and Peng both married classmates. Their husbands practiced law, but they did not. Only Du and I became lawyers. I was in Shanghai, and Du went to Songjiang. I joined the Shanghai Lawyers' Union, which had over one thousand lawyers as members. I accepted all cases, but mostly women sought my help, usually because they were being oppressed and bullied. Even women from Beijing came to me. The daughter-in-law of a member of the Beijing Supervisory Committee came to me because her husband oppressed her and her parents-in-law bullied her. She came crying at my door. I mediated this case finally.

I got married when I was about thirty years old, which is late. But when we were in school, it was different: most students married late. People with knowledge are different; they can't be controlled by parents. If you arrange

---

9. Qian Jianqiu was a longtime friend of Zhu. Qian went to Taiwan in 1949 and was the director of the Committee on Women's Work in the Central Committee of the GMD in 1960s. The women's movement both Qian and Zhu worked in was the one led by the GMD.

marriage for me, I will escape. But my second sister failed to resist her arranged marriage. The matchmaker told us nothing at all about the man, who was in Beijing; she just showed us his picture. When my sister finally saw the real person, she disliked him. My parents also regretted the arrangement. When someone from the man's family came to pursue this marriage, my father pounded the table and said, "Go to the *yamen* [county court] to carry her!"[10] But the matchmaker said, "If you break the engagement, your daughter will be the loser." Thus we had to honor the agreement, and my sister was carried away in the sedan chair in that kind of situation. This event made a lasting impression on me. That is why I married late. Wait a little bit, pick and choose: I had many classmates. In those days, when there were so few female students at the university, male students often smiled and slipped a note into your desk drawer. When you waited for a bus, he would wait for the same bus, too. The next day he would write a letter to you. I ignored all those approaches. None of the male students interested me. How you dealt with that kind of situation depended on your ability. I avoided that kind of thing and married late. Many of my classmates paired and divorced shortly afterwards. Both Peng and Ying ended up that way.

After I left home for school in Shanghai, my parents did not dare interfere with my life. They arranged my sisters' marriages, but not mine. I returned home only on vacations and stayed just a short while. They knew that if they tried matchmaking for me, I would never visit home. They knew my personality, so they did not even try. I got married after I graduated from college. My husband was a doctor who had been to Southeast Asian countries. I got to know my husband through a friend. I had been a teacher for a while. I just taught a two-hour class on Chinese every week in the Wuguang Girls' School while I was in college, but later, when I was practicing law, I became principal of the school and joined the Education Association. He joined in the association, too, after he returned from Singapore, and we knew each other for several years before we decided to get married. We informed our parents, and they attended our wedding. Even though I was an adult, my parents still asked me if he was a reliable man and what kind of family background he had.

When I got married, my parents gave me a big dowry. It included sixteen quilts, eight trunks full of clothing for four seasons, and sets of jewelry. A dowry of only two trunks was all a poor family could provide; marrying off a daughter could cost a third of a family's fortune. And my parents

---

10. By traditional custom, the bride was carried to the bridegroom's home in a sedan chair. Here, Zhu's father showed his readiness for a lawsuit.

had four daughters! When the grandchildren were born, my parents also had to give sets of clothes, hats, and shoes. Jiangsu people all had this custom. My three sisters also got the same dowry, about several thousand silver dollars for each of us. The youngest one went abroad soon after her wedding, so she did not want her dowry. The man's family also had to give betrothal gifts, about two or three thousand silver dollars, including jewelry. I was an enlightened person because of the student movement, so I did not accept betrothal gifts, which was quite different from my two elder sisters. I just accepted rings. My husband's family was quite rich and was also from Changzhou.

After graduation my schoolmate Qian Jianqiu went to America and got a Ph.D. She became a lawyer when she came back home and married an overseas Chinese. I worked with her in the national salvation movement. Before liberation she asked me to go to Taiwan with her, but I did not go. I joined Guomindang in 1928, when I was in my third year at the university. Both parties were trying to recruit students. Guomindang was led by Sun Zhongshan and had overthrown the Qing dynasty. There was nothing wrong about that, and it was in power. The Communist Party did not have much influence yet. We heard many rumors about the Communist Party, such as they share property and wives. Several of my classmates and I joined Guomindang, and because I joined as a student, there was a stamp on my diploma that entitled me to the position of *zhifu* [prefecture magistrate] if I wanted to be an official. The position was higher than the county magistrate. I worked for Guomindang first, and then He Xiangning urged us to join the second United Front. I worked with He in the second United Front, but I worked with Qian in the Guomindang-led national salvation movement. The situation back then was different. After the Japanese were defeated, the Communists and Nationalists failed to achieve a peaceful agreement, which left a small potato like me out of luck. Ever since 1949, I have been asked to stay at home. I was only forty-eight years old then, and the legal retirement age for intellectuals was fifty-five. At the time of liberation I was extremely popular. I was the principal of Wuguang Girls' School. Lawyers could be principals while practicing the law. I was the head of the Women's Association and on the board of many women's organizations. But just at the prime of my life, I was forced to take a break. The rest of my life was wasted, until 1983. The Educational Bureau of the new government took over all the schools after 1949, so I was unemployed. In 1953 I was under surveillance. Then in 1955 I was arrested; two years later, I was released.

I have two children. My husband was a doctor of internal medicine. I got married in 1930 and had my first child three years later. Both my husband and I had our careers, so we hired a wet nurse to take care of the baby. I have a daughter and a son, and each of them had a wet nurse. When they were weaned, we found baby-sitters for them. We had two female servants and a male chauffeur. One female servant did the cooking and washing, the other cleaned the house and took care of the kids. Our income was enough to pay for all this. We had a car, which rusted in the street after liberation. We had several houses, including my husband's clinic.

My income from law practice was pretty good. But I was different from other lawyers. I did not charge poor clients. Some defense attorneys would not go to the court without being paid, charging two hundred silver dollars for each court appearance. I never did anything like that. Shi Liang was not that way either; when she defended Communists, she charged only thirty silver dollars per case. I joined a group of volunteers from our lawyers' union. If the accused did not have the money to hire a lawyer, the court would appoint one from this volunteer group. I often did pro bono work this way. I would go to the court so long as a case seemed reasonable, just, and winnable, even if I had to pay for my own transportation. If the client was from a rich family and had a car, I would charge. The fees were regulated by the lawyers' union. For example, the counseling fee was one hundred silver dollars a year, or, in some cases, fifty silver dollars. I did legal counseling, too. Some of my old classmates asked me to be legal counselor for their businesses, and I agreed to do so free of charge They were your old classmates and you could not charge them. Sometimes, a friend would ask me to be the legal witness of her marriage, and I could not charge her a fee. In another case, a friend was abused by her husband and asked me for my certificate of legal counselor. I just signed a certificate for her without charge. She framed it and hung it on the wall in her home. When her husband knew that she had a legal counselor, he did not dare abuse her anymore. I was quite unique in the sense that I did not charge for each service. That was why even women from Beijing would come to see me. I was a board member for many women's organizations, and many women came to ask for my help when they were oppressed. They were beaten by their husbands or mothers-in-law, and they had no income themselves. How could I charge them? I could only do all I could to help them because they had such miserable lives. I ended up doing voluntary work often. Anyway, our family income was pretty good, and I could afford to work pro bono. Moreover, the pay for domestic servants was much lower than it is today. Today, servants are paid more than intellectuals. We intellectuals are downgraded.

Most of the cases I accepted were civil law suits—property disputes and the like. In the past, women had no share in the family property. All property left by parents went to the sons, not to the daughters. Also, in cases involving divorce or division of family property before the parents' death, women would usually be taken advantage of. As a lawyer who *shenzhang nüquan* [promoted women's rights], I represented women in those cases. Normally I would have both sides come to my office to mediate first. If we failed to reach an agreement, then we would go to court. So my law firm was very busy.

In the 1930s I had my own law firm. I rented an office in a big building and went there to work every day. I left my home in the care of the nanny. People learned about my firm from newspapers. We lawyers did not advertise; instead, we printed a statement in newspapers when we agreed to be legal counselors for businesses. I did everything all by myself. I was independent and did not rely on anyone. I had an equal relationship with my husband. I wouldn't have married him if he had been an old-fashioned man, or if he had been a high official; I would never be a *taitai*. We were equal. We went to work every morning and came home every evening. Our children were taken care of by nannies. He never had the idea that he earned enough money so that I should stay at home. For us, the man had his career, the woman had her career, and neither relied on the other. When he met me, I was already a career woman, so he was used to that. In the old society, women who did not have their own careers had to rely on men; even buying a needle required dependence on men's income. I understood that you must be able to earn money in order to be independent; I had seen my aunts and their husbands, and I knew that in the feudal society, women all depended on men. I didn't think it was right, and that is why I came to Shanghai to study and learn law. Of course, not many women of my generation did as I did. My grandson's teacher saw information about me on the form that describes his family background and was surprised, "What? Your parents are both college-educated, and your grandparents are both college-educated! You must be extremely intelligent." Actually we are not especially bright, we just had a college education.

My schoolmate Qian Jianqiu became a member of the Nationalist central committee in Taiwan. She and I worked together during the War of Resistance. We mobilized women to work for the War of Resistance, so women's work was included in the war effort. We ran the magazine *Zhongguo funü* [Chinese women] in 1938, but we stopped after 1941 when the Japanese occupied international concessions in Shanghai. Qian was hunted by the Japanese, and she hid in my home. She was a filial daughter. One day she decided to go home to see her old mother and was arrested by the Japanese. She was loyal to her friends and did not sell anyone out. I tried hard to rescue her. She was later released. When the victory came in 1945, Qian became the top leader of the Women's Association, and I was second to the top.

I met Liu Wang-liming in those meetings of the Women's Association. She was in the women's movement, and I worked for both the salvation movement and the women's movement. I was in the party, but she was non-partisan. That is why her organization failed to develop and was restricted to the Christian group. In the Women's National Salvation Alliance she was insignificant and had no leading position. Later she stopped coming to meetings and asked a young woman Chen to attend instead. So the history she wrote about the women's movement was not comprehensive and too narrow in scope. She just wrote from her own experience. After China won the War of Resistance, the women's movement developed quickly. During the four years before 1949, the women's movement increased on a grand and spectacular scale.

During this period the municipal headquarters of Guomindang had a committee on the women's movement that occupied a big office with many desks. Mainly we ran vocational schools. I thought there were too few women's vocational schools, so I wanted to establish one. The Educational Bureau approved the proposal, but then liberation came. The goal of the committee on the women's movement was to unite women and obtain political power. In the early thirties I went to Nanjing with several women members of Guomindang to petition the government for more seats for women in the National Congress. Because the War of Resistance broke out shortly thereafter, the petition came to nothing, and I joined the war effort. After the war was over, I became a councilor in the Shanghai government. Guomindang wanted to hold another National Congress and elect the legislature, and the Women's Association was allowed to send women representatives to the Congress. Many of my female friends were running to be representatives to the congress or as candidates for the legislature; because the quota in the Women's Association was filled up, I ran as a candidate for the legislature in the lawyers' union. The candidates had to be approved by the Central Organization Department of the party. I sneaked to Nanjing to check if my name was approved. A friend of mine working there told me that my name was on the candidate list, but in the end I did not get the seat. I lost to another woman candidate, Fang, who was also in our lawyers' union. There was only one seat for women. She had not thought of running for the legislature at first. But after seeing me running for office successfully, her family encouraged her to run for it, too. She was from Ningbo with ties to people from Fenghua.[11] So she used personal connections to the concubines of the big shots. I did not have that kind of connections, and I would not have used them even if I had had them. I worked hard during the War of Resistance, volunteering my time and effort and donating a lot of money. I ran for the position and wanted to be involved in politics because I was patriotic. If I hadn't been, I would not have wanted to participate in politics, because I disdained the corrupt government. I just relied on my votes, and many people voted for me: the votes from Wuxi lawyers' union were all for me. I did not use inside connections. I am an upright person. That is why I did not go to Taiwan with the Nationalists in 1949.

The May Fourth movement was mainly students giving speeches in public. It did not last long. Then came the New Culture Revolutionary Movement—they dropped the word "revolutionary" later. When the New Culture movement began, many magazines appeared. I came to Shanghai under the influence of the New Culture movement. I wanted to see the world. In Changzhou, there were few new magazines; but in Shanghai, there was no restriction on your life, especially when parents could no longer control you. The New Cultural movement made me decide to go to university. High school was not enough. Feeling that I lacked knowledge, I decided that at least I had to finish college. At the time I did not dare to think of going abroad. Not everyone had the opportunity to go abroad. I was just thinking about what university to attend. Art? No future development. Chinese? Every one knows Chinese. Foreign language? It did not seem so important at the time. The most important thing was to overthrow feudalism. I believed in Sun Zhongshan's *sanmin zhuyi* [Three Principles of the People], and I could recite "The Will of Sun Zhongshan."[12]

The women's movement began after the May Fourth era. Without Guomindang there would be no women's movement. Would the Qing dynasty let you have a women's movement? When the War of Resistance broke out, more women's organizations came into being. Guomindang established an office to register the new organizations. The Social Bureau of the municipal government would send a woman representative to attend the founding ceremony of each women's organization. I was the head of one organization, Zhonghua Funü Guofanghui [Chinese Women's National Defense

11. Fenghua was Chiang Kai-shek's hometown.
12. The Three Principles of the People are nationalism, democracy, and people's livelihood. They were formulated by Sun Yat-sen as the basis of GMD ideology. "The Will of Sun Zhongshan" is a famous political document that Sun left to his party.

Association]. Each organization sent one representative to attend the meetings for representatives from all women's organizations in Shanghai. The representatives were all equal. Later, when He Xiangning came to Shanghai, she suggested we form a Shanghai branch of Funü Weilaohui [the Women's Consolation Society].[13] She was a senior woman, so we let her be our leader, even though she did not represent any organization. She relied on us because we were the leaders of various women's organizations. In Nanjing, Song Meiling [Madame Chiang Kai-shek] formed the Women's Consolation Society and was regarded as the national leader of the women's movement.

The way we formed our organizations was that several friends got together to discuss the issue. We wrote a charter, using other organizations' charters as reference. The goal of our organization was to join the women's movement. Women need political power. Without political power, how can women be liberated? No power, no place to speak: the government ignores you. That is why women should obtain more legislative seats: so they can speak out on women's behalf. Without political power, what's the use in trying to change things? The goals of our organization were similar to those of other organizations: to participate politically, to liberate women, to achieve equality between men and women, and to ensure equal education. In feudal families, only boys were educated, not girls, which was wrong. Women's organizations all had similar goals: equal educational opportunity, economic independence—that is, women should have jobs, and equality between men and women. This was called pursuing nüquan [women's rights or feminism]. We sent an application to the Social Bureau for approval of our organization, and they sent a person to our meeting to check up on us. We were Guomindang members; we would not propagandize Communism, so our application was approved.

What did we do after the organization was formed? One thing we did was help a group of refugees whom the government was unable to help. The Shanghai public had to help these people, and we women donated time and money, collected clothes, and so on. I also ran a rescuing training course in our living room on the first floor. Many female students volunteered. At that time students were very patriotic and volunteered their service with-

---

13. He Xiangning (1878–1972) joined the Revolutionary Alliance in 1904 when she was in Japan. Her husband, Liao Zhongkai, was a senior leader of the GMD and was assassinated in 1925. Although without official titles, He had prestige and influence in the GMD. He's leading roles in many historical events are mentioned in the following narratives.

out our mobilization. The war against Japanese invaders was going on, and many wounded soldiers of the New Fourth Army [Communist troops] came to Shanghai. There weren't enough nurses in the hospital to meet the army's huge demand for medical care, so we trained nurses and sent them to the Women's Consolation Society, and He Xiangning assigned them to various hospitals. We also collected donations and bought clothes, soap, toothbrushes, toothpaste, towels, socks, and so on. We borrowed sewing machines and made big sacks in which to put all the goods. And then we sent these sacks to He Xingning's home, which was close to my house. I knew our donations were sent by He to the New Fourth Army, but we did not say anything because it was the time of United Front. When He Xiangning left after the Japanese invaded Shanghai, the Women's Consolation Society became the Shanghai Women's Association of Relief. Xu Guangping and Huang Dinghui were in charge of the general work, and Li Qiujun and I were in charge of relief.[14] We set up the Jianchen Refugee Factory to produce towels. Thus we helped some refugees. We did all kinds of things. Only in this way could we improve our social status and pursue *nüquan*. Otherwise, if we could not do the things men could do, how could we ask for *nüquan*? We could not be equal. Whatever you men can do, we women can do, too. We worked for charity. We were involved in popularizing education in order to get rid of illiteracy. We did lots of things.

In sum, *nüquan yundong* [the women's rights or feminist movement] began after the May Fourth movement. Women's minds were enlightened, and women began to understand somewhat: "Oh, human beings are actually equal. We used to be oppressed. Only men had rights. You men have rights, so why do we women have no *nüquan*?" Thus there is *nüquan yundong*. How was I influenced by the May Fourth movement? The May Fourth movement's goal was to overthrow the old feudal system and transform the old ideas into new and progressive ideas. What were the new progressive ideas? That men and women should be equal. How do you achieve equality? Through education and by pursuing *nüquan*. Thus it started. *Nüquan* was pursued first, then patriotic and national salvation movements all came into being. Shi Liang, who worked in the National Salvation Association,

14. Xu Guangping (1898–1968), Lu Xun's wife, rose to prominence in Shanghai public life after Lu Xun's death in 1936. For a brief discussion of Xu Guangping, see chapter 1.

Huang Dinghui is one of the narrators in this book. See chapter 8. Li Qiujun was an artist. Besides her role in organizing relief efforts, she donated Chinese paintings made by herself to raise money for the resistance. Her paintings depict women's efforts in the war.

and my teacher Shen Junru were arrested. They were among the famous *qijunzi* [seven noble persons].[15] I was not in open opposition like them, but I joined the Patriotic Association. It could not be a crime to be patriotic. This was more subtle. Actually, I sympathized with the progressives. I just did not have the strength to overthrow the rotten Nationalist government. In my mind and heart, I was not content with them.

Influenced by the May Fourth movement, I decided to attend the university. But what I saw in my relatives' families affected me, too. I saw husbands hit wives. My aunts were treated that way. I thought to myself that I would never put up with that—I would speak for justice. I didn't know much at the time, but that's what I thought. You could also hear a lot of stories about women's oppression. Neighbors would talk about whose husband broke her head and whose mother-in-law abused her terribly. Hearing and seeing these things got on my young nerves. So I wanted education. High school education would not do: it had to be university. I wanted to protect women's rights, so I studied law. There was no point in learning to paint— you'd just look at the painting by yourself. Only by studying law would one be able to speak on others' behalf and ensure that justice was done. Don't oppress me, we are all equal. That is how I was influenced by the new intellectual wave. My mind changed gradually. I did not need anyone to teach me. What I saw and heard in society taught me. Then my mind was shaken. Then the desire to organize grew. Individual persons had no strength. We had to organize. Originally I wanted to pursue *nüquan* for myself. Then the nation faced crisis, and I became involved with the national salvation. But later the two could not be separated. *Nüquan* and patriotic national salvation merged into one movement.

If you did not step into society, you would never understand anything and never participate in charitable or volunteer activities. Only when you worked in society would you be able to understand this set of ideas. It was the *nüquan* organizations that donated time and effort, organized social movements, and did public work. If you did not understand *nüquan*, how would you be able to do all these things in public? Fund-raising, charity,

15. The "seven noble persons" are Shen Junru, Li Gongpu, Zhang Naiqi, Zhou Taofen, Wang Zaoshi, Sha Qianli, and Shi Liang. They were leaders of organizations in the national salvation movement and were arrested on November 23, 1936, by the GMD government on the charge that their activities harmed the republic. Their arrests caused an uproar of protest in China. The CCP and many nonpartisan celebrities joined the effort to rescue the seven imprisoned people and to create a powerful public opinion that condemned the GMD government. The seven leaders were later praised as the "seven patriotic noble persons."

and volunteer activities were all included in the women's movement. We also published *Zhongguo funü* [Chinese women]. I was the editor and wrote many articles when there were not enough submissions to fill an issue. We printed many copies and sent them to each school. We voluntarily funded the magazine, and friends donated money: this one gave fifty silver dollars; that one's financial situation was better so she gave one hundred silver dollars. That is why after the War of Resistance the government asked me to be a councilor. I made contributions to society, and I fulfilled my obligations. The position of councilor was only honorary, lacking real power, though you could make propositions. Of course, they did not necessarily accept your propositions.

Many women did numerous things in those years. Some women could not donate money, so they donated work. When Shen Zijiu's women's magazine ran into financial problem, we helped too.[16] Shen was in the Communist Party. Our women organizations were like a cooperative. So long as one worked for women, we helped each other. Shen and I were old friends, and we often met in those meetings of women's organizations during the War of Resistance. She did not represent a women's organization, but she was the editor in chief of a women's magazine. So she attended meetings. Our magazine lasted until the Japanese arrested Qian Jianqiu. Then I began to help refugees, and later we handed the relief work over to the YWCA.

I not only made donations then, during wartime, but I also do so now. In 1958 when the government called for all women to participate in social production, I was excited to see women having jobs. I wanted to do something for women's liberation, so I gave the first floor of my apartment to the neighborhood committee. They used it to run a nursery to help working mothers. Not long ago some provinces had natural disasters and the government called for donations. I gave a donation. I also donated two hundred yuan to the Hope Project.[17] The Wenshiguan donated over ten thousand yuan and was praised by the government. The most important thing is to popularize

16. Shen Zijiu (1898–1989) was a prominent activist in the 1930s in Shanghai. She was the editor in chief of the *Shenbao* [Shanghai news] supplement *Women's Garden* in 1934, and in 1935 she started a new women's magazine, *Funü shenghuo* [Women's life]. *Women's Life* became a major vehicle of Communist Party policy on the women's movement during the War of Resistance. Shen joined the CCP in 1939. She was in the leading body of the All-China Women's Federation after 1949 and the editor in chief of the ACWF's journal *Xin Zhongguo funü* [New Chinese women].

17. The Hope Project is a national project to help children in the poor areas go to school. The Wenshiguan asked its members to donate, and two hundred yuan is the maximum donation.

education. Our goal was to help women get an education. When you have knowledge, you can get a job. Then you can have economic independence. Only then will you be able to have equal rights in society. Otherwise, how do you achieve equal rights? To pursue equal rights, you have to send a representative to speak for you. If you don't raise your concerns, will the rights be given to you? Leaders won't just hand them to you. Look at the situation now: there is only one woman in the Politburo. Shanghai only has one female deputy mayor. I used to call the Chinese People's Political Consultative Conference the "raising hands" conference, because the conference members were just asked to raise their hands to show their support for whatever issue the government raised. Now they are allowed to make suggestions to the government. The chair of the Shanghai People's Political Consultative Conference was Xie Xide, and the current chair is a woman, too.[18] So women can only have leading positions in the Chinese People's Political Consultative Conference. Even the Communist Party treats women this way today. It was harder for women to pursue political power in the time of Guomindang.

At the time when I formed my organization, Guomindang was open to different political opinions and welcomed the political participation of mass organizations. Many women's organizations were established, the heads of each organization met frequently in meetings, and that's how I got to know all those women activists. In 1938 when my schoolmate Qian Jianqiu became the director of the Women's Movement Committee of Guomindang, she invited me to be a member of the committee. I also became the standing board member of the Shanghai Women's Association, which was subordinate to the Shanghai Women's Movement Committee of Guomindang. The Shanghai Women's Movement Committee was an official organ of the government, whereas the Shanghai Women's Association was a mass organization like today's Women's Federation. The Shanghai Women's Association was supposed to join women's activities, just like other women's organizations did. But we also organized women's associations of all circles, such as the Shanghai Women Lawyers' Association, which included senior female law students, Women Workers' Association, Women Educators' Association, and even housewives' associations. On Women's Day in 1946, women from different organizations held a parade that packed the Nanjing Road. Back then, we did everything on a grand scale. Many women who heard of the Shanghai Women's Association came to us for help. Even af-

18. Xie Xide is a woman, renowned as a physicist and the former president of Fudan University in Shanghai.

ter a few decades of Sun Zhongshan's Revolution, women's situation was only a little better than it had been during the Qing dynasty. Many women were oppressed by their husbands and came crying, asking for help. We would mediate those cases. If mediation was to no avail, we helped the women go to court and provided free legal service. This was to do justice for women, to pursue *nüquan*.

The members of Shanghai Women's Association were not all Guomindang members. Some were Communists. At that time factories and schools everywhere had two factions: Communists and Nationalists. When I was the principal of a high school, I had students who were Communists. I made a rule that the school should be nonpartisan. I was just interested in education, not in recruiting party members. If the Communists had underground activities, I just ignored them. The two party leaders were talking about coalition; why should members of the two parties be hostile to each other? We both had one common goal: to love our country and to save it. I would support whoever did a better job leading the country and whoever really tried to save it. Even though I joined Guomindang, I thought of myself as nonpartisan. The dean of studies at my college was Mao's friend, and several of my students were Communists. They talked about the corruption of Guomindang. I was influenced by them and disliked the corruption of the Nationalists, too. That is why after liberation I was arrested but released two years later. They told me that I had a criminal position but no criminal deeds. My criminal position was being a member of the Women's Movement Committee of Guomindang. Because I had never urged my students to be anti-Communist, or interfered with Communist students' activities, or recruited my students to join Guomindang, I was judged as having no criminal deeds and released before my sentence was up. I asked them, "If I committed no criminal deeds, why should I be imprisoned? What was my crime?" They said, "Don't you want to defend yourself?" I said, "I am a lawyer. You should have legal grounds to imprison a person." Now who would compensate me for the two years I spent in prison? When I was sentenced to prison, I asked them, "How can you sentence me if I committed no crime?" The judge said, "You are a counterrevolutionary." So he sentenced me to seven years in prison. [Zhu laughs hard here.] Just because I was a Guomindang member and not a Communist, I was regarded as a counterrevolutionary. It was extremely funny, and there was nothing I could say to them. I was released two years later because I was often sick in prison. I was allowed to go home to receive medical treatment.

In 1962 I was notified that I "had served my sentence and was released officially." But in 1966, when the Cultural Revolution began, my home was ransacked. All our collections of valuable paintings and my jewelry were taken away by people from the neighborhood committee. To make it worse, the Red Guards ordered my husband to close his private clinic. Thus we had no income at all and had to rely on our children's little salaries. We lived in extreme hardship during those years. I was rehabilitated after the Cultural Revolution. I did not petition for rehabilitation right away, because I saw that many Communists had not yet been rehabilitated and I did not think they would have time to look into my case. I gave them some time to finish their own household chores before they could address outsiders' business. I am sensible; I used to be a lawyer. I waited until the Communists were rehabilitated. In 1979 I sent my petition to the Shanghai Municipal Court, asking them to review my case. I listed the things I did for women and for the salvation movement during the second United Front under He Xiangning's leadership. It took only a few months for them to rehabilitate me. They were quite nice and came to my home to investigate the case. Then they issued the judgment, which said, "The original judgment should be overturned because it did not follow the suitable law." Thus I was thoroughly rehabilitated. In 1983, I was appointed as a member of Shanghai Wenshiguan. Since then, I have received a monthly salary and enjoyed free health care.

Today March-the-Eighth Red Flag Carriers and Premier Teachers are selected nationwide, which is different from our time.[19] How many women can be selected as Premier Teachers or Red Flag Carriers? Will those who aren't selected feel encouraged to advance? Others will be discouraged. Extolling a few but suppressing a group is a bad method. In our time, when women demanded emancipation and pursued *nüquan*, we wanted to enhance women's status as a whole. What is the use in promoting an elite? Will putting one woman in the government mean we have achieved equality between men and women? In the past we hoped every woman would rise up and join the Patriotic Association, the National Salvation Association, and so on. The Nationalist government also just had one or two women representatives. In my time, things changed a little, and a women's committee came into being instead of just one or two women working individually. Our

19. "March-the-Eighth Red Flag Carriers" is a title given to a small group of select women from different districts and cities. These women usually have exceptional achievements in their respective occupations. The process of selection is controlled by different levels of the Women's Federation. March the Eighth is the International Women's Day and has been celebrated in China since the National Revolution of the mid 1920s.

"Premier Teacher" is a title given to the highest level of teachers in the classification system of elementary and middle schools.

generation won some equality between men and women. Now we no longer do anything for it. Let the next generation continue to pursue it.

INTERPRETATION: FEMINIST GOALS AND POLITICAL MEANS

Zhu Su'e is the only Nationalist Party member among my interviewees. Her party identity is a prominent thread that weaves in and out of her life story. What interested me was not only how her party affiliation affected her fate, but also how feminism was linked to her party membership. Moreover, Zhu is one of only a few women activists in the GMD who chose to stay in the mainland in 1949. Her story, therefore, represents a unique perspective on the women's movement after the May Fourth era in the People's Republic of China.

Like Lu Lihua, Zhu Su'e had the opportunity to go to school as a little girl. In her case, however, she did not have to be disguised as a boy. People in the small city where she lived, a center for women's learning in Qing times, were used to sending girls to old-style private schools. And her father thought that both boys and girls should have an education. Zhu emphasizes that her father was open-minded because he had been trained in law. It is possible that her father had new ideas about gender equality. But Zhu also calls our attention to the fact that in the newly established Western-style public school, the Women's Normal School, the great majority of students were from elite families. Even as the daughter of a banker, her status was below that of other girls in the school. As a little girl, Zhu was keenly aware of the differences between her family and her friends' families. The status symbols marked by the size and style of houses were too obvious to be overlooked by anyone. Zhu thinks that she was able to go to the modern school because of her father's open-mindedness and that other people of her class were afraid to let their daughters be tainted by Western-style education. However, because being in a modern school meant mixing with girls from elite families, her father's decision could also have been the result of his own status-consciousness. Moreover, because that city was accustomed to girls being educated in the old-style private schools, her father's willingness to send daughters to any school might be less a sign of open-mindedness than a bow to local tradition: female education was a symbol of family status in Changzhou.[20] In any event, when the local elite began to

20. For a study on the importance of women's education in some areas, including Zhu's hometown, Changzhou, during the Qing period, see Susan Mann, *Precious Records: Women in China's Long Eighteenth Century* (Stanford: Stanford University Press, 1997).

send their daughters to the public normal school, her father did follow their lead.

It is no surprise that the elite should take the lead in sending their daughters to public school: the modern discourse on female education was created by leading members of the Qing intellectual elite such as Kang Youwei and Liang Qichao, and that discourse targeted the social elite. It was easy for the elite class of Changzhou to move their daughters from old-style private schools to new Western-style public schools, especially when that move was defined as a patriotic gesture in the nationalist discourse. Backed by the elite, modern public schools for women developed rapidly after the early 1910s, despite suspicion of and resistance to Western influence elsewhere in the society.

Unlike Lu Lihua, Zhu did not participate in May Fourth activities. Although the city where she lived was only a couple of hours away from Shanghai by train, Changzhou's cultural environment and political scene differed vastly from that of the big treaty port of Shanghai. When Lu Lihua and thousands of students were experiencing those exhilarating days by participating in demonstrations and meetings, petitioning, and making speeches and newspaper headlines, Zhu Su'e in Changzhou saw only a few students standing on benches making speeches in the streets. Still, some people in the quiet small city—especially the younger ones—were stirred by the May Fourth movement. Shi Liang, the young woman who went to speak in the streets with Zhu's sister, later went to Shanghai and became a famous activist during the War of Resistance.

Zhu herself was stimulated by the New Culture movement that intertwined with the May Fourth movement. Her decision to leave home was made under the influence of the New Culture. This young woman absorbed the New Culture's opposition to the traditional family system. She was discontented with her situation at home. Seven decades later, she still remembers well the New Culture phrase "revolt against the family," which stimulated her to take action against her parents' decision that she, rather than her elder sister, should drop out of school to take care of her mother. Zhu was unhappy about leaving school. But she had no way to express her discontent, because in the Confucian morality it was a daughter's obligation to be filial to parents. Although she felt it unfair that her sister would continue school while she had to stay at home, and although she even cried over the situation, she could not articulate any of these reactions until these "new ideas" got into her head. Then she was able to view the situation in a new light. The issues had changed. The question was not "Should she fulfill her obligations?" Instead the question became "Should she continue to be con-

trolled by her parents?" The New Culture emphasis on individual autonomy and independence encouraged this young woman to make a decision
that she had never dared to make before: to leave home. She chose to enter
a boarding school in Shanghai so that her parents would no longer be able
to control her.

Zhu was stimulated not only by the New Culture ideas, but also by the
excitement in Shanghai. She was obviously aware of the limitations of a
small city and of the opportunities in a big city; therefore, she "wanted to
see the world." Her future independent life was made possible largely because of this move to Shanghai. The importance of her move to Shanghai
is clear when we compare her to her sister, who was two years older and
more active than she in the May Fourth movement. Having finished her
normal school education, her sister remained in their hometown and was
unwillingly carried away in a sedan chair into an arranged marriage. By contrast, in Shanghai Zhu was able to "pick and choose," and she married a
man of her own choice when she was twenty-nine years old. In a small city
like Changzhou, a woman who broke an engagement became a pariah, which
was the reason why Zhu's father had to force her sister to marry. But in
Shanghai after May Fourth, numerous young men and women escaped their
arranged marriages and found a haven there. In this city where political radicals and cultural bohemians gathered in large numbers and Westerners
demonstrated their outlandish lifestyles, young people could flaunt breaking an arranged marriage as a sign of their own modernity. So to some extent, even a different location could make a dramatic difference in the personal lives of two sisters.

But it was Zhu's own determination that brought her to Shanghai. Zhu's
move to Shanghai in itself says something special about this young woman.
As she puts it, "I am different from others in a way. I am quite stubborn."
She illustrates her stubbornness with her childhood memories. In her formative years, the tragic lives that her two aunts and other women led made
deep impressions on Zhu Su'e's mind. In the interviews, she repeatedly describes women's sorrows caused by their husbands' infidelity and decries
the violence that she saw and heard in her childhood. The misery of women
around young Zhu made her cry, made her angry, and most important, made
her determined: "I would never put up with that!" Her stubbornness, or
her strong personality, is revealed here. Many women with strong personalities before Zhu must have had similar feelings when seeing other women's
suffering. Many who decided that they would not accept such a miserable
life committed suicide. For the strong women of Zhu's generation, however,

suicide was far from the only way out. In Zhu's case, as a literate young woman she was equipped with New Culture ideas. The New Culture movement enabled her to name women's oppression. Moreover, new terms such as "oppression," "human rights," and "equality" not only provided her a way to analyze the abuse of women around her, but also opened new horizons. She learned that a woman could live a different life, a life that was equal to a man's. She saw that the route to that different life was through higher education. She decided to take that route, to pursue a life without the miseries that so many women had experienced. Her determination to leave home was based on the combination of a strong personality, indignation over the misery of other women, and a sense of new opportunity. At the same time, the decision itself signifies the emergence of new consciousness in this young woman. For Zhu, leaving home was, in this sense, a crucial step toward achieving a new subjectivity.

It is interesting to note that other women's narratives also show that they were deeply affected by the oppression of women they had seen in their early years. The women who moved them were usually their mothers or close relatives. Witnessing other women's sufferings motivated these young women to strive for a different life for themselves. The New Culture's critique of women's oppression in Confucian culture therefore touched a sensitive chord. In fact, for these women the most meaningful progressive idea promoted in the New Culture movement was the concept of equality between men and women as imbedded in women's rights, or *nüquan*. For every one of them, the slogan of equality between men and women aroused memories of women being treated as far less than equal—indeed, far worse than that. Hence their pursuit of gender equality was a personal goal, not consciously or directly related to the grand goal of modern nation building, which male elites used to justify the pursuit of gender equality. In Zhu Su'e's words, "Originally I wanted to pursue *nüquan* for myself." Although the idea of *nüquan* gained legitimacy in China through nationalist discourse, many women like Zhu viewed women's equal rights from a personal perspective. It was this personal attachment to *nüquan* that generated the high tide of women's feminist activities in the 1920s. Yet this personal attachment to *nüquan* did not fit the Marxist framework, and thus it was labeled bourgeois once the Communist Party was established.

Zhu did not join any women's organization in the 1920s. Instead, she chose to study law as a means to fight for women's rights. This unconventional choice made her both a beneficiary and an advocate of New Culture feminism. Law school and the legal profession were opened to women as a result of the New Culture feminist demand for equal education and equal employment, and by choosing a career in law, Zhu moved quickly into the ranks of the new women.

New Culture feminism did something even more important than create new social positions for women: it reconstituted women's subjectivity. Women like Zhu, who did not directly participate in feminist organized activities, nonetheless were strongly influenced by feminist ideas. The language Zhu uses in her narrative is full of New Culture feminist phrases. "Equality between men and women," "human beings are equal," "promoting women's rights (*shenzhang nüquan*)," "women are human beings," "independence," and "self-reliance"—these are words not just for expressing ideas but for describing her life. Her choice of law as a profession had the aim of promoting or protecting women's rights. Her pursuit of higher education enabled her to become an independent career woman, and with that independence she enjoyed gender equality, at least at home. She stresses that she would neither marry an old-fashioned man nor become a *taitai* (Mrs.), which was a quintessential May Fourth feminist stance. In Zhu's youth, many officials and wealthy men married young students because an educated wife was a symbol of status and a sign of modernity. Some elite girls' schools were even nicknamed "*taitai* school" because many of their graduates became wives of prominent men. By definition, *taitai* was a wife who took her husband's identity as hers and who had no job or social position of her own. For the generation of young women who were influenced by feminism, being a *taitai* would be the biggest insult to their independent personhood.[21] Zhu conveys this strong sentiment in the interview by proudly emphasizing her independence in her marriage.

As a young career woman who enjoyed independence and equality, Zhu's life also demonstrates that the liberal feminist approach to women's liberation produced tangible results for this group of women. She pursued *nüquan* for herself, and with the new educational and professional opportunities opening for women, she was able to live a life drastically different from that of her aunts, or her mother. Zhu's story shows that the feminist phenomenon in early-twentieth-century China had a social as well as an economic base. Metropolises like Shanghai offered new occupations and pro-

21. The feminists who joined the Communist Party later found themselves in a dilemma over this issue. Their husbands became high officials, and on some diplomatic occasions they were addressed as "Mrs. So-and-So." To avoid this humiliation, many women refused to accompany their husbands to such events. See Jin Feng, *Deng Yingchao zhuan* [A biography of Deng Yingchao] (Beijing: Renmin chubanshe, 1993), 581–589.

fessions, which in turn gave birth to a new middle-class. Meanwhile, the development of women's education produced a large number of educated women, who were concentrated heavily in the port cities. In fact, Shanghai in the early twentieth century had more girls' schools than any other place in the country.[22] Although this group of women had not initiated the feminist discourse in China, they were undoubtedly the major constituency of feminism. When male New Culturalists raised the issue of gender equality, young educated women were eager to put into practice feminist demands such as equal education and economic independence. In other words, the feminist ideas made sense to, and attracted, a particular audience in a particular social environment. In this case, the feminist discourse enabled educated women to join the budding middle class in early-twentieth-century China.

Here a telling contrast with the United States emerges. In the United States at the turn of the century, professionalization was largely a process that created male monopolies, leaving educated women to find a niche for themselves by creating professions associated with "feminine" values.[23] In China, the association of feminism with modernity provided legitimacy for women to move into all kinds of modern professions in the 1920s and 1930s. In Shanghai, women bankers, entrepreneurs, doctors, lawyers, writers, editors, journalists, teachers, nurses, school principals, and movie stars became integral components of the modern society. Jiang Qing and Ding Ling were only two of the famous career women who went to Yan'an from Shanghai in the thirties, but many female celebrities stayed in Shanghai.[24] There are no statistics on the exact number of career women in Shanghai or in the nation as a whole. Nevertheless, the narratives of career women such as Zhu

22. In 1907 twenty-two provinces in China had, altogether, more than four hundred girls' schools. Many girls' schools in Shanghai enjoyed national fame, attracting students from all over the country. The Patriotic Girls' School that Zhu entered was a very famous one created by the renowned educator Cai Yuanpei.

23. For American women's efforts to enter traditionally male professions, see D. Kelley Weisberg, "Barred from the Bar: Women and Legal Education in the United States, 1870–1890," *Journal of Legal Education* 38 (1977): 485–507; Rosalind Rosenberg, *Beyond Separate Spheres: Intellectual Roots of Modern Feminism* (New Haven: Yale University Press, 1982); and Barbara Miller Soloman, *In the Company of Educated Women* (New Haven: Yale University Press, 1985).

24. Jiang Qing was a movie star in Shanghai before she went to the Communist base area. She became Mao Zedong's wife when she was in Yan'an. Ding Ling was a famous writer who also went to Yan'an during the War of Resistance. For recent publications with information on Shanghai career women of this generation, see Dong Zhujun, *Wode yige shiji* [My century] (Beijing: Sanlian shudan, 1997), and Pang-Wei Natasha Chang, *Bound Feet and Western Dress* (New York: Anchor Books, Doubleday, 1996).

and Lu show us that in the national salvation movement, career women were an important social force.[25]

Zhu Su'e regards herself not just as a career woman, but also as an activist in the women's movement. She did not join women's organizations in the 1920s during the high tide of feminism. However, in the national salvation movement she organized the Chinese Women's National Defense Association, worked for a women's magazine, and served as a board member in Guomindang's official women's organs and in women's umbrella organizations like the Shanghai Women's Association for Relief. Rather than seeing these activities as a form of participation in the national salvation movement, Zhu defines what happened in the War of Resistance period as a blend of the women's movement and the patriotic national salvation movement. She argues, "If you did not understand *nüquan,* how would you be able to do all these things in public? Fund-raising, charity, and voluntary activities were all included in the women's movement." She emphasizes that only when women worked in the society could they understand *nüquan* and patriotism. It seems that *nüquan* (women's rights, or feminism) included not only the right to be in the public arena, but also the right to work for the country. Thus, participation in the national salvation movement as a member of an independent women's organization was perceived by woman activists as an important part of the women's movement.[26]

As we see in this study, narrators of all political orientations use the same language—*jiuguo* (save the nation) and *kangRi* (resist the Japanese)—to express their foremost concerns during this period. But this is not to say that women were manipulated by the nationalist discourse in the 1930s. Rather, women identified with the nationalist discourse out of self-interest. It could

25. The narrators' descriptions are confirmed by many recently published works in China, which do not have the same focus as this study but which nevertheless portray women's enlarged social roles in the 1930s. In *Deng Yingchao zhuan,* Jin Feng describes Deng's efforts to unite women of different political orientations for the War of Resistance effort. The source material she uses can also be interpreted as showing a struggle between the GMD and the CCP to win the allegiance of renowned career women and their organizations. See Jin Feng, *Deng Yingchao zhuan,* 262–274.

A History of the Shanghai Women's Movement, which focuses on the CCP women's role in the women's movement, lists many women's organizations and prominent women activists in this period. Even though it depicts an increase in women's activism, Zhu Su'e objects to its omission of non-Communist women—a criticism that further supports the conclusion that the 1930s were an unprecedented age for women's social activities.

26. Not only Zhu Su'e and women activists of her generation hold this view. Contemporary Chinese historians present identical opinions. All the recently published

be argued that by contributing to national salvation, women were working for their self-interest, because they did not want to live under Japanese rule. Lu Lihua's case has shown us how the Japanese invasion destroyed her school and how she subsequently turned from a school principal into a patriotic activist. But there is another inner logic that links women's patriotism to women's interests. Historically, it was through the vehicle of nationalism that Chinese women were able to move into the public arena. The national salvation movement allowed women to expand their social space on an unprecedented scale. It was during this period that women's organizations mushroomed and women's activities expanded into all aspects of social life. As Zhu states clearly, "We did all kinds of things. Only in this way could we improve our social status and pursue *nüquan*. Otherwise, if we could not do the things men could do, how could we ask for *nüquan*? We could not be equal. Whatever you men can do, we women can do, too." From the perspective of expanding women's social space, the national salvation movement did not thwart, but rather helped, the feminist cause. This may also explain why so many Chinese women activists of various political orientations regard their prominent role in the War of Resistance as an important chapter in the history of the Chinese women's movement. For them, all organized activities that empowered women and led to enlarged social space for women are part of the actual achievement of women's social advancement and, therefore, are defined as a women's movement.

If Chinese women activists and scholars have reached a consensus on women's prominent role in the 1930s, they nevertheless differ in their views about who took the lead in the Chinese women's movement and what constituted that movement. Because of her involvement with the GMD, Zhu's perception of the history of the Chinese women's movement often reflects the GMD's position. Some of her views would be rejected by Communist historians. For example, Zhu claims, "Without the GMD, there would be no women's movement. Would the Qing dynasty let you have a women's movement?" She also emphasizes that the women's movement reached its peak after the War of Resistance and before 1949. Zhu's view, which credits the GMD for the existence of the Chinese women's movement, not only

---

histories of the Chinese women's movement in the mainland regard women's participation in the national salvation movement as a glorious page in the history of the women's movement. See All-China Women's Federation, *Zhongguo funü yundong shi* [A history of the Chinese women's movement] (Beijing: Chunqiu chubanshe, 1989), and Shanghai Women's Federation, *Shanghai funü yundong shi* [A history of the Shanghai women's movement] (Shanghai: Shanghai renmin chubanshe, 1990).

reflects the official position of the GMD, but helps to explain why many feminists joined the GMD.[27]

The GMD, with Sun Yat-sen as its founding father and with its leading role in overthrowing the Qing dynasty, maintained the image of a revolutionary party even after Sun's death. To feminists, the GMD's record on gender equality seemed quite respectable. The Revolutionary Alliance, the original form of the GMD, placed gender equality in its platform when it was founded in 1905. In 1912, however, when the Revolutionary Alliance was reorganized to form the GMD, it dropped the principle of gender equality from its original platform in reaction against the surge of women's suffrage activism. This reneging on an early commitment to gender equality became an obscure past to women of the May Fourth generation, especially because the GMD endorsed gender equality again in 1924 when the first United Front was formed. In general, the GMD was no less receptive than the CCP to a feminist agenda used to mobilize women for a national revolution. At the first Congress of the GMD in January 1924, one of the three female representatives, He Xiangning, proposed a bill to "confirm the principle of men and women being equal in law, economy, education, and society; and to promote the development of *nüquan*." The bill was passed, and gender equality was written into the Declaration of the First Congress. In order to organize women's activism more effectively, on January 31, 1924, the first executive committee and supervisory committee of the GMD resolved to establish in the central executive committee a Women's Department, modeled after the organizational infrastructure of the Soviet Union. Afterward, women's departments were established at all levels of the party hierarchy, and female Nationalists worked together with many female Communists in those departments to promote a party-led women's movement in the National Revolution. In October 1924, the Women's Department in the Central Committee of the GMD formed a Women's Movement Committee to facilitate the development of the women's movement. The leading role of the GMD in promoting the women's movement was thus solidly established during this period.[28]

Because of the joint efforts of the GMD and the CCP to harness and institutionalize the emerging women's movement for the purpose of the Na-

27. Many of the May Fourth feminists later joined either the CCP or the GMD. The student activist Wang Xiaoying, for example, who organized the Women's Suffrage Association in Beijing in 1922, later became a member of the Shanghai GMD headquarters and played a prominent role in Shanghai women's organized activities in the 1930s.

28. The information on the GMD's organizational changes in respect to the women's movement is provided in *Zhongguo funü yundong shi*. An official history

tional Revolution, the women's movement became much more complicated. When many May Fourth feminists joined either the CCP or the GMD and promoted a party-led women's movement, the May Fourth feminist organizations and other nonpartisan women's organizations were either co-opted or overshadowed by the party-led women's movement after 1924. When the United Front failed in 1927, each party kept its women's department or women's movement committee. And ever since, each has claimed that it has played a leading role in the Chinese women's movement. The New Culture feminist discourse made the "women's movement" such a badge of modernity in China that any political force claiming to be progressive would grab it.

As the GMD became the dominant political party in China after 1927, it further consolidated its control over the women's movement. Propaganda in this period praised the GMD's role in women's emancipation and promulgated new principles for women to follow. In *Funü wenti lunwenji* [A collection of papers on women's problems], published in 1933, the female author Lü Yunzhang expounds the GMD's policies on the women's movement:

> Because the women's movement is a political and social movement, it obviously has to be helped by political parties in the country rather than act in disregard of other people's opinions and go its own way. Among the political parties, none surpasses Guomindang in terms of promoting the women's movement, respecting *nüquan*, and protecting women's interests. Under the leadership of Guomindang, the women's movement of the past made great progress, and women's status has improved substantially. From now on, the women's movement should stand under the banner of the Three Principles of the People [*sanmin zhuyi*] to pursue the interests of the party and women.[29]

---

of the Chinese women's movement written by the historians in the People's Republic of China, the work nevertheless presents information on the GMD's role in promoting the women's movement. This is not only because the authors are trying to write a comprehensive history of the women's movement—an intention that is evident in the broad scope and lengthy period the work tries to cover—but also because the two leading female figures in the GMD who promoted gender equality and the women's movement in the National Revolution, He Xiangning and Song Qingling, both sided with the CCP after 1927 and held high positions in the People's Republic of China after 1949. Discussing this part of the GMD's role entails no political risk in the contemporary People's Republic of China. See All-China Women's Federation, *Zhongguo funü yundong shi*, 61, 158–160. For further information on women's activities during this period, see chapter 8 in this study.

29. Lü Yunzhang, *Funü wenti lunwenji* [A collection of papers on women's problems] (Shanghai: Nüzi shudian, 1933), 69.

Lü suggests several principles for women to follow. Women should be guided by the GMD's leadership as they engage in their organized and planned activism. Women should pursue mental emancipation and behavioral reform and make their own lives simpler, more scientific, and more like those of the common people. Women's organizations should not only work for self-interest, but should also respect the broader interests of the society and the nation.

These principles convey several messages about the women's movement under GMD rule. First, the GMD intended to subsume all the women's activities under its "planned" leadership. Though this intention demonstrates the party's wish to control all aspects of society, it can also be interpreted as the feminist Nationalists' vision of a more effective women's movement. Zhu Su'e's story may help us to understand the position of many women working in different levels of the women's departments and the women's movement committees in the GMD's hierarchical structure. In their view, the political power of the GMD could be used to serve women's interests. Just as many feminists joined the CCP out of their belief in the CCP's line on women's emancipation, many feminists joined the GMD out of their belief in women's political participation. The control of the women's movement by each party was not merely a manifestation of male dominance; it was also perceived as the "correct route" to women's emancipation by feminists in both parties. In other words, women who worked in the women's departments or women's committees in the GMD and the CCP supported their respective party's role in "leading" a women's movement and worked hard to keep their party in this leadership position.

Second, Lü's emphasis on women's reform echoes prominent themes in *The Ladies' Journal* (see chapter 2). It should be pointed out that women's self-reform was also a major theme in the CCP line on women's emancipation—a theme strongly advocated by the Women's Federation in the People's Republic of China. This suggests that feminists in the dominant political party more or less identified with the ruling class and took a condescending view toward the masses of women. And yet Lü's statement also contains a warning against elitism within the female constituency of the GMD. The assertion that women should live a life "simpler, more scientific, and more like that of the common people" indicates the class background of women in the GMD. In fact, although Lü did not use a Marxist concept of class to analyze Chinese women (a common practice by feminists in the CCP), she was aware of the gap between the female constituency of the GMD and women of the lower classes. For example, Lü criticized activists in the women's movement for being "more or less ladylike" because they were unable to endure hardship in striving for women's interests. She suggested that urban educated women should try to be elementary school teachers in rural areas in order to contact rural women and to promote gender equality. She also recommended that in order to effectively lead a women's movement nationwide, the GMD should start two pilot sites for the women's movement, one in the city and the other in the countryside.[30] However, the awareness of the gap between rural and urban women did not lead to action on the GMD's part to overcome that gap. This may indicate that the urban-based GMD women activists were too removed from the lives of rural women to make special efforts to bridge the gap.

Third, although the GMD tried to control the women's movement, it did not ban nonpartisan feminist organizations in society, nor did it adopt the CCP's exclusionary practice of defining feminism negatively. Rather, the term *nüquan* was seen as having a history associated with the history of the GMD. Therefore, the term continued to be used in GMD members' writings and retained its positive meanings for Zhu Su'e, a GMD feminist, and Lu Lihua, a feminist in the GMD-controlled area. Because it stands for a feminism that demands gender equality without advocating that the existing political and economic system be overthrown, *nüquan* kept its legitimate position under GMD rule. Lü's principles reveal a situation in which the GMD's control of women's organized activities coexisted with the possibilities of women's spontaneous activism. Within the scope of those principles set forth by the GMD, women were allowed to organize by themselves. In this sense, the May Fourth heritage of women's free association survived in the Nationalist era. This social and political condition enabled the upsurge of women's activism in the 1930s. By comparison, the CCP's control of the women's movement was much tighter and more comprehensive. Since the Red Base Area era, the CCP's official women's organization, later known as the Women's Federation, has been the only legitimate "representative" of women's interests and women's voices. This largely explains the fate of many former women activists in the Maoist era. When women's social space was drastically reduced after 1949, Chinese society had no place for those women activists who could not function within the state-run institutions. The experiences of former activists Lu Lihua and Zhu Su'e illustrate this point.[31]

30. Ibid., 72.
31. Barlow states that in the People's Republic of China no one can represent women except the Women's Federation (Tani E. Barlow, "Theorizing Woman: *Funü, Guojia, Jiating*," in *Body, Subject, and Power in China*, ed. Angela Zito and Tani E.

Zhu's story illustrates women's activities in a GMD-led women's movement. In her memory, the peak of the women's movement came after the War of Resistance, even though many women's organizations had been extremely active before the Japanese invaded the foreign concessions in Shanghai. From her description, we see an institutionalized women's movement revived in Shanghai after 1945. The Women's Movement Committee of the GMD not only occupied a big office but also consolidated its control of women's organizations in all walks of life. Considering the fact that Zhu was a member of the Women's Movement Committee in 1945, her perception of the "peak" might be influenced by the more prominent role she played in this period. Although she had been active in the war years, the women's coalition organizations were represented by big names such as He Xiangning and Xu Guangping. Other minor stars were easily eclipsed. Moreover, the party coalition during the war years gave the Communists and nonpartisan activists a large role to play in the Nationalist-controlled areas, whereas after the war, with the breakup of the second United Front, the Women's Movement Committee of the GMD had the leading position all to itself.

Zhu's narrative also reveals the motivations for her involvement in both the GMD and the women's movement. When Zhu explains why she joined the GMD rather than the CCP, one reason she gives is that the GMD was in power. She volunteers the information that, because she was a Nationalist Party member who graduated from a university, her diploma bore a stamp that entitled her to the position of prefectural magistrate. Although she became a lawyer rather than an official after graduation, that stamp must have meant much to a young woman who had mingled with little girls from official families during her childhood. Her political ambition, however, is expressed within the feminist framework. "To pursue equal rights, you have to send a representative to speak for you. If you don't raise your concerns, will the rights be given to you?"

Obtaining political power was thus for Zhu a necessary part of her struggle for equal rights. And yet her involvement with women's organization reflects her sober assessment of the political situation. "At the time when I formed my organization, Guomindang was open to different political opinions and welcomed the political participation of mass organizations." So Zhu formed the Chinese Women's National Defense Association, not only to contribute to national salvation but also to gain representation in the govern-

---

Barlow [Chicago: University of Chicago Press, 1994]. Both Lu Lihua and Zhu Su'e's oral histories confirm this point.

ment. As the head of a women's organization, she quickly connected with a few other women representatives to form a delegation to Nanjing to petition for more female seats in the National Congress. And as the head of a women's organization, she became a board member of two Shanghai women's coalition organizations, the Women's Consolation Society and the Women's Association for Relief. When her friend Qian Jianqiu became the head of the Women's Movement Committee in Shanghai, Zhu was asked to be a member of the committee. Thus, through her activities in the women's organizations, she became an official in the Shanghai GMD headquarters. Zhu's experience seems to verify one of the CCP's criticisms of the "bourgeois women's movement"—that is, many upper-class women formed women's organizations mainly to become officials in the government. When the GMD power structure was for the most part closed to women, the women's movement supplied a valuable access to the power structure. It was hard for women in the GMD to reach the center of power. Zhu shows us that the Women's Movement Committee became an area within the power structure that was carved out and occupied by women. Working in this women's area provided some of the best moments in Zhu's life.

Zhu never anticipated that she would have to pay dearly for her brief involvement in the GMD power structure. Her golden age ended abruptly in 1949. She was deprived of the right to work from the time she was forty-eight years old, and she spent two years in jail after 1955. "The rest of my life was wasted," as she puts it. Rehabilitation came only when she was almost eighty years old. As a member of the Wenshiguan, she has enjoyed some social status and benefits. But nothing can compensate for the precious years she has lost. At ninety-four, her mind is still sharp and quick, she talks with a lawyer's eloquence, and she laughs hard when describing the absurd sentence she received in 1955, as if she were talking about a ridiculously funny case that involved someone else. Along with her remarkable resilience, however, is a deep regret that she makes no attempt to hide. Her narrative is asserted with phrases such as "But just at the prime of my life, I was forced to take a break," "Half of my life has been wasted," and "I made a mistake to study law as my career; I should have become a writer." Like numerous women with similar experiences, Zhu takes consolation in seeing that hers is not the worst case. Many others did not survive the persecution.

Zhu Su'e and Lu Lihua knew each other ever since they were young. Although one was a GMD member and one was nonpartisan, the two have always been on friendly terms. In conversation that I have not included in her narrative, Zhu expressed her respect for Lu, saying, "It was not easy for a young girl from the countryside to create an enterprise. I admire her daring and resolution." Zhu also commented,

> Lu is very open-minded. She is different from me. She had no one to restrict her. Her parents lived in the countryside. So she had very wide social connections and numerous male friends. She did not care. Unlike her, I was surrounded by both senior and junior generations [in the 1930s Zhu's parents and siblings moved to Shanghai]. It would not do for me to be like her. Plus, she was running a school and had to find celebrities for the school board. So she was very good at socializing with all kinds of people, men and women. I was a lawyer. I did not have to network like she did.

The two women maintained their friendship until Lu's death, even though in the 1950s Zhu did not dare visit anyone and cut off contact with her circle of friends for a long time. After the Cultural Revolution, Lu consulted with Zhu on how to get her school property back from the government. Zhu hoped that Lu would at least be able to recover her property in Jiangwan, where there used to be a nice swimming pool that Zhu and other women friends frequented in their youth. But in the end, Zhu commented, the government did not return the school property to Lu. Instead, it granted her a position in the Wenshiguan. This shrewd and ironic observation reveals the sharpness of this ninety-four-year-old woman.

On one of my visits to Zhu, I mentioned *A History of the Shanghai Women's Movement*. She was interested in the book, so I loaned my copy to her. The next time I saw her, she was very upset. She said to me, "I have read most of the book. There is no need to finish it. I see they only write about Communist women and the things they did. Other women's contributions are not mentioned at all!" The book does not mention Zhu Su'e, even though she was very active in the national salvation movement, and her assessment of the text is accurate. The history written by the Shanghai Women's Federation presents a picture of female Communists' activities in Shanghai before 1949, with little mention of other women. I cannot forget Zhu's deep disappointment at a women's history that omits women on the grounds of political orientation. Her narrative here enriches our understanding of women like her and reveals their contribution to women's social advancement. What is more, Zhu Su'e's story points out the inherent weakness in CCP historiography. History is used to glorify the party's past. This political line has been extended to the study of Chinese women's history in the People's Republic of China. In an age in which CCP censorship continues to regulate the pen of historians, the repressed story of Zhu Su'e poses a challenge to the official history of the Chinese women's movement.

6 Wang Yiwei (1905–1993): Editor in Chief

Wang Yiwei, 1989

Wang Yiwei welcomed me warmly into her tiny room of seventy square feet and apologized for the smallness of the space when I sought a place to put down my bag. As a Shanghai native, I am used to tight little rooms; still, it hurt me to see this old woman in such confined conditions. But my sad thoughts were soon diverted to the Chinese paintings and calligraphy covering her walls. Wang proudly told me that except for one scroll of calligraphy, she had done them all herself. On her bookshelf I spotted a novel that was a best-seller in China that year. Wang said she had read it already. During our conversation she took out several thick albums of photos to introduce me to her family and friends, and I realized that Wang's intellectual and social life was not confined by this tiny room. Her biting comments on contemporary politics, which she told me not to tape, revealed the liveliness of her mind and her close observation of China's social development.

Looking at her frail body, I marveled at her mental vitality and emotional exuberance.[1]

NARRATIVE

Let me tell you my love and my hatred. Love and hatred emerge from solid ground. What drew me to the women's movement and caused my lifelong concern about women is their oppression by feudalism and their oppression by men.

I was born in a feudal family. My mother bore seven children, two boys and five girls. My father was not a member of the bourgeoisie but from a medium-income family in Fuzhou. He entered a naval school and then enrolled in the naval academy that Li Hongzhang established in Tianjin, Beiyang Naval Academy.[2] He eventually became a general under Yuan Shikai. Because I followed my father to different places, I have a mixed accent that makes it hard to figure out where I am from. I am the fifth child. Before me there were two sisters and two brothers, and after me there were two sisters. My eldest sister and one of my younger sisters died in their childhood. The two brothers died, too. So out of seven children, only three sisters were left. My mother did not know how to raise kids. She was a very decadent person and only knew how to enjoy herself all day long.

I was born in 1905 in the modern way: in a hospital, a famous hospital—the Red House Women and Children Hospital, which had just been built in Shanghai. I am modern and full of creativity because I was created in that hospital [she laughs]. My mother was good at enjoying herself and trying modern things. By the time I was born, my eldest brother had died. My second brother followed my mother to the hospital. He liked me very much, but my crying scared him. He was only four years old. He ate the rich food my mother was eating—the food they feed *chanfu* [women who have just delivered their babies]. It gave him indigestion, and he died because of that. His death was a heavy blow to my mother. Even worse, after me, my mother had two more girls but no boys. The fortune-teller said my *ming* [fate] was

1. The narrative is constructed from interviews conducted on February 18, February 20, March 1, and March 10, 1993, and from Wang Yiwei's autobiography and memoirs. Three months after my last interview with her, she had a stroke while talking to a friend at home. She passed away shortly thereafter.

2. Li Hongzhang was the governor-general of the Hebei region, one of the most powerful officials in the late Qing dynasty. Facing the increasing presence of Western powers in China and the decline of the Qing empire, he initiated a series of self-strengthening programs, including establishing the North China Navy.

so hard that I ate my brother up.[3] My mother believed this. Hence I had not only bad fortune but also got a nickname. My mother said I was the one who ruined my brother, that I ate my brother up, so I was called *saozhouxing* [comet].[4] My mother felt sad for the rest her life, which was bad for me. I endured this kind of pressure from the moment I was born. My status in my family was lower than my younger sister's. She was prettier than I and did not eat her brother up.

My father was thirty years older than I. When he was thirty-nine, my mother was not yet thirty-six. There is one day in my childhood I will never forget. It was during the Spring Festival when my family was in Beijing. My father was sitting on the *kang*, and his sister, who was visiting us, was sitting on the other end of the *kang*.[5] My aunt said to my father, "Congratulations. This year you are going to be forty. But you don't have a son yet. No son, no offspring: that is most unfilial. You should think of a way to have a son. My sister-in-law is very understanding. She won't blame you." Hearing these words, my mother's face turned to ashes, and she jumped up from her seat and went to her own room. I followed her and saw her weeping in bed. When she saw me standing by her, she hit me and cursed, "You *saozhouxing*! Get out!"

In the second half of that year, my mother quietly went back alone to Fujian. She was very smart. Knowing that my father would take a concubine, she thought, "Instead of him finding one, I will find one for him." So she went to Fujian to buy a maid from a landlord's home with seventeen silver dollars. When she took her back to Beijing, everyone praised my mother's virtue in getting a concubine for her husband. This maid was both ugly and stupid, but her belly won her credit: in ten months, she gave birth to a boy. As soon as the baby was born, my mother took him into her arms and regarded him as hers. We addressed the concubine "Yi'niang." Giving birth to a boy did not change Yi'niang's humble status. She still had to do housework from morning to night and was treated the same as the other servants.

3. A widespread superstitious belief in China is that a person with a hard and strong *ming* will wither the life or lives of his or her family members or spouses. People who are seen as having such hard *ming* are usually female.

4. In Chinese astrology, the appearance of a comet foreshadows disaster. Therefore, *saozhouxing* (comet) is the name for people who are thought to bring disasters. Women are more likely than men to be called *saozhouxing*.

5. In northern China, houses were built with brick beds that could be heated through the stove in the kitchen. A *kang* (brick bed) had more functions than a bed. Because it was a heated area, most indoor activities were carried out on the *kang*, including having meals.

My mother was depressed and developed a stomach disease that could not be cured. Someone advised her to take opium as a cure, so she became an opium addict. She played mah-jongg as well. Such a fallen woman. She abused the concubine: asked her to serve her opium, wash her feet, and feed her refreshment. Every night she made trouble for her until two a.m. and then slept until noon. Although we had maids at home, my mother didn't want them to help her. She wanted only the concubine to serve her. I disliked seeing my mother torture her like that. My father did not want the concubine to serve him. Sometimes he smoked opium with my mother. He was kind of a henpecked man. My mother was very jealous and very beautiful. She learned characters by herself and read novels. She would smoke opium and ask my cousin to tell stories to her. After she died, we found a case full of books under her bed: *The Dream of the Red Chamber, Water Margin*, and so on. She read everything. Anyway, in that terrible family environment, I felt sympathy for my mother, pity for Yi'niang, and hatred for my father. I made a heartfelt promise to myself: "I will win glory for my mother. I will win glory for all women. When I grow up, I will be a woman who is stronger and better than men."

My father was exhilarated to get a chubby son. He worked harder and was soon promoted by the president of the Beiyang government, Xu Shichang. He became the commanding officer of the Songhua River area. Then we left Beijing, following him to Harbin, where he and his fleet were stationed.

We Fujianese pay attention to education. Many families hired private tutors, and my father sent me to elementary school. When we moved to Harbin, he hired tutors, and we did not go to school anymore. Although I was a girl, my father paid attention to my education because he saw that I was smart. He was the top officer, and his subordinates volunteered to be my tutors. They instilled new ideas in me. There was an old man who used to be the editor in chief of *Yishibao* [Social welfare daily] in Tianjin. He taught me how to write newspaper articles. Another man about fifty years old was a *juren* in the Qing dynasty. He taught me *Mencius* and classic Chinese. I read *Mencius* seven times. Mencius's political view of *junweiqing, minweigui* [that the monarch is less important than the people] was deeply imprinted on my mind. He also taught us works of the eight major essayists in the Tang and Song dynasties.[6] My sister studied with me. She read

6. The eight major essayists are Han Yu and Liu Zongyuan in the Tang dynasty, and Ouyang Xiu, Su Xun, Su Shi, Su Zhe, Wang Anshi, and Zheng Gong in the Song dynasty.

the *Analects of Confucius,* and I read *Mencius* and *The Book of Songs.* We read Liu Zongyuan, too. We read many essays. But we did not read Tang poetry. He trained me like a boy. Both of my parents brought me up as if I were a boy. My sister and I studied from nine o'clock in the morning to nine o'clock in the evening, only stopping for meals. After eating, we went right back to studying.

All in all, my family did not treat me badly, but they favored the other children more. I had a wet nurse who kept nursing me until I was six years old. She did that because she wanted to keep her rice bowl. She told me that my parents were partial to my other siblings and that I was not given my share in good things. That is why I had bad feelings toward my parents. And I studied hard, shutting myself up in the study. When I was sixteen, I thought to myself, "I must study hard. I must study more diligently than my younger brother. I will go abroad to study." That old tutor who taught me *Mencius* read a lot and was very progressive. He read *Dongfang zazhi* [The eastern miscellany], a very progressive magazine published by Shanghai Commercial Press. He told us what he read and encouraged me to go to Shanghai to study. It is also an old idea that girls should be like Mulan and Xie Daoyun.[7] So I said to my father, "I am not going to marry. You don't have to give me a dowry. You can spend the money for a dowry on my education." My father saw I was smart, and his subordinates did some apple polishing, saying I was very smart. My parents wanted to bring me up as a *nü zhuangyuan* [female Number One Scholar]. Thus my father agreed to my request to attend Zhongxi Girls' School [McTyeire School], a famous missionary school in Shanghai. I went from Harbin to Shanghai under my father's guard's protection. That is the first part of the story: how a woman like me, born in a feudal family, can be so progressive. It was because of the family situation.

I left my family and came to Shanghai in 1921. But after I entered the famous Zhongxi Girls' School, I did not like it. It was an American missionary school, and except for Chinese literature, all classes were taught in English. Three years of training gave me a solid foundation in English, but I was not used to their highly Westernized education. What gave me real headaches were the prayers and reading the Bible every morning and the half a day spent every Sunday listening to sermons in the big auditorium. Moreover, most students were from bourgeois families. Song Meiling [Madame Chiang Kai-shek] graduated from there. Students were usually chauffeured to

7. Xie Daoyun was a famous female poet of the eastern Jin dynasty (317–420 A.D.).

and from school and wore stylish dresses. Everyone had a close friend; after class they all walked on the sports ground in pairs like lovers. Only I was a loner, staying in the dorm all the time, reading. Most graduates from Zhongxi went to America, and I attended Zhongxi in hopes of going abroad. But because I did not like this church-run school, I left it when my father was transferred to Beijing. I entered the Jinshi High School in Beijing, China's first coed high school, which was led by General Feng Yuxiang. The teachers were from five missionary schools and quite progressive and anti-imperialistic. I was elected the secretary of the student union and participated in student activities. I also joined the protest on March 18, 1926.[8] One of my classmates was killed when the Duan Qirui government ordered guards to fire at the protesters. That incident made me very angry.

After I graduated from high school in 1927, the Northern Expedition took place. My father stepped down from his post in the Beiyang warlord government, and the government paid him a monthly allowance as if he were on vacation. My elder sister's husband was the director of a shipbuilding institute in Fuzhou. He came to take our whole family back to Fuzhou so that my parents could be cared for in their old age. I did not want to return to my hometown with them; I wanted to pursue my studies and independence. But my family no longer had money for my higher education or for sending me abroad. Instead, I had to work to support them.

So I passed exams and enrolled in a nurse training class affiliated with the Yanjing University. A graduate of that class could make eighty silver dollars a month right away, the same as a junior doctor. We did our internship in the Peking Union Hospital [an American Christian hospital]. Secondary training classes and university-level medical classes were all at the Yanjing University, and graduates all went to the Peking Union Hospital to do internships. In the entrance exams for both levels, I ranked first; therefore, I got a scholarship. The university students did not rank as high as I did. If I had continued to study a year and a half more, I would have succeeded. The doctors there all said that I was a genius and should learn to be a doctor, not a nurse. When the training class reached the part about giving shots and helping empty the bowels, I was unhappy. I said to myself, "This is not my goal. My goal is to defend my mother against the injustice done to her. Why am I learning medicine?" I had learned everything and even bathed a rickshaw man. I got infected with some germs. Once there was a

8. This was a mass protest organized by the underground Communist Party in the north against the Duan Qirui government's concessions during the confrontation between the Chinese army and Japanese government.

woman patient who had a sore on her head, which was highly contagious. I was asked to give her a bath. She was about to die, and I was asked to give her a bath! Isn't it outrageous? But I had to bathe her. In the middle of the bath, she died. I was so scared! What is more, race was a problem in the Peking Union Hospital. When we were walking, we had to follow the head nurse, and when getting into the elevator, we had to let foreigners get in first. That made me feel inferior to foreigners. I wrote a letter to my classmate, who was at Nanjing University. I quit the nursing school and ended up in the history department of Nanjing University. Meanwhile, I kept up a correspondence with a classmate in Fudan University, who told me that the department of journalism would open up to female students that year. I thought studying history would not help me to realize my dreams, so I transferred to Fudan. That year [1928] there were about a dozen female students in the department of journalism.

I was like a beggar during those years in Fudan. My brother-in-law, who was transferred from Fuzhou to Shanghai, provided some of my expenses; a cousin's husband and one of my father's friends also helped me. In addition, I worked as a tutor. My younger sister got married then. She had not been to formal school but just read poems at home. At twenty-three she was beautiful but still no husband. My parents forced her to marry a rich banker who was thirty-six years old and already had five children when she was only twenty-three. I wrote letters home to my parents, trying to help my sister resist this marriage, but to no avail. She married and moved to Shanghai. While I was in Fudan, both my elder and younger sisters supported me financially. Once we three went out in my sister's car [each of them had a car]. I was sitting between my two sisters, and they said, "Look at you. If you got married, you would have a car, too." But both of them had a lot of agony in their marriages.

My father had been the supervisor of Chinese students in America during the First World War. He had had many students abroad who would make suitable husbands. After he returned to China, he gave each student an assignment—my female cousins were all married to them. My elder sister's first choice was the one who later became the minister of the navy in the Nationalist government. She fell in love with him right away when she saw his picture. She asked my father for that man. But my father thought the guy was too handsome. He said handsome men would "change heart" [be unfaithful], which was not good. So he picked another student ten years older than my elder sister. She was twenty at the time, and he was thirty. They got married. He had studied submarines in America and was very knowledgeable. When my father was the commander in Harbin, my brother-in-law worked for my father. Later, when my father was not working, he relied on my brother-in-law.

But what a bastard my brother-in-law was! The men before liberation were thoroughly rotten![9] We Fujianese have the custom that all brides should have dowries. My sister's dowry included a maid. When she was pregnant with her first child—my niece—my brother-in-law had sexual relations with the maid! How terrible! Before the end of my sister's *yuezi* [a month's rest after delivery], she discovered that the maid was pregnant. My sister was so upset that she has had heart disease ever since. The maid eventually had an abortion and was sold to someone else. But my brother-in-law did not repent. When they came to Shanghai, he frequented brothels. My younger sister's husband was not clean either. He, too, had been sent abroad as a student by Qinghua University. He was introduced to my sister by my cousin. These are enough examples. My cousins also had bad marriages. That is why I decided not to marry.

Why did I establish *Nüsheng* [The women's voice]? Why did I join the women's movement? Because of my family background. It was not that I had some special aspiration. As Mao Zedong said, the environment determines everything. I did not think much of men's and women's equality. I thought of revenge. I was born like a bomb, ready to explode, to take revenge. In my youth I was muddleheaded, just pursuing high scores. When I was in Zhongxi Girls' School, I was shut up in school even on Sundays. I did not even know about the May Thirtieth Massacre. My mind changed in high school in Beijing and in Fudan. There were some Communists in Fudan. Chen Wangdao was a professor in Fudan; he was the first to translate *The Communist Manifesto* into Chinese.[10] He had a close student who still keeps in touch with me. In those years I began to be aware of the national crisis and learned some Communist views on women's issues.

How did I start *The Women's Voice*? My teachers in the department of journalism were all from newspapers. Upon my graduation in 1932, our teacher Pan Gongzhan, who ran *Chenbao* [The morning news], got a job for my classmate Guo Zhenyi, editor of the women's column in *Chenbao*. I got an idea and talked to Guo, "Would you please give me a title as a guest correspondent?" She agreed and printed a business card for me. Thus I be-

---

9. As noted earlier, "before liberation" means before 1949. The People's Republic of China was founded on October 1, 1949. In mainland China, people use "liberation" to refer to that date.

10. Chen Wangdao also wrote many articles on women's emancipation in the May Fourth era. He is quoted in chapter 2.

came a correspondent for *Chenbao,* interviewing famous women activists for the column. Although my brother-in-law the banker had already promised me a job in the bank, I wanted to work for newspapers. The first person I interviewed was Liu-Wang Liming. She was the wife of the president of the University of Shanghai and director of Jiezhihui [the Chinese Women Christian Temperance Union], a Christian women's organization that promoted birth control, advocated abolishing bad habits like smoking opium, gambling, and visiting brothels, and encouraged women to serve society. She was over thirty years old, and I was twenty-seven. We liked each other right away. At that time, the Temperance Union published *Jiezhi yuekan* [The temperance monthly], which was supported by an American church. After my interview of Liu-Wang Liming was printed in the newspaper, she met with me again. She told me that she was unhappy with *The Temperance Monthly.* She wished to be free from the influence of religious groups or political parties and to be independent in society. She suggested that I work with her to run an independent women's magazine by women activists. The magazine would promote our own ideas and openly discuss women's issues in order to mobilize our sisters at the bottom of the feudal society to rise up and take their fate in their own hands. Because this was just what I wished, I happily accepted her proposal.

Liu-Wang closed *The Temperance Monthly* and diverted the money to *The Women's Voice.* But that was not enough. I was responsible for the rest. Where could I find money? I convinced my banker brother-in-law and several other bankers to run advertisements in our magazine, which gave us the funds we needed in order to publish. After two months' preparation, the first issue of the biweekly *Women's Voice* was published in October 1932. Because the magazine featured women speaking for women, educated women were our only potential readers. We printed over two thousand copies of each issue. I did the marketing myself, going to newsstands personally to sell magazines.

Not long after we began publishing, Liu-Wang and I began to disagree. By that point, I believed wholeheartedly in Communist ideas. I had initially pursued equality between men and women because of my family background—so I went to school, but I did not know what the women's movement was. I thought it was women receiving education and doing things like Bing Xin or Lu Ying.[11] But after my contact with Communists in Fudan, I saw that our nation was facing a crisis and that Chinese people were en-

---

11. Bing Xin and Lu Ying became famous during the May Fourth period; they were part of the first generation of female professional writers in modern China.

during worse and worse hardships. Women were oppressed at the bottom of society, struggling for their survival. I realized that I should not be concerned only with my own future, but should link my personal fate to the interests of our nation. When I graduated from Fudan, the national salvation movement had just begun, and it developed rapidly. I became devoted to the movement. When I started *The Women's Voice*, I did not at all think that I was working in the women's movement; I just thought we should act and be patriotic together. In the editorial for the first issue, I wrote, "The historical mission of *The Women's Voice* is to mobilize working women and all the patriots to participate in the great national liberation movement." In another issue, I wrote an article titled "Our Standpoint and Attitude," which stated, "The most tragic phenomenon in human society is the sharp class division between the poor and rich. On the one side, the proletariat labor all day but live in hunger and cold; on the other side, the bourgeoisie sit around, enjoying leisure and luxury." I called for eradication of this unjust phenomenon and advocated a common world through socialism. I stated that all those groups and individuals who hindered social progress were our enemy and all those who sympathized with oppressed women and the proletariat were our relatives. "The mission of this journal is to be a powerful tongue for our comrades." My views were identical to the Communist Party's ideas. But the party did not acknowledge my effort.

The Women's Voice attracted a lot of attention, including the attention of Communists. One day Xia Yan visited me in the women's apartment where I lived.[12] He gave me a copy of *Women and Socialism*, which he had translated. After reading that book, I believed even more strongly in the Communist ideas about women. I thought their ideas on women's liberation were more systematic, and I accepted the theory that private ownership was the root of women's oppression. In Fudan I had accepted Communist ideas about women's liberation—that women should go out into society, that marriage should be monogamous, that human beings should all be equal, and that women's liberation should be linked with social revolution. After I read *Women and Socialism*, I pushed our magazine to devote less space to discussing women's situation and more space to calling upon women to go beyond family boundaries and participate in the social

---

12. Xia Yan (Shen Duanxian) was the first to translate into Chinese the entirety of *Women and Socialism*. The book was written by Augustin Bebel, a German socialist. Just as it had influenced European socialist policy on women's liberation, the book became the central canon of the CCP's discourse on women's liberation. The early translation of excerpts of the book appeared in the journals that promoted women's emancipation, including *The Ladies' Journal*, during the May Fourth period.

revolution. After liberation, when I saw what the Communist Party did, I gradually realized that I had made a mistake. The Communist Party just used the women's movement. Actually, they did not even have a women's movement; they just used women. But at that time, because I was influenced by the Communist Party, I did not get along with Liu-Wang, who was immersed in the women's movement and not affected by Communist Party ideas.

After two years of working together, we broke up. Several things led to the breakup. Liu-Wang always thought *The Women's Voice* belonged to the Temperance Union and asked me to print information on Temperance Union activities in each issue. I did not always do this. And the articles she liked were ones I did not want to print, because our ideas differed. She was more religious, and I leaned toward the Communists. But the Communist Party did not hold me in high regard because not all my ideas were the same as theirs. Later, Liu-Wang promoted old-fashioned ideas about women and asserted that every woman should first be a good wife and virtuous mother. I believed that vulgar good-wife-and-virtuous-motherism hindered women's emancipation. Instead, I called for women's participation in social revolution. At the time, Liu-Wang's Temperance Union lacked money, and *The Women's Voice* did not make a profit, so it became a burden. In the end we broke up, and *The Women's Voice* became independent—meaning it no longer had a backer. In the first issue after *The Women's Voice* became independent, I openly declared my position:

> We believe that women's problems are one link in the problems of
> the entire society. Until we solve these social problems, women's problems will never be thoroughly solved. Conversely, without a thorough
> solution to women's problems, social problems cannot be thoroughly
> solved. Currently, the Chinese women's movement has two tendencies:
> on the one hand, it advocates new good-wife-and-virtuous-motherism;
> on the other hand, it pursues narrow feminism. The former is a yoke
> over women that some men try to utilize; the latter is a tool that a few
> opportunists employ for their own benefit. Neither is the way out for
> the majority of women. We should not only refuse to cooperate with
> them but also oppose them firmly. What we need is a women's movement that can immerse itself among the masses and that seeks the
> liberation of humankind through the national liberation movement. . . .
> We hope that, from now on, with the efforts of the public, *The Women's
> Voice* will become the "voice of society."

What I meant by "narrow feminism" was those women who only wanted equality between men and women.

After *The Women's Voice* became independent, the first problem I faced was financial. In order to raise enough money for the journal, I called on our contributors and friends. Through personal connections, we invited famous movie stars like Zhen Junli and Hu Die to give voluntary performances. We collected a large sum of money by selling tickets to their performances. I also went to Nanjing and Qingdao to see my father's good friends who were then in the Nationalist government. The minister of the Navy Department and the Mayor of Qingdao both generously donated money. My younger sister also kept giving me money from her private savings. Thus I managed to run the magazine on my own.

I invited many famous writers to contribute to our journal. Of them, many were Communists. But because *The Women's Voice* promoted Communist ideas and criticized the Nationalist government, it gradually faced stronger and stronger censorship. It often took a long time for our articles to pass the official censorship, which affected our printing schedule. Sometimes our articles were cut so much by the official censors that we had to leave blank spaces in the final printed page. One night a friend came to tell me that my name was on the black list of the Shanghai Municipal Council. The censorship grew worse and worse, we had fewer and fewer contributors, and our financial resources were almost depleted. Finally *The Women's Voice* had to stop publishing in late 1935.

In July 1937, the Lugou Bridge incident occurred, and the War of Resistance broke out nationwide.[13] I was working in a post office in Shanghai. Some friends encouraged me to go back to the media in order to mobilize mass resistance against Japanese invasion. At the same time someone wrote an article criticizing me for "asking others to resist the Japanese, while she escapes the real struggle." These opinions stimulated me to rejoin the battle. I quit the post office job and went to Guangdong. In a bookstore in Shaoguan, I saw the monthly magazine *Guangdong funü* [Guangdong women], which was published by the Guangdong Women's Association. It printed a brief biography of Lenin, which indicated to me that the magazine was progressive, so I wrote a story about Guangdong women's life as I saw it on my trip and sent it to the journal. I also told them I used to be the editor in chief of *The Women's Voice*. The story was printed right away and I was asked to see Lu Suying, the director of the Culture Department of the Women's Association. Lu had graduated from Zhongshan University and

13. On July 7, 1937, Japanese troops bombed the Lugou Bridge (Marco Polo Bridge) and adjacent area, close to Beijing. After the incident, Chiang Kai-shek declared the War of Resistance against Japan.

was supportive of the Communist Party. Portraits of Marx, Lenin, and other revolutionaries hung on the walls of her room. She appreciated my views in *The Women's Voice* and invited me to be the editor in chief of *Guangdong Women*. Thus I began editing *Guangdong Women* and had the same position I had held at *The Women's Voice*. This job gave me great satisfaction.

However, because the journal was run by the provincial government, many of the staff were Guomindang members. They were unhappy to see this new editor in chief and looked at me jealously. After I had edited two issues, we heard that the Japanese were coming to Guangdong. The provincial government moved to Guangxi, and *Guangdong Women* ceased publication. I contracted malaria, so I said good-bye to Lu and returned to Shanghai. Then I was invited by a friend to be the editor of a women's column in the *Damei Evening News* in Shanghai. I wrote most of the articles for the column, which mainly called for women to join the War of Resistance. But before long, the editor in chief of the newspaper was assassinated by the Japanese and the newspaper was forced to close down. After that, I taught in Zhongxi Girls' School for a few years.

When *The Women's Voice* was independent, Guan Lu, a female poet, wanted to take it over. She was a Communist Party member, and maybe she was sent by the Communist Party to break into *The Women's Voice* when they knew it was without financial backup. At the time, I did not know that she was a Communist, and when she came to our meetings and tried to grab control of the journal, I rejected her efforts. In the early 1940s, after Shanghai fell to the Japanese, a journal appeared that looked identical to ours and was also named *The Women's Voice*. But this *Women's Voice* advocated surrender and the Greater East Asian Coprosperity Sphere.[14] Its editor in chief was Japanese, and Guan Lu was on the list of editors. I was busy teaching at the time and unaware of this fake *Women's Voice*. I learned about it from a friend's letter and found it at a bookstand. I realized that because I had refused to let her get her hands on *The Women's Voice*, Guan Lu was very unhappy with me. Now she had insulted *The Women's Voice*, throwing mud at it by using its name for a traitor magazine. Seeing this fake *Women's Voice*, I decided that some day I would revive our *Women's Voice*, expose those traitors, and regain the reputation of *The Women's Voice*.

After the Japanese were defeated, Guomindang returned to Shanghai.

14. The Greater East Asian Coprosperity Sphere was an idea that legitimized the Japanese invasion of China. According to this idea, China should become a producing country of crude materials for Japan and accept Japan's martial leadership in order for both China and Japan to rise in the world power structure.

Guan Lu's sister, Hu Xiufeng, whom later I learned was a Communist, was extremely popular with Guomindang. Hu's husband was Li Jianhua, once a famous sociology professor in Fudan. According to newspapers at the time, Hu was his fourth wife. Li was sent by the Communist Party to be the director of the Social Bureau after the war. Hu also ran a magazine called *Xiandai funü* [Modern women]. Because she was an activist in the women's movement before Shanghai's fall, she certainly knew *The Women's Voice*. She also knew of my conflict with Guan. When I tried to revive *The Women's Voice*, I at first failed to get the necessary stamp of approval from the Social Bureau. I think it was Li and his wife who obstructed the approval. But I eventually registered the magazine with the help of my student. When I was teaching in Zhongxi, I was popular with students. One student's mother knew a woman, Lu, who knew a big shot in the Guomindang Propaganda Department. This woman, Lu, had read *The Women's Voice* and thought I wrote beautifully. When she learned that I had a problem in registering *The Women's Voice*, she offered to help. My student introduced me to her and she wrote a letter to the big shot. Within one week we got the Social Bureau's approval. But in the Cultural Revolution, that registration became a problem: I could not explain when asked, "Why would the Guomindang government approve of your journal?" Some people thought I had a close relationship with the Guomindang.

After the Japanese surrendered, my younger sister gave me five hundred silver dollars to revive *The Women's Voice*. I invited several former contributors who were still in Shanghai to work together. In October 1945, *The Women's Voice* resumed publication, this time as a monthly journal. In the first issue I wrote, "Under the Japanese occupation, beautiful clothes were grabbed to cover an ugly corpse. The name of our journal, *The Women's Voice*, was used to spread various poisons. Fortunately, intelligent people are able to tell the difference between black and white, true and false. . . . Now we have won victory in the War of Resistance. In order to secure a permanent victory and accomplish the great cause of nation building, we should more actively promote the women's liberation movement." In the first few issues, in order to emphasize women's contribution to the War of Resistance, we printed stories of women who performed heroic deeds during the Japanese occupation. One of my students did an interview with Qian Jianqiu, who was a Guomindang member. I printed the story because I thought all women who had made contributions to the War of Resistance should be praised. I also printed articles written by Guomindang members, because I thought they were also patriotic. This was different from the Communist Party's views. In a sense *The Women's Voice* changed its nature. During the

War of Resistance, it followed the Communist Party and just wrote about patriotism, as if women joining the patriotic movement were the same as working for the women's movement. After the war, I printed few articles contributed by Communists, but more women's articles and even the Guomindang's articles.

The Women's Voice often printed exposés of men who abandoned their wives and married young beautiful women, of intellectual women who broke up other families in order to live a luxurious life, and of rascally literary men who philandered with women in the name of courtship. Because of this, many people were offended, and they criticized The Women's Voice as "narrow womanism" that specialized in cursing men. I guess I just had one label on me. My mouth was full of curses about men. When men with various political backgrounds came to see me—Communists, Nationalists, or traitors—they would give up talking to me because we could not agree on anything. Although I also scolded Jiang Jieshi [Chiang Kai-shek] badly, the Communists would not pay attention to me. They thought I was of no use to them. The Guomindang knew I did not have a political background, so they just ignored me. They totally looked down upon women, ignoring them just as you would ignore a barking dog. But The Women's Voice put top priority on national interests. Once, Tian Han's wife came to tell us about Tian's extramarital affair with a woman. Tian was a Communist big shot. Because at the time the Nationalist newspapers were using the affair to attack the progressive forces, we did not print anything to support Tian's wife, even though we were very sorry for her.

For a short time after The Women's Voice was revived, I collaborated with the publisher Kang Dan. I was responsible for the editing, and he was responsible for the marketing. Gradually, Kang tried to interfere with the editing, so we parted ways. Around that time, Liu-Wang Liming returned to Shanghai from Chongqing. After the war her mind had changed a lot. She accepted new ideas and no longer promoted good-wife-and-virtuous-motherism. She said to me that we did not differ too much and that she was happy to see The Women's Voice revived. So we collaborated again. As in our first collaboration, she was the director of the journal and I was the editor in chief. A lot of the office work was done by the staff of the Temperance Union. And we changed our editorial policy. In order to promote women's interest in writing, we decided to print only articles written by women. We printed stories written by women from all fields—education, performing arts, medicine, law, cinema, and art.

I also participated in social activities with Liu-Wang. We joined the progressive forces to protest the Guomindang's sabotage of the United Front and to protest the impending civil war. The Guomindang tightened their control. Liu-Wang was a prominent member in the Democratic League and was on the wanted list. She had to escape to Hong Kong before it was too late. One of our regular contributors, Geng Xinzhi, had just finished an interview of Shi Liang, the famous woman activist and lawyer. The interview was already in print when Shi Liang had to escape, too. Before she left, she told us to withdraw the story. We had to destroy the laid-out type right away. Although Liu-Wang told me to try our best to continue the journal, the political situation made that difficult. Plus, we again faced fiscal problems. Geng Xinzhi suggested that we ask for donations from friends and acquaintances, and many people donated things like books, paintings, and antiques. But when we tried to hold an auction of these donated goods, we failed. The ongoing civil war caused such inflation that few people had enough money to buy these things. In 1947, under all kinds of pressure, *The Women's Voice* once again had to stop publishing. The situation afterward was so chaotic that we lost all the issues we had published during my second collaboration with Liu-Wang. I do not even remember which was the last issue.

Then I worked as a tutor to support myself. After liberation Li Jianhua changed from the head of the Guomindang Social Bureau to the head of the Labor Bureau of the Communist government—and so his wife Hu once again cut a very smart figure. That is why I did not go out to look for jobs: I was afraid that Hu would persecute me if she found out where I was. I continued to make a living by teaching a few students at my home. Guan Lu was jailed after liberation. But in recent years Guan's name has become prominent again. Many articles praised her as a heroine, and they also wanted to write her story into a TV series. I do not believe that a Communist would use her real name to work for the Japanese and promote the so-called Greater East Asian Coprosperity Sphere. I don't understand how a person can be a traitor one day and a Communist heroine the next. The Communist Party is so complicated. I am very upset about it. I did not think I would be able to get the story straight. I wondered how I could make future generations know the truth about Guan Lu and our *Women's Voice*. I got the idea to set up a tombstone for myself.

In 1990 I had a tombstone set up on the Phoenix Mountain, Suzhou. The epitaph was written by a friend. It reads as follows.

> Ms. Wang Yiwei devoted her life to the women's liberation movement
> and patriotic anti-imperialist struggle. In 1932, when the Japanese
> invaded China, Wang rose up to unite progressive women like Liu-
> Wang Liming, organized the Women's Voice Society, and established
> the journal *The Women's Voice*. Contributors included Liu-Wang

Liming, Yang Meizhen, He Xiangning, Pen Zigang, Huang Biyao, Jin Shiyin, Zhang Naiqi, and Shen Zhiyuan. *The Women's Voice* played an avant-garde role in the national salvation movement and received strong response from its readers. Therefore, after Shanghai fell, the Japanese used the prestige of *The Women's Voice* to publish a fake "women's voice," which propagandized the traitorism of the Greater East Asian Coprosperity Sphere. It instilled in the Chinese the poison of surrendering and attempted to eliminate the Chinese nation and race. But the result was quite the opposite. The crazy Japanese were thoroughly defeated and driven back to their home. Today, we Chinese have stood up and women have been liberated. In the process of pushing the wheel of history forward, Ms. Wang has made her own contribution.

There is a better epitaph that has been written but not inscribed. I asked my friend, artist Xie Chunyan, to write this one in 1990:

Spring water comes out of the gully, and a fragrant orchid grows in the valley. Here rests in peace Wang Yiwei *xianshen* [a respectful term for a senior person], a remarkable person. *Xianshen* was born to an old and well-known family in southern Fujian. Bright and sharp, a young rebel against old Confucian ethics, she struggled for freedom and independence. Although tasting bitter fruits in the process, she never regretted her actions. This is the first remarkable thing about her. Growing up in a chaotic world, with her sole wisdom and courage, she created *The Women's Voice*, promoting women's liberation and never yielding to men. In the War of Resistance, working with Wang Liming, He Xiangning, and Shi Liang, and calling for national salvation, she had no regard for her own life and death. This is the second remarkable thing. In her old age, with her ailing body but warm heart, she taught students and made Chinese paintings. She did not step out of her little room but served as a matchmaker. Many people have benefited. This is the third remarkable thing. It is rare for people to have three remarkable things. Wild weeds cannot cover her spirit, and pure wind will reveal her essence. Her lofty aspirations will never die.

I myself wrote these lines in 1983: "Sickness has accompanied me every year in my hard life, but I am unwilling to die without fulfilling my life's goal." It cost me two thousand yuan to have this tombstone made. I was just worried that these women would be forgotten. After liberation the Communist Party only gave recognition to its own kind of women's movement. Other women's movements are not recognized at all. But even Sheng Zijiu and Shi Liang did not promote the women's movement; they just did things to follow the Communist Party and to overthrow the Guomindang, things totally unrelated to women. Most people have the misconception that anything involving women is a women's movement. According to the Communist Party, following the party is women's liberation. I once believed in that, too, but what I was actually involved in was the national salvation movement. I did not do much for the women's movement. After liberation, I gradually realized this. The Communist Party still does not give women important positions; it just uses women to promote the party. The women's movement died after liberation. A women's movement should never let men lead, because a women's movement led by men can never be thorough. It was after liberation—shutting myself up in my little room, reading newspapers, and watching what really happened—that I reached this conclusion. These are all my own thoughts. When I ran *The Women's Voice*, I just parroted the Communist Party. But now, I know what women's liberation truly is. In feudalism and capitalism, women were not treated as human beings, but as decorations, slaves, and tools for reproduction. Feudalism and capitalism promoted the notion of the good wife and virtuous mother. My idea of women's liberation is that women are human beings, just like men, and they should have equal positions. Although the Communist Party says that men and women should be equal, they do not practice what they preach. The Communist Party promoted movements such as the youth movement and the women's movement only for the purpose of telling you what they wanted you to do. They are hanging up a lamb's head but selling dog meat. Chinese women are still not liberated, and everywhere women are oppressed. Many husbands still oppress women very severely. Factories kick women out, and universities refuse to accept female students. What kind of women does the government most need today? What they praise most are the ones who make lots of money. Women should be business managers, following the government's policy! If you know how to make money, to open a company and to be a manager, the government will extol you.

In the Guomindang period, women were also discriminated against. When I taught in Zhongxi Girls' School, they did not hire married women. They only wanted single women. The principal of the school was an unmarried woman. Many working women were just like vases for decoration. The highest positions women could attain were as school principals and lawyers. That is why, when I heard of the Communist Party, I was attracted to it. But personally, I did not encounter any discrimination. In the school I was treated the same as male teachers. When I edited the journal, I only contacted women. Men would come to see me. At that time I was extremely popular. Many men sought me out. But because I was not pretty, they stopped coming after their first visit, and I never returned their visits. I was very proud.

When I was running *The Women's Voice*, a man in Zhejiang saw the journal. He wrote to me and became a contributor—and that is how I got to know my ex-husband, Lu Hefeng. He was a high school graduate and a minor staff member in the Guomindang county government. We did not marry right away. We got to know each other and had a relationship. Later, we got married. I asked my brother-in-law to find him a job in Shanghai doing financial work. I married him because I thought he loved *The Women's Voice* and was concerned about it. But actually he was the worst type of bad guy. In the Communist Party there are a lot of honey-lipped people who behave worse than feudal lords in marriage. I often said that Guomindang members were bad because they had concubines. But the Communists are even worse. They just abandon their first wives. Under feudalism, when a man had several wives, proper status was given to the first wife. But in the Communist Party the first wife is totally abandoned. She is divorced and given a "hat" [political label] as a sign that she has an ideological problem. Lu was not a Communist Party member but favored the party. He was like the Communist Party. His words and deeds did not match. He was no good in any respect. He could not rise in literary circles, so he wrote articles concerning women's problems to cut a smart figure. He was extremely bad. He just wanted to use *The Women's Voice* to publish his articles. The views he expressed in his articles were all false, not genuine. He was absolutely a male chauvinist. The Communist Party members are all that way. I heard many stories of Communists having concubines. I did not want to contact any man who had concubines. Wasn't Mao that way too? During the War of Resistance, I learned of the affair between Mao and Jiang Qing. That changed my opinion of the Communist Party. Lu was just the same as Mao, only he was unable to climb up the political ladder. So he wanted to use *The Women's Voice* to help him climb up. Back then, many men pursued me. Chinese men were all that way. That is why I despise them. They oppress women in their actions, but in words they say they support equality between men and women. Tian Han's wife came to see me. Several more women came to talk about their husbands' affairs. Those men all oppressed their wives. Guo Moruo had seven wives. At his memorial all seven turned up with their children, which made his last wife furious. When I quarreled with Lu, he said, "We want several women. Men need refreshments as well as meals." I was so outraged that I threw his hat at him. He was such a male chauvinist that he even hit me. We soon divorced.

I did not have children. Once I went to see a gynecologist because of an illness, and she said, "If you want children, I can help you have them. It is easy." But I said, "I do not want children. I want to work for revolution and to air women's grievances." This was fine with Lu because he was a leftist. Leftists did not want children. I did not think much of my own marriage. I was just devoted to the cause of women's equality. I think women have their own ideas and their own personalities. In contrast, in the old society, by depending on men for food, women had to obey men in all things. As the folk-saying goes, "If a woman marries a chicken, she has to follow the chicken. If she marries a dog, she has to follow the dog." I think in the future, the family will be dissolved. Family will be just like friends: it's not easy to have a lifelong friend, is it? Sometimes you even break up friendships.

I became a member in the Wenshiguan in 1962. Because there were many artists there, I began to learn painting from them. And I began to compose poems. I had never been interested in those things when I was young. But for a long time I lived in fear—especially when Hu Xiufeng became the leading figure in the Shanghai Women's Federation—because I did not know what the Communist Party thought of my activities before liberation. So I kept a low profile. After the Cultural Revolution, when Shi Liang died, Shen Zijiu and Hu Yuzhi wrote a memorial article for her. In that article, they mentioned *The Women's Voice* and me. It was only at that time that I realized the Communist Party did not regard me as a counterrevolutionary. I was so relieved that I began to get involved in public activities. I always want to do things for women. I think women should raise their educational level. So I volunteered to teach many young women in my spare time. I also helped women find jobs, and I did matchmaking. Some young women asked me to matchmake for them, so I asked them, "Why do you have to get married?" They said they did not know, they were just feeling empty. When they reach a certain age, they just want to marry. But if women know it is not good to have men as company, why do they have to marry?

The Wenshiguan pays a lot of attention to artists but not to me, a person who was in the women's movement. Yet in 1984, they asked me to write a memoir of *The Women's Voice*, because Deng Yingchao asked Wenshiguans all over China to dig out those people who contributed to the women's movement before liberation. If she hadn't done that, nobody would know me. Deng made a great contribution to the women's movement, and she was the one who truly promoted the movement. Zhou Enlai's name became so big that it overshadowed Deng. She ran the periodical *Nüxing* [The women's star] in the 1920s. And I ran *The Women's Voice* in the 1930s. I asked a friend to write an article on *The Women's Star* and *The Women's*

Voice. When the Shanghai Archive was established a few years ago, celebrities' materials were collected, and at first they wanted to include me. But someone said that I did not have a mass following, and thus they dropped me. I was very angry. I had run my journal for such a long time—I did not have a mass following? However, I donated the issues of *The Women's Voice* I had to the archive. I also made photocopies of some articles in those issues, either written by me or other contributors. They are in these two big albums that I want you to have.[15]

When I was looking for the journals to donate, a friend of mine, Chen Yongsheng, gave me a copy of *The Women's Voice* that she had kept. I have known Chen for a long time. She knew Liu-Wang and came to the Temperance Union to attend meetings. She was a physical education teacher and had been to an American university. Under Liu-Wang Liming at that time there were many women like Chen. They got an education, went abroad, and then returned home to climb the social ladder. Those women were individualists. They did everything for their own self-interest, without regard for the benefit of the society as a whole or for women in general. Self was their first priority. Back then, few people struggled for the good of society as a whole. That is why our journal did not sell well. I have another friend, Cai Muhui, who was Chen Wangdao's wife. When I was running *The Women's Voice*, she was running *Nü qingnian* [The green year]. She was the head of the YWCA in Shanghai. She saw that *The Women's Voice* was successful, so she wanted me to work with her. My salary was only sixty

---

15. Wang Yiwei had the two big albums of photocopied articles from *The Women's Voice* ready for me when I paid her a second visit. She also tried to give me a third album that was full of family photographs taken since her childhood. I did not accept the third album, because it seemed a family treasure; I thought that I could always come back to make duplicates of the photos. I soon regretted this decision. After I learned of her death, I went to her apartment, where her helper remained. But all her belongings had already been removed by her few immediate relatives, whom I was unable to trace. I wonder if Wang knew only I would cherish those personal documents as much as she did. I went to the Shanghai Archive to look for *The Women's Voice* after Wang's death. But I was told that they did not have the journal. My citations of *The Women's Voice* are from the two valuable albums Wang Yiwei gave me. The East Asian Collection at the Hoover Institution has four issues of *The Women's Voice* published in 1945 and 1946. These rare copies are a proof of Wang Yiwei's tenacious struggle to revive the journal in a time of tremendous social and political turmoil. The library also has *The Women's Voice* published during the Japanese occupation. Wang Yiwei thought this fake *Women's Voice* was run by the Japanese. Because of the involvement of Guan Lu, an underground CCP member, in this magazine, it is not clear if it was run by the Japanese or was a cover-up for CCP activities.

silver dollars, and she would have paid me one hundred silver dollars, but I did not take that job because it was a church-run magazine and I strongly oppose religion. I think Christians are hypocrites. That is why I went to a high school that was antireligious.

In the year I was born, the Revolutionary Alliance was established. In the year I came to Shanghai, the Communist Party was established. And Fudan was also formally established in the year I was born. The timing seems to indicate that I should have become a great person, but in the end I was just a nameless little pawn. When I was studying in the Nanjing University, its fortieth anniversary occurred, and I acted in a drama during the celebrations. I played two roles: an old prostitute and a man. At Fudan I also acted in dramas. I was not good at acting, so I did not become famous.

I see more and more clearly that the Communist Party just used the women's movement to reinforce its own leading position. On my part, I used politics to reach my goal of equality between men and women. I joined the national salvation movement, but I did not forget about women. That is where I differed from the Communist Party, and that is why neither the Guomindang nor the Communist Party wanted me. So in the end I am shut up in this seven-square-meter *tingzijian* [a small room designed for storage, common in Shanghai-style buildings], just given a mouthful of food. I am such a poor person. I am really a *gulao* [lonely old person]. I am politically lonely as well as lonely in family and career. My life is a tragedy. If I had been a man, my father would have taken me abroad with him when he went to Europe. If I had not leaned toward the Communist Party, I would have gone to the United States. But because I was influenced by the Communists in Fudan, I was pro-Soviet and anti-America. I taught three years in Zhongxi Girls' School. Most of my students are in the United States, and they have achieved a great deal.

INTERPRETATION: FEMINISM
IN BETWEEN THE CCP AND THE GMD

When I was looking for old woman activists in Shanghai, one of my friends told me that in her neighborhood there was an old woman who used to be an editor of a women's magazine. When I was introduced to this old woman, Wang Yiwei, she greeted me with great enthusiasm and said, "You have found the right person. I am a specialist in the women's movement. You cannot find anyone else like me." Wang regarded herself as a woman activist who became involved in the women's movement by editing women's magazines. In several interviews, she spoke very little about things unrelated to that part of her life. Instead, she constructed a life story centered around her identity as an editor in chief of the journal *The Women's Voice*, even though she spent only approximately five years altogether working for women's magazines or writing for women's columns in newspapers. Before she became a member of the Wenshiguan, she had worked as a teacher, a tutor, and a post office worker. But these experiences are unmentioned in the epitaphs written at her request. Obviously, being the editor in chief of *The Women's Voice* was the most meaningful and satisfying experience in her long life. It seems that, for Wang Yiwei, her experience as editor did not merely illustrate, but rather *constituted* who she was. She examined her family background and her childhood in light of how she eventually became an activist in the women's movement.

In Wang Yiwei's story we see again the two chief factors that brought women in the early twentieth century into the struggle for women's liberation: women's oppression in the family and a discourse on gender equality. In her narrative, Wang presents a fine analysis of the impact her family life had on her. As a daughter who allegedly cost her brother his life, Wang endured tremendous psychological pressure during her childhood. The chain of events she recalls is gruesome: her birth led to her young brother's death; the only son's death led to her father's acquiring a concubine; and the existence of the concubine led to her mother's incurable disease and eventual addiction to opium. In the story, Wang Yiwei, her mother, and the concubine—three women of different generations and social status— were victims of a patriarchal and patrilineal family system. Growing up in this oppressive system that favored male heirs, Wang determined to fight back by being better than men. Witnessing her mother's sorrows motivated her to aim high and to achieve more than her half-brother in order to win glory for her mother as well as for all women. Her professed interest in women's issues surely originated in these early personal experiences.

Wang's parents fostered Wang's ambition in both negative and positive ways. They were sorry that she was not a boy. However, they brought her up as a boy and hoped that she would become a female Number One Scholar. It was not unusual in Chinese culture for families without a son to rear a daughter to be a surrogate son, either for practical reasons, as when Lu Lihua's father groomed her to be the heir of the family business, or to serve their own psychological needs.[16] Such young girls usually endured psychological pressure for being female, yet at the same time they received en-

16. For a story of a surrogate son told in first person, see Buwei Yang Chao, *Autobiography of a Chinese Woman* (New York: John Day Company, 1947).

couragement and differential treatment that implied they were special and promising. Judging from the cases of Lu Lihua and Wang Yiwei, we have reason to believe that these lucky daughters were likely to become strong women. Such a girl would strive hard to achieve more than an ordinary son would achieve, in order to make her parents proud, as well as for her own self-satisfaction. In the turbulent sociopolitical transformations of the early twentieth century, these select daughters' ambitions would be realized by gaining a position in the men's world.

But educational opportunities were not necessarily only given to select daughters as a special treatment. Wang Yiwei emphasizes that her parents regarded her as especially smart and paid attention to her education. When she asked to go to the famous girls' school in Shanghai, her father agreed right away. But her two sisters also had private tutors, even though they did not go to universities. Wang's explanation is that private tutoring for girls was a common practice in Fujianese families. Regional differences may in part account for differences in stories of women's education. In Lu Lihua's area, no girls had received any education before her. In contrast, in Zhu Su'e's hometown, girls' education in an old-style school was taken for granted. Wang Yiwei was in a situation similar to Zhu's: Changzhou and Fuzhou, where Zhu's and Wang's families originated, were both listed by the historian Ho Ping-ti as prefectures boasting unusual academic success in Ming and Qing times.[17] It seems that regions producing more scholar-officials were historically more likely to favor girls' education. Perhaps private tutors for girls in scholar-official families had become such a status symbol in these areas that other families with financial resources followed their example. Thus the story of women's oppression in the patriarchal family is sometimes paradoxical, as is illustrated in Wang's narrative. A daughter seen as an ominous comet (saozhouxing) might also be treated as a potential Number One Scholar. She was capable of bringing credit as well as disaster to her family.

Wang Yiwei's exposure to the discourse of gender equality is different from that of Lu Lihua and Zhu Su'e in several ways. Because she was a few years younger than the other two women, the May Fourth movement did not leave as deep an impression on her as it did on them.[18] Moreover, be-

17. Ping-ti Ho, *The Ladder of Success in Imperial China* (New York: John Wiley and Sons, 1964), chapter 6. According to Ho, there were obvious regional differences in academic success in Ming and Qing times. And both southern Jiangsu and Fujian were ranked high when the numbers of *jinshi* from different regions were compared.

18. According to the findings of psychological research, events occurring during the transition to adulthood are more meaningful than those in other periods. In this sense, the May Fourth movement was not a cohort-defining event in the life of Wang

cause her father was a high-ranking officer in the Beiyang warlord government, she might have been deliberately shielded from student activism. But progressive ideas nonetheless broke through her seclusion in the commanding officer's mansion. One of her tutors subscribed to an influential journal published by the Shanghai Commercial Press, and he told his young students of what he read in the magazine. New Culture messages passed to Wang through this channel. This same tutor not only introduced Wang to a Western-style girls' school, but also encouraged her to emulate ancient female role models: Mulan and the famous poet Xie Daoyun. Like many Chinese male scholars, the tutor acknowledged women's talent. As a man with progressive ideas, he welcomed the emergence of new women who would contribute their talents to public service. Interestingly, encouraging his female students to aim high did not mean that this old man had made a revolutionary break from the past. Rather, as Wang astutely points out, "It is also an old idea that girls should be like Mulan and Xie Daoyun." A modern Xie Daoyun, however, could not be content with learning inside the inner chambers. The tutor encouraged Wang to pursue her dream of an education abroad and thus advised Wang to go to McTyeire School, an American missionary school built to attract girls from elite families, as the first step toward fulfilling that dream. This was a path that had been traveled by many women from elite families since the beginning of the twentieth century. Many of the female students who returned from abroad, including those who returned from Japan, were establishing respectable careers in China's urban areas when Wang was encouraged to follow in their footsteps. An education abroad had become a secure route to high social status for both men and women.

Because she was living in Harbin, a northern city distant from the center of the New Culture movement, Wang knew little of the ongoing new intellectual currents. In her words, she was "muddleheaded," focused only on pursuing high scores. Her description of this early stage reflects little influence from nationalism, liberalism, or feminism. Nevertheless, her role models included the famous May Fourth new women, Bing Xin and Lu Ying, professional writers of the 1920s. As Wang emphasizes in her narrative, "I did not know what the women's movement was. I thought it was women receiving education and doing things like Bing Xin and Lu Ying." Wang correctly connected these new women with the women's movement. Bing Xin

because she was not yet fourteen years old. See Abigail J. Stewart and Joseph M. Healy, Jr., "Linking Individual Development and Social Changes," *American Psychologist* 44, no. 1 (1989).

and Lu Ying both received a college education and developed an independent career, and equal educational and career opportunities for women were among the prominent themes of New Culture feminism. Thus, through famous new women of her time, Wang learned messages of New Culture feminism. She took these women as role models that pointed her on the road to self-realization. Hence, Wang's childhood ambition to be better than men was achieved in response to New Culture feminism: receive a high education and become an independent career woman.

Yet the road to self-realization was, for Wang, a bumpy one. Studying in the prestigious girls' school proved less exhilarating than Wang had expected. McTyeire School was an upper-class school, and the majority of students were from Shanghai's wealthy families.[19] Although Wang was also from an upper-class family, she differed from the main student body in significant ways. She had grown up mostly in the north, in cities such as Beijing and Harbin, which means she probably was distinctively different from Shanghai girls in accent, clothes, and even in the foods she preferred. Moreover, up to the age of sixteen, she was conversant with Chinese classics but had little knowledge of Western culture. Now, suddenly, landing in that American missionary school, she surely experienced cultural shock. The few years in McTyeire School left her with many negative memories. She liked neither the stylish students nor the heavily Westernized curriculum and became antireligious because of her experience in the missionary school. Under these circumstances, her father's transfer back to Beijing was good news, because she was able to leave Shanghai and join her family in Beijing. What she did not realize then was that, in leaving McTyeire School, she left the track to the realization of her original dream to study abroad—a dream whose loss she regretted until the end of her life.

In the Jinshi High School in Beijing, she began to confront leftist ideologies. She liked her antireligious teachers and classmates. In the interviews, she repeated the point that Jinshi was a very progressive school that transformed her mind. She began to be influenced by nationalism and communism. After graduation from high school, Wang drifted from a nursing school in Beijing to the history department in Nanjing University, finally landing

19. In a recent study of Shanghai women in the 1930s, Su Su reports that entering the McTyeire Girls' School became such a status symbol that parents spent fortunes to make social connections that would help their daughters enroll in the school. Unlike other girls' schools established by missionaries, McTyeire Girls' School targeted girls from wealthy families from the very beginning. See Su Su, *Qianshi jinsheng* [The previous generation and life today] (Shanghai: Yuandong chubanshe, 1996), 66–67.

in the department of journalism in Fudan University in Shanghai. There she stayed, enduring financial hardship in order to graduate. The school obviously suited her. The major presented her with the opportunity to become a journalist—a career only recently opened to women. Her talent in writing was to be utilized, and her mission to win glory for her mother and for all women would be fulfilled by being one in the first generation of professional female journalists. And Fudan left another mark on her: it had attracted a group of progressive professors who, she later realized, were actually senior Communists.

Her attraction to communism was logical. In her narrative Wang presents a set of answers to the question she must have asked herself many times: How can a person from a feudal family like mine be so progressive? From what she has constructed, we may easily trace the development of a Communist sympathizer. The "feudal family" both oppressed her and fostered her ambition to be better than men. Given that ambition, she was frustrated to see that in her time the highest social positions for women were only as school principals and lawyers. Under those circumstances she welcomed radical social change, or even a communist revolution that promised gender equality in all aspects.

Wang's exposure to the Chinese Communist ideas, including the CCP line on women's liberation, is manifested in her narrative at both conscious and unconscious levels. She explains clearly that her acceptance of CCP ideas began during her years in Fudan and that, as editor in chief of *The Women's Voice*, she wrote many articles "identical" to the CCP line. However, since liberation, she has been disenchanted with the CCP. In her old age she is very critical of the CCP and has reevaluated the CCP's gender policy as well as her own siding with the CCP. At the same time, her conversance with CCP language often shapes her own account. For instance, her criticism of her mother is expressed using phrases such as "a decadent person" and "a fallen woman"—terms that convey the tone of Chinese Communist moral condemnation of bourgeoisie. Although she is deeply sympathetic to her mother's tragedy, she cannot help using the CCP line to judge her. In her reevaluation of the CCP, Wang concludes that women were used by the CCP in the social movements that it promoted. Nevertheless, she calls women of her generation who pursued career achievements rather than political or social involvement "individualists," evoking the full negative connotation of the Chinese Communist discourse. In short, Wang's narrative reflects both a revolt against and a conformity to the CCP discourse. It often expresses the conflict and confusion of a woman who has found that she has to reassess the most cherished part of her life.

One of the major Communist theorists, Chen Wangdao, was Wang's professor at Fudan, and through him Wang became familiar with the Communist theory about women's liberation. Her "parroting" of CCP rhetoric is best represented in her writing in *The Women's Voice* after she broke up with Liu-Wang Liming. There she criticized Liu-Wang for promoting good-wife-and-virtuous-motherism as well as "narrow feminism." She called for women's participation in the national salvation movement, a theme emphasized by the CCP during that period. Wang did not talk much about women's issues after she broke up with Liu-Wang. "What I was actually involved in was the national salvation movement. I did not do much for the women's movement." This self-criticism, uttered by Wang in our last interview, seems to contradict a remark in the first interview, when she said, "I am a specialist in the women's movement." Actually, Wang was employing different frameworks to present her past experience in these two cases. As she comments, "Most people have the misconception that anything involving women is a women's movement." This "misconception" was shared by both Communists and Nationalists, as Zhu Su'e's narrative illustrates. As we saw in the previous chapter, the enlargement of women's social space in the national salvation movement conflated women's self-interests and those of the nation. In this sense, Wang in the 1930s was working for the women's movement as well as the national salvation movement.

Running *The Women's Voice* was the most meaningful experience for Wang Yiwei. It was the peak of her career, bringing her tremendous personal satisfaction. But more important, it allowed her to participate in the national salvation movement and the women's movement. What I want to stress here is not only that these movements empowered many women like Wang, but also that women's participation in the War of Resistance has been acknowledged by the CCP. In fact, many female activists on the Left in the national salvation movement later rose to high positions in the People's Republic of China. They have also been recognized as leaders of the women's movement in CCP official works. After 1949, Shi Liang and Shen Zijiu, the two famous activists Wang came to know in the 1930s, became the first minister of justice and a member of the standing committee of the All-China Women's Federation, respectively. Therefore, by emphasizing her role in the national salvation and women's movements in the thirties, Wang expresses her identification with the CCP's dominant discourse. In the epitaphs, and in her autobiography and memoirs, she never fails to stress this part of her history. Wang is not unique in presenting a narrative that conforms to the party's line. Even Zhu Su'e, a Nationalist, emphasizes her activities during the period of the United Front and praises the CCP for women's liberation in her autobiography. In the People's Republic of China, everyone knows what to say publicly to be politically correct. But when Wang presents herself as a follower of the CCP line, her purpose is not simply to pass censorship, but to call for the party's recognition.

The complicated nature of Wang's narrative lies in her ambivalence toward the CCP. The part of her life that she is most proud of is the time when she followed the CCP line. If she still believed in the CCP line about women's liberation—as many women Communists of her generation do, or as her own written works indicate—her narrative constructed here would be more consistent. But she is bitterly disillusioned with the CCP. The Communist Revolution brought her no social advancement, nor did it achieve the promised goal of gender equality in all aspects. Looking back at her own past effort as a Communist sympathizer, she feels that she was used. As a result, her reappraisal of the CCP cannot but contradict her effort to construct herself as a person who devoted herself to the women's movement. Actually, her sharp criticism of the CCP's women's movement led to a self-criticism of her own role in the thirties: "I just parroted the CCP," and "I did not do much for the women's movement." Yet the epitaphs inscribed on her tombstone reveal none of these misgivings or reappraisals of her past.

The epitaphs show clearly what concerns Wang most. In contemporary China, it is unusual for a tombstone with an epitaph to be erected before a person's death. For Wang, buying it was a big decision. To set up the tombstone, as she emphasized in the interview, she spent two thousand yuan—equivalent to six-months' salary. She talked about the tombstone in the first interview, mentioning it to support her claim to be a person specialized in working for the women's movement. But the full meaning of the tombstone became clear only in subsequent interviews, when she began to talk about Guan Lu, who apparently affected Wang's life in important ways. According to Wang, Guan once tried to take over *The Women's Voice* when it was in financial trouble. Wang's rejection of this attempt caused resentment in Guan. After Shanghai fell under the Japanese occupation, Guan used the name of *The Women's Voice* to sell traitorism. Wang was concerned that her history would be tainted by this incident. In "Recollections of *The Women's Voice*," written by Wang in 1984 and published in *Shanghai Local History Source Materials* in 1986, Wang described the appearance of the counterfeit *Women's Voice*. In 1984 she also dictated a more detailed memoir of *The Women's Voice*, which was printed as a pamphlet in 1987 by the magazine *Daqian shijie* [The world] as source material for reference. In the pamphlet, she discussed the connection between Guan Lu's intention to take over *The Women's Voice* and the appearance of the false issue of *Women's*

Voice. She also emphasized that it was this imitation *Women's Voice* that made her determined to revive her own magazine.

Guan Lu affected her in another important way. Hu Xiufeng, the wife of the director of the Social Bureau in the GMD period and the head of the Shanghai Women's Federation in the Communist period, was Guan's sister. Wang believed that Hu had obstructed the registration of *The Women's Voice* after the War of Resistance. Moreover, because after liberation Hu was a high official in the government and her husband was the head of the Labor Bureau, Wang feared persecution if Hu should learn of her whereabouts. Because of this fear, Wang did not go to the government to apply for a job.[20]

Understandably, Wang was extremely upset to see the person she offended and despised suddenly became a Communist heroine in the late 1980s. It turned out that Guan Lu was an underground Communist instructed by the CCP to play a role in the fake *Women's Voice*. Possibly, she acted as a "cultural traitor" to cover her espionage during the Japanese occupation. Like many other underground Communists, Guan was imprisoned for a long time after liberation as a result of the power struggle within the CCP.[21] She was rehabilitated along with other persecuted Communists after Mao's death. Guan attracted the media's attention after her rehabilitation because she had been a famous female poet in the thirties in Shanghai, and because of the new discovery that she had actually not been a "cultural traitor" but a Communist spy. The new official definition of Guan's activities in the thirties has put Wang in a difficult situation. If Guan has always been a loyal Communist, Wang's dispute with her must be politically incorrect. Moreover, if Guan was instructed by the CCP to take over *The Women's Voice* or to use the name of *The Women's Voice* for the sake of the party's cause, there would be no point for Wang to condemn her as she

20. Wang's fear was not necessarily well-founded. In *A History of the Shanghai Women's Movement*, published in 1990, *The Women's Voice* is mentioned as one of the progressive women's magazines in the Nationalist period. Hu Xiufeng serves on the advisory board of the Committee on the History of the Shanghai Women's Movement, which is responsible for the publication of the book. Given her senior position, Hu had the power to cut the paragraph on *The Women's Voice* if she really had negative views toward the journal or Wang Yiwei. Shanghai Women's Federation, *Shanghai funü yundong shi* [A history of the Shanghai women's movement] (Shanghai: Shanghai renmin chubanshe, 1990).

21. Guan Lu's role in the War of Resistance, the CCP's underground activities, and the fate of many underground workers after 1949 are described in Wang Chaozhu, *Gongchen yu zuiren* [The hero and criminal] (Shenzhen: Haitian chubanshe, 1993).

did in her memoir. In short, if Guan, the rival of Wang, was a Communist heroine, who was Wang? Although people's attention was on Guan, the heroine, and no one even mentioned Wang Yiwei, the old lonely woman living anonymously in a shabby tiny room, Wang saw in Guan's rehabilitation a big shadow cast on her own identity. It was against this background that she got the brilliant idea of setting up a tombstone in order to depict her own identity and to record history as she saw it. In this sense, the tombstone represents the old woman's resistance of the CCP line. Paradoxically, and understandably, the resistance was made in the CCP language.

Wang's tombstone aimed not only at getting the "story straight," but also at gaining recognition for what she had done. In my interviews, Wang complained often that although she had propagandized the CCP line in *The Women's Voice*, the CCP did not acknowledge her effort. She also criticized the CCP for only recognizing their own kind of women's movement. "Other women's movements are not recognized at all." She named several women activists in the epitaphs because she was "just worried that these women would be forgotten." She certainly includes herself in "these women." To remember "these women" at a personal level is Wang's effort to acknowledge the value of her own work and that of other non-Communist women activists who have long been obscured in the People's Republic of China.

Wang's effort also throws light on the complicated nature of "the women's movement" in China. As a woman activist in the 1930s, she knew there were different kinds of women's movements; after all, she and Liu-Wang Liming split up because they had different opinions about what constituted such a movement. Now, as a critic of the CCP in her old age, she is unhappy with the CCP's presentation of the history of the Chinese women's movement. By making Communist female activists prominent in their history of the women's movement, the CCP has devalued or obscured many prominent women activists who were non-Communists and in most cases did not follow the CCP line about that movement. Wang's strategy for breaking the party's hegemony over the history of the women's movement is to place obscured women activists, including herself, in a prominent position on that tombstone.

Given the limited space on the tombstone, and concerned to identify her own history with the party's cause, Wang used the official language to describe those obscured women's activities, rather than presenting them as individually distinctive identities. For instance, she situated the creation of *The Women's Voice* in the context of the national salvation movement, a movement promoted by the CCP. Her efforts and the efforts of Liu-Wang in the 1930s were depicted as centering on the national salvation. But in the interviews she was much freer to discuss the differences among the women activists of her time. When I asked about Liu-Wang's role in the 1930s, Wang emphasized that Liu-Wang "was immersed in the women's movement and unaffected by Communist ideas." In the interviews, Wang did not use the term "narrow feminism" to describe Liu-Wang's activities, as she had done in the editorial she wrote in *The Women's Voice* after she broke up with Liu-Wang. Liu-Wang's nonpartisan feminist stance in this period was also confirmed by Zhu Su'e. In her interviews, Zhu emphasizes that Liu-Wang was in the women's movement, whereas Zhu herself joined both the salvation movement and the women's movement, and that Liu-Wang was nonpartisan, whereas Zhu was a GMD member. These women described a scene of political contestation in which women activists were consciously aware of each others' different political positions. The national salvation movement was a contested sphere for the two parties and a central political stage in China. Though many women activists were ready to play a role on this stage, it seems that Liu-Wang tried not to be involved. The on-and-off relationship between Wang Yiwei and Liu-Wang Liming, as Wang described it, certainly carries much meaning in Wang Yiwei's individual history. It also sheds light on the larger scene of the women's movement in the competing discourses on women's liberation before 1949.

Liu-Wang's case demonstrates that although the New Culture feminist activities were still alive before the Japanese occupation of Shanghai, they were at a low ebb and confronted with increasing pressure from the CCP. The Japanese invasion provided a great opportunity for the CCP to increase its influence in urban areas. With the worsening national crisis, increasing numbers of city dwellers—especially the educated people—were attracted to the CCP's call for resistance as well as to its nationalism. The national salvation movement became an ideal vehicle for enabling the CCP to reach its potential followers as well as to increase its influence. Wang Yiwei was one of those who responded, supporting the CCP line in the national salvation movement. In 1932 when she graduated from university, Shanghai had just experienced the first direct confrontation with Japanese invaders, the battle of January 28. In order to support the Nineteenth Army's resistance against the Japanese, women in Shanghai organized to rescue and cure the wounded, collect donations, make winter clothes, and so on. Although the battle ended after one month, the national crisis was ever so real to Shanghai people. The national salvation movement, in which the underground Communists played a leading role, rapidly became the focus of the urban residents. Under these circumstances, it was easy for women like Wang to accept the CCP's argument that national liberation was the precondition of women's liberation and that the goal of the women's movement at the moment was national salvation. Wang emphasizes that, when she started *The Women's Voice*, her aim was to urge women to be patriotic together, which was apparently different from Liu-Wang's idea for a women's magazine. Fresh out of Fudan, where underground Communist intellectuals had made a deep impression on her, Wang unhesitatingly spread the ideas she learned in school.

Wang has never been a Communist Party member. However, because she accepted Communist views, she drew a distinct line between correct and incorrect positions, just as a Communist does. *The Women's Voice* was mostly financed by the Chinese WCTU, but Wang was not happy to see it follow Liu-Wang's line and promote "narrow feminism." "Narrow feminism," as expressed in Liu-Wang's work, never called on women to join the revolution to overthrow the GMD government in order to achieve women's liberation. Rather, "narrow feminists" believed that improvement in women's situation was possible only through gradual social evolution. Rapid changes in urban and middle-class women's lives in the single decade since the May Fourth era—changes that included more educational and employment opportunities, less gender segregation, and greater autonomy in their personal lives—lent confidence to those who held "narrow feminist" beliefs. But their position could not be reconciled with Wang Yiwei's. Wang believed that "following the CCP was women's liberation." She states frankly that she was attractive to the CCP because there was limited opportunity for women under the GMD government. In other words, Wang hoped and believed that a Communist revolution would create a society that placed no limit on women's social advancement. It was mainly because of this belief that she finally declared independence from Liu-Wang's WCTU. She took over *The Women's Voice* to propagandize the CCP line and deny "narrow feminism" a voice.

Wang's voluntary support of the CCP line illustrates the increasing influence of the CCP. In the thirties, many educated women such as Wang chose to follow the CCP's route to women's liberation. The New Culture liberal feminist discourse, which had been overshadowed by the nationalist discourse in the National Revolution of the mid 1920s, lost further ground to the CCP's nationalist discourse in the mid 1930s.[22]

22. In *A History of Shanghai Women's Movement*, chapter 6 to chapter 8 illustrate Shanghai women's activities for the underground CCP during the national salvation movement and the War of Resistance. According to the book, many women activists joined the CCP in this period.

The interesting twist in the relationship between Liu-Wang and Wang coincided with significant changes in both women's personal lives. During the time between their first and second collaboration, both experienced personal tragedy. Liu-Wang's husband was assassinated by Japanese agents, and Wang's husband proved an unworthy man who cheated her and abused her. The death of Liu-Wang's husband made Liu-Wang more sympathetic toward the CCP and the party's firm resistance stance. But the betrayal of Wang's husband cooled Wang's enthusiasm for the CCP. Wang's husband Lu was a leftist, a supporter of the CCP. But Wang bitterly discovered that this man did not practice what he preached. He claimed that he was for gender equality, but in his personal life he treated women as sexual objects. Lu's betrayal opened an old wound deep in Wang's heart. Ever since childhood, she had resented her father for taking a concubine. As a matter of fact, she resented any man who had a concubine. Now she found herself in her mother's situation, or even worse. She comments poignantly, "Under feudalism, when a man had several wives, proper status was given to the first wife. But in the Communist Party, the first wife is totally abandoned. She is divorced and labeled as having an ideological problem." This statement does not directly describe her own situation, but it was made when she was talking about her ex-husband. It is obvious that in the painful discovery of her husband's extramarital affairs and consequent divorce, Wang compared her own life with her mother's. And it is obvious that the pain caused by Lu made her even more intolerant of any unfaithful man. Thus when she heard of the affair of Mao and Jiang Qing, her disillusionment with the CCP began in earnest.[23]

In order to understand Wang's bitterness toward the CCP, the impact of her ex-husband's betrayal should be further explained here. In the first two interviews, Wang gave me the impression that she had never been married. Later she mentioned that not long before, a magazine named *Nüsheng* [The women's voice] had been published in Guangdong province without consulting her. She was pretty upset about that and showed me a copy of the magazine, in which there was an article with her pen name and another name: Lu Hefeng. She said that Lu sent in this piece without telling her. So I asked who this Lu was. Only then did she reluctantly say that he was her ex-husband. I was surprised and wanted to know more. But she offered only a few comments and said, "This man had no influence on *The Women's*

23. After he began to live together with Jiang Qing, Mao divorced He Zizhen, his third wife, a veteran of the Red Army who married Mao in the Jinggang Mountain Base Areas and followed him to Yan'an through the Long March.

Voice. That is why I did not mention him." I protested, "But he must have influenced your private life." Wang described his male chauvinism, his affairs, and his hitting her, all in brief but angry words. Then abruptly she stopped. It was obviously too painful for her to continue her story and therefore too painful for me to continue asking further questions. We left it there.

It was shocking to me that half a century later that failed marriage remains a psychic trauma for Wang. It was apparent that her omission of Lu was not because Lu was insignificant but because he had wounded her too deeply for her to talk about him with detachment. I realized that she had tried to convey the point that "men in the old society were truly rotten" by talking about her mother's, sisters', and cousin's unfaithful husbands. But her strong resentment toward those "rotten" men did not merely grow from observing other women's agony; rather, it came from her own tragedy. She was an ambitious and proud woman who wanted to be better than men. She did not want to follow her mother's or her sisters' steps, living in an unhappy marriage without self-fulfillment. She aimed to be an independent new woman who demanded equality with men in society. She finally dropped her misgivings about marriage to marry Lu because he claimed to be a supporter of gender equality. Because of Wang, this man from Zhejiang with a high school education got his articles published in a Shanghai periodical and even secured a job in Shanghai. Theirs could have been a new type of marriage in which the wife was not dependent on her husband for a living or social status. But when Lu began to have affairs, Wang not only felt cheated but also used. Moreover, Wang found that Lu had actually put her in the same loathsome situation that her mother and sisters endured. This was certainly too humiliating for the proud Wang to mention.

Wang revived *The Women's Voice* after the War of Resistance to disperse the clouds created by the false *Women's Voice*. But her revived magazine clearly demonstrated Wang's changed views. She no longer consciously followed the CCP line. Instead, she emphasized her own concerns. A comparison of two editorials she wrote may illustrate her new position. In the first issue after she declared independence from the WCTU in 1934, Wang wrote, "We believe that women's problems are one link in the problems of the entire society. Until we solve these social problems, women's problems will never be thoroughly solved. Conversely, without a thorough solution to women's problems, social problems cannot be solved thoroughly. . . . What we need is a women's movement that penetrates the masses and that seeks the liberation of humankind through the national liberation movement." In 1945 Wang asserted in the first issue of the revived *Women's Voice*, "We always believe that women's problems are embedded in broader social problems. Only with women's liberation can national problems be truly solved. . . . Now we have won the War of Resistance. In order to obtain a permanent victory, to accomplish the great cause of nation building, we should more actively push the women's liberation movement from now on."[24] Obviously, the 1945 statement reversed the logic in *Women and Socialism*, a book that the underground Communist Xia Yan gave to Wang and that she once used to guide her editorial works. Now that the national crisis was over, she implied, women's liberation should precede everything else. At a moment when both the CCP and the GMD were ready for a showdown, Wang's nonpartisan tone reveals her distance from the CCP.

Wang knew very well that the revived *Women's Voice* no longer followed the CCP line. Although it printed stories of women in the Soviet Union and articles criticizing the GMD government, it did not follow the CCP in calling women to join the political battle between the revolutionaries and reactionaries. Rather, its themes sounded echoes of "narrow feminism." The magazine extolled women's contributions to the war, regardless of their political background. The editor in chief organized a series of discussions on subjects such as "Women's Political Participation," "Women's Education," and "Intellectual Women's Prospects." Moreover, *The Women's Voice* became famous for its exposés of unfaithful men and philanderers. The discussion on "Wives of the War of Resistance" (*kangzhan furen*) organized by Wang reveals her aversion to unfaithful men.[25] She condemned those men who used separation caused by the war as an excuse to abandon their wives and children. "Some people called *The Women's Voice* 'narrow womanism' that specialized in cursing men and being biased toward women, and said that men should create a 'Men's Voice' in revenge."[26] Clearly, "*The Women's Voice* changed its nature," in Wang's own words. Significantly, in her official autobiography and epitaphs, Wang emphasized the role of *The Women's Voice* in the national salvation movement, but she only briefly mentioned or omitted the revived *Women's Voice* in the 1940s.

24. Wang Yiwei, Wo yu Nüsheng [*The Women's Voice* and I] (Shanghai: Daqian Shijie, 1987), 14–16, 20.

25. *Kangzhan furen* was a term for women who married or lived with men who had been separated from their legal wives by the war during the years of Japanese occupation. In most cases, the women had previously been unmarried. In some cases, they were ignorant of the men's previous marriages.

26. Wang Yiwei, Wo yu Nüsheng, 23. "Narrow womanism" (*xiaai funü zhuyi*) is another way of saying "narrow feminism." "Feminism" had been translated as *funü zhuyi, nüzi zhuyi*, and *nüquan zhuyi* in the May Fourth era. In the 1930s there was no fixed translation for feminism. However, under the influence of the CCP discourse, *funü zhuyi* and *nüquan zhuyi* became associated with the adjective "narrow."

Meanwhile, Liu-Wang Liming changed her negative views toward the CCP and became a Communist sympathizer. Now she could better understand Wang's previous pro-Communist position, just as Wang began to endorse Liu-Wang's former "narrow feminism." They realized that they differed much less than they had thought, and they were able to collaborate with one another again. Wang was grateful that Liu-Wang was once again supporting her. Although the second collaboration did not last long because of the ongoing civil war, and although Wang never saw Liu-Wang again, she continued to regard Liu-Wang as her comrade and to highly value their friendship. Over four decades later, Wang used the tombstone to express her deep feelings for Liu-Wang. She wanted future generations to remember not only her but also Liu-Wang Liming. After all, Liu-Wang was the person who enabled her to have that cherished experience, although the phrases in the epitaph sound as if Wang took the full initiative to create *The Women's Voice*.

The cooperation of Liu-Wang and Wang ended in 1947, but its impact on Wang is lasting. Before the end of Wang's life, she proclaimed her own ideas of a true women's liberation and derided the CCP's false women's liberation. "Women are human beings, just like men, and they should have equal positions." She stressed that most women activists of the thirties were not really working for the women's movement, but that Liu-Wang was truly working for the women's movement. From criticizing Liu-Wang as a "narrow feminist" to recognizing Liu-Wang as a leader of a true women's movement, Wang Yiwei has walked a unique path that the CCP would call regression. For Wang, the path reflects her years of exploration and times of disappointment. When the Communist Party failed to fulfill its promises after liberation—or even earlier, when CCP leaders proved to have a double standard—a disenchanted Wang began to look for alternative routes to women's liberation. She is groping for language with which to criticize the CCP's women's liberation movement and point a different route. However, she only knows the New Culture feminist language. For her, this is not a simple return to New Culture feminism. Rather, it demonstrates that the New Culture feminist discourse still serves as a reference point. Or more accurately, it serves as a medium for women to express their disappointment over unfulfilled dreams and their critique of the CCP's gender policy.

7   Chen Yongsheng (1900–1997): Educator

Chen Yongsheng, 1935

Chen Yongsheng, 1995

On my first visit to Chen Yongsheng, I was accompanied by my friend Li, who had an administrative post in the Wenshiguan. After Li introduced me to Chen, we three chatted for a while. Chen told Li that she wanted to run an English class so that she could earn extra income to pay for a house-keeper. She asked Li if the Wenshiguan would be interested in this idea and would provide her with the necessary assistance. Li and I exchanged a look, both amused by this ninety-three-year-old woman's idea. But Chen was serious. I began to understand the idea's significance only after I heard her life story.[1]

1. The narrative is constructed from interviews conducted on February 24 and March 24, 1993, and January 8, 1995, and from her autobiography in the Wenshiguan publication.

NARRATIVE

I was born in 1900, in Changsha, Hunan province. My father passed exams as a *xiucai* and then passed exams to go abroad.[2] He was sent by the Hunan provincial government to study economics in Japan. Huang Xing, the Xinhai revolutionary, was sent to Japan with my father. My father was already married when he went to Japan. My mother never went to school, but she taught herself Chinese characters. She could read novels like *The Legend of White Snake,* and she told stories to my father's mother. My mother bore eight children, two of whom died at a young age. I was the third child and the eldest girl. My mother let my elder brother, at the time the only son, be adopted by my uncle's wife, who was widowed. This showed my mother's open-mindedness. My mother's family ran a grocery store. My paternal grandpa owned a southern food store. He had seven sons and one daughter by his second wife, my grandma. My uncles all had been to Japan. Our whole family was not very traditional and more inclined to Western ideas. No woman of my generation in our family had bound feet because my father had been to Japan and Japanese women did not have bound feet. When I was born, my father did not want me to have bound feet. Two of my uncles' wives and daughters had been to Japan, too. But in Japan, men and women took baths together, and my aunts-in-law were not used to that, so they came back home with their daughters.

It was the custom in Changsha that every household should open doors for spirits on July 1 of the lunar calendar. Starting on that day, families should prepare to receive the spirits of their ancestors. On July 4, offerings should be displayed: several big square dinner tables were placed in the spacious living room and covered with refreshments, fruits, and other good food. July 15 was the day to send your ancestor spirits away, and paper money was burnt for them to spend. To prepare a pack of money for each ancestor, all the children in our household were kept busy writing ancestors' names on the wrapping. Just as my family was setting off firecrackers to receive our ancestors, my mother gave birth to me on July 10. Everyone said, "This girl has a good *ming* [fate] because she is sent by our ancestors." They got a fortune-teller who said, "This little girl is extraordinary! She will accomplish great things in the future." My eldest brother died as soon as he was born. My second brother was three years older than I and was adopted by my uncle's wife. I was the third child and a girl. Usually a girl in this situation would not be loved. But my family loved me. My father loved me very much,

2. See note 5 in chapter 5 for information on Chinese scholarly titles.

making all sorts of pet names for me. My second brother told me this in a letter in his old age.

My family was a big one, like the one Ba Jin describes in *Family*.[3] We all lived with grandpa in a grand house. We had a chef. When coal came, it formed a mountain. We ate from the big pot, but each family also had a small stove. My grandma had never been to school, but she was rich. Her sons were all very filial to her, greeting her every morning and every night. Her birthdays and the Spring Festivals were big occasions with many guests. A tutor taught all the children. I joined the boys to study, but I do not remember what we read. When my father became a *juren* after he returned from Japan, he was appointed an official in the Department of Transportation in Beijing. We stayed in Beijing from 1908 to 1911. My father endorsed equality between men and women. He sent all his sons and daughters to school. I went to an elementary school in Beijing. I remember paying respect to Confucius in school. Every first and fifteenth day of the month, we kowtowed to a portrait of Confucius. In Beijing all children went to school, including girls. I do not know why, but in Beijing my father dressed my brothers, my sisters, and me in boys' clothes. I loved school and never missed a class.

After the 1911 Revolution we returned to Hunan. Because he studied economics in Japan and was a friend of Tan Yankai, who became the governor of Hunan, my father was appointed the deputy director of the Treasury of Hunan province after 1911. But my grandma did not want her son to be an official, and my father did not like being an official, either. He soon quit and started a real estate company. We bought a big house and then no longer lived with my grandma. I had been to Zhounan Girls' School as a boarding student since I was six years old. After returning from Beijing I went to Gudaotian Girls' School. In my generation, if the family's financial state allowed, the girls were all sent to school. My father had been to Japan where girls went to school, so it went without saying that the girls in my family should go to school. We went to school in a *jiaozi* [sedan chair]. My female cousins went to school, too. Several of them worked as accountants after graduating from secondary schools. Two cousins did not work after getting married. Most women stopped working after getting married. Among all

3. Ba Jin (1904–) became one of the most famous writers after the publication of his novel *Family* in the early 1930s. The novel, based largely on his own extended family, is regarded as the best literary representation of Chinese extended families in the early twentieth century. *Family*, a product of the New Culture literature, touched millions readers of the May Fourth generation.

the women in my generation of our big family, only my sister and I went abroad for a higher education.

When I was sixteen years old, I decided not to marry. I had two reasons. One was patriotic. When I was graduating from the elementary school attached to Changsha Women's Normal School, Japan imposed Twenty-One Demands on China.[4] Xu Teli, who was a teacher in my school, cut his finger to write a letter in blood protesting the Japanese demands.[5] This event deeply disturbed me. Japan was a small country, and yet it tried to bully China. Chinese were called the sick men of Asia and were said to lack the strength even to grab a chicken. A strong nation depends on a strong race, and to have a strong race, women's education and the health of women's bodies are important. We should improve women's health. Physical education was the way to national salvation. That is why I wanted to devote myself to physical education. My second reason was that a woman's life was too hard. She had to raise children and follow her husband no matter what kind of man he was. I saw many women with many children, but their men were absent from home, fooling around with other women. Women could not get a divorce as they can now. Suffering and living like a widow, but with a husband—how hard a woman's life was! Women had no status. That is why I decided not to marry.

At first I thought my uncles were very honest and even sacred. I worshipped them. But in the end they brought concubines home. That made me very mad. My father had a concubine, too. That is why my mother died young. She was very unhappy. She died at age forty-two, in 1919, when I was studying in Shanghai. My brother was in Shanghai, too, and my sister was in Suzhou. After receiving the telegram that told us she was ill, we went home, but she died before we got there. She had an ulcerous sore on her skin. Chinese medicine might have cured her, but my father sent her to a Western hospital. Western medicine had no cure for that.

At first my father kept his concubine outside the home. We children did not know that he had a concubine, and the adults did not know either, be-

4. When Western powers were distracted by the World War I, Japan decided to expand its power in China. In January 1915, Japan issued the Yuan Shikai government the Twenty-One Demands, which included extensive economic, commercial, and administrative rights for the Japanese in China. Yuan yielded to Japan's demands, which prompted nationwide anti-Japanese rallies and a boycott of Japanese goods. In the Western way of calculating age, Chen Yongsheng was not yet fifteen years old when she graduated in 1915.

5. Xu Teli was a famous teacher even long after he wrote that protest letter in blood. One of his students who was strongly influenced by his patriotism and progressive ideas was Mao Zedong.

cause he hid her from us. When my uncle brought his concubine home, my father brought his home, too. Making good friends is very important. Bad friends have a bad influence on you. It is like eating an olive: you have a taste first and then want more. An honest man will turn bad. My father's concubine was originally a prostitute. She was not very young, but this kind of woman knew how to make men happy and serve men well. One's own wife would be OK during courtship. But after being married for some time, each person reveals their true nature and does not handle the other as carefully as before. Men just want you to pamper them. My mother did not know that kind of stuff. Also, she did not have enough energy to take care of all those children, let alone to take care of my father. We had servants to help, but she still had to manage servants. When I saw things like this in my family, I did not want to marry. Besides, once a woman married and had children nobody wanted to employ her anymore. Even if her beauty was used as an asset to a job, just as a *huaping* [flower vase] is used temporarily, no employers wanted her after she was married.[6] Women had no status. That is why I have remained single. I had never heard of celibatarianism at that time.[7] It was my own idea to remain single.

There is another reason I remained single. I thought women had not been liberated and become truly equal to men because of the family name. Married women were called "Mrs. So-and-So," but married men did not have to change their names. It is very hard for a woman to endure pregnancy and have a baby. She should receive recognition for all her work. I have tried in vain for many years to find a man who could understand this idea. Who would be willing to do that? To marry me and take my name, while I took his? Men did not like that idea. They felt it was like changing the signs on their shops. In 1930–31, I was the chief executive of the YWCA in Hangzhou. Once I was asked to give a talk to students at Zhijiang University. My topic was "Our Own Personal Problem." What was our own personal problem?

6. *Huaping* (flower vase) is a term used by Chen's generation to refer to women hired as decorations to a business or enterprise. Many employers used young women to present a modern image or to attract male clients. In this context, the term is derogatory. The practice has became popular again, given the development of China's economic reform since the 1980s. However, young women who are hired to entertain or attract male guests or clients are no longer called *huaping,* but are given new titles such as *gongguan xiaojie* (Miss Public Relations) and *liyi xiaojie* (Miss Hospitality).

7. "Celibatarianism" was one of the widely discussed topics in the May Fourth era. Many young men and women seriously explored the possibility of remaining single in order to avoid the pain of marriage and to devote themselves entirely to revolution.

The problem of the surname. As the old saying goes, "If a woman marries a chicken, she has to follow the chicken; if she marries a dog, she has to follow the dog." She thus loses her own personhood. I told my audience that I would not be anyone's appendage. I attacked inequality between men and women. Men can do a thousand or ten thousand wrong things, and no one says they have committed a crime. But if a woman just talks to a man once, that isn't allowed. Today a woman can talk to men outside her family, but her husband may quarrel with her once she returns home. "Why did you have dinner with others?" the man will ask. "But why can you if I can't?" the woman will argue. I discussed the surname problem with Americans when I was in the United States in the late 1940s, but they only said, "Oh, I haven't thought about it." I just want to be myself and I do not want to depend on others.

Once my family tried to match a man up with me. The man was from a wealthy family in Hunan. My parents said that the man would go abroad and I could go with him. But I was determined to study physical education and to achieve big things, to *tiyu jiuguo* [save our nation with physical education]. I had that ambition, and I did not want to marry. My parents did not try that kind of thing after that. My father had made his mistake in taking a concubine, so he did not dare raise the issue of my marriage. I would have fought him if he had.

My father was the founder of Qunyi Shushe [Qunyi Publishing House], which had one bookstore in Shanghai, another in Tokyo, and another in Changsha. It was the third largest publisher at the time, smaller only than the Commercial Press and Zhonghua Press. Mao Zedong and Yang Kaihui often went to his bookstore in Changsha.[8] The bookstore in Shanghai was located close to the Commercial Press. It was quite large and had many books. My father also translated Japanese books into Chinese. He was a learned man. I now regret that I did not learn much from him, but I resented him at the time, because he kept a woman and caused my mother's illness and early death. My uncle got to know Chen Duxiu in Shanghai, so Qunyi Shushe became the distributor of *New Youth*.[9] But I did not read *New Youth*. When I was sixteen, I came to Shanghai to enter a physical education school; that was just shortly after *New Youth* began. Because my interest was in

8. Yang Kaihui was Mao Zedong's first wife, who was killed by the Nationalist Party in 1930.

9. On September 15, 1915, Chen Yongsheng's uncle Chen Zishou discussed with Chen Duxiu the issues relating to the publication of *New Youth*. See Tang Baolin and Lin Maoshen, *Chen Duxiu nianpu* [A chronicle of Chen Duxiu's life] (Shanghai: Shanghai renmin chubanshe, 1988), 68.

physical education and because no one told me to read *New Youth*, I never read the magazine. My pursuit of equality between men and women came from my observation of women's situations around me.

What helped me decide on my career as a physical education teacher was the performance given by some women teachers. Three female graduates of Chinese Women's Gymnastic School in Shanghai came to Changsha. They taught physical education in several schools. Although they did not teach in my school, I heard of them and saw them. This aroused my interest and concretized my idea of strengthening our race. I decided to go to Shanghai to enter the school from which they had graduated. My parents did not interfere with me. They had great confidence in me; whatever I wanted to do was fine with them. And my paternal uncle was working in the Shanghai branch of Qunyi Shushe. At that time we were still in one big family, so my uncle was there to support me. I went to Shanghai by boat with my maternal uncle. When we got off the boat at the Shiliupu dock, I got lost. Fortunately I spoke Mandarin. In the end I found Qunyi Shushe by myself. I lived with my uncle's family. Later my uncle took me to look for that gymnastic school, but we failed to find it because it had closed. So my uncle sent me to the Patriotic Girls' School, which had been established by Cai Yuanpei and had a physical education course. After half a year, the gymnastic school was reopened, so I went there for a year. The training there was in the Japanese style because the teachers had all studied in Japan. We had courses on dumbbells, gymnastics, sticks, ball games, and *wushu* [martial arts]. There was no track and field yet.

After I graduated from China Women's Gymnastics School, I taught there for half a year. Then I entered the Physical Education Normal School run by the YWCA in Shanghai. Its first principal was an American, and the second was a Chinese who was a graduate from Wellesley in Boston. Her fiancé had courted her for eight years, and she was about to get married. That is why she left the school. Another American came to be the principal. The school had a gymnasium and a tennis court. Its standards were higher than the school I graduated from. It required a four-year middle-school education for enrollment and two years to graduate. I did not have a middle-school diploma—I had only finished elementary school and had been in physical education training for a year and a half—but they accepted me anyway because I had already attended courses there and I knew the principal. There were not many students: in my class there were only a dozen girls from all over the country. Many women did not want to be physical education teachers because it would be inconvenient after they got married and had babies. I entered the school in 1918.

The following year the May Fourth movement broke out. I participated actively in the student movement. I became a member in the communication department of the Shanghai Students' Union and made speeches and petitions, burned Japanese goods, and participated in other activities. The activities did not last very long. I graduated from the school the next year.

Upon my graduation a friend of mine, whose brother-in-law was the president of Beijing National Women's Normal University, recommended me as a physical education teacher there. Today this would be called *kaihoumen* [going through the back door]. In the fall of 1920, when I was twenty years old, I arrived in Beijing. I was appointed the chair of the physical education department. Some students were older than I. I gave physical education classes to about one hundred students from different departments. It was a prestigious school. Lu Xun taught there after I left, and Wu Yifang was my colleague there. She was the chair of the English department. She stayed there for only one year and then went to the United States to study. She graduated from the University of Michigan and later became president of Jinling Women's College in Nanjing. My pay was enough to support myself. But I was very sad because my mother had just died in December 1919. She had often said that she did not want to depend on her sons, but rather on her daughters. Unfortunately, she had died before my graduation, and I had no opportunity to provide for her.

When I was in the Physical Education School of the YWCA, I had a close friend, Ma, who was from Shandong. We were roommates. Ma's father was a doctor. When she was born, her father served as a midwife. Her mother died when she was young. While we were at school, her father died, and she went home to attend his funeral. When she came back, she was behind in the course work. Our principal asked me to coach her. Thus we became very close. Before graduation we discussed the prospect of going abroad, and she suggested that if she passed the provincial exams for sending students abroad, she would take me with her. The provincial government allowed the scholarship to be used by two persons. After I taught in Beijing for a year, she passed the exams. I quit the job and prepared to go to the United States with my friend, but before leaving, I found that the government had a rule that students going abroad had to take a first-class cabin on the ship. I could not afford the fare and did not want to ask my family for help, so I missed the opportunity. My friend went to the University of Texas at Austin and got a Ph.D. in chemistry.

I did not return to Beijing National Women's Normal University. The government was so poor that it could not pay teachers at eight national universities, and those teachers went on strike. A student of mine from Hubei introduced me to Hubei Women's Normal School, so I went to Hubei to teach. I was very popular among my students: they often came to my room to chat in the evenings. But that gave rise to troubles, because a woman supervisor thought I was a Communist. The Communist Party had just been founded in 1921. I did not like the situation with this suspicious supervisor. When a classmate of mine from the Shanghai YWCA introduced me to Guangdong Women's Normal School, I was happy to leave Hubei for Guangdong. The principal of the Guangdong school had studied in Japan and was the elder sister of Liao Zhongkai.[10] Liao Zhongkai's daughter was my student there. I again taught physical education, but before long I did not feel comfortable there. Perhaps it was because this school was pro-Communist Party—although at the time I was unaware of the political situation. I just felt that I did not fit in. After a year I quit the job and returned to Shanghai. Back then, it was not unusual for a young woman to travel alone, and I did not fear anything. I did everything all by myself. A lot of women had begun to work, most in nursing and teaching, in order to support their families.

When I returned to Shanghai, another opportunity to go abroad came along. My friend Ma had been in Texas for a couple of years. She stayed with a professor whose name was Miss Lavender. Miss Lavender belonged to a Baptist church and had a good Baptist friend, Dr. Hardin, who was the president of Baylor College for Women. Miss Lavender told Dr. Hardin that Ma had a close friend in China who wanted very much to study in the United States, and she asked if Dr. Hardin could offer me that opportunity. Dr. Hardin wrote me right away, offering me a full scholarship for four years. I became the first and only Chinese student at Baylor College. Because I lacked a high school diploma, which Baylor required, I first attended a high school for a year, mixing with much younger students. Then I began my undergraduate study at Baylor. Baylor had a good curriculum and fine facilities for physical education, but it did not grant degrees for physical education. I had to obtain a degree, so I chose English as my major. I had to take courses on poems, essays, and short stories. I was not the type of person who liked literature. I had to study very hard. I took many courses, including home cooking and housekeeping. I was active in student affairs and became the chair of the international students' union. I was baptized there. In 1927 I got a B.A. in English. The president was very proud of me because I was the first Chinese person to graduate from Baylor.

10. Liao Zhongkai (1877–1925) was an early leader of the Nationalist Party and He Xiangning's husband.

After I graduated, I found a job as a governess in a naval officer's home. But the family treated me like a servant, so I quit the job and returned to Shanghai. I also came back because my family was having financial problems. My father had failed at stock trading, and I had to look for a job to help my family. I met an overseas Chinese couple from Burma at a party, and when they learned of my credentials, they asked me to teach in an overseas Chinese night school in Burma. I went to Burma and became the sole person responsible for the school: I taught both English and Chinese and was the principal as well as the office worker. In short I did everything. Because the climate there was too hot, I often had eye infections. The pay was just enough to support myself, and I did not have any money to send to my family. I quit the job after working there for one year.

I returned to Shanghai in 1928 and got a job in Zhongxi Girls' School. I taught physical education there rather than English. In Shanghai there were too many English majors and not enough physical education teachers. That's why I was very popular in the old society: my expertise was in high demand at the time. The husband of one of my classmates was the head of the Education Bureau of Shandong province. Because I had a major in English and a minor in education when I studied in the United States, my classmate recommended me to her husband, and I became the principal of Shandong Number One Women's Normal School. I left Shanghai for Taian in 1929 and became the first female principal in Shandong. I took my younger sister with me. In Shandong I met Miss Gallaher, who was the chief executive of the YWCA in China. We became friends, and things there were fine, but my sister suddenly fell ill. She had appendicitis and was sent to the hospital to have surgery right away. She had total anesthesia and needed intensive care. I was her sister, and I had to take care of her at night. Miss Gallaher's home was close to the hospital, so I asked her if I could stay with her in order to take care of my sister. Miss Gallaher agreed. Of course, because she was an American, I paid rent.

I left Shandong after being the principal for one year. I was not the right person for the job. All those personnel problems and administrative work were too difficult for me. Plus I was from another province. As an outsider, I was more or less excluded by the native people. No one was behind me. Although my friend's husband gave me the position, I could not always trouble him with my problems. Moreover, there was a Guomindang headquarters there. They required the students and the entire faculty to recite in unison "The Will of Sun Zhongshan" every Monday in a big auditorium. I could not remember "The Will" well. A Guomindang member and a teacher collaborated to create an unpleasant atmosphere for me. I was not used to the life there, either. During my one-year term, I had the lavatory remodeled to make it cleaner and built a public bathroom. I only did these two things. In Shandong, a man who had also studied in the United States proposed to me. I told him I was not interested in marriage. He said, "Women should work in the kitchen at home. What's the point in being a principal?" I totally ignored him.

Then Miss Gallaher recommended me to be the chief executive of the YWCA in Hangzhou. I liked the job, which involved many social activities. But I disliked one thing: the local YWCA's funds were obtained from donations, and I had to spend a lot of time going to board members' homes to ask them to donate. Most of the board members were housewives who had no control of money. I felt it wasted my time. Moreover, my salary was paid from the donations, and it consumed a large portion of the donations. I did not think it an appropriate thing to do. So when the one-year contract ended, I left the position. When I was working in the YWCA, I also worked as a substitute physical education teacher in the Humanities College of Zhejiang University. Then at a West Lake Exhibition held in Hangzhou, I encountered Liu Zhan'en, the president of the University of Shanghai. He invited me to teach physical education in his school, so I returned to Shanghai in 1931. I got to know Liu-Wang Liming, who invited me to their meetings, and I became a board member of the Temperance Union.

At the University of Shanghai, I was the physical education teacher and the deputy supervisor of female students. I encountered some unpleasant things there, too. After all, women had no status. A male professor was able to have his whole family live in a nice house, but a single woman was treated totally differently. I and another single woman who taught chemistry and had studied in Germany lived in the dorms with the students. We had to rush for our turn in the bathroom. I did not like it. We negotiated with the administration and after that were allowed to share an apartment building with unmarried foreign female teachers. Still, many of the female students made me uncomfortable. The ones from rich families often asked the chef to add special dishes for them. I was a poor teacher who could not afford to do the same—my salary then was about one hundred silver dollars, not much. Anyway, women were taken advantage of everywhere. Although I did not like the situation in the university, I stayed until the battle of January 28, 1932. Then the Japanese occupied the original school site, and the University of Shanghai had to move downtown. Because the school no longer had space for physical education, I wasn't needed. I offered to teach for free, but the school administrator said there was no place for a physical education class.

My family faced a further financial predicament. My elder brother had run a printing house in Zhejiang, but business was bad, so he eventually went bankrupt. He sold all his possessions to pay off his debt and became a proletarian. My two younger brothers, who had been working for him, were now also out of jobs—plus my elder brother had a teenage son, so altogether there were three boys who needed to be fed. Because I had lost my job at the University of Shanghai, I decided to take the three boys to Hong Kong with me. We traveled to Hong Kong as refugees in a third-class cabin on a boat. Hong Kong people were patriotic and received us warmly. For a short while I stayed at the YWCA and the boys stayed at the YMCA; then we went to my friend's home in Guangzhou. She found jobs for my two brothers, and I got a teaching job in a girls' school. Only my nephew had no job, and he wanted to return to Shanghai because the war had ended there. I also wanted to return to Shanghai, because I had rented an apartment there before going to Hong Kong.

After I returned to Shanghai, I had nothing to do, so I often went to a gymnasium run by some Europeans. There I met a Mr. Huang, who had also returned from the United States. He had no job and volunteered to help at the gymnasium. One day Mr. Huang invited me and a Miss Li to dinner. Miss Li was a teacher in Shanghai Municipal Council Girls' School. When she learned that I was a physical education teacher, she said that at the moment her school needed a physical education teacher. The very next day, the school called me and I went for an interview. I was hired right away as a substitute teacher. After the summer vacation, I became a permanent teacher. The school was created by the famous modern educator Chen Heqin and run by the British Shanghai Municipal Council. All the teachers [over a dozen total] were female college graduates. Some had received an education in the West and Japan. The goal of the school was to make its students future career women. Students were from various family backgrounds.

It was the top school in Shanghai. The pay was higher than at other schools. As a person who had gone to school in the United States, I started at 240 silver dollars a month, which was more than my previous salaries as a principal and university teacher, and the pay increased every year. I taught six hundred students. The principal gave me a free hand in my teaching; thus I could be creative and do things according to my own ideas. Only then was my talent and knowledge fully utilized. And my dream of promoting physical education in China was realized, too. I initiated many physical education programs that were forbidden in other girls' schools at the time—things such as rings, rope climbing, box horse, and all kinds of ball games.

I also trained girl students to give bicycle performances, several students riding on one bicycle doing gymnastics. When people at the time mentioned the Shanghai Municipal Council Girls' School, they would say, "Its physical education program is the best among such programs taught at many schools." I not only gave physical education classes, but also taught students to be fine human beings. The recently elected chair of Shanghai Political Consultative Conference, Chen Tiedi, is a graduate of Shanghai Municipal Council Girls' School. I stayed in this school from 1932 to 1943. I was able to stay there for such a long time because my working environment was fine and the pay and treatment were good. I was able to rent an apartment by myself. My brothers and sisters often came to stay with me, and I frequently entertained friends in my big apartment. I hired a live-in housekeeper. When I had friends over for dinner, she would cook for us. Back then, domestic help did not cost much—unlike today, when it costs more than my income. My friends and I would often go out together after work. Sometimes we would take a taxi to see movies or eat dinner in restaurants. Sometimes we visited each other. I lived a comfortable life then, much better than now. That was my golden age.

Another good thing happened during this period. After my elder brother went bankrupt, he gave me a world bank savings lottery ticket. In the spring of 1934, I won the first prize with that ticket. The newspaper printed my name. I won eleven thousand silver dollars. Rich people in Shanghai were often kidnapped, so I put the check in the bank right away. But that money was soon spent, and I am a proletarian now. My elder brother got three thousand dollars to pay off his debt to a widow, my younger sister got three thousand dollars to study in the United States, my younger brother got one thousand dollars to study in Japan, and I spent two thousand dollars attending the eleventh Olympic Games in Germany in 1936. The Chinese government organized an inspection delegation to the Olympic Games. The delegation included physical education teachers from high schools and universities all over the country. With a friend's help, I was able to join the group, but I had to pay for the trip by myself. In the group there were twelve women, including me, all of whom were college graduates and spoke English. Our delegation visited Germany, France, Italy, Czechoslovakia, Hungary, Austria, Denmark, and Sweden to inspect physical education in these countries. After we returned to China, I published *A Diary of the Trip in Europe*, which described the state of physical education abroad.

In 1943, when the Japanese occupied our school, our principal resigned and I resigned, too. I went to Chongqing and got a job as an office worker in an industry and business institute. In 1945, I quit the job and accompanied my younger sister to Lanzhou. My sister had been in the United States from 1935 to 1939, then returned to China and worked for the YWCA. Now she was sent by the YWCA to establish a new branch in Lanzhou. It was not convenient for her to go on the long trip alone, so I accompanied her. Shortly after we established a school in Lanzhou, the Japanese were defeated. Having heard the news of victory, we decided to return to Shanghai. But by then the Shanghai Municipal Council Girls' School was controlled by the Guomindang. I did not want to go back to that school; I was not interested in politics, I just wanted to teach physical education. That is why I suffered a lot later. You do not interfere with politics, but it will interfere with you.

As soon as I arrived in Shanghai from Lanzhou, I met a friend of mine, Yu Qingtang, at the railway station.[11] Yu had also gotten an education in the United States. One of her friends was a big shot in the Nationalist government and was looking for a head for the Shanghai prison's female section. Yu was offered the job but wasn't interested, so when she saw me, she recommended me right away. The following day the prison officials sent a car to my apartment to pick me up. I was not interested in the position because my goal was to work in education. But they said that this was a place for education, too, that all those female prisoners should be educated before they were finally released. Because I did not have a job at the time, I accepted the offer. Every day I rode my bike from the west of the city, where my apartment was located, to the east of the city, where the prison was. After one month, they urged me to move to a house the government provided for me. When I went to look at the house, I was surprised to see the doors and windows wide open, whereas none of the other prison administrators' houses were that way. This was a sign of intimidation. In prison administration, corruption was rampant. When I was at the post, I set an example by refusing bribes and embezzlement. Many people hated me for doing that. I thought to myself, I am only in my forties and I still have ambitions to fulfill. I do not have the energy for this kind of mess. So I wrote a letter of resignation as soon as I got home. And I did not go to work the next day.

At that time the former principal of Shanghai Municipal Council Girls' School was running the Western Girls' School in Shanghai. He invited me

11. Yu Qingtang (1897–1949) obtained a Ph. D. in education from Columbia University in 1922. She returned to China to promote public education and established the Chinese Society of Social Education. She was a professor at several universities and served as president of Jiangsu Provincial Education College. She was appointed the director of the social education bureau in the Department of Education when the People's Republic of China was founded.

to teach physical education in the school, and I accepted the offer. There were Russian students, Western students, and many Chinese students in the school. That was in 1946. By May, I had already organized sports games in the school, which attracted some attention from the media. I was not yet forty-six. I was thinking of going abroad again. I had been thinking for decades that physical activities were important for human beings. But what about people who could not do physical activities? I wanted to go to the United States to see how Americans taught disabled people. Therefore, I entered Columbia University to study special education. I used my savings and what was left of the lottery prize to pay for my trip to and education in the United States. There I stayed with an American friend and did some housework for her. My living expenses did not cost much. In 1948 I got a M.A. in special education. My thesis was on "Establishing China's First School for Disabled Children."

I returned to Shanghai in 1948, preparing to set up a special education school. Meanwhile, Chen Heqin appointed me director of the Shanghai Special Children Institute. I also taught physical education in a girls' school for a while. On June 1, 1949, I opened China's first school for disabled children, fulfilling my promise at Columbia University. From an old man I rented the first floor of a building with three big rooms for classrooms. The faculty, including myself, were all volunteers. I rode my bike back and forth between the school where I taught physical education and the school for disabled children. After one year the government increased the land tax, and my landlord asked for more rent. I did not have money to pay for that. Through friends I got help from Zhao Puchu, who was in charge of relief and welfare in Shanghai. He gave me a tearoom in a garden, which enabled us to continue the school.

I was happy to have this new environment for my school, but just then something unthinkable happened. I had offended a teacher by refusing to let someone she knew who had TB live in our school. She and another teacher plotted to take over the school with the help of their friend who worked in the Education Bureau. I am Hunanese. I have this type of personality: if I fit in with the place, I stay; if not, I simply depart. The school was created by me, but if someone else wanted to take it over, I did not have to hold on to it. I could do something else. So I resigned. But they did something indecent. They brought in a reporter from *Wenhuibao* [an official Shanghai newspaper] and encouraged children to make false accusations against me, saying that Principal Chen abused children. On June 1, 1951, *Wenhuibao* printed an article attacking me, and the Education Bureau declared that I was fired. It was ridiculous that I was fired from the school I created myself. The school did not cost the government any money, but provided needed services to those disabled children. I did such a good thing but was fired by the government. Those *tubaozi* [country bumpkin] cadres lacked the ability to reason. Because it was not long after liberation, I was afraid of the Communist Party. Moreover, I had received an education in the United States, and the Korean War was going on. I could do nothing at a time when all the thinking was one-sided. People who did not know the truth thought I did terrible things. My whole life was ruined by this incident. The reason I am accepted by the Wenshiguan is because the Communist Party did me a disservice.

After leaving the school, I studied Russian for two years. I did not have a job, and my sister in the United States supported me. In 1954, a friend of mine introduced me to the Shanghai Second Military Medical University. I taught therapeutic physical education there. I liked this job, and I made suggestions in order to improve my work. But the president of the university and other colleagues distrusted me because I had studied in the United States. They would not let me do anything I initiated. They would not even allow me to read patients' files when I worked in the hospital with my students. I was very unhappy. In 1955, when the campaign against counter-revolutionaries began, I was put in a special session to be evaluated. The treatment then was much better than it was later, during the Cultural Revolution. Six months after they began, they finished checking up on me and said that I did not have political problems. They did not fire me, but I no longer wanted to work there. That was not a place for me. When I quit the job, I asked for a vehicle to transport my luggage back to my apartment downtown. They gave me a horse cart. I had to follow the horse cart on my bike. Some colleagues helped me load my luggage, and then they took buses to my home to help me unload things and carry them to the third floor. But during the Cultural Revolution people made this into a story, saying I was fired and sent home under escort as if I had committed a big crime.

I could not live without working, although with my sister's support I had no financial worries. Two months later, in April 1956, I went to study traumatology from Wang Ziping, the famous Chinese medicine doctor and martial arts master. I thought it would be nice for a person specialized in physical education to master traumatology. I was Wang's favorite student. But soon I became the rival of his son-in-law, who was also his student. My position as a person educated in the United States made him uncomfortable, so he tried to make the situation bad for me. I did not want to put up with that, so I left Wang Ziping after one year.

In 1957 I went to Beijing to learn *qigong*.[12] Liu-Wang Liming introduced me to the *qigong* therapy institute. Later I opened a massage clinic in my apartment. Many people came to my clinic, including movie actors, directors, and school principals. I did that, not for the sake of the money, but to have something to do. I ran the clinic until the Cultural Revolution. Then they said I was running a clinic without a license, and the clinic was forced to close. My home was ransacked when the neighborhood people came to "sweep off the four old things."[13] I did not have any bad labels, so these people came to ransack my home merely out of jealousy. They saw I had many possessions all to myself and I lived in a big apartment by myself. One thing eventually became my crime. I bought a portrait of Chairman Mao, and a person I knew wrote some sentences on the back of it. Later I was mad at the person so I tore apart the portrait. Someone, who was supposed to be a friend, saw me doing that and reported this to the neighborhood committee. That was a crime in the Cultural Revolution. They hit me and asked me to sweep the streets. The person who reported me later died a sudden death. All those people who persecuted me in the Cultural Revolution have died. I moved away from that neighborhood after the Cultural Revolution because I did not want to see those people anymore. Although they gave me a list of things they took away, I never got those things back. I also lost all my old photos. I tore them up myself because I thought they would cause more trouble for me. I did not want to live in that kind of society anymore, so why should I cherish those photos? I regret doing that very much. I used to have cases of photos from traveling abroad. Now I only have my diploma from Columbia University, which was underneath a newspaper in a drawer and thus overlooked by the people doing the ransacking. Otherwise, I would have nothing to prove my credentials. A copy of *The Women's Voice* I bought in the 1930s was also left, which is lucky for Wang Yiwei. It is a proof of her accomplishments in the past. I gave the journal to her after the Cultural Rev-

---

12. *Qigong* is an art and skill to train *qi*. It is a method by which the practitioner gets physical and mental exercise through bringing into play his or her subjective initiative. *Qi*, in Chinese a homonym of "air" or "breath," refers to a kind of nutritive substance within the body. It is closely related to but entirely different from the respired air. As a medical keep-fit activity, *qigong* has a history of several thousand years in China. See *Chinese Qigong*, a volume in the series *A Practical English-Chinese Library of Traditional Chinese Medicine*, ed. Zhang Enqin (Shanghai: Publishing House of Shanghai College of Traditional Chinese Medicine, 1990).

13. "Sweep off the four old things" was a campaign at the beginning of the Cultural Revolution. The slogan refers to old customs, old habits, old culture, and old thinking.

olution. I just console myself with the thought that I am much better off than those people who lost their lives in the Cultural Revolution.

In my youth I met many men who showed an interest in me. But because I had determined not to marry, I felt no more interest in men than in women. Early in the May Fourth movement, a young man wrote to me, saying that he wanted to make friends with me. I said, "What are you doing here, making revolution or making friends?" I just treated those men as ordinary friends. I have never met any man who expressed respect for my devotion to my career. Unless God creates one for me, I don't think such a man exists. A few years ago I was invited by a young couple to their son's birthday celebration. I bought some gifts and wanted to write their son's name on the gifts. Then I discovered that their son had both parents' surnames. That is the only case I have ever seen. I have never met any man who would do the same thing. In the old society, I remained single, and nobody tried to mind my business. The situation is different today. After liberation, no one can remain single because people around her will all show their concerns. In the past, everyone had freedom. Moreover, many places preferred single women to be physical education teachers.

I think women's life today is harder than women's life before. In theory, men and women are equal, and women are half of the sky. In reality, women suffer unspeakable miseries. Women who want to devote themselves to careers cannot have a happy family life. Men, foreign or Chinese, are the same. They all think women should serve them at home. As a result, women have to cook, take care of their children, and look after their old parents at home. At the same time, they have to work hard outside the home. They endure too much hardship. In the past, most career women had domestic helpers who shouldered half of the burden.

I knew many women activists in Shanghai, because in the War of Resistance we all participated in patriotic activities. I was just a common follower. I joined the Women's Association and attended their meetings. Because I was very busy with my heavy teaching load, I did not do too much in public. Only those women with social connections had the chance to hold responsible positions. Since I was sixteen years old I have wanted to save the nation through physical education. Now I see that physical education and sports are prospering. I have not done much, but others have done a lot. I am happy, too. Although I was very much traumatized by the Cultural Revolution, I have never stopped helping others. In the Cultural Revolution I volunteered to cure people with my skill in traumatology. After the Cultural Revolution, since 1977, I have taught numerous students to speak American English for free. My students are spread out in all walks of life both at home and abroad. I am an old woman now, but my mind is still young and vigorous. I hope my life is one that contains nothing to be ashamed about.

INTERPRETATION: INDIVIDUALISM AND NATIONALISM

Chen Yongsheng, in Wang Yiwei's opinion, is an individualist who only cares about her own self-interest. Wang's opinion is based on the fact that Chen was not a prominent activist in the 1930s in Shanghai. Although Chen once joined the Women's Christian Temperance Union, she was involved in few women's organized activities. In this respect she is different from our other narrators. And yet her case is relevant to our study of feminism of the May Fourth era. In fact, her life story demonstrates striking similarities to the experiences of other educated women studied here, as well as provides telling evidence for the influence of feminist discourse on that generation of educated women.

Chen is from a family that followed the new intellectual trends in the early twentieth century. Her father and uncles had all studied in Japan. Her father was involved in the 1911 Revolution and was a founder of the progressive Qunyi Publishing House. Through her uncle's relationship with Chen Duxiu, one of the founders of the CCP and the editor in chief of *New Youth*, Qunyi Publishing House became the distributor of *New Youth*. In this family, which was "not very traditional and more inclined to Western ideas," no women of Chen's generation had bound feet and all received an education. Chen entered Zhounan Girls' School as a boarding student at age six, a fact she emphasized in both her autobiography and interview. Zhounan Girls' School was a private school established by Zhu Jianfan, an educator who received his higher education in Japan. Zhu believed that "the premise of revolution is enlightening people; and the precursor of revolution is women's emancipation." He turned his family compound into a school when the Qing government ruled against private girls' schools. After the 1911 Revolution, Zhu openly declared that the goal of the school was to "aim at women's emancipation, and to bring up talented women in order to revitalize China." The school enrolled a group of students who eventually became prominent figures in early-twentieth-century China. Xiang Jingyu and Cai Chang, the two famous CCP leaders of the women's movement, and Ding Ling, the famous writer, all graduated from there.[14] To mention an ed-

14. Su Ping, *Cai Chang zhuan* [The biography of Cai Chang] (Beijing: Zhongguo funü chubanshe, 1990), 15–17. For more information on Zhounan Girls' School and Zhu Jianfan, see chapter 8 in this volume.

ucation in Zhounan Girls' School is to emphasize one's progressive background in mainland China.

But Chen did not stay in Zhounan Girls' School long, and unlike other famous alumnae, she did not become a politically oriented woman activist. However, the strong theme of patriotism that Zhounan and other girls' schools stressed stands out in Chen's narrative. Chen's view of women's emancipation was formed through the lens of nationalism. Her devotion to women's physical education was stimulated by Japan's Twenty-One Demands and Xu Teli's protest letter in blood. "A strong nation depends on a strong race, and to have a strong race, women's education and the health of women's bodies is important." Her conviction about physical education as a means to national salvation was so strong that she determined to remain single in order to devote herself to the cause of women's physical education. National interest was certainly the driving force in her career development, a fact overlooked by women activists like Wang Yiwei. Wang's comment about Chen reflects the CCP's negative views toward those who tried to maintain an independent position in China's confusing political wars. Chen would never think of herself as an individualist who was only concerned about self-interest. She had made her own choice about the way to national salvation. Concentrating on her career rather than on other social or political activities was her means of contributing to the well-being of Chinese women and the nation. It seems that the hegemony of the nationalist discourse in early-twentieth-century China left few educated women of that generation free of nationalist concerns.

Interestingly, as in Lu Lihua's case, Chen's concern for national well-being was harmoniously connected to her self-interest. National salvation required educated women to contribute, and career women like Chen happily found their self-realization through service to the nation. Teaching women physical education became such a key modern profession that Chen found herself "very popular" and her expertise "in high demand." Young women with one or two years of physical training could find teaching positions in provincial girls' schools or national women's colleges. At twenty years old, Chen became the chair of the department of physical education at the prestigious Beijing National Women's Normal University—even though she at that time lacked a high school diploma. These expanding employment opportunities and relaxed attitudes toward women's academic credentials were created by the urgent need to strengthen the nation by building a strong race. Women's bodies, according to the nationalist discourse, were the key vehicle to reach that goal. Understandably, women hired in those posts were aware of their mission as well as their bright prospects. That

Chen often shifted her posts shows her constant effort to find a suitable place for herself at a time when physical education teachers were in high demand.

Beyond the nationalism that educated women learned from their male mentors, women had their own personal experiences to help them make choices. Again, like many other women of her generation, Chen's life was strongly affected by the women's pain that she witnessed. It was shocking to Chen when her father and uncles—the enlightened and enlightening intellectuals she worshipped—brought concubines home. She interpreted her mother's early death as a consequence of her father's acquiring a concubine. Apparently, her father's behavior caused no less trauma for her than for her mother. Chen emphasized in the interview that at sixteen she decided not to marry for two reasons: patriotism and women's sufferings. She could remember the time of her decision so accurately because of the Twenty-One Demands and her teacher's blood letter. Understandably, the women's suffering she had witnessed and the pain her father and uncles had caused her were the grounds for that decision. When the teenage girl with a saddened heart was suddenly stimulated by the national crisis and her teacher's heroic deeds, she found not only a way to national salvation but also a way out of her own predicament: to devote her life to physical education in order to strengthen the nation. Thus a woman's resistance to gender oppression was legitimately expressed in the language of patriotism.

Chen's experience here is strikingly similar to that of Lu Lihua, Zhu Sue, and Wang Yiwei, whose striving for a career was also stimulated by women's tragedies in their families. The shared experiences of these women, and the importance of the early experiences in these women's own accounts, may help us understand the relationship between women's personal experiences and their receptivity to a certain ideology. From these women's life stories, we identify a variable in their susceptibility to nationalism and feminism: their early experiences of gender practices. No matter whether they took the form of the double sexual standard, or the family system favoring male heirs, the gender practices generated anger, frustration, and pain in these young girls. Nationalism and feminism assisted their revolt against the oppression of women, a concept that articulated their childhood experiences and feelings. Embracing these empowering discourses, rebellious young girls became courageous new women. The construction of a new subjectivity in women is a process that involves not only the circulation of a new discourse, but also a group of women unhappy with the status quo. In other words, without an audience made receptive by their own personal experience, even a circulating discourse cannot create new subject positions.

As a revolt against the oppressive marriage system, Chen's decision to remain single was not uncommon in her generation. Wang Yiwei also decided not to marry because of unhappy marriages in her family. The opening of career opportunities made these women confident of an independent life, and the nationalist discourse legitimized their patriotic devotion. It was no longer unthinkable for an educated woman of the early twentieth century to live by herself. Many young women thought of their own celibacy as a wise and necessary choice, and women activists who regarded themselves as the pioneers of women's emancipation were particularly prone to choosing a celibate life, because the cause of women's emancipation required their total devotion. Moreover, it was almost impossible to obtain a happy marriage in the existing social system. The pioneers of women's emancipation had no time or energy to experiment on their own marriages.[15] Such a view was popular among the May Fourth young women as well as among young men who wanted to devote themselves to revolution. Although most failed to stick to their vows, some women did remain single and built outstanding careers.[16]

Young Chen soon learned a new language to add new meaning to her decision to be celibate. The most frequently used phrases in New Culture feminism—"independent personhood" and "appendage"—were used effortlessly by Chen in her interviews. To maintain independent personhood and not to be anyone's appendage became the core of Chen's subjectivity. At sixteen, celibacy for Chen was an ideal combination of devotion to the nation and escape from women's sufferings. At thirty, when she gave the talk on women's personal problems, she had a new perspective on the issue of celibacy. She was consciously pursuing independent personhood. And she was able openly to attack gender inequity. Like other women studied here, Chen is unable to name any particular book or magazine that gave her new

15. Celibacy was one of the problems in the national debate. The view cited here was presented by a woman activist Zhang Ruomin. See Zhang Ruomin, "Jixianfeng de nüzi" [Pioneering women], in Wusi shiqi funü wenti wenxuan [Selected articles on women's problems in the May Fourth period], ed. All-China Women's Federation (Beijing: Zhongguo funü chubanshe, 1981), 49–58.

16. Cai Chang, her brother Cai Hesen, Xiang Jingyu, and Mao Zedong vowed not to marry when they made their youthful decisions to devote their lives to national salvation. All of them broke their vows before long. See Su Ping, Cai Chang zhuan, and He Huzhi, Xiang Jingyu zhuan [The biography of Xiang Jingyu] (Shanghai: Shanghai renmin chubanshe, 1990). The most famous unmarried career woman was the renowned gynecologist Lin Qiaozhi. Beginning with that generation, single women with remarkable achievements have enjoyed public respect for their devotion to their careers.

ideas. However, she learned to use the New Culture feminist language and to abide by its principles.

It is interesting to note that Chen never mentioned how much she was enlightened on gender issues during her stay in the United States. On the contrary, in interviews she referred to American women twice, only to show that they were unable to think what she was thinking. Chen mentioned that women students at Baylor College for Women would have parties every weekend and be very excited if they got dates, saying, "Oh, I am going to have a date tonight!" Chen imitated the girlish voice she heard seventy years ago to stress the simplemindedness of her American classmates. None of her American classmates had experienced what she had been through. She had long ago decided not to marry, because she had seen too much misery in marriage. Men to her were just ordinary friends. No man could excite her unless he treated her equally and would agree to let her keep her surname. She definitely did not meet such a man in the United States. Worse still, when she brought up the question of surnames to her American friends the second time she was in the United States, none of them had ever thought about it. In short, Chen never encountered feminism during her stay in the United States, even though she was concerned about gender issues. This might be because her American classmates in the mid 1920s were young women in the age of jazz and flappers rather than the cohort of suffragists. Moreover, a fundamentalist school in Texas was an unlikely place to get exposure to feminism. And her second trip to the United States was after World War II, when antifeminism rather than feminism was the rising tide and most American women were eager to be Mrs. So-and-So. Therefore, this Chinese woman of the May Fourth generation was unable to discuss gender issues with her American friends.

Chen received a higher education in the United States, an experience different from other interviewees. How has that experience contributed to the formation of her subjectivity? Chen's good command of American English shows a Western cultural background. But except for that, she sounds very much like other educated women of her generation who have never been abroad. She emphasizes her patriotism, her devotion to her career, her service to other people—all the qualities that have been confirmed by official discourse in the People's Republic of China. More telling is her relationship with her family members. She always refers to her kin as her family. Although she has remained single all her life, mentally she has never separated herself from her natal family, and physically she welcomed her brothers and sisters to live with her when she had a big apartment. She regarded it as her responsibility to take care of her brothers, sisters, nephews, and nieces. When she won the lottery prize, she divided it among her siblings. In her old age she still feels sorry that her mother died shortly before she was able to provide for her. Her concept of family and of her obligations to her kin shows no tint of American individualism.

In everything Chen says, only one phrase is typically American: "I just want to be myself." She says it in Chinese, yet it is easy to detect its foreign origin, for Chinese people without exposure to Western culture would be unlikely to use the awkward translated phrase *zuowo ziji* (be myself). Interestingly, she used the phrase when referring to her determination not to be an appendage to any man. Because she had made her decision to be single long before going to the United States and had learned the concept of independent personhood in the May Fourth era, "to be myself" was not an American concept that enlightened her and changed her behavior; rather, it was an American idea that she could identify with and that she could grasp in her own way. Many American women would say "I just want to be myself" without questioning their status of being Mrs. So-and-So. But Chen's understanding of being herself is being an independent woman who, at the very least, would keep her own surname in marriage. Independent personhood (*duli renge*) and "being myself" have an obvious affinity. Independent personhood was an alien concept introduced by the New Culturalists in promoting Western individualism. In Chen Duxiu's early usage, the phrase "independent personhood" was meant to convey the basic elements of individualism, such as independence, autonomy, and individuality. But once "independent personhood" entered the Chinese discourse, it acquired its own concrete meanings tied to its specific historical and social context. Because the phrase was popularized through the New Culturalists' advocacy of women's emancipation, it has had a clear gender dimension ever since. It appears mostly in the context of discussing women's issues. For May Fourth women, it signified an independent life demanding equality with men in all aspects. Not surprisingly, Chen projected her understanding of independent personhood onto the phrase "being myself."

One of the most striking characteristics of Chen's life is that she enjoyed free physical mobility. She moved from school to school as a student as well as a teacher. Once she was past childhood, she made all her own decisions as to which school to attend and which job to quit or to take. After she graduated in 1920 and before she went to the United States in 1923, she drifted from Shanghai to Beijing, to Hubei, to Guangdong, and finally back to Shanghai. Significantly, she did not define her frequent shifting of posts as trying to "be herself"; instead, she attributed it to her Hunanese traits. "If I fit in with the place, I stay; if not, I simply depart." In her perception, her moves were a matter of temperament rather than a conscious search for an abstract self. Chen did not use an American cultural framework to explain her experience. She is just another strong-willed Chinese woman who happened to be born into an age that allowed women's social mobility and into a family that encouraged young girls' independence. Chen remembers well that her mother did not want to depend on her sons but rather on her daughters. It is possible that her mother saw in her strong-willed daughters great potential—or perhaps she merely wanted her daughters to aim high. Whether the mother expressed that wish out of confidence or as a stimulus, she saw the possibility that her daughters might live a life different from hers. In short, rather than a Western education, it was family background and a historical moment that enabled Chen to live a mobile and independent life.

Although culturally her education in the United States did not visibly affect Chen's life pattern, socially the label of "returned student from the United States" (*Meiguo liuxuesheng*) made important differences in her life. In the years before 1949, the label was a credit that brought benefits for her. She secured a position as a principal of one girls' school, and in another school she was paid higher than those who did not have a Western degree. A Western education was obviously welcomed, and many Western-educated women returned to China. Actually, under the dominance of a nationalist discourse, almost all students who went abroad in the early twentieth century returned to China. The purpose of their study in the West was to strengthen China. It is telling that in 1928, when Chen returned to Shanghai with a B.A. in English, she could not find a job teaching English. Although schools of different levels were all offering English classes, the metropolis still had more people with English teaching credentials than it needed.

After 1949, her identity as a returned student from the United States put Chen at a disadvantage. The CCP fanned strong anti-American sentiment in the country when the Korean War broke out, and that sentiment caused Chen to lose the disabled children's school that she had recently established. Gone with the school were her dreams and her respected social status. She became a person stigmatized by scandal. In her words, her life was ruined by this incident. Although she found a job a few years later, she was never again trusted. When the anti-counterrevolutionary campaign occurred in 1955, she had to endure an investigation. This strong-willed woman refused to put up with more. She quit her job, as she had done numerous times in the past. But this time, the situation was different: after liberation, she no longer had job opportunities. In her mid fifties, the resilient Chen began to learn a new trade—traumatology—and opened a clinic by herself. Although she was glad to provide service to people, as a self-employed person in Mao's era Chen became a marginal woman. It was not until after the Cultural Revolution that the government restored her social respectability by accepting her as a member of the Wenshiguan—an acceptance that she believes was a form of compensation for the loss that she endured.

Chen's unique experience before 1949 finally gained her some social recognition and special treatment by the government in the 1990s. In China's campaign to host the Olympic Games, Chen was discovered as an old patriot who had fought all her life for the development of China's physical education and sports. In the rising nationalist sentiment surrounding the Olympic Games, Chen's attendance at the Olympic Games in 1936 and her return to China after studying in the United States made her an excellent example of Chinese patriotism in association with the Olympic Games. Chen was invited as a distinguished guest to attend the opening ceremony of the East Asian Games in Shanghai in 1993. She was interviewed by reporters from newspapers and magazines. She supported the government's bid to host the Olympic Games. And she was genuinely happy to see physical education and sports developing rapidly in China. Depicting Chen as an old patriot is no distortion. In a very real sense, Chen embodies the nationalist sentiment of strengthening the Chinese race that has persisted throughout twentieth-century China.

As a prominent old patriot who returned from abroad, Chen was visited by Shanghai's vice-mayor Gong Xueping before the Spring Festival in 1995. Gong felt sorry to see this ninety-five-year-old woman living alone in a messy apartment. He told the officials of the Returned Overseas Chinese Office to hire a domestic helper for Chen. But Chen declined, saying, "I am poor, but I do not want the government to pay for a domestic helper. I would rather not have any helper. I have a good command of English. I can do translation work to pay for a domestic helper." Her wish to use her expertise in English to earn money to pay for a domestic helper—an idea she expressed the first time I met her, two years before—was finally realized. Through Shanghai officials' effort under the mandate of the vice-mayor, both the *Shanghai Qiaobao* (the Shanghai overseas Chinese newspaper) and a Shanghai law firm hired Chen as their English consultant. Thus, Chen continued to uphold to the very end the principle of independence that she maintained throughout her long life.[17]

17. During my visit to Chen on January 8, 1995, she told me of the vice-mayor's recent visit. She got to know Gong Xueping at the opening ceremony of the East Asian Games in 1993. The story of Gong hiring a domestic helper for Chen appeared

As a career woman Chen shares many similarities with other career women of her generation. National salvation and independent personhood constituted the core of the subjectivity of this group of educated women. In their double pursuit of making a contribution to the country and maintaining an independent life, they were consciously aware of ubiquitous gender discrimination in the society. Nevertheless, they were able to make great strides in their careers. Indeed, after the late 1920s, career women became a prominent social force in China's metropolises. Equal higher education and equal employment, promoted during the May Fourth era, were institutionalized quickly thereafter. These women's narratives demonstrate that, so long as individual families did not thwart their daughters' dreams for a career and could provide them with an education, it was relatively easy for the women to enroll in secondary vocational schools or universities. And with that educational background, women who did not want to be a Mrs. So-and-So could smoothly become a member of the respected new social group, career women (*zhiye funü*). Huge differences between the life of the "new woman daughter" and her mother testify to the rapidly changing gender relations in the early twentieth century. Although career women constituted only a very small percentage of the population, the very existence of this social group proclaimed the end of centuries-old gender segregation as a dominant social practice as well as a ruling ideology.

Ironically, these pioneers of Chinese women's liberation were not valued during the Maoist era when the state claimed women's liberation to be a high priority. Their patriotic devotion did not necessarily make them politically correct in the eyes of the CCP. Their self-reliance and career achievement only proved that they did not belong to the oppressed proletarian class. The fact that they had not joined the Communist Revolution disqualified them from the ranks of the new elite. A Western education or affiliation with the GMD further removed them from the center stage of social life. In the Maoist transformation of Chinese society, the career women as a group did not fit into any of the categories in the CCP's class stratification. They were therefore dispersed into different classes. A few career women with remarkable achievements were granted honorable positions and were able to continue their professions because they were needed in the new so-

---

in *Xinmim Wanbao* [Shanghai evening news], February 14, 1995, with the title "Ni'ai zuguo, zuguo geng'aini" [You love the country, the country loves you more]. The story emphasizes Chen's patriotism and the vice-mayor's concern for the people. As for Chen's refusal of the helper offered by the government, the reporter attributes this to the old woman's "stubbornness."

ciety. Many fell into the category of bourgeois intellectuals. If they continued to work in state-owned institutions, they had to go through a lifelong transformation under the guidance of Marxism and Mao Zedong Thought. Many others who could not find a niche in the new social structure—women such as Chen Yongsheng, Wang Yiwei, Zhu Su'e, and Lu Lihua—had to discontinue their careers and live a marginal life. The career women or the new women as a social category, which had existed since the May Fourth period, was hence obliterated in the Mao era.[18]

18. Not until 1989, when *A History of the Chinese Women's Movement* was published, was there a section on career women of the twenties and thirties in this official women's history. Career women's important role in promoting Chinese women's social advancement before 1949 was acknowledged. This signified a meaningful change from the Maoist era. See All-China Women's Federation, *Zhongguo funü yundong shi* [A history of the Chinese women's movement] (Beijing: Chunqiu chubanshe, 1989), 283–288.

8 Huang Dinghui (1907–):
Career Revolutionary

Huang Dinghui, 1995

At eighty-six, Huang Dinghui looks like an energetic lady barely past sixty. Her clear eyes, delicate features, and little dimples accentuating her smiles made me picture her as a petite beauty in her youth. She has a pleasant and resilient voice that allows her to talk for several hours at a stretch. She speaks rapidly and with an animated expression. A simple question of mine often prompts a monologue from her. She has too many interesting personal stories to wait for my prompt. In her own words, "The things I have experienced are more than enough for two books."[1]

NARRATIVE

I was born in Liuyang, a famous town with a revolutionary heritage. Mao Zedong led an uprising at Wenjiashi in Liuyang and went to the Jinggang Mountains in 1927. Liuyang has not only beautiful landscape, but also many outstanding people. The educational level in Hunan was comparatively high.

---

1. The following narrative is constructed from interviews conducted on March 22, 1993, and January 12–13, 1995, and from Huang's unpublished autobiographies.

Even the pedicab drivers and porters learned *Sanzijing* and *Qianziwen*.[2] There were no beggars in Liuyang because the people were all hardworking. In every household, women spun or wove cotton or linen. There was a folk song: "Weaving linen at six; spinning cotton at seven; embroidering at nine or ten." Hunan embroidery is famous internationally. Men did farming, women did weaving; both worked hard.

My mother's family name was Li. Her father was a doctor who practiced Chinese medicine. She was illiterate but had a very good verbal memory. My father taught her to recite many articles, so words flowed from her mouth as from the pen of a master. She was married to my father at age eighteen. My father had previously had two marriages. Both of his wives had died without leaving any children. My father was nineteen years older than my mother. My mother bore seven children—five boys and two girls. I was the eldest. I was born on July 20, 1907. Shortly after the 1911 Revolution, my father became the dean of Yuelu Academy; he kept the post for two years. Tan Yankai was the president of the academy. My mother stayed at home, doing housekeeping. We hired a maid who cooked and cleaned. The water was carried by a man we hired.

Because my father was an enlightened man, he let me go to school when I was six years old. My childhood was very happy. I was unaware of sorrows, worries, or sadness in the world. When I was born as the first daughter to my father, he was already over thirty years old. He cherished me as a pearl in his palm. A few years later, my mother gave birth to my brother. My parents did not show partiality to their sons.

When my mother married my father, he asked her to unbind her feet right away. She cut her wrapping cloth. According to the custom, my feet should have been bound when I was six. In our hometown, girls a few years older than I all had bound feet. When they saw that I did not have bound feet and played with boys, they thought I was odd. My mother talked to them about the disadvantage of bound feet. My father often said, "Women should have equality. And eliminating the pain of bound feet is the precondition of equality between men and women." I could read and sing, which most rural girls could not. Because I went to school in the town, I was more open-minded.

My father was the only son of a poor family. He went to school with financial help from his mother's family. He was very bright and able to compose poems when he was only twelve years old. He could be called a person with

---

2. *Sanzijing* [The three-character classic] and *Qianziwen* [The thousand-character classic] are two classic texts for teaching Chinese to beginners.

talent but without luck. He made friends with all those famous scholars of his time. They composed poems for each other. My father and Tan Sitong were classmates.[3] My father's book was recently reprinted in the mainland and in Taiwan. My father was in the democratic revolution of the old type.[4] He was a *yougong*, one of the rank who, like *juren*, were entitled to enter the exams for *zhuangyuan* [Number One Scholar] in Beijing.[5] He did not pass the exam for *zhuangyuan*. Tan Sitong had passed the exam a year before. My father then worked for Tan Sitong as his assistant [*mufu*]. Tan's son was my father's student. A lot of Xinhai revolutionaries were his students, too, because he was once a teacher of the Hunan Yuelu Academy. Today he would be like the dean of an education school.

Together with Tan Sitong and other progressive people in Liuyang, my father once ran an orphanage. Liuyang had the custom of female infanticide. When a daughter was born, she was called *peiqian huo* [a losing investment] because the family had to give her a dowry but would receive no bride-price. The second daughter might be kept, but the third one would definitely be abandoned. After the orphanage was set up, many baby girls were sent there. Because father and his friends popularized the idea that infanticide was a crime and that girls could participate in farming when they grew up, gradually the incidence of female infanticide was reduced.

My father no longer wanted to make revolution after the failure of the Xinhai Revolution [1911 Revolution]. He believed in *shiye jiuguo* [saving the nation through business enterprise]. When he was at the Yuelu Academy, he wrote a report to Tan Yankai, proposing the development of mining and railways in Hunan. Later he worked on a mine project but failed. When others tried to use his failure to exclude him from his position, he quit. Then Tan Yankai, the governor of Hunan, asked him to work on the

3. Tan Sitong (1865–1898) was a famous reformer of the late Qing. In his major work, *Renxue*, he attacked the three basic principles of Confucianism. He also advocated gender equality. See chapter 1 in this volume for a brief discussion of Tan.

4. In Maoist analysis, the 1911 Revolution was a bourgeois revolution, a democratic revolution of the old type (*jiuminzhu zhuyi geming*). The second stage, a democratic revolution of the new type, was led by the CCP and marked by the May Fourth movement.

5. *Yougong* belonged to the category *gongsheng*—an academic degree that in Qing times conferred a social status similar to that of *juren*. *Gongsheng* were the holders of the first degree, who were selected for further studies at the Imperial Academy or for eventual minor official appointment. See Ping-ti Ho, *The Ladder of Success in Imperial China* (New York: John Wiley and Sons, 1964), 27–29. Huang's reference to "exams for *Zhangyuan*" is slightly misleading; it should be "the exams for *jinshi* degree." *Zhuangyuan* is a title given to the scholar who ranks first in the exams for *jinshi*.

Zhuping Railroad. Later he was promoted by Zhan Tianyou, the superintendent of the Yuehan Railroad, to be in charge of building the railroad between Guangdong and Hankou. When the section between Wuchang and Changsha was completed, the Northern Expedition began. Then, because of my involvement in the Communist Party, my father was demoted and sent to the Longhai Railroad in Zhengzhou. He contracted tuberculosis there. Worrying about me and unhappy about his own position, he died shortly afterward, at age fifty-nine.

My father worked for the railroad for eighteen years. When he worked at the Zhuping Railroad, he made 60 silver dollars a month. Later when he was transferred to the Yuehan Railroad, he made 180 silver dollars. Our family expenses amounted at most to 100 silver dollars. My mother saved some money to buy land and houses in Liuyang. That was the way of people in those days. She herself was very frugal. She knew that my father was old, and she had to manage the big family and her children's education. But later we were classified as a landlord family. Originally we were from poor families. My mother raised us strictly. With her frugal household management, she was able to send three of my brothers to college. My sister had a high school education and married a college student who became a diplomat for the Nationalist government. My other two brothers died as martyrs in the revolution.

I went to the Girls' Elementary School of Liuyang County. It was the only girls' school in the county. I remember wearing a black skirt and a white shirt and carrying my own lunch box. I went to school when I was six years old and graduated when I was eight. It should have taken four years to graduate, but because my grades were very good, I skipped a year. My memory has been excellent ever since I was a child. Father taught me Tang poems when I was very young, and I still remember them. My father was away from home and came back only once every other year. He taught me and gave me quizzes when he was on vacation at home. When he was away, my mother asked me to write letters to him on her behalf. My father would correct my mistakes and send my letters back to teach me. I learned to write letters when I was still an elementary school student. Later, he became my primary teacher; he taught me all that I know about classics. My father supported my going to school. My family also supported my joining the revolution. He was only sorry that I was a girl, because he thought that if I were a boy my family would be prosperous. He was past thirty when I was born. The brother born right after me was in poor health, but I was very healthy. After that brother came my sister. My father always thought I was very bright and often said to me, "If you were a boy, you would surely bring glory to our ancestors." As a person belonging to the democratic revolution of the old type, he had some feudal ideas.

My elementary school in Liuyang was very progressive. The honorary principal of my elementary school was the wife of Tan Sitong, and our teachers had all studied in Japan. These teachers left a deep impression on me—that is why I have neither bound feet nor pierced ears. The physical education teacher, Chinese literature teacher, and so on, were all women. At school I liked to sing "Mulan ci" [Ballad of Mulan] and "Man Jiang Hong ci" [Lines for the Man Jiang Hong melody].[6] After we sang these poems, the teachers told us about Hua Mulan and Yue Fei, so from elementary school, I received a progressive and patriotic education. Moreover, my family was patriotic and democratic, too. That's why I have this foundation. My teachers were all single and stuck to *dushen zhuyi* [celibatarianism]. They were devoted to girls' education and strove for women's equality and freedom. They also said that after their education in Japan, they were no longer used to a lot of the social conditions at home. Therefore, it was hard for them to find a spouse.

In the elementary school I excelled in gymnastics, classical Chinese, and other courses. I was at the top of my graduating class. When the worker from my school sent my degree to my home, he set off a string of firecrackers. My mother was very happy and gave him a red pack [money wrapped in red paper]. Then we set off our own firecrackers, too. Our neighbors all knew that I graduated from elementary school. They said I was *xiucai* now.[7] As one of the first graduates from the girls' school in my hometown, I was much honored. My mother held a three-table dinner party to treat the neighbors who came to congratulate me. The neighbors also bought firecrackers as congratulatory gifts.

When I was eleven years old, Hunan was flooded. At the time my father was working at the Yuehan Railroad, so we moved to Wuchang to join him. To board the boat, we had to walk across a long narrow plank that connected the boat to the shore. I carried my third brother, who was nine years younger than I, on my back and walked bravely across the plank to the boat. My mother's feet had once been bound, so she could not walk normally. Also, she had fallen into the river as a child, so she was afraid of water. She had to be supported by two people as she walked across the plank. During the

---

6. "Man Jiang Hong" [Lines for the Man Jiang Hong melody] is a poem written by the famous patriotic general Yue Fei of the Song dynasty. The poem expresses Yue's strong desire to drive away invaders and to keep the nation intact. Together with the "Ballad of Mulan," it became an important text in the nationalist discourse.

7. As noted earlier, *xiucai* refers to a scholar who passed the imperial examination at the county level in the Ming and Qing dynasties.

trip she had terrible sea sickness. Fortunately, I had no such problem. I have never been sick on a boat, plane, or vehicle. Then we arrived in Wuchang. Because Yuehan Railroad allowed the family of employees to ride the train for free, I took a ride to Changsha, where my maternal uncle worked. When I was twelve years old, I went to Zhounan Girls' School there.

I do not have any diploma. The most famous school I entered was Zhounan Girls' School. The principal, Zhu Jianfan, was famous. Both he and his wife had been educated in Japan. In 1990 I returned to the school to attend the celebration of the eighty-fifth anniversary of Zhounan. Now there are over one hundred Zhounan alumnae in Shanghai, including the wife of the former mayor. But there is no one but me left from the class of 1919.

At Zhounan Girls' School, Mr. Zhu Jianfan's teaching methodology was very enlightened. He let students form a student union and read books other than textbooks. Every week he gave a lecture on politics. Ever since my childhood, I had loved to hear about Chinese history. Mr. Zhu talked about modern Chinese history: how the Qing dynasty failed to resist foreign invasions and signed many unfair treaties, and how in the feudal society men were favored and women were looked down upon. He said, "Why did I open this girls' school? Because my wife and I decided that we would work hard for women's emancipation. Although the women's emancipation movement has been in place for a few years, it is important to popularize education. If women are all educated, they will be able to be independent and become useful people in society." I had heard my elementary teachers talk about equality between men and women, but no one had expressed this idea so thoroughly as Mr. Zhu. He told us about those unfair treaties and linked them to the contemporary situation in China. He thus aroused our patriotism. We received an enlightened education about antifeudalism, antiwarlordism, and anti-imperialism from him. We have a saying, "When you drink water, think of the source." I would say that, without Mr. Zhu's enlightenment and without my participation in the May Fourth movement, I would not have joined the Northern Expedition, left my family, or opposed my arranged marriage to pursue my self-emancipation. Mr. Zhu and the May Fourth movement raised my consciousness to pursue women's liberation and the liberation of all humankind.

A few months after I came to Zhounan, the May Fourth movement broke out. Thus, I joined the May Fourth movement when I was only twelve years old. I was in the lowest class—there were three classes altogether. Each class elected a representative to run the qiangbao [newspaper on the wall], which reported the information on demonstrations. I was elected by our class because my essays had always been praised by our teacher in class and posted on the wall. Our principal, Mr. Zhu, was very revolutionary. He encouraged students' involvement in the movement. He said, "You students should be in the vanguard, and we faculty will back you up." He encouraged us to form the students' union. I was in the three-person leading group that belonged in the students' union, responsible for the newspaper on the wall. I followed others to march and make speeches.

Every movement experiences a period of naïveté. In the early stage of the Communist movement, workers hated machines and smashed them. In the May Fourth movement, wherever we saw Japanese-made glass, we smashed it; wherever we saw a Japanese-made umbrella, we cut it. We went to stores to check on who was selling Japanese goods, denounced the bad merchants, and marched them in the streets with high hats on their heads. At the time Mao Zedong established the Xinmin Xuehui [New People's Study Society] and led the movement behind the scenes. Later the Changsha Students' Union sent a notice to us saying that we should register the Japanese goods and owners of those stores and send the goods to the Municipal Education Bureau for auction, so the money could be used to help poor students and private schools. It corrected the leftist tendency. Like the May Fourth movement, the Cultural Revolution was very naive at the beginning.

I learned the slogan of women's emancipation during the May Fourth movement. The May Fourth era was the beginning of the New Culture movement. We all began to have some consciousness in this period, but our consciousness was kind of fuzzy at that time because the party had not yet been established.

Lenin once said, "Even a brief participation in a revolutionary movement is equal to scores of years of social practice." Although my participation in the May Fourth movement lasted only a few months, the people's unity, high spirits, and righteous indignation were extremely exciting, enormously encouraging, and profoundly educational.

The students who worked in the students' union decided not to go home for summer vacation, so I wrote a letter home to tell my parents of this decision. Among my father's students, some were patriotic leftists, some were reactionary, and some were in the middle. One of his former students happened to be dean of studies in our school. We called him Dwarf Lou. He asked students to vote on the question whether you were for or against going home. I voted against going home. Another question was if the students' union was good. I said it was good. He secretly wrote letters to our parents, saying that the students who were against going home were bad. Although my father was an enlightened man, he did not know what I was doing at school, and it made him uneasy. He asked my brother to come and fetch me, saying that my mother was sick. When I got home, my mother had just had my fourth brother and was in poor health. Because I was the eldest, I had to take care of her and my siblings. She was very sick and was hemorrhaging. Her life was in danger. I had to stop going to school after that summer vacation.

I stayed at home to take care of my mother. Gradually she recovered and taught me sewing and knitting. My father arranged my curriculum: I studied classics on odd days, and history on even days. I read history books by myself, and I finished *The Twenty-Four Dynastic Histories*. My father taught me *The Four Books* and *The Five Classics* every morning before he went to work. He checked my work after he came home in the evening. During the day, I helped my mother with the chores and had no time to read books. In the half hour before my father's return, I sat at the desk and read the texts twice. When he came home, I recited them loudly for him. I strongly disliked those old books, but I had to read them.

I also took a correspondence course in English run by the Shanghai Commercial Press. My father taught me Chinese classics, and a tutor taught me math. With that English course, I thought I would be able to complete my education as if I were at school. From the Shanghai Commercial Press, I learned of *The Short Stories Monthly*, whose editor in chief was Mao Dun [Shen Yanbing]. I subscribed to it, the only new magazine I read in that period.

Before I was ten years old, my parents arranged a marriage for me. The man they chose was the son of my father's former classmate Mr. Li. Li's son was four years older than I, and the Li family wanted me to marry their son when I was only eighteen. But once we married, I found that I could not bear it, although the man's parents and four siblings all treated me very nicely. He had not yet graduated from college, but he had already had an affair with his maid and was addicted to opium. He often stayed out late. When he came home late at night, he would sometimes kick the maid and blame her for being too slow to open the door for him. I had never seen him before we married, though his younger sister was my classmate in Zhounan. She once said to me, "You are so nice, but my brother has a hot temper." My heart sank even though she had not told me about his opium problem. But the marriage was arranged by my parents, so I could not say much. My mother prepared my dowry, and on the wedding day my father ordered a special carriage from the railroad to send me and the dowry away. It was a grand ceremony.

Once my father came to Changsha on errands, and he visited me. I did not have a private conversation with him that day, but I sneaked him a note I had written beforehand. The note said, "Please send a letter saying mother

is ill and asking me to go home. I will tell you everything once I get there."
I did not want Li's family to hear me complain about their son. When my
father returned home, he sent a telegraph saying that my mother was seriously ill and that I should come home immediately. My uncle came to accompany me home. I left Li's home without taking any of my dowry back.
I had been married to Li for over a year.

My father knew the story of Qiu Jin. Now he realized that I was experiencing the same situation as Qiu, who married an unworthy man. He recommended that I read the *Biography of Qiu Jin*, saying to me, "You should
have high aspirations. Because you are unhappy with the marriage, you
should pursue an independent life." He supported my decision to leave that
man. He had only known the parents, not their son. He wrote a letter to the
family, telling them that his daughter was going to stay at her natal family
to wait and see if her husband would redress his wrong doings. He encouraged me to prepare myself for college entrance examinations. If I had not
been born into this enlightened family, if my parents had not been so open-
minded and loving, or if the man I married had been a good man, then I
would not have joined the revolution. That would be the end of my story.
I would be doomed to a common person's life without all the vicissitudes I
eventually experienced.

Staying at home, I read many books. I liked *The Romance of the Three
Kingdoms*. I did not care much for *The Dream of the Red Chamber*. Maybe
I do not know much about romance. Although I am a woman, people said I
was tough like a man. Anyway, reading love stories was not my hobby. But
I did read *The Sorrows of Young Werther* translated by Guo Moruo. I
thought the story expressed the sorrows and perplexity that young men and
women experienced in the feudal arranged marriage. I also liked Mao Dun's
novels.[8]

Six months after I returned to my home in Wuchang, the Northern Expedition began. A cousin of mine joined the Wuhan Railroad Workers'
Union. He knew that I was depressed by my unhappy marriage and often
brought flyers for me to read. Thus I learned about the workers' movement,
the peasant movement, and the women's movement in Guangzhou. I also
learned about the activities of Mrs. Liao Zhongkai and Song Qingling.[9] One

8. Both Guo Moruo and Mao Dun (Shen Yanbing) were famous New Culturalists who joined the National Revolution. Huang came to know both in Wuhan. For
a discussion of Mao Dun's role in *The Ladies' Journal*, see chapter 2.

9. Mrs. Liao Zhongkai was He Xiangning. See footnote 13, chapter 5. Song Qingling was Madame Sun Yat-sen.

day my cousin showed me a flyer that announced the strike of female workers in British- and American-owned tobacco factories. Because I had experienced strikes during the May Fourth period, I crossed the river to show
my support and consolation to the striking sisters. That was June 15, 1926.
I donated fifty silver dollars to them—savings from pocket money my father had given me. There I met Li Zifen, the head of the Communist Youth
League of Hubei province. He asked about my situation and what new publication I had been reading. I told him that I had read *The Short Stories
Monthly* edited by Mao Dun, Guo Muruo's translation of *The Sorrows of
Young Werther*, and the *Biography of Qiu Jin*. I also told him of my unhappy marriage. After he heard my account, Li showed his sympathy and
introduced me to Zhang Yun, the director of the Women's Department. I
took Li's note to Zhang, who welcomed me warmly. She said, "I welcome
you to the revolution and your leave from your husband's family. You
should cut your hair first." I said fine, thinking it was the same as in the
Xinhai Revolution when all revolutionaries cut off their pigtails. I was very
happy and went right away to cut my hair at a barber's. I told my parents
after I got home. They thought it was a miracle that I was able to meet a
good woman leader. They agreed that I should leave home right away and
live with my comrades. My motivation for joining the revolution was to
oppose arranged marriage.

After June 15, Li Zifen talked with me several times and showed me the
constitution of the Communist Youth League. He asked me if I intended to
join the Youth League. I said, "Oh, yes. I very much need the help of leaders and the organization. It will be decisive in raising my political consciousness." So Li introduced me into the Youth League. Many young men
and women joined the Youth League, and we were all very excited. I became
Zhang Yun's secretary. We worked during the day and took the Youth League
class from seven to nine every evening. After attending these training sessions, which were specially set up for newcomers, my vision was broadened.
I began to understand that the purpose of joining the revolution was not
just to pursue self-emancipation, but to strive for the liberation of women
all over the world. The party's constitution stated that we pursued the liberation of all humankind. Compared to the Three Principles of the People,
Communism was more thorough and more advanced.

In October 1926, the Northern Expedition Army reached Wuchang, and
Wuhan became the center of the National Revolution. In those days, we studied Marxism and Leninism, Bukharin's *Marxist ABC*, and Bebel and Marx's
theory on women's liberation. Many leaders came to lecture on different
subjects. We also heard Mrs. Borodin talk about how women in the Soviet

Russia participated in its revolution.[10] We learned that if Chinese women wanted to have a thorough liberation, we had to overthrow the power of husband, of gods, of clan, and of reactionary government, and we had to oppose feudalism. Without political organization, without joining the Communist Party, one's actions were individualistic heroism, which would not succeed in a great cause. One chopstick breaks easily. But ten chopsticks bound together cannot be broken. Unity is power. In order to realize our dream, we must have organizations, leadership, convictions, theories, and policies; tens and thousands of people should be united as one, following discipline, overcoming difficulties, and advancing wave upon wave.

I had always admired Qiu Jin. Song Qingling and He Xiangning were also my role models. Once I joined the revolution, I thought of myself as a legendary woman. That is why I changed my name to "Mulan" when I joined the Youth League. I thought, "My father is aged, and have no older brothers," so instead I joined the army—that is, I joined the National Revolution. In the beginning I was individualistic. Many women of similar background joined the revolution because of the conditions at this historical moment. Without the tide of history, you would have no way to break away from the family. There would be no organization or leadership. What could you do by yourself? If you were depressed, you could only blame your own fate. I happened to be born into that great time of revolution, and I happened to be in Wuhan.

Li introduced me to Wan Xiyan. Wan was our teacher and also the director of the Propaganda Department, the editor in chief of *The Hubei Daily*, and later the editor in chief of *The Republic Daily*. He had a college education and was a talented writer. He often spoke with me after class to explain revolutionary theories. Once he told me that we should eliminate individualistic heroism. Because my name was Huang Mulan, he thought that it meant I admired Luoman Luolan.[11] At that time I had not yet heard of Luoman Luolan. I told him that my name meant I admired Hua Mulan, who

10. Borodin, whose original name was Mikhail Gruzenberg, was the Comintern agent in China. He acted as Sun Yat-sen's special adviser, pushing for the first alliance between the CCP and the GMD.

11. Luoman Luolan is the Chinese name for Romain Rolland (1866–1944), a French writer and Nobel Prize winner. His works were translated into Chinese during the New Culture movement. In modern China his name has been associated with his novel *Jean Christophe*, which is a saga of an artist's heroic individual struggle in capitalist society. In the Maoist discourse, *Jean Christophe* is viewed as a book glorifying bourgeois individualism. Romain Rolland is a familiar name to any Chinese interested in Western literature.

joined the army for her father's sake. Wan Xiyan told me that we Communists believed in collectivism, and we joined the party for the revolution and for the people, not for anything else.

Li Zifen, Wan Xiyan, and Zhang Yun all helped me. Zhang taught me how to draft slogans and constitutions for women's associations. Because I had an education, I learned those skills very fast. I even acted in a drama, playing the role of a little daughter-in-law. It was the first time that I had acted on stage. In the National Revolution, I felt that I was totally changed. I was able to give speeches without looking at a draft. I was able to write articles, organize masses, and act in the play. I felt that I was developing fast in many areas. Certainly I had deep gratitude to the party and the Youth League and to those leaders who taught me and helped me to mature.

Three months after I began my work in the Women's Department, I was appointed the director. The Women's Association was subordinate to the Women's Department. At the time, both Mao Zedong's wife, Yang Kaihui, and Liu Shaoqi's wife, He Baozhen, were working in the Women's Association. The Women's Department was composed of a director, two secretaries, and three staff members and was in charge of the three adjacent cities of Wuchang, Hankou, and Hanyang. I was younger and had less seniority in the revolution than most of my subordinates. But I was able to make speeches and to write articles effortlessly. I was good at quickly learning leaders' talks by heart. I had so many suitors that love letters filled up my drawer. Those suitors said that they had heard my speeches and really admired me. I usually ignored those letters.

Through the Women's Association, which was like today's Women's Federation, we contacted women, spread the ideas of women's emancipation, and helped solve women's problems. We opposed arranged marriages and keeping of domestic slaves. Many women slaves and abused wives came crying for our help. We educated the men who abused their wives. I was very thrilled in those days, working from morning till night. We were in the high tide of revolution and had much to do.

On November 12, 1926, the Youth League nominated me to be transferred as a party member. At that time, the Youth League members were transferred to the party in groups. Later in the winter of 1926, the organization decided to send me to study in Moscow.[12] Funds to support this study came from the National government. I went to Shanghai first, preparing to leave there for Moscow. But Dong Biwu telegraphed me, asking me to re-

---

12. "The organization" is the term party members use to refer to the CCP.

turn to Wuhan.[13] Qu Qiubai and Yang Zhihua came to talk to me.[14] I said that I wished to study in Moscow for one year and then return to work. They sent my answer back to Wuhan. But Dong telegraphed again, saying they still wanted me back because three people working together were unable to do the job I had handled all on my own. Qu Qiubai talked to me. He said, "We party members should follow the party's instruction. You can go to study in Moscow in the future." So I returned to Wuhan. No one expected that six months later the situation would change. For the moment, however, I played a role in the revolution on a spectacular scale.

Before I left Wuhan on that aborted trip to Moscow, Wan Xiyan had fallen in love with me. But I did not want to get married: I wanted to get an education and a degree. My parents supported my decision to go to Moscow and they prepared a fur coat for me. If I had gone to Russia at that time, I would have been Jiang Jingguo's classmate.[15] I told Wan later, "I would not be your wife today if I had gone to Moscow." Some people thought that Wan had not wanted me to go and thus had persuaded Dong to call me back. But the real reason I was called back was that three people could not finish the work I normally did alone. I shouldered three important positions and had over a dozen titles. In 1937, when I was in Shanghai, I also had over a dozen titles.

Once back in Wuhan, we ran a training session for women cadres. The Women's Associations in Hubei selected women cadres to send to the session. At the end of the program, we gave certificates to students, and they returned to different locations to work. The training session lasted for three months, during which students studied the history of the workers' movement and the history of international women's movements. Wan Xiyan lectured on opposing *funü zhuyi* [womanism]. In the women's emancipation movement at that time, many women were strong in their work but kind of conceited and disdainful toward men. Those women had experienced unhappy marriages and insisted on celibacy. Opposing womanism was mainly opposing women's *dushen zhuyi* [celibatarianism]. Wan also talked about a shared devotion to revolution and encouraged young women to marry. Women who stuck to celibatarianism usually set excessively high standards

13. Dong Biwu (1885–1975) was one of the founders of the CCP. During the National Revolution, he was the chair of the CCP's Wuhan Committee. After the founding of the People's Republic of China, he was one of the top leaders of the country.
14. Qu Qiubai (1899–1935) was an early CCP leader. Yang Zhihua (1899–1975), Qu's wife, was one of the CCP leaders of the women's movement.
15. Jiang Jingguo was Chiang Kai-shek's son and the president of the GMD after Chiang's death. He studied in Moscow and married a Russian woman.

for men. Many women joined the National Revolution with an intention to be celibate, but many of them later married Guomindang officials.

We also closed brothels, and the Women's Department shouldered the responsibility of educating and supporting the former prostitutes. We promoted the movement to unbind feet and the movement to sweep away illiteracy, and we forbade people to abuse maids or keep concubines. We did a lot of things.

I was appointed the chair of the Preparatory Committee for the celebration of March Eighth, Women's Day, in 1927. The National government decided to have a big celebration in Wuhan, and although I was still very young, I was entrusted with this important task. I was in charge of organizing the celebration. On March 8, over a hundred thousand women gathered in the city's central square. We had a meeting first, which was attended by many prominent people in both the Communist Party and the Nationalist Party. Song Qingling, He Xiangning, and Liu Yazi were also present.[16] I was the chair of the meeting, which was a great honor that the party and the people gave me. Many people who were present still remember me today because of that occasion. After speeches, the meeting ended, and over a hundred thousand women marched in front of the grandstand where important guests were watching and then paraded downtown.

The Central Military Political Academy opened a branch in Wuhan. The school had enrolled women and formed a Women's Brigade shortly before Women's Day. The Women's Brigade had over two hundred female students. Dressed in army uniforms, they participated in the Women's Day celebration. When they marched valiantly and spiritedly past the grandstand, we felt very proud of them. Everyone applauded them, and they were a big hit that day. One of the female students was Xie Bingying, who later became a famous writer.[17] Xie and I met each other again in 1991, and we have corresponded since then. The women's parade on Women's Day became national news, not only because of its grand scale, but also because of an incident during the parade. The reactionaries in Wuhan hired young prostitutes

16. Liu Yazi (1889–1958) was a poet and a member of the Revolutionary Alliance. He once served as a secretary to Sun Yat-sen. As a leftist GMD official, he opposed Chiang Kai-shek after the failure of the alliance between the CCP and GMD. Later Chiang expelled him from the GMD. After the founding of the People's Republic of China, Liu was a member of the Standing Committee of the National Congress.

17. Xie Bingying joined the Northern Expedition and wrote about her experiences in the army in *Congjun riji*, which has been translated into many languages. See Hsieh Ping-ying, *Letters of a Chinese Amazon: And War-Time Essays* (Shanghai: Commercial Press, 1930), and *Autobiography of a Chinese Girl* (Boston: Pandora Press, 1986).

to jump into the parade topless. Although they were quickly driven out of the parade, the incident exploded into the news nationwide. The reactionary newspapers said that Wuhan women had a naked parade.[18]

On March 8, I paraded during the day and got married at night. We did not have a ceremony; we just published a statement in the newspaper, saying, "We two have common goals and would like to become a couple for life. This is to inform all our relatives and friends." We did not mention our previous marriages. Afterward, many people followed our example. Back then, political power was in our hands: we were free to divorce and free to marry, and no one could sue us. That day after the parade we had a small gathering at headquarters. Dong Biwu announced our marriage, and our comrades applauded and congratulated us. As Wan Xiyan was called the "king without a crown" because he was in charge of all the journalists, so I was called the "queen." Comrades jokingly passed the word around that the "king" and the "queen" were married. When we finished that busy working day, we went home to get married.

Wan Xiyan had visited my family a few times. My parents liked him. Wan discussed revolutionary theories with my father, who thought Wan was very knowledgeable and talented. When my father was sick, Wan invited a famous doctor to examine him. My father was a believer in Sun Zhongshan's Three Principles of the People, thinking it a great idea to unite Russia and the Communist Party and to help peasants and workers. Therefore, he and Wan had much in common to talk about. At first, Wan did not reveal his identity as a Communist Party member. After my plan to go to Russia was canceled, Wan took some leaders to see my father. My father was more enlightened and liked Wan very much. He approved of my marriage. After we got married, we lived in the French concession in a house that my father rented to store his books. In those busy days, my mother came to stay with us and help keep house.

When Wan and I married, I told him about my previous arranged marriage. But he concealed his own arranged marriage from me. I did not learn about it until after liberation. The Wan family were big landlords, and Wan had married a woman with the surname Sai, who had a daughter with him. After liberation, when I was reunited with my son, he told me that he had a sister. That woman got a certificate for martyrs' families and received special treatment from the government after liberation.

---

18. The incident is the theme of a nonfiction book titled *Shihai Gouxuan* [Exploring in the sea of history] (Beijing: Kunlun Press, 1989). The author, Jing Lingzi, interviewed many contemporaries, including Huang Dinghui.

After Jiang Jieshi's betrayal, the National Revolution failed. The Communists could no longer stay in Wuhan openly, and party members were dispersed or transferred quickly. Wan Xiyan and I were told to register with the party organization in Nanchang, and I decided to leave home and follow Wan to Nanchang. We took a boat and arrived in Jiujiang in July 14, 1927, along with members from the Instruction Regiment. We carried many confidential documents with us. On the boat, Wan noticed that some suspicious people were paying attention to us. He decided that we should divide into two groups. He and I went to Mount Lu, and other people carried documents to Nanchang. Wan Xiyan was in poor health, exhausted from his heavy workload. He had a sore throat and diarrhea. Because we did not yet know about the planned uprising, we went up to Mount Lu and vacationed there for ten days.

After leaving Mount Lu, we went to the Grand Hotel in Nanchang to make connections with the party organization. That was either July 28 or 29, a few days before the uprising. Chen Tanqiu, the chair of the Jiangxi provincial committee, told us that the Central Committee had decided that Wan Xiyan and I would not join the uprising but go underground. Wan Xiyan became the director of the Propaganda Department of the Jiangxi provincial committee, and I was the secretary to the Jiangxi provincial committee. Thus we began underground work and formed an underground party organization. The party supported us financially. We did not have salaries. We moved in with an old couple named Xu whose children were also party members. They ran a small grocery store, selling soy sauce, oil, and other ingredients. Chen Tanqiu and Wan Xiyan told people that they were the old couple's nephews and changed their names to Xu Guodong and Xu Guoliang. We lived in a back room of the store. I often stayed up late at night to write confidential reports. It was not convenient to do those things in the daytime.

We were in a very dangerous situation. The Guomindang soldiers came to search every once in a while. At first, because I was still young, I blushed and got scared, but Chen Tanqiu taught me how to keep my poise even when confronting the collapse of Mount Tai. When the soldiers came to search, I sat on the bench and lowered my head, wiping a kerosene lamp without looking at them. Chen Tanqiu dealt with the soldiers. Holding a water pipe and wearing a little mustache, he looked like an old man rather than someone in his early thirties. He answered the soldiers with the air of a landlord. He was in charge of everything, telling us not to be scared. By his example, I learned how to handle that kind of situation. Chen Tanqiu also taught me how to write confidential documents and how to contact other comrades secretly. I received training in underground work from Chen Tanqiu. This work required one to endure a lot of hardship and risks. When the party issued the August 7 Declaration, which was drafted by Deng Xiaoping and reviewed the party's achievements and weaknesses in the first alliance with the Guomindang, we had to deliver the document secretly to all the party branches. Chen Tanqiu was disguised as a landlord who went to the countryside to collect his rent, Wan Xiyan was disguised as a shop clerk, and I was disguised as an ordinary housewife. We went to many places to deliver the document. It was very difficult.

In January 1928 I gave birth to a boy. Three days after the birth, Wan Xiyan came to the hospital to say good-bye to me: the Central Committee had appointed him chair of the special committee of Ganxi'nan. His younger brother Wan Xixian, as a member in the Front Committee, was already in the Jinggang Mountains. Wan Xixian's name appears in the first volume of *Selected Works of Mao Zedong*. His name is more prominent than his elder brother's. Wan Xixian was the first one sent by the party to open the Jinggang Mountains Base Area. He successfully persuaded two Nationalist regiments, whose leaders were from the same hometown as Wan, to rise up and take over the Jinggang Mountains. After the takeover, Zhu De led the group from the Nanchang Uprising to the Jinggang Mountains, and Mao Zedong led the group from the Wenjiashi Uprising to the Jinggang Mountains. The so-called Union of Zhu-Mao in the Jinggang Mountains took after Wan Xixian occupied the area. Wan Xixian was later killed by Wang Ming.[19] The history of our party is very tortuous and complicated.

The order for Wan Xiyan's transfer came before the birth, but because he saw that I was about to go into labor, he postponed his departure for a few days. It was my first delivery and quite slow. I was sent to the Women's Hospital in Nanchang when my contractions began, and it was three days before the baby was born. Three days after that, Wan came to the hospital. Because there were other people in the ward, he had to whisper in my ear. "I am leaving," he said. "You will be taken care of by my brother and sister-in-law and our uncle and aunt ['brother and sister-in-law' were Chen Tanqiu and his wife, and 'uncle and aunt' were that old couple]. I am going to do things that I am not familiar with [guerrilla warfare]. Because I have only worked with a pen, I am not sure if the business will go smoothly. If anything happens, you should send our child to Huangmei. Let his grandparents take care of him."

Wan Xiyan was from a landlord's family. Early party members were all intellectuals with a college education. They became Communists because

19. Wang Ming (Chen Shaoyu) was the CCP's top leader in the early 1930s.

they accepted Marxism and Leninism. It would be hard for families other than landlords to send their children to college, so many early Communists were from landlord families. His hometown was in Huangmei, Anhui. "Don't you feel sad," he said. When I heard him saying that, I felt very sad and tears fell from my eyes. He wiped them away with a handkerchief. "*Chanfu* [women who have just delivered babies] should not cry. Listen to brother- and sister-in-law [the organization]." With those words, he left.

He left in January and died in a battle in April. In between, I received no letters from him, nor did I learn of his death right away. I had hemorrhaged and was in a poor health. Fortunately, Chen Tanqiu and his wife and the old couple took good care of me. I rested for two months before I returned to work. In the third month I went to the river bank to wait for a boat that served the party's underground traffic. I went there once, twice, and many times more, but I failed to see the boat, which was supposed to carry messages to me. It was not until July, when Chen Tanqiu was about to be transferred, that he told me of Wan's death. The organization had known the bad news early on, but because I was sick and this would be a heavy blow to me, they did not want to let me know. Finally, when they had to leave and could not continue to take care of me, they had to tell me the truth. Chen Tanqiu said to me, "To raise the orphan is a small thing, but the party's cause is a great thing. Turn agony into strength. Our cause is long-term. You should try to contact your family." He was very good at *zuo sixiang gongzuo* [doing thought work].[20]

When the newspaper reported Wan Xiyan's death, saying that the Communist bandits and their leader Wan Xiyan had been shot to death, my parents thought I was dead too. They cried very hard. People in the Wuhan Women's Association read the newspaper, and they cried, too. They felt very sad that the most perfect couple ended up like this. My father liked Wan Xiyan very much, thinking he was talented and respectful to senior people. He felt very sorry for me, because I had been married only a few months. Chen Tanqiu wrote a letter to them on my behalf, telling them that I did not go to the Jinggang Mountains—instead, I had given birth to a boy and was in good shape. My parents were so happy to receive that letter. After Chen told me that he had written to my parents, he suggested that I con-

---

20. *Zuo sixiang gongzuo* (doing thought work) is a basic phrase in CCP terminology. It appears frequently in Huang Dinghui's narrative. It refers to psychological work performed by party members. Usually, the one in a senior position does thought work on the one in a junior position. The thought work is composed of one or several talks that usually aim at persuasion.

tact my family and ask them to send the child to my husband's family. Wan's was a big family in Huangmei with many big houses. The baby could grow up in the big landlord family and continue Wan's family line.

In January 1929 the Central Committee transferred me to Shanghai. I wrote my parents, saying that I was going to school in Shanghai. Of course they knew I was to work for the party. I said it was inconvenient to take the baby with me and asked them to come to Jiujiang and get him. Soon my mother, accompanied by my second brother, arrived in Juijiang by boat from Hankou. I was scheduled to sail from Juijiang to Shanghai that same day. We had only half a day together at the dock. Three generations held each other and cried hard, unable to separate. From the time Chen left in July to the time I was to sail, I had lived for six months on my own, unable to cry aloud or wear mourning clothes. Every night in bed my tears dripped onto my baby's face—my baby, who did not know that his father was dead. That was an extremely painful period—the first heavy blow in my life. Leaving this child felt as if I were seeing him die. I cried hard. My brother was already a member of the Communist Youth League. He said to me, "Sister, don't you worry. We will send the child to Wan's family. You take care of yourself." The baby was only one year old and did not know anything. [Huang's eyes fill with tears as she tells this part of the story.]

The baby stayed with my family for a few months. After receiving a letter from them, Wan Xiyan's father came to pick up the baby. He was an enlightened landlord; otherwise, he would not have sent both sons to the university and let them be revolutionaries. I did not see my child again until after liberation, when he was already a young man. He left Huangmei in the War of Resistance when he was only thirteen. Then he drifted to Chongqing. There he entered a telegraph operator training school and became a telegraph operator in a post office. He was not told about his father's death or his mother's whereabouts. That was the only way to do it, because he could be protected by that landlord family. He did not know anything at all until after liberation. He found me by the end of 1949.

In 1929 I went to Shanghai and became the confidential secretary of the Central Committee. There I became reacquainted with the man who would become my second husband, He Chang, a member of the Central Committee, who I had met in Wuhan when he was attending the Central Committee's conference.[21] Because I was the secretary who took notes for the party

---

21. Huang does not regard the man in her arranged marriage as her husband; hence she said "second" rather than "third" husband here. Also, she told me about this part of her life before she mentioned her arranged marriage.

conference in Wuhan, I got to know all those Central Committee members. Peng Pai was the director of the Peasant Department, Zhou Enlai was the director of the Organization Department, Li Lisan was the director of the Propaganda Department, and so on. I had met them all in Wuhan.[22] At that time, I had been married to Wan Xiyan. Now He Chang told me, "We all envied you and never expected that comrade Xiyan would die so soon." Because I had been the confidential liaison between the Central Committee and the regiments, the committee members all knew me and had a high opinion of my work. They knew I was from a scholarly family and had played a dynamic role in Wuhan before suddenly becoming a member of the underground, enduring hardship and danger but performing very well. Now Wan Xiyan had died, yet I still continued my work. They thought I was quite remarkable.

He Chang began to do thought work on me. He said, "Proletarian women don't have the concept of *congyi erzhong* [following one husband to the end of her life], nor do they wish to set up a *zhenjie paifang* [chastity memorial archway]. You are a proletarian woman. I believe you do not have such feudal ideas. When you and Wan Xiyan got married, you did not have a ceremony. People all said you were pioneers of antifeudalist marriage." His implication was that I should marry him. He was from Shanxi and only one year older than me. He began to work after graduating from high school and was one of the founders of the Communist Youth League. In Wuhan we often had parties at which we sang revolutionary songs and told stories. He was the liveliest one on those occasions, telling stories of the revolutionary history of the Soviet Union. He was very handsome and outgoing. After several private talks between us, we wrote a report to the Organization Department, which at the time was headed by Zhou Enlai. Because the organization planned to send him to work in Hubei, we began to live together in a hotel before his departure. We had no ceremony—just the party's approval. We were married secretly, unlike my previous marriage, when Dong Biwu made a loud announcement and people applauded and congratulated us. This time very few people knew. Afterward, He Chang went to Hubei.

After He Chang and I got married, I encountered X.[23] He said sarcasti-

---

22. For more information on these early Communist leaders, see Benjamin Schwartz, *Chinese Communism and the Rise of Mao* (Cambridge: Harvard University Press, 1951).

23. On second thought, Huang asked me not to expose the man's name. She said, "In my life story, it is not necessary to talk about others' bad behavior." I am following her wish, only using the letter X to refer to the man.

cally, "You put yourself under the patronage of a bigwig." He Chang was a member of the Central Committee, a position higher than that held by X. But I had been unaware of X's infatuation with me, and I did not marry He Chang for his position. Hearing that kind of remark, I was furious. But I had no one to talk to. I was still mad the next day, when I took a pedicab home after a meeting. Because I was preoccupied with my unhappy thoughts, I got off the pedicab without taking my purse. There was a notebook in my purse. Although I used a special code to take notes at the party meetings, it was a terrible mistake to lose that notebook. I ran to chase that pedicab as soon as I realized I had forgotten my purse, but it was in vain. I reached the Bund, walking aimlessly. I wept by the Huangpu River for some time. I thought to myself, "Why do women who have joined the revolution still have to bear insults from male comrades?" Feeling terribly wronged, as well as frightened by the consequences of losing the notebook, I jumped into the Huangpu River.

I was rescued by policemen and sent to a *Jiliangsuo* [penitentiary]. Again and again I was asked why I tried to commit suicide. I had to make up a story, saying that I was dumped by my lover. Next day the Shanghai newspaper printed the story with the title "Young Woman Dumped, Jumped into the River, and Rescued." I said that I had a cousin in Shanghai and gave a pseudonym of a comrade. Zhou Enlai saw it in the newspaper and sent the comrade to pick me up. When I saw Zhou, I told him everything. He criticized me for being unable to bear wrongs and for lacking a strong Communist commitment to the revolutionary cause. He said, "We Communists should devote our lives to the cause. If we died in our struggle against our enemy, then it would be a worthy death that would weigh heavier than the Tai Mountain. But a death for a trivial reason would be unworthy and lighter than a feather." He suggested that I put this incident behind me, and he said that he would not tell anyone, including X. He said finally, "Anyway, in the penitentiary you were thinking of the organization and asked our comrade to get you. After you were rescued, you still wanted to follow the party. That was good." Actually, in the penitentiary I had struggled to decide: should I go home or return to the organization? I thought for a long time and decided that I could not go home. Li's family had been to my hometown to look for me once. My mother was afraid that they would find me, so she did not allow me to go home. It was all because of that arranged marriage that I had to follow the party faithfully no matter what happened to me.

When He Chang learned about what had happened, he thought it was because I was unhappy with him. I had to tell him what X said to me. Then He Chang just said, "There is nothing wrong with him just because he carries a torch for you. You should not take his remarks to heart." He Chang tried to console me, which made me feel better. In the party there was a rule that anyone who made a mistake would be sent down to work at the grassroots level, so I asked to be sent down to work in a factory.

I am the type of woman who became pregnant as soon as I lived with a man. It is very strange. When I was pregnant this time, I was sent to a textile factory to experience the workers' life and to join a workers' strike. The strike was organized by Li Weihan, Li Tieying's father. He was then a member of the Political Bureau and the chair of the Jiangsu Provincial Committee, which was located in Shanghai. He was also the chair of the Shanghai Committee. He led the strike of two hundred thousand workers from the Shanghai textile industry in 1929. That year was called "the year of victory of the anti-imperialism struggle," as if the revolutionary high tide was reviving. Actually it was not yet. The purpose of the strike was to improve workers' conditions and to force the national capitalists to give in a little bit. In order to call workers to prepare for May First, International Labor Day, I was sent out to distribute leaflets. I was almost done and had only one leaflet left when a policeman caught me. "What is in your hand?" he asked me. "A piece of paper I picked up from the ground," I said. But he put me in the police station. That was on a Saturday. On the following Monday, I was sent to court. This was in the British concession, so they had the so-called civil system, in which they provided voluntary defense attorneys who took turns defending the accused. I insisted that I was illiterate and did not know what the paper was. I said, "Such a nice piece of paper. I could use it for wrapping things." And I told them that I had just come to Shanghai from the countryside and had not worked in the factory very long. I was twenty-two years old, but I told them I was only seventeen, which was not yet the legal age. I was quite petite. The judge asked me in a severe tone, "Don't you know this is a Communist leaflet?" I put on a dumb look, as if I could not understand him. He said, "OK, I don't blame you this time. You should know Shanghai is very messy. A lot of bad guys. Don't be cheated. And don't pick up things you don't know about." Thus I escaped.

When my comrades learned of this, they all said I was sharp-witted. I knew how to use my wits because I had been trained well as an underground liaison: I was not scared of confronting those people. But now that the police in West Shanghai had caught me, it was not safe for me to stay in West Shanghai anymore, so I was transferred to the Hengfeng Textile Factory in East Shanghai. This was during the time when workers in the silk industry had just begun their strike. Women workers in Shanghai filatures were well-dressed, wearing silk stockings and nice clothes, and Shanghai women textile workers were quite pretty. It was easy for us to be disguised as workers but not as peasant women. In the Hengfeng Factory, the boss was a Hunanese. There were five Communist Youth League members and three party members in the factory. A factory worker named Liu Axiu was away on sick leave, so party branch gave money to Namowen [the Number One], who then allowed me to replace Liu Axiu as an apprentice at the factory.[24] But my job for the party was to contact workers and to kindle a strike.

On July 1 we distributed leaflets. A Youth League member who was an electrician turned off the electricity and cut the wires at midnight, and I climbed to the roof and threw down a bunch of leaflets. By the time the police came and the wires got repaired, the workers had stopped working. The factory management was scared because they did not know how many Communists were present. I pretended to be illiterate, asking an old worker to read the leaflets to me. The old worker had experienced the May Thirtieth Incident and had strong feelings for the Communist Party.[25] He told me, "This was distributed by the Communist Party, calling for a strike. They raised several demands." He knew everything.

I was elected as one of the workers' representatives. We went to filatures to learn about their strike situations and came back to tell the workers in the cotton textile factories. We passed information back and forth. Pretty soon, workers in the cotton textile industry joined the silk workers' strike. Thus we achieved success: two hundred thousand textile workers were on strike. I was the representative of the apprentices, and I and seven other representatives sat down to negotiate with management in a tea house. But before we finished negotiating, several dozen truckloads of police came to arrest us, driving away thousands of workers who tried to stop the arrest. We were all arrested and incarcerated at the Longhua Headquarters.

That was in July 1929. I was in prison for one hundred days. My second son was conceived in June, and he accompanied me in my belly during the prison time. Fortunately, I was wearing loose clothes, and the pregnancy did not show much after a hundred days. Moreover, all the eight representatives were very loving to each other in prison. Because I often vomited and had no appetite for food, the women in our cell knew I was pregnant. They would not let me fetch water from the well or wash clothes. But prison life

24. "Number One" (Namowen) refers to a head supervisor in factory workshops. The term is British slang that entered the Chinese language after China's opening of treaty port cities.

25. For reference to the May Thirtieth incident, see note 16 in this volume's introduction.

was hard anyway. I had a serious stomach problem afterward. He Chang had been transferred to Guangdong to be the chair of the Southern Area Bureau, and he did not know I was pregnant. After I was released, he learned about it. The baby was born very thin, no comparison to my first son. When the second baby was born, I could not produce milk, and this child has had poor health ever since because of the poor nutrition we experienced in prison. He had surgery later because of his poor heart condition. I had to do party work in prison, because a few days after I was arrested, Peng Pai was arrested and sent to the same prison. Peng Pai was the head of the peasant uprising in Hailufeng, a member of the Central Committee.[26] I knew him back in Wuhan. He was on the wanted list of the Nanjing government, and his true identity had been betrayed by a renegade. He had no way to deny that he was Peng Pai, and he was prepared to die. As he was sent to prison, he sang revolutionary songs all the way.

There happened to be a squad leader working in the prison who used to be a subordinate of Peng Pai in the peasant uprising in Hailufeng. He had joined the National Revolutionary Army in Guangdong, and after the Northern Expedition failed, he found this job in the Longhua Headquarters through his relatives. When he saw Peng Pai, he hurriedly lowered his head. Peng Pai recognized the man and later spoke to him quietly at night. "Your position here is very good. It would be very difficult for us to insert anyone in this position. You should help the political prisoners and try to improve their lives here." If he could give the prisoners even one more drink of water, that would be a good thing to do. The squad leader told Peng Pai that there were a few jailers willing to pass along a message for five silver dollars, and Peng Pai wrote a letter to the Central Committee telling them not to attack the prison to rescue him, because the prison was too well guarded. If the rescue plan failed, not only would he die, but many others would die, too. The squad leader sent the letter for him.

Peng Pai also asked who was in the female cell. The squad leader told him there were eight women who had been arrested for striking. Peng asked if anyone was literate. The squad leader answered, "They all claim to be illiterate. But among them there is a petite woman who is very lively." Peng Pai told him to ask my name. Because he was on our side, I told him, "My name is Huang Mulan." I had been using Liu Axiu's name as a disguise.

26. For a discussion of Pen Pai's role in the National Revolution, see Christina Kelly Gilmartin, *Engendering the Chinese Revolution: Radical Women, Communist Politics, and Mass Movements in the 1920s* (Berkeley: University of California Press, 1995).

Peng Pai remembered that we had met at the Central Committee conference in Wuhan. In *Peng Pai's Collected Works*, published after liberation, there are two letters that mention Huang Mulan. Peng contacted me through the squad leader and told me to continue the party's work in prison.

Besides the eight of us women workers in our cell, there was a robber's wife whose husband got a life sentence. Because she thought that nobody would want a criminal's wife, upon her release she asked the head of the prison for permission to work in the prison, washing and mending for the jailers. In the prison it was like this: including the head of the prison, everyone deceived his superior but not his subordinates. The prison staff passed information or things for the prisoners in and out of the prison for the sake of money. They also helped themselves to packages sent to prisoners. The head of the prison allowed this woman to stay. As soon as we entered prison, we called this woman *ganma* [nominal mother]. We told her, "You are not a robber. Because you were so oppressed by this bad government, you went to rob. When we workers and peasants win power, your husband won't have a life sentence. He will be released." We described a rosy picture of the revolutionary situation to give her hope. She had never had so many girls calling her *ganma*, so she treated us very nicely.

When we appeared in court, I presented demands raised by the apprentices, and other women presented demands raised by the workers. We testified that the Number One beat and scolded workers and took liberties with women and that we had no time to eat or go to the lavatory. We talked about our sufferings and demands for improvement. The judge ordered it all to be written down and asked us if we were literate. We answered no. He asked each of us to draw a cross. We drew an irregular cross with deliberately shaking hands. Not only did the judge have sympathy for us, but the guards with guns standing by were sympathetic, too. That is class sympathy. The guards working in the prison only made three silver dollars a month, and that pay was usually delayed for six months, during which time they were just fed in prison. That is why they were willing to send letters for us, taking five silver dollars for each message. At that time a hundred *jin* of rice cost three silver dollars.[27]

Among the eight women workers, two were party members and three were Youth League members. The other three knew of our party affiliations. We established a party branch in prison. With the assistance of the squad leader we tried to help all the political prisoners communicate with each other

27. Two *jin* are equal to one kilogram.

and make their stories consistent. We eight were locked in the same cell, but others were locked up separately. So we wrote notes to them at night, and *ganma* acted as look-out for us while she sewed. When she saw someone approaching, she would cough a little. Hearing the signal, we would jump under the quilt and pretend to be asleep. I was constantly in a state of anxiety and nervousness, which is why the baby had heart disease. If we were discovered, we would be killed, and other prisoners would be implicated.

Peng Pai was executed in ten days. He had no trial; he just waited for the order of execution. During those ten days, he did many things in prison. He asked the squad leader to inform each political prisoner that Peng Pai was there and tell them three things: one, be patient and do not go on hunger strikes or protest in any way, because that would be to the prisoners' disadvantage; two, do not reveal your true identity; and three, try your best to ask friends or relatives outside to help you. Peng Pai died a heroic death. He shouted revolutionary slogans on the way to his execution. The soldiers who were to execute him shivered because they had learned of his story from the squad leader and thought he was a hero. Everyone in the prison shed tears. My first husband had sacrificed his life, and now Peng Pai, a man I knew personally, was sacrificing himself, so I was very sad. In our cell, some cried, and some hummed the "International."

We were released when the workers won the strike. We received a glorious welcome home from the Workers' Union. Wang Ming had visited us in prison, claiming to be my cousin; he had brought pickled vegetables for me and told us that they were still negotiating outside and that we would be out soon. After I was released, He Chang telegraphed the Central Committee, asking to transfer me to the Southern Area. He Chang was the chair of the Southern Area Bureau, which was located in Hong Kong and was in charge of Guangxi and Guangdong. Deng Xiaoping at the time was the chair of the Guangxi Provincial Committee.

I delivered the baby in Hong Kong, but I had no milk. That was in 1930. Seven days later, He Chang was transferred to be the chair of the Northern Area Bureau. He gave our child to a Lu who was a small business owner. At that time, drinking cow's milk was regarded as a privilege. He Chang said that because I did not have milk and the baby was so thin, it would be better to let the child be raised in a family who could afford to give him cow's milk. He gave the baby away first, then came back to do thought work on me. "It is a feudal idea to raise children for the security of one's old age. Predecessors must plant the trees so that successors may enjoy the shade. The enemy is not yet eliminated; how can we talk about family? We all deserted our families to join the Communist Party. Who can afford to have children and a family?" Well, he had already sent the baby away—how could I not listen to him? So I followed him to Tianjin.

Because workers' strikes were victorious nationwide in 1929, the Li Lisan line emerged in the party. Li Lisan called for "striving for victories in one or a few provinces first and organizing big strikes in big cities." He formed an Action Committee, of which He Chang became a member. To prepare armed uprisings in big cities, they started to buy ammunition, but the enemy discovered what they were doing before they finished their preparations. Peng Pai had known that a failed attack on a prison would cause huge losses. Workers' strikes might make capitalists give in a little, but the Nationalist government had troops and police in big cities, which made them many times more powerful than we. Li Lisan regarded the victories of workers' strikes everywhere as the revival of a revolutionary high tide. He underestimated the power of the enemy and overestimated our own strength. Li ordered Mao Zedong to attack Wuhan from the Jinggang Mountains, but Mao Zedong did not carry out the order because he thought we lacked the strength to succeed—and because he did not receive the message until a few months later, when the situation had changed.

He Chang followed Li Lisan's call for uprising in the cities. He was a close friend of Li Lisan, because they had worked together in Anyuan. I was the liaison and passed the order of the Central Committee from Shanghai to He Chang, who arranged everything according to the order. But before the uprising was realized, a traitor betrayed us. The one responsible for purchasing ammunition was arrested and confessed. The Li Lisan line only lasted for a few months. The same failure occurred in Wuhan, Guangzhou, and Qingdao. In all of those cities, the plan was discovered by the enemy before the uprising materialized. Then Zhou Enlai, Wang Ming, Zhang Wentian, and Qin Bangxian returned from Moscow to reshuffle the Central Committee. In October, He Chang and I came to Shanghai to attend the Third Plenary Session of the Sixth Central Committee. He Chang made a deep self-criticism and asked to go to the red base areas to join the guerrilla war effort, a request that was approved. He kept his title as a member of the Central Committee. Li Lisan was sent to study in the Soviet Union. Wang Ming was put in charge of the party. Wang Ming was very tyrannical. He Chang was demoted from his original positions in the Central Political Bureau and the Northern Area Bureau and made the chair of a township committee.

In the winter of 1930, I was appointed the head of the Rescue Department in Shanghai. Around that time, because of Gu Shunzhang's betrayal, many comrades were arrested.[28] He Chang's best friend, Guan Xiangying, who was in charge of the Youth League, was arrested, too. The reasons for my appointment were twofold: first, I had been in prison and had connections there; and second, my father had many connections in the Nanjing government. Why was I not demoted? Because in Tianjin I had a miscarriage, so I did not participate in preparing the uprising. Moreover, I disagreed with the order when I learned about it. While in prison, Peng Pai had spoken against attacking the prison, and I learned that lesson. I did not think it was feasible to follow the Russian model and have armed uprisings in the cities. In his self-criticism to the Central Committee, He Chang reported faithfully what I had said to him. He said, "I am not as good as Mulan. From her experience in prison, she realized that our enemy would overpower us. We really underestimated our enemy's strength this time and took action blindly." Because he highlighted me positively in his self-criticism, the Central Committee appointed me to be the head of the Rescue Department. Wang Ming also knew me from that strike. They thought I was capable and decided to keep me in Shanghai.

But because He Chang was going to the Jinggang Mountains, I wanted to resign my post and go with him. I did not want to obey the order to stay in Shanghai, and I cried for three days and nights. I wanted to go with He Chang. I was afraid that if I did not, things would end up like they had with Wan Xiyan: once separated, we would never see each other again. He found it difficult to do thought work on me, so he asked a party member we both knew to talk to me. This comrade, Wu Defeng, was in charge of underground liaisons, and he later became the director of the Legal Committee working with Zhou Enlai. He told me, "We will send you there later. Your skin is so fair, and there is no way that you can be disguised as a peasant. It wouldn't be safe for both you and He Chang and the people who would have to protect you." On their way to the red base areas, people had to go through underground traffic stations located in peasants' homes, so they had to be disguised as peasants. He Chang was dark-skinned, whereas my face and hands were very fair and soft. It would be easy for He Chang to be disguised as a peasant with bare feet, but not for me. "You have to wait until we open another route safer for you to take," Wu said, "For the moment, you two have

28. Gu Shunzhang was an alternate member of the political bureau of the Sixth Central Committee, in charge of security work in the party. Because he knew the party's underground networks, his betrayal led to many arrests and deaths in the CCP. Gu was arrested by the GMD on April 24, 1931. Huang's new assignment occurred during the summer of 1931, as she recorded in one of her autobiographies.

to separate for a while." So, there was no choice. To ensure the safety of He Chang and the peasant traffic stations, I had to stay.

I had told He Chang, "I have endured the hardship of being a factory worker and a prisoner; I am not afraid of hardship. They sent away my two children, and now I am told to separate from you. I won't do it. I will never do it!" He Chang said, "I know your love for me and your loyalty to the party. But you should know that you don't belong to me. Bourgeois love means you belong to me and I belong to you. But you don't belong to me. You belong to the party and to the people. You should understand the party's organizational discipline. The Central Committee has decided that I leave and you stay to do rescue work. If you rescue one general from our enemy's prison, won't that be a great contribution to the party and the people? If you follow me and something happens, both you and I will be killed. I would not regret it if you died of love for me and I died of love for the party. But how can we let the party down? The party has made the assignment; how can we refuse to obey?" So, there was no choice. I just cried. We separated in May. He waited to be sent away, and I waited for my special assignment. [Huang cries as she tells this part of the story.]

The party assigned me a special task. Pan Hannian was responsible for internal affairs, and I was responsible for public affairs.[29] I came to know this lawyer, Chen Zhigao, whose father was a judge. He was a progressive lawyer involved in rescuing the famous *qijunzi* [seven noble persons].[30] He was a student of Shen Junru, who was also a progressive lawyer. So we began the project of rescuing Guan Xiangying.

In Shanghai, before I married Chen Zhigao, I was called Miss Huang. I concealed my marriages to Wan Xiyan and He Chang and only let people know who my parents were. My father had died but my family still had status, and I was regarded as a maiden from a scholarly family. But I could not

---

29. After Gu Shunzhang's betrayal, the CCP reorganized the leading body of security work. Pan Hannian was appointed the director of the second office, in charge of collecting intelligence and counterespionage. In later years, Pan played a major role in the party's underground work and acted as a special liaison between the CCP and the GMD on many occasions. After 1949, Pan was appointed as the deputy mayor of Shanghai, but he was later accused as the head of a counterrevolutionary group and imprisoned in 1955. Pan was released from the prison in 1962 and sent to a labor camp. In 1967 he was imprisoned again, and in 1975 he was again released. He died in a labor camp in 1977. Pan was rehabilitated by the CCP in 1982. Many underground CCP members in Shanghai were implicated in Pan's case. Huang Dinghui is one of them. For an in-depth study of Pan Hannian, see Wang Chaozhu, *Gongchen yu zuiren* [The hero and criminal] (Shenzhen: Haitian Press, 1993).

30. For the "seven noble persons," see note 15 in chapter 5.

hide my true identity from Chen Zhigao, because the rescue work had to be done through him, and Zhou Enlai told me not to hide anything from Chen except for the part about He Chang. Because I had been exposed in Wuhan during the National Revolution, and because I still needed help from Song Qingling, He Xiangning, Liu Yazi, and other famous people I got to know in Wuhan to rescue our comrades, I could not conceal that part of my history. Thus my story was that I had joined the National Revolution in Wuhan but gave up my party membership afterward. Those who had known me back in Wuhan thought I got remarried to Chen Zhigao. Others just thought I was Miss Huang. Friends and relatives of the Chen family all thought I was a maiden. Although I was already over twenty years old and a mother of two, I was able to pretend to be a maiden. I was beautiful in my youth.

When I started to visit the Chen family in order to rescue Guan Xiangying, Chen's parents saw me for the first time and liked me right way. I mentioned my father and friends of his such as Tan Sitong. Chen's father was an enlightened man, too, and he had rescued members of Sun Yat-sen's Revolution Alliance. My parents were Buddhists, and Chen's parents were Buddhists, too. I told them that I had come to Shanghai to go to college but had failed the exams and now was looking for a job. When they learned that my classical Chinese was excellent, they asked me to be their young daughter's tutor.

After a few visits, I told Chen's father that my cousin was in prison and needed his help. Chen's father had been a judge for eighteen years and had numerous connections, and the judge in the Longhua Headquarters was his junior. He called that judge to his home and told him, "Miss Huang is my *gannüer* [nominal daughter]." Actually, I had not yet made him my *gandie* [nominal father]. "Her cousin is an honest businessman. You go check up on the case. If they really caught the wrong person, let my son bail him out." That judge just kept nodding his head and promised to check. But the secretary in the court wanted a bribe, so he postponed the approval of bail for three months. Chen Zhigao went to inquire about the case. The judge said he was not opposed to releasing the man, but the secretary said his confession had problems. Zhigao said, "Well, let's change the confession." The judge said that the secretary was an opium addict and wanted some benefit. Chen's father also smoked opium, so they gave the secretary the best Yunnan opium. Thus the confession was changed and Guan Xiangying was released on bail.

I recalled what He Chang had said: "To rescue a general is a great contribution to the party." Guan could be regarded as a general. He was a member of the Political Bureau and the general secretary of the Youth League. I made my contribution. So I entered a hospital run by the underground party network and waited there to be picked up by He Chang.

He Chang died in 1935. He knew I rescued many people, so he did not come to get me. He was the kind of man who could forget about his family for the sake of his country and forget about his private life for the sake of the public. He knew I was in Shanghai, but he thought I could make a greater contribution there than in the red base areas. He did not send liaisons to get me. We never corresponded. And he died a heroic death. The party has published *A Biography of He Chang*, as well as Wan Xiyan's biography. They were both excellent leaders of the party. But I was just doing underground work, all the time rescuing party members, the famous seven noble persons, other nonpartisan people, and refugees.

I only lived with Wan for nine months, and he left soon after our child was born. I lived with He Chang for two years, from 1929 to 1931. The two were excellent party members. I benefited tremendously from their mastery of Marxist theories. Although they were my lovers, I regarded them with respect as though they were my mentors.

I met Chen Zhigao in 1931, when the national salvation movement began. He and I both wrote articles advocating resistance to the Japanese invasion. Chen was quite progressive. Although not a Communist, he had read *Capital* earlier than I did—he read a French version while in college. He had many books on Marxism and Leninism in his room. After I got to know him, I often went to borrow books from him. Busy accomplishing tasks assigned by the party, I had not spent much time studying theory, although I had joined the party early. On Chen's bookshelf, I found *The Biography of Marx, The Biography of Engels, The Philosophy of Marxism*, and so on. After the failure of the National Revolution, many left-wing intellectuals got involved in translating and publishing Marxist works. Now, as an underground worker in Shanghai, I had time to read those works.

I did not hide from Chen the fact that I had a child from my marriage to Wan Xiyan. To many people who had known Wan Xiyan and me, I was Wan's widow. Yet Chen still wanted to marry me, and he was eager to help me with rescue work. He sent gifts to those in charge of the cases, invited them to dinners, and posted bail for the arrested. He showed great enthusiasm in each case. My heart was torn: I did not want to marry him. That is why we knew each other for four years before getting married. My frequent contact with him was natural, because I was his parents' nominal daughter and, therefore, his elder sister.

Despite the rumors, it is not true that Chen fell in love with me at first sight.[31] He loved his classmate Peng. But Peng's parents did not agree to their marriage, and Peng married someone else before Chen married me. While he was courting me, several other women comrades fell in love with him. Because many cases were presented to Chen Zhigao by comrades who claimed to be my relatives or friends, these comrades all knew Chen Zhigao. He was young, handsome, generous, gentle, and very popular with everyone. We all called him Jia Baoyu.[32] I tried to persuade him to marry another woman he loved. I said, "I was married and have a child. She is a maiden and younger than me. You should marry her." He answered, "No. Both my parents like you. You are chosen by my father. You also get along well with my siblings. You are from a scholarly family and you have roots. We don't know her family background. I have no way to check on other women's family backgrounds." He thought other women were true Communist members and that I had left the Party. He said that his family would not approve of those women and that he would not be able to tell his parents how he got to know those women, whereas I had been acquainted with his family for several years.

His parents already regarded me as their nominal daughter, and the organization let me use my parents' names to formally take them as my nominal parents. The organization paid for a ceremonial banquet in Da Hongyun Restaurant. Three dinner tables were full of Chen's relatives and friends—Chen's was a prominent family in Haining, and the Qianlong Emperor had visited the family four times.[33] Before I married Chen Zhigao, I used Chen's family connections to reach Shanghai's social elite and carry out the rescue work. In four years I had twice run away from Chen Zhigao's proposal. And twice, the organization asked me to come back because comrades had been arrested and needed me to use Chen's connections again. Chen Zhigao was a very smart person. He rescued many people without getting involved in those cases directly. His father had many connections, so he used those connections and asked his friends to look into those cases.

31. Huang said in the first interview that Chen fell in love with her at first sight. It is possible that Chen liked her right away, even though he was at the same time in love with another woman.

32. Jia Baoyu is the main protagonist in the Chinese classical novel *The Dream of the Red Chamber*. Jia loved to be with female relatives and maids instead of in a men's world. "Jia Baoyu" is often used to refer to men who are popular with and surrounded by women.

33. Chen's family genealogy is recorded in Library of Congress, *Eminent Chinese of the Ch'ing Period (1644–1912)* (Washington: GPO, 1943), 96–97. The visits of the Qianlong Emperor (1736–1795) to Chen's ancestors are also mentioned in the section under Ch'en Shih-kuan.

I was reluctant to marry Chen for several reasons. First, I was not fit for his family; second, my true identity was unknown to them; and third, I had married again and again. The previous two husbands were excellent leaders of the party, and those marriages were approved by the organization. But to marry someone who was not our own comrade—even though he was a progressive person—seemed not so good to me. And to have one more marriage was not so good, either.

Although we joined the revolution, we still had a strong feudal mentality. For instance, in my hometown Liuyang if a woman wanted to remarry, the clan hall would drown her. The head of the clan would not allow that. And the woman's name would be deleted from the clan genealogy. I had already been in a wedding sedan chair before marrying Wan Xiyan. So when I married He Chang, I did not tell my family. My mother never knew of that marriage. When I married Chen, I did not tell him of He Chang and my first marriage. I did not tell him of He Chang until 1938. My mother did not allow me to go home because the Li family had been to my hometown to look for me. I did not formally divorce him—they knew only that I had joined the revolution. The situation left me no choice: I had no place to withdraw to and nowhere to go. I had to follow the organization dearly. I was not allowed to go to the Jinggang Mountains because my skin was too fair. So I had to do whatever the party asked me to do. I married Chen because I decided to sacrifice myself. Because Chen had rescued a Communist Central Committee member and spent so much money to do things for the party, I thought the party would forgive me when the victory came.

Chen and I met in 1931, and he proposed to me in 1933. That year my brother had some trouble in school, and my mother wanted me to go home, so I decided to go home to ask my mother's opinion on Chen's proposal. The organization knew that I had not been home for a long time, so they sent comrade Zhao to accompany me home. Chen's mother told Zhao to ask my mother if she would agree to this marriage. When my mother learned of Chen, she said, "Because this is a good family that has rescued many Communist Party members, you should make your own decision."

In 1935 after the party told me of He Chang's death, I married Chen Zhigao, with the party's approval. One of the marriage witnesses was from the party. I made three requirements of Chen. First, he should continue to support our work. Second, we should not interfere with each other's activities. I would attend the party activities that I could not let him know about. If he tried to interfere with me, how could we get married? Third, when the Communist Party won a final victory, I would reunite with my son. He agreed to everything as long as I agreed to marry him. He did not know about my relationship with He Chang. The son by He Chang did not get to see me until after liberation. I told Chen everything only after my parents-in-law died and his siblings all went to the United States.

My mother-in-law never knew I was a Communist. She died when she was fifty-nine years old. During the War of Resistance, when people from different organizations had meetings at my home, she made refreshments for us late at night. If I went out to attend activities at night, she sat up all night, chanting the name of Buddha for my protection. We had an excellent mother-in-law and daughter-in-law relationship. The whole family was involved in the resistance efforts. I used my connections with He Xiangning and Song Qingling to attend activities run by the Nationalist Party, and I was involved in the "left-wing" cultural activities through the connection with Guo Moruo. My true identity was safely covered by those activities.

My original name was Zhangding. During the National Revolution I changed my name to Mulan because I had loved to sing the "Ballad of Mulan" ever since elementary school. When I joined the National Revolution, I thought of myself as a legendary woman. But in my autobiography I have to be modest. I changed my name to Dinghui during the War of Resistance. This name was my father's idea. My grandfather was a Taoist and practiced physiognomy. He had told me of my fortune long ago: I had the appearance of nobility; calamities would be turned into blessings; but I would experience the disaster of imprisonment. My father, who was a Buddhist, only knew some of my misfortunes in 1931, such as Wan's death and the failure of the National Revolution. He wrote me these words: "Ding was born with *hui* [intelligence], but she is deep in disasters. She should be protected by the favor of Buddha. I wish for her both intelligence and good fortune." Because Chen's mother and Chen were both Buddhists, I used the cover of Buddhism to carry out my underground activities. That is why I changed to this name with Buddhist overtones.

In those years I worked directly under Zhou Enlai, and Wu Defeng passed messages back and forth between the Central Committee and me. The party had not sent me alone to Chen Zhigao; his legal secretary was sent by the party, too. Chen's law firm was turned into an underground traffic station without his knowledge. The secretary kept the files of the comrades we rescued and was responsible for sending those comrades to another underground traffic station. Other underground liaisons came to deliver messages and stay in the law firm overnight where it was safe.

Once Chen Zhigao's classmate, who worked in the police station of the British concession, told him that they had just arrested a Communist big shot, the chair of the Political Bureau, Xiang Zhongfa, and that he had talked.

Chen Zhigao told me. I was the only one in the party who knew this. I quickly told Pan Hannian, who then told Kang Sheng, who reported it to Zhou Enlai. The next day, Zhou Enlai and three other top leaders met with me to hear my report on the case. It was the party's order that I stay with Chen Zhigao.

When the War of Resistance began, I wanted to go to Yan'an. I did not think that I should stay in Chen's family for too long because I had concealed my true identity. In 1938, after a quarrel with Chen, I sneaked out of his house, moved to the Cangzhou Hotel, and booked a ticket to Hong Kong from the China Travel Agent. I planned to go from there to Chongqing and then to Yan'an. But it happened that Chen's brother's relative worked in the China Travel Agent. In booking passage, I had used a pseudonym but kept my surname, so when they searched the reservations by date, they found the surname Huang. They located me at the hotel and sent me home. Unaware of my true reason for leaving home, my mother-in-law thought it was because Chen and I had quarreled. She blamed her son and welcomed me home.

In mid July 1937, Chen and I helped establish a refugee camp in Zhendan University. Chen had previously joined the International Relief Association. Although the refugee camp was affiliated with the International Relief Association, the staff was largely composed of Communist Party members and was turned into a recruiting station for the New Fourth Army. Chen worked with the head of the international settlement to get the Japanese Headquarters's permission to let refugees through the Japanese blockade, on the grounds that the refugees would return to the countryside to produce grain. Under this cover, three thousand men were recruited from scores of refugee camps in Shanghai and sent to the New Fourth Army. I have a picture taken of me in the refugee camp together with other underground Communist Party members. I cherish this photo, because it testifies to my work in this period.

I made another initiative at the time. The Japanese Headquarters issued a "Good Citizen Card" to each person they allowed to pass through the blockade, and we gave some of those cards to our underground liaisons, who were therefore able to go back and forth freely. That is why in 1938 Zhou Enlai sent Liu Shaowen to Shanghai with a letter for me, praising our work and disagreeing with my plan to go to Yan'an. In the letter he also openly thanked Chen for his efforts, and thus the direct relationship between Chen and Zhou was established.

In this period I was also involved in other activities. He Xiangning asked me to organize a women's consolation society on her behalf. I did not have any organization of my own, but I connected twenty-two women's organizations in Shanghai and became one of the board members of the Shanghai Women's Consolation Society. I helped raise a lot of money from big shots in Shanghai.

In 1942 I was arrested at Qujiang ten days after I gave birth to a son. Qujiang is at Shaoguan, where the Guangdong provincial government located after Guangzhou fell to the Japanese. Chen was there as a member of the Central Relief Committee in charge of relief work for Guangdong and Fujian. We helped many famous refugees from Hong Kong return to Chongqing. The route was dangerous, so we arranged for protection from Dongjiang guerrillas. Then a rumor broke out in Hong Kong, saying that we had taken over the movie star Hu Die's possessions when she retreated along that route. The rumor made Chen mad, and he wanted to resign from his post. I traveled to Chongqing with my two young daughters to meet with Zhou Enlai in the Eighth Army Office at Zenjiayan. The day after I arrived in Chongqing, Deng Yingchao called me and sent a car from the Eighth Army Office to pick me up. Had it not been for that car, the Guomindang secret agents would not have found me. I told Zhou about the situation and my worry that gossip would reveal to the Guomindang our relationship with the Dongjiang guerrillas. Zhou answered that the Guomindang had not found out yet and that we should continue our work. He said that it was a very important location and that we should hang on there. So I returned to Qujiang.

I gave birth to a son in Qujiang. After returning home from the hospital, I ran a high fever. The hospital sent a nurse, Miss Lu, to take care of me. I believe this Miss Lu was an underground Communist member. One night ten days after my baby was born, three men appeared suddenly, demanding to see me. Chen was not home yet. Miss Lu wanted to stop them outdoors, but they ran into my room and began to drag me away—at which point, Miss Lu said that I was very sick and that she must go with me. After a short discussion, the men decided that their superiors would not approve if I died on them, so they allowed Miss Lu to come along. When we reached the railway station, I saw that Chen was already there.

My baby died shortly afterward. I lost two sons. In 1948 when our company went bankrupt [Huang describes the bankruptcy later], I was pregnant, and as a result of the terrible stress, that baby was premature and stillborn. In 1942, because both Chen and I were arrested, the party sent Liu Shaowen to Qujiang to take our two daughters away. Miss Lu followed me to the Guomindang secret jail in Hengyang and stayed there for forty-two days. Once a week two jailers escorted her as she walked ninety *li* to the town to buy eggs, cotton, gauze, and other things for me. I was very sick and had a terrible backache. Miss Lu took good care of me in jail. Then she returned to the Qujiang hospital. She must have been a Communist Party member; no one else would have had the courage to go to jail with a patient.

It turned out that the head of Hengyang prefecture, Zhou Kuilong, was a Nationalist whom Chen and I once bailed out from the police station in the Shanghai French concession. We had given him three hundred silver dollars for his trip home. When he found out that we were locked up, he pleaded with Dai Li for our release.[34] But Dai telegraphed him back, saying that Jiang Jieshi had ordered that Chen and Huang be sent to Chongqing. Zhou then came to see us in jail and told the head jailer that we were his saviors and should be treated well; thus we were given good food, allowed to have meals together, and were able to discuss our future statement in court.

Six weeks later we were sent to Chongqing, where we were imprisoned for two years. Chen was locked in a favored treatment cell, because Dai Li wanted to recruit him to work for the Investigation Bureau that Dai directed. I was locked up with fifteen other women in a big cell. The women were all illiterate, and some were unsure of why they had been imprisoned. I helped those women write legal petitions, and a few were released.

The Guomindang secret agents asked me why I went to Zenjiayan and if I was collecting intelligence for the Communists. I said that I had given up my party membership long ago and that a family like Chen would not put up with a Communist Party member. They knew that I did many things to support the Communists, but they lacked evidence that I was still a party member. In my statement, I argued that if I opposed the Communist Party, how could I face my son by Wan one day? The secret agents knew that I had a child with Wan, so I told them that I went to Zenjiayan to look for my son by Wan Xiyan and that I did not want Chen to know this. I said that Chen and his family did not know about my marriage to Wan. They then made an excuse for arresting me and Chen: they said that we took Hu Die's possessions and that Chen embezzled from the relief fund. Because we had transferred funds to Communists and the Dongjiang guerrillas that we could not account for, we were sentenced to seven years in prison. Chen's brother, who worked for Bai Chongxi, bailed us out two years later.[35]

34. Dai Li was the deputy director of the investigation bureau in the Military Committee of the GMD, in charge of secret agents within the GMD military.
35. Bai Chongxi was the deputy chief of staff of the Nationalist Military Committee in that period.

With Chen Zhigao I have three daughters and one son. Altogether I have six children. Chen Zhigao went to Taiwan after 1950. Why did Chen go to Taiwan? At the preparatory meeting for the Chinese People's Political Consultative Conference, Liu Shaowen proposed that Chen and I be members of the conference committee. The nomination was opposed by some people who misunderstood something Chen and I had done in the War of Resistance.[36] We had acted under the party's instruction, and Liu Shaowen knew that very well, yet at the time of the preparatory meeting Liu was unable to tell the truth, because Taiwan was not liberated. Thus we were deleted from the nomination list. Liu came to Shanghai to visit us and apologized for having failed to nominate us. Chen and I were in a terrible shape with our recent bankruptcy, and we had no income, but Chen just said, "Others misunderstand, but so long as you can testify for us, it will be fine. I don't care about the title of committee member anyway." What else could we say? There might be other reasons that Liu did not tell us. There might be personal grievances toward us. It is possible that we had offended some people because we were too straightforward.

Another thing compounded Chen's decision to leave. X—the one who attacked me for my marriage to He Chang—now became the leader of the Bureau of the East Area of China.[37] Because Chen Zhigao had a plan for international trade, I went to see X. When he heard of Chen's plan, he laughed, saying, "Oh, now the capitalist is begging us." He said sarcastically, "Well, you have become a bourgeois *taitai*. Enjoy your fortune." How could I tell Zhigao this? I took a pedicab home by myself, with tears rolling down my cheeks. (We lost our car and chauffeur when our company failed.) I did not tell Zhigao anything, but later he learned about it from his women friends. He asked me why I did not tell him. He said, "If he does not recognize your party membership, then all my efforts for your sake have come to nothing. All those years, whenever your people came, I gave them money and offered them service. I have acted like a bodhisattva. Now it all amounts to nothing. OK, I have lost all my money and should start all over again. I will leave the country and enter the petroleum business, which will benefit our country and you."

Chen Zhigao knew what was to come and asked me to go with him. He

---

36. Huang wished to omit the details of the particular activity in which she and Chen were involved. She believed that, even today, exposure of that activity would not be in the CCP's interests.

37. The East Area of China as an administrative division included Shandong, Jiangsu, Anhui, Zhejiang, Fujian, Taiwan, and Shanghai. The division was established in 1950 and rescinded in 1954.

said, "Your party's rectification campaign in 1942 was ferocious. Can you endure that if that happens again?" I said, "Yes. Why should I be afraid of that? The things I have done were all ordered by the party. What bad things have I done? I have saved underground party members, nonpartisan people, and refugees. You have done the same. You have rescued so many people." He said, "Well, if that kind of thing happened to me, I would not be able to endure it."

Before liberation Chen had been the chief executive manager of his bank. Once I wrote a big check to donate to a foundation proposed by Song Qingling, but it was discovered by the Nationalist secret agents, and the Nationalist government took away the bank's license. When our customers read in the newspapers that the bank lost its license, they withdrew their savings. To pay our debt, we had to borrow money, but it was a time of drastic inflation. The ones who borrowed money from the bank did not pay back in time, whereas we had to pay others high interest. Chen quickly went bankrupt. Because he was unable to pay the debt, the creditors ripped off his leather coat and cut his hair. He said, "A person can be killed but can't be insulted." So now, facing dreadful prospects, he decided to leave the country.

We had rescued more Nationalists than Communists during the War of Resistance. Many people Chen rescued asked him to do business in Hong Kong and Southeast Asian countries. He wanted to go to the south to work in international trade so that he would be able to pay our debts and keep our house, which he had designed and was the only property we had left. Our children were still young, so he wanted to make money. We reported to the Central Committee. Nie Rongzhen sent a letter summoning him to Beijing to discuss important issues.[38] Chen made three proposals to Nie: one, to instigate the Nationalist air force to revolt; two, to help draw foreign currency to China; and three, to get petroleum for China. Chen left China with these missions and with the Central Committee's acquiescence. Before he left, he told Liu Shaowen that he felt uneasy about leaving me like this, but Liu said to be at ease, that Zhou Enlai would testify for me. Thus reassured, Chen left. I thought very naively that in ten years he would return, when Taiwan was liberated—that whatever I was going through at the time was a show put on for our enemy. He left in 1950. I did not expect my imprisonment in 1955, nor did he.

38. Nie Rongzhen was the vice-chair of the Military Commission of the Chinese People's Revolution and deputy chief of staff of the Chinese People's Liberation Army. He became the vice-premier and the director of the National Defense Council in 1956.

He wanted me to go with him, but I did not want to. My face was too red [the GMD suspected that Huang was a Communist], and I thought my party membership would hurt Chen's work outside. So I let him take his former girlfriend Peng with him, and I paid the debt that she left behind. People said I was very generous. Chen Zhigao and Peng had been in love with each other when they were in college, but she married a physically abusive man with whom she grew dissatisfied. When she tried to commit suicide, we rescued her. Later she divorced that man. I thought Chen was only forty years old, and he would marry again anyway. If I let him take this woman, he would be grateful to me. He did say I was remarkable. I told him to go with her and leave the company to me. I had been the chief secretary of the company, and after Chen left I became the head of the board. I sold his house and paid off our debt. I have never seen him since. But we talked on the phone once when I was in Guangzhou after my rehabilitation in 1980 and he was on a trip in Hong Kong. Chen Zhigao told the Guomindang that he would not be anti-Communist nor would he be an official; he just wanted to be a lawyer. And he did become a lawyer—a successful one, who attended international conferences in Geneva and defended Communists in Taiwan without charging them fees. He was a real Buddhist. A true Buddhist does not read script or worship the Buddha but accumulates merit in this and the other world.

He had said to me, "My lot was tied to yours in the previous life. That is why I fell in love with you at first sight. I would be willing to sacrifice myself for your sake." He never wanted to divorce me, but I divorced him in 1953 because I would be suspected otherwise. They thought that if you were loyal to the party, you would not hesitate to end a relationship with someone in Taiwan. When he received my letter telling him of my divorce decision, he sent me a letter written in his own blood. It said, "Let the gods and spirits of my ancestors know that I will never fail in my obligations and will never divorce." But he was there. Certainly, he had to go because he did not want to endure our party's scrutiny. He had very complicated social connections. Chen Zhigao died in Taiwan in 1988. My children did not let me know that right away. After I learned of his death in 1989, I held a memorial service for him in Shanghai. His ashes were sent back and buried with his parents.

After Chen left, I had to sell our house to pay our debt. The government bought the house. Then I began to work as a secretary to Zhao Puchu in the Relief Committee. Zhao was nonpartisan but had worked with us before liberation. He knew of my relationship with the party and did not regard me as his subordinate. In 1953 I went to Beijing to see Zhou Enlai, but I failed to see him. I called Sister Deng, who sent a note to me, saying, "You should go back. Wuhao will do what he promised."[39] But in 1955, I was arrested along with Pan Hannian. Pan Hannian's meeting with Chen Lifu on Mount Lu had, in fact, been ordered by Mao Zedong and Zhou Enlai, but under the scrutiny of the leftist line, everyone who had any relationship with the Nationalists was in trouble. Even intellectuals who had no relationship with Nationalists were in trouble in 1957, let alone we underground workers who had so many complicated social connections.

I had known that I would be locked up. I had made a second trip to Beijing in 1955, because my second son was about to have a heart surgery there, and I stayed at the home of Wu Defeng, who was then the vice-chair of the Supreme Court. I learned that underground party members had to write confessions in confinement. Wu did not think his court should issue a warrant against me because he knew about my liaison work before 1949 and our liaison network had never been sabotaged. Wu's wife called up Deng Yingchao, asking if Mulan could write a confession at her home instead of in confinement, because Wu could testify to my role as a liaison. I was in the next room when she made the call, so I could hear their conversation. Deng answered, "Luo Jianbing is already in confinement.[40] Pan will be confined, too. It is not appropriate for Mulan to confess at your home. We can give our testimony for her." Thus, I knew I would be taken to confinement. My conscience was clear, although I knew that some people were attacking me and opposing my nomination in the Chinese People's Political Consultative Conference. I came back home and got everything ready. I thought it would be all right to go through this confession process. I did not expect that mine would be regarded as a counterrevolutionary case and I would be locked up for such a long time. I was in prison for eight and a half years.

The first few years, I was locked up in Deshengmen—which was not a true prison but a place that was used as accommodations for Number One Scholars in the imperial system. In 1959 we were removed to the newly completed Qincheng, which had eight buildings—four for the last emperor and Nationalist officers, and four for Communist high officials. We were treated quite nicely in that prison. The budget for each person's food was forty-five yuan a month. Mao Zedong even inspected the prison and told the head man-

39. "Wuhao" was Zhou Enlai's pseudonym, which he used when he was in charge of underground work in Shanghai.
40. Luo Jianbing was a female CCP underground worker. She was also implicated in the case of Pan Hannian because she once worked as Pan's assistant.

ager to take good care of us because we would be entrusted with important tasks in the future. I was released in 1963 and placed on probation for three years. Then I wrote a petition to review my case. Before my case got reviewed, however, the Cultural Revolution began. The Red Guards came to search Chen's family belongings because they learned that Chen was in Taiwan. They took away many antiques that had been passed down from Chen's ancestors, including gifts from the Qianlong Emperor. I was beaten up by the Red Guards, and three of my ribs were broken. Then I was sent back to Qingcheng prison again for another eight and a half years. Fortunately, my injury was looked after properly and healed in prison. I was released in 1975, along with Nationalist generals who had led armed insurrections against the Guomindang in 1949. Altogether, I was in prison for seventeen years after liberation.

When I was first sent to prison, my youngest daughter was nine years old. By the time I was finally released, she was almost thirty years old. All those years, my children lived on a government subsidy before they got jobs. I was in prison not only because of Pan Hannian but also because I married a banker who left for Taiwan—and because his siblings and my siblings were in Taiwan and the United States.

After I was released in 1975, I wrote four reports to the Central Committee, pleading for rehabilitation. Then my brother came from Thailand to see me. As a big petroleum businessman, he met leaders in the Central government while he was in China, and that helped my rehabilitation. I was rehabilitated in 1980 and appointed as a councilor to the Shanghai municipal government. I became a member of the Shanghai Political Consultative Committee in 1981. Now I am retired from that position, but I am still a councilor to the Shanghai municipal government. This is a permanent position that provides for the aged. So now I have to be provided for as an old woman. What else can I do? I was almost seventy years old when I got out of prison.

Zhang Yun was the one who introduced me to the party. She was the director of the Women's Department in Wuhan, and I became her successor three months after I met her. After my rehabilitation, she apologized to me for refusing to see me in 1953—she had refused because she heard a lot of gossip about me back then. But now, she realized how easily people could be hurt by slander, because she herself had been locked up for eight and a half years on the basis of others' false accusations. She told me to write down all the things I had done under the instruction of Zhou Enlai. So I wrote sixteen things and sent the report to Deng Yingchao. That was in 1982, long after Zhou's death.

Several ministers in the Central government used to be my subordinates in the 1930s. But because I was married to Chen, who went to Taiwan, my standing plummeted after liberation. So far I have not recovered my previous high rank, but the seniority of my party membership has recently been acknowledged by the party: I am now recognized as having been a party member since 1926. This is the result of several reports I wrote to the Central Committee. My only aim was that my seniority in the party be acknowledged; I did not care about the privileges that go along with it. I used to be the head of the Rescue Department, which is equivalent to the position of a minister. After liberation, I was only given the position of *kezhang* [head of an office]. I did not argue about that at all. It was a very hard time for me: our company went bankrupt, my husband left for Taiwan, I was responsible for the four kids, and I endured heavy political blows. I persevered. What was in my mind? I was just thinking that both Wan Xiyan and He Chang had died, but now we had won the victory and their dreams had finally come true. The people were happy now, so I should not be bothered by my personal loss. I have never given up my party membership, and Zhou Enlai said that he would testify to my party membership when we won victory. That is why I went to Beijing in 1953, but it was not until recently that I was acknowledged as having been a party member since 1926.

The teachers in my elementary school repeated to us the purpose of education. "You should become useful people in society after your education. You should strive for independence and equality between men and women." Later, when I was in Zhounan Girls' School, I learned more of those ideas. In the May Fourth movement I absorbed the ideas of anti-imperialism and antifeudalism. When I experienced an unhappy marriage, I left that family to pursue an independent life and my self-emancipation. After I joined the party, my consciousness was raised to the higher level of pursuing women's emancipation and the emancipation of human beings all over the world. If I had not experienced the May Fourth movement, or had not absorbed the ideas of anti-imperialism, antifeudalism, and equality between men and women, I would not have felt so dissatisfied with my first marriage. After I left that family, I just wanted to enter a college and pursue an independent life. The teachers in my elementary school all remained single.

If there was truly equality for women today, there would be no need for the current laws that protect women's and children's interests. Certainly many women have accomplished a great deal. Lenin said, "Revolution will not succeed without women." We learned this sentence as soon as we joined the revolution. The propaganda at that time all said that women constituted half of the population and that without women's participation and consciousness, the success of the women's movement and revolution would be impossible. Today we should say after all, we have achieved much. For instance, the women's movement in the National Revolution aimed first at prohibiting footbinding. Hubei was more backward than Hunan, and many women at that time were still having bound feet. My feet were not bound and my ears were not pierced. And I went to school at six. I only suffered the pain of arranged marriage, and without that experience I would not have joined the revolution.

Before I joined the revolution, I studied *The Twenty-Four Dynastic Histories*. I am familiar with Chinese history. I am a combination of Confucianism, Taoism, Buddhism, Marxism, and Leninism. That is why I enjoy helping others and would be willing to sacrifice myself for others' benefit. Now, in retrospect, I realize the law of the unity of opposites. As the essence of the inner world, different philosophies have connections with one another. The correct attitude toward all philosophies is as Chairman Mao said—reject the dross and assimilate the essence. When I was very young, my father taught me Confucian texts. One of Confucius's quotations is "Only women and lowly men are difficult. If you are close to them, they will have no respect for you; if you are aloof toward them, they will complain." Hearing those words, I asked in protest, "Daddy, did Confucius have no mother?" Father replied, "Oh, yes. He had a very virtuous mother. You should read *Lienüzhuan* [The biographies of exemplary women]. You will see that the most important thing to all those men with great fame is what they learned from their mothers." I raised that question because I had learned the ideas of equality between men and women in elementary school.

I am working now to inform the next generation. I have written several versions of my autobiography to pass down. I have also written many articles and testimonies for Wan Xiyan, He Chang, and other comrades. He Chang's son said to me, "Mom, if you had gone to the Jinggang Mountains with Dad, you would have been a martyr, too. It is better the way it is. We are grown up now, and you should enjoy a good life." But I thought to myself, "If I had gone to the Jinggang Mountains, I would be a *martyr* now. I would not have the rest of the story as that of a ghost." My father did not want to teach me poetry. He thought that in history women with both beauty and talent often had bad fortune, so it was better not to teach me poetry. At the end of his life, he wished I would convert to Buddhism. But I love to write poetry and articles. The problem is that whenever I write and recall my past, all the old feelings come back again. That is not good for my health. However, I cannot give up writing. This is my whole life. Whether I am a heroine or not, history will judge.

INTERPRETATION: THE MODERN MULAN
AND THE ROAD TO A CCP-LED WOMEN'S MOVEMENT

Unlike the previous four women, Huang Dinghui is a Communist Party member. It is important to understand that her paramount concern in the interviews as well as in her unpublished autobiographies is to prove that she has always been a CCP member, since the day she joined the party in 1926. Because of this concern, she consciously places herself within the discourses of the CCP. She has written several versions of her autobiographies: the longest and most detailed is only for the party, because it is full of confidential information that she thinks would not be in the party's interest to release; the medium-size one, which is from the tapes she dictated and paid to have transcribed, is written for publication and was shown to me; a shorter one she completed in 1987 serves as an outline to solicit interest for publication; and a brief one in the form of poem was written in 1990 for her son by He Chang. Her autobiographies are full of CCP language that I am unable to present fully here because of space limitations. Except for some information I have selected from her unpublished autobiographies, the narrative presented here is largely based on my interviews with her. In my view, Huang's speech reveals more conflicting subject positions than her writings, in which she strives to construct a single identity— a loyal and faithful Communist Party member, an identity that the party long refused to acknowledge.

Because Huang was involved in the underground work of the CCP, her experience includes many complicated and intriguing stories. Some puzzles are entirely beyond my ability to solve, because I lack access to the CCP's confidential files. However, it is not my priority to delineate Huang Dinghui's role in the underground CCP organization. And to my relief, Huang asked me to omit some stories involving the secret struggles between the CCP and the GMD, for fear of leaking information to the GMD. Therefore, I have cut those stories out of her narrative not to manipulate her oral history for purposes of my own, but rather to respect her wishes.

It is necessary to note that my follow-up interview with Huang occurred after an almost two-year interval. When I visited her at her sickbed early in 1995, I could hardly recognize her. She had aged terribly, now looking her real age, and had lost so much weight that she looked much smaller. All I could recognize was her voice. When she began to speak, I also noticed changes *in* her. She no longer spoke only the CCP language. Other voices from deep inside of her emerged now and then. She became more introspective. She was less concerned about presenting an image of a Communist heroine, more often revealing her discontent and grievances over un-just treatment she had received. Toward the end of the interview, she explained her drastic change by telling me that a terrible family tragedy had occurred after my first interview with her. I realized that the tragedy had devastated her. As she said, "I endured so many vicissitudes in my life. Now at such an old age, I have to face such a terrible blow. How can I bear it?" Because Huang did not wish to publicize her family tragedy, I can only report that the tragedy destroyed her health and shook her profoundly. It affected the interview by causing her to be much less rigid about expressing conflicting views toward her own life.

Despite much deletion, Huang's narrative is still rich and meaningful. For the purpose of this study, I focus on the following issues: first, the relationship between the May Fourth feminist discourse and the early CCP line on the women's movement; second, the constituency of the women's movement in the National Revolution period; third, the meaning of Hua Mulan to May Fourth women; and fourth, the transformation of a May Fourth woman into a Communist.

Feminism and the National Revolution

During her long-term imprisonment after liberation, Huang Dinghui must have repeatedly reviewed her life. When writing several versions of autobiography after her rehabilitation, Huang constantly pondered the question "What made me a Communist Party member?" When I asked her about her life, she had ready answers to most of my questions. She used vivid examples to illustrate her colorful experiences, stressed key events to emphasize the milestones in her long and tortuous life, and provided analyses of the inner logic or motivation behind her actions and choices. For a large part of my interviews with Huang, I was simply a fascinated audience, listening attentively to her effortless monologue.

Huang emphasized at the end of the last interview that "If I had not experienced the May Fourth movement, or had not accepted the ideas of anti-imperialism, antifeudalism, and equality between men and women, I would not have felt so dissatisfied with my first marriage" and stated that "I . . . suffered the pain of arranged marriage, and without that experience I would not have joined the revolution." These plain statements clearly remind us of the connection between the May Fourth discourses, women's new subjectivity, and the new women's participation in the revolution.

At twelve, the young Huang's involvement in the May Fourth movement was brief but unforgettable. She quickly absorbed new ideas. The person who made the deepest impression on her was the principal of Zhounan Girls' School, Zhu Jianfan. Just as Lu Lihua remembers Ma Xiangbo's talk on national salvation, and Chen Yongsheng remembers Xu Teli's protest against the Twenty-One Demands, Huang Dinghui can still recite what Zhu Jianfan said in class over seventy years ago. Zhu's lectures were enlightening to Huang because it was the first time she heard someone link women's emancipation to national salvation. Until then, she had had no personal experience of gender inequity. The elementary school teachers' talks on men's and women's equality did not impress her much. But Mr. Zhu opened her eyes. Women's emancipation was not simply unbinding women's feet or ceasing to pierce women's ears. (Huang was already emancipated in those respects.) Women's emancipation required women's equal participation in building a new, strong nation. The young girl who had admired Hua Mulan since elementary school was certainly touched by the prospect of stepping into a men's world to achieve great things.

The student movement after the May Fourth Incident provided the first opportunity for young girls like Huang to move out of their sheltered life and get involved in public affairs. The themes of anti-imperialism, antifeudalism, and gender equality blended perfectly to allow young patriotic female students to enter the public arena with confidence and self-esteem. In the process, young female participants were remolded by May Fourth discourses. The heightened consciousness of gender equality and the vision of an independent and useful life made many a young woman such as Huang feel that their arranged marriages were unbearable.

Unlike Zhu Su'e, Chen Yongsheng, and Wang Yiwei, who refused to allow their parents to choose a spouse for them, Huang accepted arranged marriage at first and then ran away from it. This pattern was not uncommon for her generation, though it required tremendous courage for a young wife to run away from her husband's home. Fortunately for Huang and women of a similar background, the revolution provided a haven. Huang's decision to join the revolution was made easily. The very day she met those Communists, she made up her mind to join them and moved in with them right away. Although she had loving parents and a comfortable home, as a married woman she did not belong to her natal family. In this sense, she was lucky to find a new home in the *zuzhi* (the party organization), which warmly accepted her as a woman running away from arranged marriage.

How was it that a nationalist revolution had such appeal to women like Huang? The National Revolution that Huang joined in 1926 was led by the first alliance between the CCP and the GMD. The grand revolution (*da gem-*

ing) promised to overthrow imperialism in China, to unify China by eliminating warlords, and to create a democratic society. The coalition was based on Sun Yat-sen's policy to "unite with the Soviet Union, unite with the Communist Party, and help peasants and workers." Advisors sent by the Comintern had a heavy hand in helping Sun reorganize the GMD. Modeled after the Soviet organizational structure, special bureaus were formed under the Central Executive Committee to deal with workers, peasants, youth, and women. Many Communists joined the GMD and began working with GMD leftists to mobilize workers, peasants, and women in Guangdong in 1924. The first Women's Bureau under the Central Executive Committee was formed on January 31, 1924, with the goal of promoting a women's movement. Afterward, women's departments were formed in different localities and in different levels of the GMD organization. This was the beginning of institutionalization of the women's movement in China.[41]

The women's movement in the National Revolution kept many May Fourth feminist issues alive. After the tragic failure of the Jinghan Railroad workers' strike in February, 1923, the CCP began to realize that it was too early to have a proletarian revolution in China.[42] A coalition with different political factions and different classes seemed the only feasible way to achieve the goal of overthrowing imperialism and warlords—the first stage of the Communist Revolution in China. When the party tried to form an alliance with the GMD, it also began its effort to mobilize people of different social groups, including women.

In June 1923, the Third Congress of the CCP issued a resolution on the women's movement. In contrast to the one issued a year before, which emphasized the importance of a proletarian revolution for the liberation of proletarian women, the 1923 resolution divided the women's movement into two large categories: a working women's movement and a general women's movement. The general women's movement included a feminist movement,

---

41. See Gilmartin, *Engendering the Chinese Revolution*, for more information on the two parties' efforts at organizing a women's movement. Also see All-China Women's Federation, *Zhongguo funü yundong shi* [A history of the Chinese women's movement] (Beijing: Chunqiu chubanshe, 1989), 158–159. For a discussion of the alliance between the GMD and the CCP, see Jonathan D. Spence, *The Search for Modern China* (New York: W. W. Norton, 1990), 334–341.

42. The strike is also known as the "Great Strike on February 7." On February 4, 1923, the workers on the railroad between Beijing and Wuhan were led by the CCP to begin a general strike, protesting warlord Wu Peifu's suppression of the Railroad Workers' Union. On February 7, Wu's troops massacred over forty striking workers and wounded over a hundred, and more than one thousand workers were fired. With tremendous casualties but no gains, the strike ended on February 9.

a suffrage movement, and a movement to abolish prostitution. The resolution emphasized the importance of those movements and instructed:

> Our female party members should guide and unite various movements in any time and in any place. Our slogans should be "Unite women's movements in the whole country," "Break the old ethics that enslaved women," "Equal education for men and women," "Equal employment opportunity for men and women," "Women should have the right of inheritance," "Freedom of social contact between men and women," "Freedom of marriage and divorce," "Equal pay for men and women," "Protect motherhood," and "Help working class women." Besides these slogans, in order to guide one half of the population—women—to join the National Revolution, we should add two slogans of the National Revolution: "Overthrow warlords" and "Overthrow imperialism." In guiding various movements, we should be careful, first, not to look down upon those movements and regard them as a movement of Miss and Mrs., or of female politicians, and second, not to allow ourselves to be tinted too much by class ideology, so that we will not scare these women off.[43]

The resolution reflects the CCP's sober assessment of the situation of women's movements in China in 1923. The May Fourth liberal feminist discourse was influential among various women's organizations in urban areas. Women's rights and women's immediate interests were what attracted different groups of women to women's movements. Although the CCP claimed to strive for women's emancipation with the fundamental aim of eliminating private ownership, the Marxist line had few female followers at the time. A report by the CCP Women's Bureau in 1924 estimated that there were only twenty female CCP members and over forty female Socialist Youth League members nationwide. In order to attract female followers and to "guide" various women's movements toward a "correct" Marxist and Leninist line, the CCP had to adopt a liberal feminist agenda at this stage, when its activities were largely urban-based.[44]

The feminist agenda in the National Revolution was also sustained by

43. "Zhongguo Gongchandang disanci quanguo daibiao dahui guanyu funü yundong jueyi an" [The resolution on the women's movement by the Third National Congress of the CCP], in *Zhongguo funü yundong lishi ziliao* [Historical source materials of the Chinese women's movement], ed. All-China Women's Federation (Beijing: Renmin chubanshe, 1986), 68.

44. "Zhongguo Gongchandang funübu guanyu Zhongguo funü yundong de baogao" [A report on the Chinese women's movement by the Women's Bureau of the CCP], in All-China Women's Federation, *Zhongguo funü yundong lishi ziliao*, 171. In September 1926, the Central Executive Committee of the CCP issued a reso-

the May Fourth feminists who joined either the CCP or the GMD. Deng
Yingchao may be the best case to illustrate this point. Deng (born 1904)
was a prominent student activist in the May Fourth movement in Tianjin.
At age sixteen, she was " full of patriotism . . . willing to sacrifice everything for national salvation and independence, for achieving democracy and
freedom, and for opposing feudal forces."[45] Like many other May Fourth
activists, Deng was informed by the multiple and sometimes conflicting discourses of her time. Besides her activities in the patriotic movement, Deng
was also noted for her major role in promoting a feminist movement in
Tianjin. After the Feminist Movement Association was established in Beijing in June 1922, Deng and her friends formed a Tianjin branch of the Feminist Movement Association in November 1922. In December, Deng was
selected as one of four representatives of the branch to send a feminist petition to the Beiyang government in Beijing. The petition included the seven
requests in the much publicized Declaration of the Feminist Movement
Association:

1. Open all the educational institutions in the country to women.
2. Ensure that women and men equally enjoy the rights of the people
   in the constitution.
3. According to the principle of equality between men and women,

---

lution on the women's movement, calling for an alliance with different groups of
women. It admitted:

> Often we were just concerned about our own action and proposed our own
> slogans. We paid very little attention to the interests of women of different
> classes and to the proposals of different women's organizations. As a result,
> our activities became isolated and lost the sympathy of the majority of the
> masses. This was one of the mistakes in the past. Therefore, from now on we
> should pay special attention to the united front of different classes of women
> and different women's organizations. In order to form this united front, we
> should, first, pay more attention to women's own interest; second, respect the
> proposals by other women's organizations in different movements; and third,
> avoid monopolizing everything and becoming involved in unnecessary
> conflicts. (All-China Women's Federation, *Zhongguo funü yundong lishi zil-
> iao*, 475–476)

For a discussion of the early female Communists and the party's gender policies, see
Christina Gilmartin, "Gender in the Formation of a Communist Body Politic," *Modern China* 19, no. 3 (1993): 299–329.

45. Deng Yingchao, "Wusi yundong de huiyi" [Recollections of the May Fourth
movement], in *Wusi shiqi funü wenti wenxuan* [Selected articles on women's problems in the May Fourth period], ed. All-China Women's Federation (Beijing: Zhongguo funü chubanshe, 1981), 5.

revise civil laws relating to husband and wife, parents and children, inheritance, property, and behavior.

4. Base the marriage law on the principle of equality between men and women.

5. Add to the criminal law clauses about "the age of consent" for marriage and stipulate that "taking a concubine is bigamy."

6. Prohibit prostitution, the sale of maids, and binding women's feet.

7. Make protective legislature for working women according to the principles "equal pay for equal work" and "protect motherhood."[46]

Deng's feminist position in this period was most clearly expressed in her article "Sisters, Rise Up!" Having witnessed her close friend's tragic death in a sad arranged marriage, Deng was more than ever determined to fight the old system. In the article printed in the Tianjin branch publication, Deng called for a women's revolt against oppression. Her analysis and argument were full of the rhetoric of the popular feminist literature at the time. She emphasized two major themes: women's right to be a "human being" and the new sexual morality:

> In the past few millennia, Chinese culture, history, institution, customs, and law have denied that women are "human beings" and have regarded them as playthings and slaves. . . . Living in the twentieth century, when humankind is seeking emancipation, we should first recognize that we ourselves are "human beings." . . . As for the marriage institution in the old ritual that looks down upon women's personhood and deprives them of human rights, we should attack it first and permanently eliminate it. . . .
>
> Madam Ellen Key once said, "Love should be the center of marriage. A marriage based on love is moral; without love a marriage is immoral, regardless how perfect its legal procedures are." . . . Married sisters, if

46. "Nüquan Yundong Tongmenghui xuanyan" [Declaration of the Feminist Movement Association], *Funü zazhi* [The ladies' journal] 8, no. 8 (1922): 126–127. The Feminist Movement Association's Tianjin branch had over six hundred members in July 1923. It was an influential organization in Tianjin at the time.

For Deng Yingchao's feminist activities in the May Fourth era, see Tianjin Women's Federation, *Deng Yingchao yu Tianjin zaoqi funü yundong* [Deng Yingchao and the early women's movement in Tianjin] (Beijing: Zhongguo funü chubanshe, 1987), 237–404, and Jin Feng, *Deng Yingchao zhuan* [A biography of Deng Yingchao] (Beijing: Renmin chubanshe, 1993), 61–67. Jin Feng claims that Deng Yingchao drafted the Declaration of the Feminist Movement that was published in Tianjin newspaper *Yishibao* in November 1922. Actually, the one that appeared in *Yishibao* was just a reprint of the declaration written by the Beijing Feminist Movement Association in August 1922. The biography nevertheless contains many revealing anecdotes about Deng's feminism.

your marriage is not based on love and now you are dissatisfied to the extent that you can not continue the relationship, I hope you will not hesitate to discontinue it. . . . You should bravely ask for a divorce and break away from a life of prostitution. Abolish the so-called chastity in the old ethics! . . .

Dear sister, rise up! Bravely rise up! Be a true independent "human being!"[47]

Deng joined the Socialist Youth League in January 1924 and became a CCP member a year later. At this stage, accepting Marxism did not mean for Deng a suppression of feminist issues. Rather, it made Deng and other CCP feminists pay more attention to proletarian women's predicament, and it offered them an analysis of the root of women's oppression—private ownership. Their Communist goal of overthrowing the existing political and economic system did not conflict with their feminist efforts to wake up their sisters and revolt against the oppression of women in all aspects of social and private life. In this period, Deng and her friends in the Feminist Movement Association, Tianjin Branch, organized a women's research group called Nüxingshe (The Women Star Society) and published a feminist periodical titled Nüxing [The woman star] and a Women's Daily that promoted the women's movement. Deng also took a leading role in the Tianjin Women's Committee to Promote a National Assembly.[48]

After the May Thirtieth Incident in 1925, Deng Yingchao, like other Communists, actively pushed public sentiment toward nationalistic concerns and toward the National Revolution. In her speech to the Shanghai Women's

47. Deng Yingchao, "Jiemeimen, qiyao!" [Sisters, rise up!], in Tianjin Women's Federation, Deng Yingchao yu Tianjin zaoqi funü yundong, 274–276. Viewing a woman's marriage without love as prostitution was a popular idea in May Fourth feminism.

48. Ibid., 381–437. The movement to promote the National Assembly in late 1924 and early 1925 was pushed by the CCP. This nationwide high tide of women's activism demanded that women be included in the upcoming national assembly. Although its major theme was a continuation of the May Fourth feminist agenda, the CCP instructed its female members to become actively involved. Through female CCP members like Xiang Jingyu, Yang Zhihua, and Deng Yingchao, who played leading roles at different locations, the CCP succeeded in diverting the attention of many feminists to the National Revolution. The movement marked the beginning of the CCP's increasing role in channeling a feminist movement into the National Revolution. See All-China Women's Federation, Zhongguo funü yundong shi, 177–186, and "Zhongguo Gongchandang disici quanguo daibiao dahui duiyu funü yundong zhi jueyi an" [The resolution on the women's movement by the Fourth National Congress of the CCP], in All-China Women's Federation, Zhongguo funü yundong lishi ziliao, 279–281.

Association in July 1925, she emphasized that the women's movement now should pay attention to four points. "First, abandon individual movements for employment, suffrage, marriage, and so on; second, join the national independence movement; third, make efforts to popularize the idea of uniting peasant and women workers; and fourth, ensure that women all over the country are well-organized."[49] The four points reflect the party's urgent need to mobilize the masses for the National Revolution. They also reveal Deng's conscious identification with the party line.

In the CCP's analysis, women's partial movements could not prevail in China's contemporary political and economic system. Only a revolution overthrowing foreign imperialism, warlordism, feudalism, and capitalism would provide a fundamental solution to women's oppression. Hence, women activists should first devote their energy and efforts to the nationalist and class struggles. In the party's effort to mobilize women's participation in the National Revolution—or rather, to compete with feminist organizations for constituencies—the practice of "othering" feminism began. Women Communists at women's gatherings and in writings for women's journals drew a line between a "partial" or "narrow" feminist movement (*xiayide nüquan yundong*) and a "women's emancipation movement" (*funü jiefang yundong*) attached to the National Revolution. With the same political mission as Deng Yingchao, the prominent Communist leader of the women's movement Xiang Jingyu warned feminists in Shanghai not to "only pursue women's rights [*nüquan*] without concern for the survival of the Chinese nation."[50] She argued that "a feminist movement cannot separate from the civil rights movement [the National Revolution] to be independent. It can only obtain true women's rights within the general civil rights movement."[51] In this line of argument, the pursuit of women's rights—or feminism—was criticized as a separation from national interests. This critique signified a departure from the New Culture definition of feminism, in which women's pursuit of equal rights and independent personhood held the key to revitalizing the nation. Detached from its nationalist

49. "Deng Yingchao zai Shanghai gejie funü lianhehui fabiao yanshuo" [Deng Yingchao made a speech to the Shanghai Women's Association], *Minguo ribao* [Republic daily], July 20, 1925, in All-China Women's Federation, *Zhongguo funü yundong lishi ziliao*, 347.

50. "Zhongguo Funü Xiehui chengli jiyao" [On the founding of the Chinese Women's Association], May 1, 1925, in All-China Women's Federation, *Zhongguo funü yundong lishi ziliao*, 387.

51. Xiang Jingyu, "Nüguomin dahui de sanda yiyi" [Three significances of the congress of women citizens], March 1925, in All-China Women's Federation, *Zhongguo funü yundong lishi ziliao*, 442.

connotations, the CCP-defined "narrow feminism" would soon lose legitimacy in CCP political discourse.

However, given its female members' involvement in various women's organizations, the CCP was also aware that a revolutionary mobilization that ignored women's immediate interests would fail. The CCP's resolutions, reports, and announcements in this period all stressed the importance of considering the needs of various women. The Resolution on the Women's Movement by the Second National Congress of the GMD most clearly demonstrates such an awareness:

II. The principle of the women's movement: Besides leading women to participate in the National Revolution, special attention should be paid to women's own emancipation. . . .

IX. In order to enforce the following items, we should supervise and urge the National Government to follow the twelfth stipulation of the party platform: "Recognize the principle of equality between men and women in law, economy, education, and society; and promote the development of *nüquan*."

    A. Legislation

        1. Create a law of equality between men and women;

        2. Stipulate women's inheritance rights;

        3. Strictly forbid the sale of people;

        4. Create a marriage law according to the principle of absolute freedom in marriage and divorce;

        5. Protect women who have run away from oppressive marriages;

        6. Create labor legislation for women according to the principles of equal pay for equal work, protecting motherhood, and eliminating child labor.

    B. Administration

        1. Improve women's education;

        2. Pay attention to peasants' and female workers' education;

        3. Open all staff positions in administration to women;

        4. Open all professional institutions to women;

        5. Prepare to set up child-care institutions.[52]

The resolution includes almost all the demands raised in the Declaration

---

52. "Zhongguo Guomindang dierci quanguo daibiao dahui funü yundong jueyi an" [The resolution on the women's movement by the Second National Congress of the GMD], in All-China Women's Federation, *Zhongguo funü yundong lishi ziliao*, 505–507.

of the Feminist Movement Association and thus illustrates the influence of the May Fourth feminist discourse.[53] More revealing, the committee responsible for submitting this resolution was composed of Song Qingling, He Xiangning, two prominent female members of the GMD, and Deng Yingchao, the young Communist who had already gained fame in her own right.[54] The three women all gave priority to the National Revolution, while at the same time maintaining a deep concern for women's lot. Of the three, Deng was the only one who had been actively involved in the May Fourth feminist movement.

It should be no surprise that the National Revolution incorporated many May Fourth themes. In the National Revolution, prominent roles were played not only by famous New Culturalists such as Chen Duxiu, Guo Moruo, and Shen Yanbing, but also by many newly emerged political stars who had been May Fourth student activists, such as Mao Zedong and Zhou Enlai. The founding of the CCP was one consequence of the popularizing of Marxism and socialism in the May Fourth era. To many culture critics and feminist advocates of the May Fourth era, the alliance of the GMD and CCP and the growing National Revolution pointed toward a viable way to realize their New Culture dreams. Therefore, the centers of the National Revolution—first Guangzhou, then Wuhan—were packed with famous people from the May Fourth era as well as from the 1911 Revolution. The leading body, the GMD, became an inclusive party that contained revolutionaries of all shades.

In all respects, the focus of the revolution was an extension and development of May Fourth nationalism. The May Fourth feminist issues—as long as they were pursued under the leadership of the two-party coalition—were neither "narrow" nor harmful to national interests. Rather, they served as a rallying point for mobilizing various groups of urban women. For the May Fourth feminists who followed political tides, the most obvi-

53. The resolution had a section of slogans for the women's movement, which included "Oppose polygamy" and "Oppose the small-daughter-in-law system." Compared to the Feminist Declaration, it omitted only the prohibition of prostitution and footbinding.

54. Song Qingling, the wife of Sun Yat-sen, had always held a prominent position in China's modern politics. He Xiangning, the wife of Liao Zhongkai—who enjoyed seniority in the GMD second only to Sun Yat-sen at the time—had also been actively involved in party politics. He Xiangning was the one who insisted on "promoting *nüquan* [women's rights, or feminism]" in the GMD's platform. Deng Yingchao, at age twenty-one, enjoyed rising national fame in her leading role in Tianjin's patriotic and feminist movements. She married Zhou Enlai in 1925, when she was transferred by the CCP to work in Guangzhou.

ous new development in the women's movement of this period—besides a new emphasis on uniting female peasants and workers—was the partisan effort to control various women's organizations. Following the Soviet model, both the GMD and the CCP were eager to organize the entire country, including women's organizations, under the leadership of the National government. After the eventual breakup of the alliance, both parties continued this organizing principle. In sum, as a result of its incorporation of feminist issues, the National Revolution witnessed a rapid growth of the women's movement in China—a women's movement "guided" by two political parties with a nationalistic agenda. Significantly, the party-led women's movement adopted the phrase "women's emancipation movement" (*funü jiefang yundong*) to denote its difference from the "feminist movement" (*nüquan yundong*). The two phrases would later become antithetical in CCP terminology.

Gender Troubles of Women Activists

The Resolution by the Second National Congress of the GMD served as a blueprint for the women's movement throughout the National Revolution. Numerous female GMD and CCP members worked enthusiastically in different levels of the women's departments. Increasing numbers of feminist activists were recruited (many of whom joined the GMD because it was the leading party of the revolution and had a prestigious founder, Sun Yat-sen), and increasing numbers of women (workers, students, housewives, and peasants) were attracted to the women's movement. Against this background, Huang Dinghui ascended the stage of the grand revolution.

Keeping the above blueprint in mind, it is easy to picture Huang's excitement when she first met those Communists. They did not look down upon this woman running away from an unhappy arranged marriage. Instead, they welcomed Huang sincerely and promoted her rapidly to the leading position in the Wuhan women's movement. She supervised activities like unbinding women's feet, cutting women's long hair, closing down brothels, training former prostitutes, helping abused wives and maids, opening reading classes for illiterate women, and so on. Perhaps what she did most was making speeches at all kinds of gatherings. She had an excellent memory. After she heard a talk by party leaders, she was able to pass their words on to the masses faithfully and effectively. Considering that radio was unavailable to the masses and that the majority of the people were illiterate, Huang's skill in making speeches or in popularizing the CCP line was extremely important. In other words, her ability to engage in revolutionary speech empowered her greatly. Moreover, she had an excellent voice. When Song Qingling made a speech to a big gathering in Wuhan, Huang served as a loudspeaker: every sentence that Song spoke, Huang repeated loudly, so that the audience could hear. It is no wonder that such a young woman was given a big role to play, not only in a drama but also on an important occasion. On Women's Day, 1927, Huang, not yet twenty years old, chaired the celebration rally with over two hundred thousand participants.[55]

Although Huang's swift rise to celebrity might be unique, she was quite representative in the sense that many young women of similar background joined the revolution. Item five in the resolution guaranteed that the revolution would be a haven to women who had run away from oppressive marriages. Whereas May Fourth feminism provided young women and young men a legitimate way to resist or escape from their arranged marriages, the revolution furnished those rebels with a material base. In her study of the female Communists in the National Revolution, Christina Kelley Gilmartin emphasizes that gender issues played a prominent role in women's decision to become Communists. "Indeed, to these women who were concerned with challenging traditional gender relationships and providing alternative role models, the party appeared more as a subculture than as a political institution. First and foremost, it facilitated their efforts to reject family controls over the marriage process and to define new social arrangements, such as free-choice marriage."[56] The phenomenon of women running away from their marriages to the revolution was also captured by the contemporary media. *The Republic Daily* reported on June 3, 1927, "Since women's associations were organized in Hubei province, recruitment has developed rapidly. Among the forty thousand members, many are asking for divorce on the basis of self-interest. According to a survey, most of the women asking for divorce are middle-class, some are petite bourgeoisie, and very few are from the peasant and working class."[57]

---

55. According to Shen Yanbing, who mentioned Huang three times in his memoir, Huang was one of the three most famous women in the revolutionary center at Wuhan. She was renowned for her beauty and her capability. In Jing Lingzi's *Shihai Gouxuan*, a report on Wuhan women in the National Revolution, Huang is depicted as a prominent figure at the time. Huang's name also appears frequently in Wuhan Women's Federation, *Wuhan funü yundong dashiji* [A record of great events in the Wuhan women's movement] (Wuhan: Wuhan Women's Federation, 1981).

56. Gilmartin, *Engendering the Chinese Revolution*, 101.

57. The report is cited in Wuhan Women's Federation, *Wuhan funü yundong dashiji*, 42.

In *Dageming hongliuzhong de nübing* [Women soldiers in the National Revolution], a collection of autobiographies by women who joined the Wuhan Central

It is quite revealing that in the women's training session in Wuhan, "Criticizing Womanism" [*Funü zhuyi de piping*] was listed as one of the lecture topics.[58] According to Huang, "Opposing womanism was mainly opposing women's *dushen zhuyi* [celibatarianism]." She emphasized, "In the women's emancipation movement at that time, many women were strong in their work but kind of conceited and disdainful toward men. Those women had experienced unhappy marriages and insisted on celibacy." Because this was the only problem named within the rank of female revolutionaries, it is possible that the percentage of women tinted by "womanism" was rather large.

A further point can be made by examining the different definitions of "womanism" offered in various contexts. Yang Zhihua, a leader of the CCP's women's movement and the wife of Qu Qiubai, pointed out in her analysis of the Chinese women's movement in 1926:

> Since the May Fourth Movement . . . a "womanist" women's movement has developed. It maintains that women's liberation should be achieved without women's participation in political movement and social movement. Instead, the object of this women's movement is men. . . .
>
> The question of women's participation in the political movement has already drawn objections from some womanists. They think that if women get involved in the political vortex, they will necessarily be used by politics and will no longer sincerely have a women's movement for women's interests. Further, they think that adding women workers' strikes to the agenda of the women's movement smacks of Communism. They often use those theories to avoid much of the work that should be done and to further split the women's movement. Actually, it is very narrow and erroneous for women's movement activists to look at things only from a perspective of the struggle between the two sexes.[59]

Military and Political Institute, some mention that they joined the National Revolution in order to revolt against arranged marriages. Xie Bingying, the woman soldier who became a renowned writer by publishing entries made in her diary during the National Revolution, commented, "I believe at that time the primary motivation of the female students who joined the army was to leave the oppression of their feudal families and to look for a better future for themselves." Xie Bingying's desire to escape an arranged marriage was the major factor in her decision to join the army. See All-China Women's Federation, *Dageming hongliuzhong de nübing* (Beijing: Zhongguo funü chubanshe, 1991).

58. The reference to the women's training session can be found in Wuhan Women's Federation, *Wuhan funü yundong dashiji*, 17. Instead of "Opposing Womanism," as Huang remembers, the lecture by Wan Xiyan was called "Criticizing Womanism." The topic is listed together with eleven others on world women's movements, Chinese politics, and so on.

59. Yang Zhihua, "Zhongguo funü yundong zuiyan" [Comments on the Chinese

According to Yang's definition of "womanism," the women who had already joined the National Revolution should not be called womanists. However, male CCP leaders such as Wan Xiyan extended her line of argument to include those women who did not want to marry. Whereas Yang argued that it was erroneous to focus only on gender struggle, Wan's emphasis in his lecture was that it was erroneous even to *perceive* gender conflict within the camp of revolutionaries. It is not clear whether those women's decisions to avoid marriage resulted from their painful experiences with men or from the influence of "womanism," or from both. Nevertheless, it is obvious that the male party leadership was quite sensitive to the gender issue and reacted swiftly to the "womanist" tendency. Wan's lecture may mark the earliest effort of male CCP leaders to silence any expression of gender consciousness within the revolution.

The women's associations organized by women's departments of the National government developed rapidly in Hubei. According to a report by the head of the provincial women's department on June 27, 1927, the membership of the women's associations in Hubei rose from two thousand to sixty thousand after the arrival of the Revolutionary Army. The reliability of this statistic is questionable, but a rapid growth in the women's movement is evident. On the same occasion, other women leaders discussed problems of the women's movement and pointed out in particular that peasant women were often suspicious of the women's movement. The growth in membership at that time was largely among urban women.[60]

The Resolution on Rural Women by the Hubei Peasant Association on June 21, 1927, stipulated that, first, different levels of peasant associations should set up women's departments; second, rural women should join peasant associations; third, in rural areas, women should not be forced to cut their long hair, and propaganda about absolute freedom of marriage and divorce should be forbidden; and fourth, women's departments should investigate rural women's life situation in order to understand their demands.[61]

Apparently, rural women were far from mobilized. Moreover, the issue of free divorce, effective among urban women, aroused a hostile response from Hubei peasants. Although it is not clear how peasant women responded

women's movement] in All-China Women's Federation, *Zhongguo funü yundong lishi ziliao,* 557–559.

60. Wuhan Women's Federation, *Wuhan funü yundong dashiji,* 50. The occasion was the opening ceremony of a women's training session.

61. Ibid., 53. As an important CCP document, the resolution is also collected in All-China Women's Federation, *Zhongguo funü yundong lishi ziliao,* 708.

to free divorce, the resolution seems to suggest that freedom of marriage and divorce was not an urgent demand of rural women. Because the CCP at this stage was urban-based and constituted largely by urban-educated men and women, it lacked a clear picture of rural life. The Hubei Resolution noted the party's early awareness of the need for a rural agenda.

However, the women's movement in the National Revolution successfully attracted many women workers. Constituted largely by a Eurocentric Marxism and Leninism, the early Communists and some left-wing Nationalists paid special attention to the growing Chinese proletariat. Close contact with factory workers by CCP female members such as Yang Zhihua enabled the CCP to address women workers' specific needs. In the National Revolution, the CCP proposed the eight-hour workday, paid maternity leave, and other protective legislation. The CCP also played an active role in supporting women workers' strikes in factories owned by foreigners, such as the tobacco factory workers' strike in Wuhan that attracted Huang's attention. Although it is unclear how women's working conditions were improved under the National government, there are documents on women workers' involvement in the women's movement in Wuhan. The following news may serve as an illustration:

> (Hankou, Reuters News Agency) The liberated women's husbands held a demonstration in front of the All-China Workers' Union today. They shouted loudly, "Down with the women's associations!" Most of the demonstrators were workers. They complained that ever since the arrival of the Guomindang—because of Guomindang's propaganda about women's freedom, freedom of choosing a spouse, women's emancipation, and so on—their wives no longer stay at home but stay out all night. They believed that their families have been destroyed by this new liberation. They demanded that their wives and other women return to the standards of conduct of the past.[62]

The husbands did not specify what their wives were doing "out." However, women workers did stay out late because of their movement activities, which was enough to arouse fear in their husbands or fiancés.[63] Historical documents show that Wuhan women workers were responsive to the call

---

62. *Chenbao* [Morning news], March 18, 1927, cited in Jing Lingzi, *Shihai Gouxuan*, 45–46.

63. In *Shihai Gouxuan*, an old man who was one of the husbands at the demonstration tells the author, "[At that time] the newspaper printed divorce and marriage statements every day. Women's associations would help a woman get a divorce in the daytime, find her a new spouse right away, and hold a wedding ceremony in the evening. Women at that time were so liberated!" (Jing Lingzi, 50).

for unbinding feet and were enthusiastic about night schools. Although freedom of marriage and divorce made their husbands nervous, the previously mentioned survey shows that women workers constituted a small number of those who asked for divorce. It is possible that most women workers joined women's associations because of other issues that concerned them. The Resolution of the First Hubei Women's Conference named two issues of concern to women workers: "Male and female workers unite" and "Female workers should join the workers' union, and male workers should not look down upon female workers." Apparently, beyond protective legislation, gender discrimination within the working class was also discussed by women workers in the women's movement.[64]

Mulan Heroism

Once Huang joined the revolution, she changed her name to Mulan—the Chinese characters mean "admiring" (*mu*) "Hua Mulan" (*lan*). She admits that she thought of herself as a legendary heroine. The revolution enabled her to follow in the footsteps of her childhood role model. For many women activists of that generation, Hua Mulan made a deep impression long before they heard the phrase about equality between men and women. In many cases, it was the subject position of Mulan that initially made these young women seek a heroic life. The life of the first Communist leader of the women's movement, Xiang Jingyu, illustrates this point.[65]

Xiang Jingyu was born to a merchant family in Hunan in 1895. From the time she was five years old, her father and brothers taught her characters.

---

64. "Hubeisheng diyici funü daibiao dahui xuanchuan wenti jueyi an" [The resolution on propaganda by the First Women's Conference in Hubei province], March 18, 1927, in All-China Women's Federation, *Zhongguo funü yundong lishi ziliao*, 767.

65. It should be noted that Mulan was not the only heroine mentioned in the nationalist discourse at the turn of the century. For example, Qiu Jin's martyrdom in 1907 immediately made her a renowned heroine in China. But the "Ballad of Mulan" circulated more widely than stories of other ancient heroines and earlier than stories of modern heroines. For the influence of Hua Mulan on many women of the generation, see All-China Women's Federation, *Dageming hongliuzhong de nübing*. As one woman soldier recalls, when she and her friend were accepted by the Central Military Political Academy, they were overjoyed, congratulating themselves on becoming revolutionary soldiers who would fight for a new world, and they "would no longer have to envy Mulan, let alone have to be disguised as men without any one's knowledge" (165). For more discussions on the impact of Mulan, see also Gilmartin, *Engendering the Chinese Revolution*, 74, 100, and 189, and Roxane H. Witke, "Transformation of Attitudes towards Women during the May Fourth Era" (Ph.D. diss., University of California, Berkeley, 1971), 45–49.

In about two years she was able to read classical texts, and she loved history. Of the stories her father and brothers told her, she loved "Mulan Joins the Army" most. Coached by her father and brothers, she learned to recite the "Ballad of Mulan." Often Xiang would gather a group of young girls from the neighborhood by the riverbank to recite the "Ballad of Mulan" together loudly. From childhood on, it was said, she "had the ambition to emulate Hua Mulan, to strive hard."[66]

According to Xiang's husband, Cai Hesen, Xiang excelled in all her classes during elementary school. In the student competitions in the school or at the county level, Xiang was always number one, "excellent in both civil and martial events" (wenwu shuangquan). "In this kind of encouraging social atmosphere, the new-style vivacious young girl blossomed. Day and night she thought of being 'the greatest person under the heaven.' She even dreamed of that while sleeping." Cai recalled, "The only desire she had was to accomplish a 'world-shaking cause.' . . . She often thought to herself passionately, 'If I fail to succeed in a great cause in the future, I will burn myself to ashes!' Whenever she was in such an impassioned mood, she burst into tears."[67]

Xiang received her education in Changde Women's Normal School, Zhounan Girls' School, and the Number One Women's Normal School in Hunan. Then she returned to her hometown to open a girls' school by herself. She made many public patriotic speeches in the May Fourth movement. Near the end of 1919, she joined the Hunan students' "Work Study Group" and went to France with Cai Hesen and his family. On the long trip to France, after numerous talks with Cai—a young Communist believer and Mao Zedong's close friend—Xiang gave up her conviction of "saving the nation through education" and celibatarianism. She became a Communist believer and married Cai in May 1920.

Xiang returned to China in early 1922 and joined the CCP in Shanghai. She immediately became involved in the party's women's work. Indeed, Xiang was the chief theorist and propagator of the CCP line on the women's movement. She wrote many articles on the Chinese women's movement, applying class analysis and displaying a strong nationalist sentiment. She

66. He Huzhi, *Xiang Jingyu zhuan* [A biography of Xiang Jingyu] (Shanghai: Shanghai renmin chubanshe, 1990), 9.

67. Cai Hesen, "Xiang Jingyu zhuan" [A biography of Xiang Jingyu], in *Xiang Jingyu wenji* [Papers by Xiang Jingyu], ed. Dai Xugong and Yao Weidou (Changsha: Hunan renmin chubanshe, 1985), 1. Cai and Xiang separated in 1926. Cai wrote the biography in 1928, two months after Xiang's tragic death. He addressed her as a "great proletarian heroine" and "the everlasting lover of the Chinese proletariat."

played a leading role in channeling Shanghai feminist energy into the National Revolution, as well as in envisioning a unified women's movement led by the CCP.[68]

Although Xiang's leading role in the CCP's women's movement was well recognized and highly praised, her husband noted that she herself "had always been unwilling to do 'women's work.'" Cai Hesen revealed that Xiang often sensed a backhanded oppression in the party: "In her view, thinking that female comrades' ability was inferior to male comrades' ability was 'terribly insulting.' The more that comrades said she was the best among female comrades, the less she was content." Cai himself admitted that Xiang's ability qualified her to shoulder the party's general directory work and that the party had revealed its "weakness" by giving her the job assignment of women's work. The reality was that in the early stages of the CCP's development, the female Communists were only assigned to do "women's work," to take charge of women's mobilization. Xiang Jingyu, dreaming of accomplishing great deeds in a men's world since her childhood, was forced to confront gender segregation within the party. Identifying her with "women's work" located her in a subordinate position far from the center of party power.[69]

But Xiang's dream of becoming a heroine still came true in the end. After over a year's study in Moscow, Xiang returned to Wuhan in 1927. She led the women workers' movement first and then was appointed the director of the Propaganda Department of Hankou. After the CCP and the GMD alliance dissolved, Xiang stayed in Wuhan to continue underground work. She was the editor in chief of a CCP underground publication. When the GMD liquidated the CCP organizations in Wuhan, Xiang was arrested in the French concession in March 1928. When she was extradited to the GMD

---

68. In contrast to Gilmartin, who offers a positive assessment of Xiang Jingyu's role in promoting the women's movement, I view Xiang's role as mixed. Xiang's efforts at achieving a unified women's movement under the leadership of the CCP marked a significant turning point in the history of the Chinese women's movement: a spontaneous feminist movement that created social space for Chinese urban women was turned into a party-controlled women's emancipation movement. Although the latter affected Chinese women's lives on a much larger scale than the feminist movement at the time, it eventually closed the social space for women's spontaneous activism in a party-state. For a more detailed argument, see my review of Gilmartin's work, "Pingjia Ke Lingqing zhu *Cong shehui xingbie jiaodu kan Zhongguo geming*" [A review of *Engendering the Chinese Revolution*], *Jindai Zhongguo funüshi yanjiu* [Research on women in modern Chinese history], no. 4 (August 1996): 343–346.

69. Cai Hesen, "Xiang Jingyu zhuan," 2–3.

Headquarters in Wuhan, thousands of people gathered in the streets to see her. She made speeches and shouted revolutionary slogans all the way. She was killed by the GMD on May 1, 1928. Xiang's heroic death and her leading role in theorizing a CCP-led women's movement qualified her to be made a Communist heroine in CCP history.

For Chinese women born at the turn of the century, the meanings of the Mulan subject position were complex. Heroism was an inspiring goal. Xiang strove to be a heroine and lived a short but heroic life. Huang Dinghui regrets even in her old age that she did not have the opportunity to become a martyr, whereas both her ex-husbands did. She still worries about whether her long and complicated life will make her a heroine in the eyes of future generations. Numerous source materials show that the appeal of heroism cuts across political orientations and class or regional differences. Without delving into psychological theory to explain why certain girls are more susceptible to heroism, what the historian can demonstrate is that, in a very real sense, it was the heroic model that mobilized the particular constellation of heroines in this generation.

Mulan heroism had a specific content at that historical juncture. It encompassed women's double struggle over nationalism and feminism. Antiimperialism, antifeudalism, and gender equality had entered Chinese discourse at the end of the Qing dynasty and become dominant themes after the May Fourth movement. A heroine could not be made outside this context. In other words, what made a modern woman a heroine was that she was able to join men in the fight for national independence and prosperity. In the dominant discourses after the May Fourth period, feminism was mainly understood as women's right (*nüquan*) to participate in the national struggle and in the public arena. If women insisted on pursuing only women's interests, they were "narrow feminists" or "womanists." They might strive heroically in the public arena for women's interests, but they would not be recognized as heroines in the early-twentieth-century discourse of Mulan heroism.

Unlike "womanists," modern Mulans perceived that their self-interest could best be served through the struggle for the national interest. Xiang Jingyu theorized this route to Chinese women's emancipation in numerous articles. Her major argument was that "women can never achieve freedom and equality alone; the Chinese nation must first achieve both."[70] National independence, therefore, was the precondition for women's emancipation. But not all women who joined the revolution believed this

70. "Zhongguo Funü Xiehui chengli jiyao," 388.

theory about women's emancipation. Huang Dinghui admits frankly that she joined the revolution for self-emancipation. In her case, political involvement offered an immediate escape from her unhappy domestic life. However, the revolution did not just provide her a shelter. More important, it brought her close to her childhood dream of being a heroine like Mulan.

Even though the Mulan subject position was strongly nationalistic, it was not unproblematic in the CCP discourse. Huang still remembers Wan Xiyan teaching her that "we Communists believed in collectivism" and that "we should eliminate individualistic heroism." The ancient Mulan clad in men's armor was able to rise to become a general in the army. The modern Mulans, however, were always seen as women in a men's world. Xiang Jingyu was frustrated when comrades said that she was the best among women comrades: how far could she have taken her great ambition in the CCP if she had not died a martyr? In the cases of Huang and many other female CCP members, the pattern has been consistent. No matter how great the ambition of their youth, they were reconstructed by the discourse of collectivism: in the collective cause of the Communist Revolution, individuals submitted themselves completely to the needs of the party and the revolution. Otherwise, they were regarded as dangerously individualistic and bourgeois. The collectivist principle applied to both men and women. The problem was that women were the ones always called on by the party and the revolution to do subordinate work rather than to play a leading role.

The Mulan subject position worked paradoxically for modern Mulans such as Huang. It made them discontented with their treatment in the CCP, while at the same time it consoled them for their sacrifice. Huang revealed many times in the interviews her grievances about the way the party treated her. Both her ex-husbands have been eulogized as Communist heroes by the CCP; but after she followed the party's instruction to do underground work, endured imprisonment twice as a result, and suffered the loss of her loved ones, her contribution was not even recognized, let alone viewed as heroic. Worse still, the party even questioned the seniority of her party membership. Thus her youthful dream of being a legendary woman like Mulan did not come true. Nevertheless, she felt herself better off than Mulan in the sense that Mulan showed loyalty to the ruler and endured hardship for her father's sake, whereas she, as a Communist, had been loyal to the party and sacrificed herself for the sake of revolution and the people. Loyalty and the ability to sacrifice oneself were prominent traits in Mulan. Embracing the role model of Mulan, modern heroines inherited those traits. After enduring tremendous pain in her personal life, Huang is still unwaveringly proud of the fact that she possesses those virtues.

The Making of a Female Communist

It is significant that during the long interviews Huang seldom used the word "independence." When she did use it, its use was meaningful. Toward the end of the interviews, in a retrospective mood, Huang said,

> In the May Fourth movement I absorbed the ideas of anti-imperialism and antifeudalism. When I experienced an unhappy marriage, I left that family to pursue an independent life and my self-emancipation. After I joined the party, my consciousness was raised to the higher level of pursuing women's emancipation and the emancipation of human beings all over the world. . . . [But earlier, when] I left that family, I just wanted to enter a college and pursue an independent life. The teachers in my elementary schools all remained single.

This statement reveals several layers of meaning. Because of the example of her elementary teachers, Huang had always known there was the option of an independent life for women. The May Fourth discourse made the prospect of independence not only feasible but desirable. Like other young educated women of the May Fourth generation, Huang aspired to an independent life through higher education—a story made familiar to us by the previous four narratives. Mentioning this option as a route to self-emancipation, Huang confirmed the influence of the May Fourth liberal feminist discourse and the possibility for women to live an independent life.

If Huang had entered a college instead of the revolutionary camp, her life story would be dramatically different. This thought must have occurred to Huang many times. When she confided to me her plan of almost seventy years ago, she was actually reviewing other possible choices in her life that she perhaps should have made. But remembering her specific situation, she dismissed the possibility that she could have made other choices. She was a fugitive from an unhappy marriage. The opportunity of higher education was open to her, but she was unsure how she would be treated by others in school or in society. The Communists welcomed her heartily and put an exciting haven within her immediate reach. Joining the revolution, also a radical subculture, was the best choice she could make at the time. As a result, she took a detour from the route to self-emancipation. Consequently, in her long talks and autobiographies, she never used the May Fourth feminist phrase "independent personhood."

Once involved in the revolution, Huang quickly became conversant with CCP language. Her long-term imprisonment after liberation did not expunge the Communist teachings she learned as a youth. On the contrary, the high value she placed on confirming her identity as a veteran party member has ensured a dominant CCP position in her consciousness. Speaking from that subject position, she saw her dream of being a legendary heroine as "individualistic" and was grateful that the party raised her consciousness to the higher level of pursuing the emancipation of women and human beings all over the world. She felt fortunate that she "happened to be born into that great time of revolution and happened to be in Wuhan." Being a member of the CCP brought her tremendous hardship, but the Communist identity gave her positive feelings and self-esteem for most of her life. All her hardship and sacrifice were worthwhile and meaningful when they were seen as part of the price paid for the great cause of emancipating humankind.

However, there were times when the Communist hold on Huang loosened. The first crisis came when she was insulted by a male Communist leader, X. X remarked that Huang had married He Chang to place herself under the patronage of a party boss. This was terribly insulting to a proud modern Mulan. She had not expected that "women who have joined the revolution still have to bear insults from male comrades." Partly as a revolt against this wrongdoing within the party, and partly as an escape from the dreadful prospect of being punished for losing the party's confidential notebook, she tried to commit suicide.

Mentioning this incident, Huang emphasized that the party leader Zhou Enlai gave her a lecture on how to be a loyal and strong Communist—a lecture that she remembered ever since. At another level, because X later played a major role in denying Huang's party membership, Huang's revelation of this incident provided a context to explain X's vengeful behavior. In interviews and in Huang's autobiographies, Communist principles were always foregrounded. She was careful not to taint the glorious image of the party by her account. Even so, the suicide incident gives us a glimpse of an extremely depressed and lonely young woman in the Communist Party. She had no language for gender politics within the party. She only knew that what she confronted was unlike what she had dreamed of in the Communist Revolution. The great cause did not appear so attractive anymore. After she was rescued from her attempted suicide, Huang contemplated the option of going home. That was another moment in her life when she had to make an important choice. But again, she decided that she had no better option than to remain in the party: "It was all because of that arranged marriage that I had to follow the party faithfully no matter what happened to me." Huang concluded her story of suicide with a mixed expression of sadness and resignation.[71]

The second crisis came when the party decided to send He Chang, Huang's third husband, to the Jinggang Mountains. Huang had only been in the CCP for a few years, but she had already born tremendous loss. Her second husband had died in battle. Both of her babies had been sent away for the sake of the revolution. Now she had to face yet another separation— this time, from her third husband, whom she apparently loved. She could no longer bear it. She protested in front of He Chang, "They sent away my two children, and now I am told to separate from you. I won't do it. I will never do it!" She resisted the party's decision and "cried for three days and three nights." Huang could not identify her self-interest with the party any more. She referred to the party as "they."

But the revolt was in vain. He Chang used CCP language to overpower Huang's individual will. The needs of the party legitimized the deprivation of individuals. An individual was a nonentity in the party, beyond his or her use as the party's tool. Although the principle of total submission was applied equally to both men and women, and both Huang and her husband suffered from their separation, Huang felt the pain much more deeply. She was a woman who "still had a deep feudal mentality." In her hometown, a woman who married twice would be drowned by her clan. Her three marriages had been a terrible burden on her heart. Now the third one was also beyond her control. At the time, she was only twenty-four years old. What would her future be? Was she going to marry a fourth time? Or must she remain single forever? Even if she did not consider the future, the immediate reality was that she had to bear the loss of another loved one.

Huang's case illustrates the fate of many female CCP members. The failure of the first alliance between the CCP and the GMD turned the CCP into an illegal and fugitive organization. Because an open mobilization of women was no longer possible in the GMD-controlled areas, except in the small red base areas, the party dropped its feminist agenda while struggling hard for its own survival. Women as a whole became an invisible entity within the party. Female CCP members such as Huang who were attracted to the party

71. Vengeful behavior such as X's was not uncommon in the CCP. The unequal power relations between genders often helped male comrades in higher positions sexually pursue female comrades. If a young woman declined unwanted attention from a male comrade who was her direct superior, she might jeopardize her chances for promotion, a better job assignment, and so on.

by gender issues in the first place had to abandon their efforts for women's emancipation.

Moreover, female CCP members experienced drastic transformation to meet the party's new needs. Instead of gathering in the gender-segregated sphere of "women's work," they were now requested to be genderless revolutionaries who should cut all family ties and responsibilities. If the female CCP members had been like the legendary Mulan, who was unmarried throughout her warrior career, it would have been easier for them to meet the new demands. However, as a result of "criticizing womanism" and because of the sex ratio in the party, few female Communists had remained single. Despite the fact that most women had husbands and children, they were told not to see themselves as wives or mothers, but as Communist revolutionaries. Their love for their families should be subordinate to their love for the party—otherwise, they were not proletarian but either bourgeois or feudalistic. Women's reduction to genderless proletarian revolutionaries was traumatic and tragic, as the story of Huang demonstrates.

Still, Huang was transformed. Repeated talks by male leaders such as He Chang and Zhou Enlai consolidated in her the dominance of the Communist subject position. That is why Huang emphasized the important "thought work" she experienced at critical moments. Each round of "thought work" sustained her through a trying period. Moreover, the accumulation of those "thought work" sessions provided Huang with canons of the CCP ideology that defined and constituted who she was. In her old age, after a long ordeal of imprisonment by the CCP, she still speaks the CCP language to define her identity. Nevertheless, she is not merely a CCP member. Rather, she is "a combination of Confucianism, Taoism, Buddhism, Marxism, and Leninism." This statement, made at the end of the interviews, expresses Huang's attempts to reconcile lifelong tensions within herself. As a Communist Party member, she has fought hard battles all her life. Now she needs to find peace in the "law of the unity of opposites." The changed political atmosphere of 1990s China and her recent family tragedy have weakened the Communist Party's dominance in her consciousness. She no longer tries to suppress other competing voices within her, and she is able to look at her life philosophically.

My last interview with Huang Dinghui was conducted in a convalescent hospital for high officials. Huang was recovering from her illness. She looked frail and weak. But she granted me the interview nevertheless. During our conversation, she took out a thick manuscript from her desk drawer. It was part of the transcript of her taped autobiography. She paid college students to transcribe those tapes. She was not pleased with the quality of the work, because the young students lacked historical knowledge of many events and people and often put in wrong words. In disregard of her poor health, Huang had been revising the transcript in the hospital. In my first interview with her two years before this, when she told me that she had written a few versions of her autobiography, I understood it mainly as her effort to win the party's acknowledgment of her seniority as a party member. But insofar as the CCP had subsequently recognized her as having been a party member since 1926, what was the drive behind her persistent determination to tell her own story?

Huang's thick, carefully edited manuscript reminded me of Wang Yiwei and her tombstone. These women who have participated in making history will not give up their struggle to claim their rightful place in history and to present a history as they have experienced it. In Huang's own words, "Whether I am a heroine or not, history will judge." "History," instead of the CCP, is the supreme judge. And Huang is determined to do as much as she can to shape this history. In the final analysis, the dominance of the party has far from subdued the loyal party member Huang Dinghui's expression of her own subjectivity, a subjectivity that has long been shaped by the prevailing Mulan-New Woman positions in the intellectual discourses of May Fourth China.

Epilogue

To recognize women as historical actors—vulnerable as men are
to forces beyond their control, striving as men do to shape the con-
tours of their lives as best they can—is to introduce into historical
work the analysis of gender relations . . .

   In seeking women's agency, we seek to recapture voices of
women in dialogue and in confrontation with men. We trust that
these voices will lend depth to our perception of what counts as
historically significant and that they will contribute information
about women even as they help us comprehend what enables and
sustains power for certain groups of men.

Introduction to U.S. History as Women's History[1]

The preceding epigraphic quotation—which came to my attention after I
had finished this study—articulates what I have striven to accomplish in
this work. What did Chinese women do in great historical events of the early
twentieth century? How did the "Chinese Enlightenment" impact or involve
women? What role did women play in the process of China's "modernization?" How did gender relations relate to the intellectual, social, and political
transformations of this century? And to what extent were gender relations
changed by women's and men's conscious efforts? Pursuing these questions, I have examined both men's and women's voices in early-twentieth-
century China. Whereas the May Fourth men's voices, expressed in their
writings, describe an exciting period of establishing their leadership in the
rapid social and intellectual changes of the early twentieth century, our female narrators depict a historical process in which women, far from being
passive followers, were both constructs and agents of historical change. The
narratives in this study testify to the existence of a social group unnoticed
by previous studies of China's Republican period. Career women emerged
from the May Fourth new women as a new social category in the early twentieth century.

   1. Linda K. Kerber, Alice Kessler-Harris, and Kathryn Kish Sklar, eds., *U.S. History as Women's History: New Feminist Essays* (Chapel Hill: University of North
Carolina Press, 1995), 7.

New Culture feminism circulated widely during the May Fourth era and provoked rapid and sweeping social changes in early-twentieth-century China. Considering the fact that it took American women seventy years of hard struggle to obtain women's suffrage, the rapid development of feminism in China and its achievements in the first few decades of the twentieth century were remarkable. This unique phenomenon was made possible by a combination of several historical factors. First of all, women's status had been associated with the future of China in the nationalist discourse for several decades. In raising the issue of women, the New Culturalists continued and consolidated an established nationalistic theme, rather than departed drastically from the intellectual mainstream.

Second, the power of the West gave a special authority to modern Chinese intellectuals who obtained a Western education. Semicolonized China was ready for a Western prescription for self-strengthening. In the pressing race against the West as perceived by most educated Chinese early in this century, China needed knowledge about Western culture. Modern intellectuals' knowledge about the West, articulated by New Culturalists in the form of universal truths, quickly won them a large audience and social prestige. Though feminism was a marginal discourse in the West, in China it was considered part of the universal truth and an indicator of a higher stage of civilization. Adopting feminism was seen as a crucial strategy for China to accelerate the speed of evolution in its race against the West, as well as a discursive practice for modern intellectuals to gain power.

Third, the disintegration of China's political power in the 1910s created a vacuum that modern intellectuals' discursive power could fill. Western ideologies were turned into subversive weapons in the hands of the New Culturalists, whose publishing activities were largely unchecked. Confucianism—the target of their attack—lacked strong political backing in this period, and therefore the New Culturalists were unencumbered in their advocacy of "heresies." The lively national debate on women's problems attracted large followings with diverse political orientations and intellectual backgrounds, indicative of the relaxed intellectual atmosphere in the early twentieth century.

Fourth, this large and diverse audience for New Culture messages was a social precondition for the swift rise of New Culturalists and for the wide circulation of feminism. A guide could not be a guide without followers, and an emancipator could not be an emancipator without those seeking emancipation. Under the impact of Western ideas, early-twentieth-century urbanization and modern education in China—including women's formal education—had prepared a major constituency for feminism: May Fourth students, male and female. Without this cohort of urban educated women and men, who were removed from the constraints of Chinese rural society, and to whom New Culture feminism made sense, the New Culturalists would have preached without an audience. These May Fourth women and men not only served as receptive audience, but also proved to be dynamic social agents who soon played an important part in the making of a feminist discourse in China.

When the National Revolution concluded this era of rapid cultural change, New Culture feminist agitation and women's spontaneous activism were eclipsed by a powerful nationalism promoted by the alliance of China's two political parties. However, feminism did not "fail" or disappear at that point. Rather, as a viable discourse, New Culture feminism continuously affected the historical processes of twentieth-century China. A whole generation of educated women with a new subjectivity were both constituted by and contributed to the feminist discourse in China. Pursuing a human life with an independent personhood, May Fourth new women not only created a life's journey drastically different from their mothers', but through their conscious, individual and collective efforts also brought or sustained institutional changes that enabled Chinese women's social advancement in the first half of the century.

The five narratives in this study illustrate new women's feminist efforts in the fields of education, law, and journalism and in other social institutions. But the sites of feminist contestation are not limited to individual women's maneuvers at the local level. Along with the growing power of political parties, feminism entered the state polity. After May Fourth, the women's movement became a badge of modernity that both the Communist Party and Nationalist Party claimed to wear. The two parties' institutionalization of the women's movement dampened the prospects for an independent women's movement in China. In spite of this, their appropriation of the New Culture feminist agenda had positive effects for women. When either party controlled state power, it incorporated women's equal legal rights into its legislation. Moreover, the parties' endorsement of women's emancipation made it possible for some women to occupy a place within the male power structure. Feminists in both the CCP and the GMD promoted women's advancement whenever they were able to do so.

From its inception, the CCP built its legitimacy by embracing women's emancipation as one of its goals. Although the party excluded feminism as the antithetical "other" in the process of seeking and consolidating political control over women, it was nonetheless a radical political organization that was shaped by May Fourth feminism and attracted many feminists.

Once the party gained political control of the nation, it implemented institutional changes that not only followed a Marxist-Leninist blueprint but also expressed May Fourth feminist ideals. In her study of the CCP's feminist history, Christina Gilmartin remarks, "After 1949 the party kept alive much of the language and rituals of women's emancipation, providing a legitimate basis within the Communist state for anyone with the determination and savvy to utilize them."[2] From the first Marriage Law in 1950, which was drafted by a group of May Fourth feminists within the party, to the CCP general secretary's speech titled "Gender Equality Is a Fundamental State Policy" in 1996, the CCP's gender policies tell a story of continuous feminist contestation within the system of the party-state.[3] Under the rubric of the party-led Chinese women's liberation, we may find practices reflecting Marxist ideas of women's participation in social production, socialist-feminist visions of public kitchens, nurseries, and other social welfare facilities for women, and liberal feminist concerns for women's equal rights in all spheres.

It is important to emphasize that even though the social space for spontaneous feminist activities was closed in the Mao era—as our narrators' stories demonstrate—much of the May Fourth feminist discourse has been incorporated in the dominant political discourse of the People's Republic of China. Even when a market economy takes priority over social and economic justice, the party leaders nevertheless must proclaim their adherence to gender equality. Gender equality and modernity were cemented so fast by the New Culturalists that no Chinese ruling group claiming to lead the nation toward modernity has openly tried to separate them. Meanwhile, women who grew up in the Mao era of gender equality have been increasingly conscious of the power of this dominant gender discourse in their negotiation with the state for women's interest.

2. Christina Kelly Gilmartin, *Engendering the Chinese Revolution: Radical Women, Communist Politics, and Mass Movements in the 1920s* (Berkeley: University of California Press, 1995), 216.

3. The Marriage Law of 1950 was drafted by the Women's Committee of the Central Committee of the CCP. Deng Yingchao and a group of May Fourth feminists played a crucial role in writing this law, which expressed many May Fourth feminist ideas. See Jin Feng, *Deng Yingchao zhuan* [A biography of Deng Yingchao] (Beijing: Renmin chubanshe, 1993), 457–461, and Deng Yingchao, "Guanyu Zhonghua renmin gongheguo hunyinfa de baogao" [A report on the Marriage Law of the People's Republic of China], in *Zhongguo funü yundong wenxian ziliao huibian* [Source material of Chinese women's movement], ed. Chinese Women Management Cadres College (Beijing: Zhongguo funü chubanshe, 1988), 2: 49–64.

For the general secretary's speech, see *Zhongguo funü bao* [China women's news], March 8, 1996.

Presenting this study to a Western audience in an age of poststructuralism and postcolonialism, I may be running against the current academic tide. Western bourgeois liberalism has been severely criticized by poststructuralist scholars. The influential critique of orientalism has called into question attempts to disseminate Western liberal values in non-Western cultures.[4] In this context, my work is likely to strike a dissonant note, because I emphasize that Western liberal concepts of human rights, equality, and independence served as a major driving force in Chinese women's emancipation in the early twentieth century.

As a woman from China, a country with a history of semicolonization, I neither worry about the taint of "cultural imperialism" nor identify entirely with intellectual concerns generated in countries with a history of colonizing or being colonized. What concerns me is what can be or what might have been useful for Chinese women in their struggle for social advancement and improvement. Historically, as this study demonstrates, the liberal concept of human rights empowered an entire generation of educated Chinese women to break away from the confinement of the Confucian cultural framework and to step into the public arena in large numbers for the first time in Chinese history. "You are a human being, and I am a human being, too. Whatever rights you have, I should have, too." At ninety-three, Zhu Su'e still recalled those phrases that had changed her consciousness in her youth. For this Chinese woman and many others, Western liberalism did not present itself as imperialist cultural hegemony. Rather, in the Chinese context, it provided a discourse of resistance, facilitating Chinese men's and women's struggles against the hegemonic Confucian framework. Western liberalism, feminism, or any other Western ideology was not imposed on Chinese by colonizers but was actively deployed and appropriated by various Chinese social groups in their pursuit of self-interest and national interest. In this process the Chinese actors redefined or resignified the meanings of foreign concepts to express their localized concerns. Moreover, women's knowledge about human rights and Western women's struggle for equal rights, as the Chinese term *nüquan* signifies, was decisive in shaping their ability to reinvent and create themselves as historical actors rather than as objects. These May Fourth women's stories illustrate a particular historical process and a unique set of dynamics in semicolonized China—a process and dynamics that cannot be reduced to or conflated with those experienced by people in colonized countries.

In contrast to what happened in the West, the introduction of Western

4. See Edward Said, *Orientalism* (New York: Vintage Books, 1979).

liberalism to China in the early twentieth century did not result in a cultural hegemony of bourgeois liberalism. Instead, Chinese Marxism in the form of Maoism has been the dominant discourse since midcentury. In the Maoist discourse, Chinese women were simultaneously empowered and subjugated. They were empowered to the extent that gender equality was legalized by the state and women were encouraged to step into the public arena for socialist construction. They were subjugated in the sense that the party became the patriarch who demanded total submission and sacrifice from women in the name of proletarian revolution. Thus, when "liberated" Chinese women played an important role in the country's social and economic life, the great majority of them had no say in defining issues related to women. The "liberated" Chinese women were reduced to a silent majority not only because the patriarchal state monopolized political power, but also because the party's overbearing class analysis and the party's myth that Chinese women were liberated deprived women of the language to name women's problems. Compared with the May Fourth new women, the urban educated women of the Mao era enjoyed more institutionalized gender equality but far less political autonomy. Significantly, whereas "equality between men and women" became a household term in the Mao era, "human rights" and "independence" lost their currency.

In the post-Mao era, Chinese intellectuals have criticized Maoism as "feudal totalitarianism," a term that suggests that Maoism maintained Chinese traditional political culture. Perhaps the most salient cultural continuity in Maoism is its open call for the subjection of individual will and individual rights in the name of proletarian revolution. The continuous suppression of liberalism in the CCP resulted in a dictatorship that culminated in the Cultural Revolution. It is not surprising that after the Cultural Revolution, Chinese intellectuals tried to revive liberalism as a discourse of resistance. In a culture that lacks the concept of individual rights, a populace yearning for social and economic justice can be used by the ruling class as a basis for despotism—a lesson that the Chinese have painfully learned in the course of the reign of Chinese Marxism. Although both liberalism and Marxism are products of the Western enlightenment that were embraced by various early-twentieth-century Chinese groups, the emphasis on individual rights has the stronger appeal to late-twentieth-century Chinese intellectuals, as they try to resist the powerful state and pursue a more humane society.

Understandably, many Chinese women and men in the post-Mao era have turned to the West for intellectual weapons, just as their May Fourth predecessors did. Emerging from the "Mao dynasty," they feel a strong affinity with New Culture intellectuals. The May Fourth cultural critique is still valid in many respects. And the sources of resistance against the Maoist hegemony can still be found in Western ideologies. For many contemporary Chinese intellectuals, the attraction of Western liberalism has been correlated with the suppression of individual freedom by the CCP. Since the May Fourth era, liberalism has maintained its edge as a discourse of resistance in China. Today, the concept of human rights is used by men to negotiate for the elimination of political persecution and for the reduction of party control. It is used by women to demand women's equal opportunity in education and employment and women's protection from violence. Even the Chinese government has appropriated the discourse of human rights to serve its own purpose. It declares that human rights for Chinese are rights to survival, dismissing the notion of universal human rights as a relic of Western imperialism. With this stance—which is ironically similar to some poststructuralists' critique—the Chinese government has successfully resisted Western pressure to democratize. The eighteenth-century bourgeois liberals could have never imagined that their invention would be used in so many innovative ways.

The story of liberalism in China illustrates that Western ideologies have always been strategically used by various Chinese interest groups for specific ends. That Chinese intellectuals were able to empower themselves by appropriating Western knowledge certainly reveals the power relations between the West and China. In the power structure of the twentieth-century world, it can hardly be imagined that social groups in the West would rise to power by circulating knowledge about China. Even in the 1960s, when Mao's revolution inspired leftist students in the West, those students remained marginal in their own societies. Ironically, this testifies to the limits on intellectual choice for marginal groups in globally powerful nations. In this sense, living at the periphery of the world economy, the New Culturalists were an enviable marginal group, because the unequal relations between the West and China added power to their resistance against Chinese culture hegemony. In sum, the story of the New Culturalists and the May Fourth new women reveals two significant points about the transplanting of Western discourse. First, even in their semicolonial positions, Chinese men and women did not adopt ready-made Western concepts blindly but played the role of historical agents in appropriating those concepts for their own specific ends. Second, the "specific deployments of discourse for specific political purpose determine the very notions used";[5] regardless of whether a

5. Judith Butler and Joan W. Scott, introduction to *Feminists Theorize the Political*, ed. Judith Butler and Joan W. Scott (New York: Routledge, 1992), xiii.

discourse is dominant or marginal in its native culture, the power relations a discourse constitutes are not fixed but contextualized. This understanding enables a Chinese scholar who is looking for sources of resistance to be open to any discourse that may serve Chinese women's interests in a particular historical context.

Apart from theoretical underpinnings, a historian's view of a historical subject is usually formed by historical documents available to him or her. My encounter with the living May Fourth new women profoundly changed my assumptions about the Chinese women's movement, the history of feminism in China, and the May Fourth women. Their oral histories have not only shaped my understanding of the new social category of career women in early-twentieth-century China, but also enabled me to discern from the multiple discourses of the May Fourth era the ones meaningful to them. Without their personal testimonies, I would have felt lost in my attempt to determine what constituted the new consciousness of new women.

Because of the availability of these oral histories, I have been able to explore the connection between texts and women's consciousness. Not all texts had an equal impact on educated women. Not all educated women responded to New Culture feminism in the same way. Something that predated our narrators' exposure to feminist discourse made them receptive to the new subject position of an independent new woman. That something was their personal experience in their early years. Although they lived in different locations and had different family backgrounds when young, their indelible early memories all highlighted gender inequality.

At the beginning of this century, Chinese culture was replete with practices that would constitute experiences exclusively for women. It was woman who had to suffer the pain of footbinding as a little girl; to be treated as a lesser being than her brothers; to face the horror of being sold as a concubine, a child bride, or a prostitute; to bear intense apprehensions on her wedding day when she was sent to live forever after with a stranger's family; to endure unspeakable anguish when her husband or her father frequented brothels or brought home a concubine; to go through the pain of childbirth and the fear of giving birth to a baby girl; to manage to survive an abusive husband with neither recourse to help nor release from the miserable marriage; and to be excluded from the men's world. Regardless of her class background and geographical location, the chances for a Chinese woman to escape all of the preceding "women's experiences" were rare, because the gender-biased system was her way of life. With or without a language to define the meanings of her experiences, she felt physical pain and mental anguish and was consciously aware that those sufferings belonged only to women.

As our narrators' stories reveal, it was the experience of suffering, the injustice they felt as young girls, and the desire to escape from women's predicament that made these young women run so eagerly in the directions toward which New Culture feminism turned them. They had had enough of life as a "Woman." Now they wanted to live as a "Human." Their flight shows us, as nothing else can, why liberal humanism had a strong appeal for them. Their flight also shows us that, if not for their shared anguish and anger at woman's lot, they would have lacked the desire to pursue a different life in the first place. A May Fourth new woman, in this sense, was made in a process constituted of the following parts: "women's experiences," a desire to escape from those experiences or to refuse to accept them as her fate, an encounter with new concepts that enabled her to name those experiences as "oppression of women," and material possibility to live a "human" life.

Though the narrators vividly demonstrate how concepts of "human rights" and "women's equal rights" empowered them, we also notice that this empowerment was far from a universal experience for all Chinese women in that period. Illiteracy, poverty, and physical isolation from the sources of information made the majority of Chinese women unaware of those empowering ideas. More important, even if new ideas had been available everywhere, not all women would have had the luxury to live the "human" life prescribed in the New Culture feminism. This "human" was not only masculine but also middle-class. The new women's ability to enjoy masculine privileges was often a function of their class standing. And the new women's active career and public life was possible often because they could afford one or several domestic servants. Though the new women achieved an independent "human" life, their women servants—though also living independently on their own labor—might not even dare to dream of a "human" life. The class stratification largely explains the fact that although women of different classes more or less share "women's experiences," only a small number of women were able to materialize a new woman subject position.

Embracing gender equality as the major tenet in human rights, the new women were proud of being able to do whatever men could do. Masculine bias inherent in the humanist position was not an issue in those days. Chinese women began to feel the oppression of masculine bias in gender equality in the Mao era, when to function like a man outside the home was no longer a personal choice but a state mandate. Under the socialist planned economy that practiced a universal low income intended to reduce class stratification, female urban professionals were no longer able to afford someone to do "women's job" at home; at the same time, domestic work was devalued and denigrated in the official and masculine value system, while women continued to carry the major burden of domesticity. Gender equality, or "assimilation to a preexisting male norm," became increasingly taxing and limiting, especially to urban professional women. It was against this historical background that urban educated women in the post-Mao era rejected the assimilatory gender equality and advocated "being a woman."[6] Thus, within a century, different generations of Chinese educated women have walked the path from "being a human" to "being a woman" in their pursuit of emancipation.

Yet our protagonists in this work never swayed in their pursuit of being a human, because the misery of being a woman was always fresh in their memory. What is more, their past experiences of striving for independent personhood, as well as for the welfare of other women and the nation, gave dignity and meaning to their lives. Even though their struggles and achievements have long been forgotten in China, these women cherish that part of their lives, even in their old age. As a historian, I cherish these women's life stories no less than they do. They help reconstruct a historical period in which many Chinese women rose up to challenge the conventions, to change gender relations, and to transform the social landscape of urban China. They unequivocally demonstrate that New Culture feminism empowered a group of Chinese women who became important social agents in the historical process of the twentieth century. I hope that, in these respects and more, the May Fourth women's meaningful experiences as constructed by both the narrators and the historian will become part of the knowledge that not only contributes to our understanding of the past but also sheds light on our current theoretical explorations in cross-cultural women's studies.

---

6. The phrase "assimilation to a preexisting male norm" is from Jane Flax, "The Play of Justice," in *disputed subjects: essays on psychoanalysis, politics, and philosophy* (Routledge: New York, 1993), 113.

Glossary

Aiguo	爱国	Chen Duxiu	陈独秀
Aiguo nüzhong	爱国女中	Chen Guangfu	陈光甫
Ba Jin	巴金	Chen Heqin	陈鹤琴
Bai Chongxi	白崇禧	Chen Lifu	陈立夫
baihua	白话	Chen Tanqiu	陈潭秋
Baihua	《白话》	Chen Tiedi	陈铁迪
bangyan	榜眼	Chen Wangdao	陈望道
Beiyang shuishi	北洋水师	Chen Wentao	陈问涛
bi	婢	Chen Yiyi	陈以益
Bing Xin	冰心	Chen Yongsheng	陈泳声
Cai Chang	蔡畅	Chen Zhigao	陈志皋
Cai Hesen	蔡和森	Chenbao	《晨报》
Cai Muhui	蔡慕晖	chiren	吃人
Cai Yuanpei	蔡元培	congyi'erzhong	从一而终
canzheng	参政	dageming	大革命
canzheng yundong	参政运动	Dai Jinhua	戴锦华
chanfu	产妇	Dai Li	戴笠
changpao magua	长袍马褂	datong shijie	大同世界
Changsha	长沙	Datong shu	《大同书》
Changzhou	常州	Deng Chunlan	邓春兰
Chen Bainian	陈百年	denglong ku	灯笼裤
Chen Dongyuan	陈东原	Deng Xiaoping	邓小平

Deng Yingchao	邓颖超	Guangdong funü	《广东妇女》
Deshengmen	德胜门	gulao	孤老
Ding Ling	丁玲	Guo Moruo	郭沫若
Dong Biwu	董必武	Guo Zhenyi	郭箴一
Dongfang zazhi	《东方杂志》	Guomin huiyi cujin yundong	
Du Yuying	杜玉英		国民会议促进运动
Duan Qirui	段祺瑞	Guomindang	国民党
duli renge	独立人格	He Baozhen	何葆珍
feiren	非人	He Chang	贺昌
feiren de shenghuo		He Xiangning	何香凝
非人的生活		He Zhen	何震
Feng Yuxiang	冯玉祥	Hu Die	胡蝶
fengmao linjiao	凤毛麟角	Hu Shi	胡适
fu	妇	Hu Xiufeng	胡绣枫
fumi'nieshimu	弗弥涅士姆	Hu Yuzhi	胡愈之
funü jiefang yundong		Hua Mulan	花木兰
妇女解放运动		Huadongju	华东局
Funü weilaohui	妇女慰劳会	Huang Biyao	黄碧遥
funü wenti	妇女问题	Huang Dinghui	黄定慧
Funü zazhi	《妇女杂志》	Huang Mulan	黄慕兰
funü zhuyi	妇女主义	Huang Xing	黄兴
gandie	干爹	Huang Yanpei	黄炎培
ganma	干妈	Huanqiu xueshenghui	
gannüer	干女儿	环球学生会	
gao nüquande	搞女权的	huaping	花瓶
Gao Shan	高山	huifu nüquan	恢复女权
Geng Xinzhi	耿馨之	Hujiang daxue	沪江大学
Gong Xueping	龚学平	Hunan	湖南
Gu Shunzhang	顾顺章	Jiang Qing	江青
Gu Weijun	顾维钧	jianquande	健全的
Gu Zhenglai	顾正来	jianyin	奸淫
Guan Lu	关露	jiaozi	轿子
Guan Xiangying	关向应	jiefu	节妇

jielie 节烈

Jiezhi yuekan 《节制月刊》

Jiliangsuo 济良所

jinguo yingxiong 巾帼英雄

jinshi 进士

Jin Shiyin 金石音

Jin Tanhe 金天翮

Jin Yi 金一

Jing Xiong 竞雄

Jing Yuanshan 经元善

Jiujiang ruli shuyuan
　九江儒励书院

junweiqing, minweigui
　君为轻,民为贵

juren 举人

kai houmen 开后门

kang 炕

Kang Baiqing 康白情

Kang Dan 康丹

Kang Sheng 康生

Kang Tongbi 康同璧

Kang Youwei 康有为

kangzhan furen 抗战夫人

keji fuli 克己复礼

kezhang 科长

Lao Qiuying 劳秋英

lao xiaojie 老小姐

Li Dazhao 李大钊

Li Gongpu 李公朴

Li Hongzhang 李鸿章

Li Jianhua 李剑华

Li Lisan 李立三

Li Peilan 李佩兰

Li Qiujun 李秋君

Li Tieying 李铁映

Li Weihan 李维汉

Li Yuanhong 黎元洪

Li Zifen 李子芬

lian'ai 恋爱

lian'ai ziyou 恋爱自由

Liang Hongyu 梁红玉

Liang Qichao 梁启超

Liao Zhongkai 廖仲凯

liefu 烈妇

lienü 烈女

Lin Zongsu 林宗素

Liu Bannong 刘半农

Liu Qingyang 刘清扬

Liu Shaowen 刘少文

Liu Yazi 柳亚子

Liu Zhan'en 刘湛恩

Liu-Wang Liming
　刘王立明

lou datui 露大腿

Lu Hefeng 陆合丰

Lu Lihua 陆礼华

Lu Suying 陆素英

Lu Xun 鲁迅

Lu Yin 庐隐

Lü Yunzhang 弓云章

Lu Zhenquan 陆振权

Luo Jialun 罗家伦

Luo Jianbing 骆剑冰

Luo Longji 罗隆基

Luo Suwen 罗苏文

Ma Renchang 马仁常

Ma Xiangbo	马相伯
Man Jiang Hong	《满江红》
Mao Dun	茅盾
Mei Sheng	梅生
Meiguo liuxuesheng	美国留学生
Meng Yue	孟悦
Mian nüquan ge	《勉女权歌》
Miao-Cheng Shuyi	缪程淑仪
ming	命
mingfen	名份
mufu	幕府
Mulan ci	《木兰辞》
Namowen	拿摩温
nannü pingdeng	男女平等
nannü shoushou buqin 男女授受不亲	
nanxing	男性
Neixun	《内训》
Nie Rongzhen	聂荣臻
nü	女
nübannanzhuang	女扮男装
Nüfan	《女范》
Nüjie	《女论语》
Nüjie zhong	《女界种》
Nülunyu	《女诫》
Nuola	娜拉
nüquan	女权
nüquan geming	女权革命
Nüquan pingyi	《女权评议》
nüquan yundong	女权运动
Nüquan yundong tongmenhui 女权运动同盟会	
nüquan zhuyi	女权主义
nüquan zhuyizhe	女权主义者
Nüsheng	《女声》
nüxia	女侠
nüxing	女性
Nüxing	《女星》
nüxing zhuyi	女性主义
Nüxingshe	女星社
Nüxuebao	《女学报》
nüxuesheng	女学生
nüyingxiong	女英雄
nüzi	女子
Nüzi canzheng tongmenghui 女子参政同盟会	
Nüzi canzheng xiejinhui 女子参政协进会	
nüzi zhuyi	女子主义
Pan Gongzhan	潘公展
Pan Hannian	潘汉年
paotou loumian	抛头露面
Pei Wei	佩韦
peiqian huo	赔钱货
Peng Ji'nen	彭季能
Peng Pai	澎湃
Peng Qingxiu	彭庆修
Peng Zigang	彭子冈
Qi Wen	绮纹
Qian Jianqiu	钱剑秋
Qian Liqun	钱理群
Qian Xinzhi	钱新之
Qianziwen	《千字文》
qiangbao	墙报
qiangzhong baoguo	强种保国
qijunzi	七君子

Qin Bangxian	秦邦宪	sishu	私塾
Qincheng	秦城	Sishu wujing	四书五经
Qiu Jin	秋瑾	Song Jiaoren	宋教仁
Qu Qiubai	瞿秋白	Song Meiling	宋美龄
Qunyi shushe	群益书社	Song Qingling	宋庆龄
ren	人	Sun Xiyu	孙熙育
Ren xue	《仁学》	Sun Yat-sen	孙逸仙
rende quanli	人的权利	Sun Zhongshan	孙中山
renquan	人权	taitai	太太
sangang	三纲	Tan Sitong	谭嗣同
sanmin zhuyi	三民主义	Tan Yankai	谭延闿
Sanzijing	《三字经》	Tang Qunying	唐群英
saozhou xing	扫帚星	tanhua	探花
Shanbei gongxue	陕北公学	tanxiong loubi	袒胸露臂
Shang Yi	尚一	Tao Lügong	陶履恭
Shanghai funü yundong cujinhui 上海妇女运动促进会		Tao Xingzhi	陶行知
		Tian Han	田汉
Shanghai qiaobao	《上海侨报》	tianfu renquan	天赋人权
shangwu	尚武	Tianjin	天津
Shen Duanxian	沈端先	Tianyibao	《天义报》
Shen Junru	沈均儒	Tianzuhui	天足会
Shen Yanbing	沈雁冰	tingzijian	亭子间
Shen Zhiyuan	沈志远	tiyu	体育
Shen Zijiu	沈兹九	tiyu jiuguo	体育救国
Shenbao	《申报》	Tubaozi	土包子
shenglang	声浪	Tushanwan	土山湾
shensheng de muxing 神圣的母性		Wan Xixian	宛希贤
		Wan Xiyan	宛希俨
shenzhang nüquan	伸张女权	Wang Changguo	王昌国
Shi Liang	史良	Wang Ming	王明
Shibao	《时报》	Wang Pingling	王平陵
shiye jiuguo	实业救国	Wang Ruoyu	王若愚
Shu Wu	舒芜		

Wang Yiwei	王伊蔚	xiucai	秀才
Wang Yunzhang	王蕴章	Xu Guangping	许广平
Wang Ziping	王子平	Xu Shichang	徐世昌
Wang Zhenting	王振庭	Xu Shiheng	徐世衡
Wan'guo gongbao	《万国公报》	Xu Yanzhi	徐彦之
Wei Chuan	渭川	Xujiahui	徐家汇
Weilaohui	慰劳会	yamen	衙门
wen	文	Yan Shi	晏始
Wen Yiduo	闻一多	Yang Kaihui	杨开慧
Wenjiashi	文家市	Yang Meizhen	杨美珍
wenren	文人	Yang Xiuqiong	杨秀琼
Wenshiguan	文史馆	yang xuetang	洋学堂
wenwu shuangquan	文武双全	Yang Zhihua	杨之华
wu	武	Ye Shaojun	叶绍均
Wu Defeng	吴德凤	Yibosheng zhuyi	易卜生主义
Wu Yifang	吴贻芳	Yin Jin	尹进
Wu Yu	吴虞	Yin Tongwei	殷同薇
Wuchang	武昌	yi'niang	姨娘
Wuhan	武汉	Yizi hutong	椅子胡同
Xia Yan	夏衍	yougong	优贡
Xiandai funü	《现代妇女》	Yu Qingtang	俞庆棠
Xiang Jingyu	向警予	Yu Youren	于佑仁
Xiang Zhongfa	向忠发	yuan	元
Xiangbao	《湘报》	Yuan Shikai	袁世凯
xianli nüxiao	县立女校	yuezi	月子
Xie Bingying	谢冰莹	Yun Daiying	恽代英
Xie Daoyun	谢道蕴	Zenjiayan	曾家岩
xin nüxing	新女性	Zhan Tianyou	詹天佑
Xin Nüxing	《新女性》	Zhang Bojun	章伯均
Xin Zhu	心珠	Zhang Bolin	章伯麟
Xinchao	《新潮》	Zhang Gongquan	张公权
Xinmin Bao	《新民报》	Zhang Jian	张睿
Xinmin xuehui	新民学会	Zhang Naiqi	章乃器

Zhang Qinqiu 张琴秋

Zhang Wentian 张闻天

Zhang Xiangwen 张湘纹

Zhang Xichen 章锡琛

Zhang Yun 章蕴

Zhang Zhujun 张竹君

Zhao Puchu 赵朴初

Zheng Junli 郑君里

zhenjie paifang 贞节牌坊

zhennü 贞女

zhifu 知府

zhishi fenzi 知识分子

zhiye funü 职业妇女

Zhongguo funü 《中国妇女》

Zhongguo nübao 《中国女报》

Zhonghua funü guofanghui 中华妇女国防会

Zhonghua funü jiezhihui 中华妇女节制会

zhou 帚

Zhou Enlai 周恩来

Zhou Gucheng 周谷城

Zhou Jianren 周建人

Zhou Kuilong 周奎龙

Zhou Shuren 周树人

Zhou Wenji 周文玑

Zhou Zuoren 周作人

Zhu De 朱德

Zhu Jianfan 朱剑凡

Zhu Su'e 朱素萼

zhuangyuan 状元

zili menhu 自立门户

zuo sixiang gongzuo 做思想工作

zuo woziji 作我自己

Bibliography

WORKS IN CHINESE

All-China Women's Federation. *Zhongguo funü yundong shi* [A history of the Chinese women's movement]. Beijing: Chunqiu chubanshe, 1989.

————, ed. *Dageming hongliuzhong de nübing* [Women soldiers in the National Revolution]. Beijing: Zhongguo funü chubanshe, 1991.

————, ed. *Wusi shiqi funü wenti wenxuan* [Selected articles on women's problems in the May Fourth period]. Beijing: Zhongguo funü chubanshe, 1981.

————, ed. *Zhongguo funü yundong lishi ziliao* [Historical source materials of the Chinese women's movement]. Beijing: Renmin chubanshe, 1986.

————, ed. *Zhongguo funü yundong lishi ziliao, 1840–1918* [Historical source materials of the Chinese women's movement, 1840–1918]. Beijing: Zhongguo funü chubanshe, 1991.

Bao Jialin. "Qiu Jin yu Qingmo funü yundong" [Qiu Jin and the women's movement in the late Qing]. *Zhongguo funüshi lunji* [Collected essays on Chinese women's history], ed. Bao Jialin, 346–382. Taibei: Daoxiang chubanshe, 1992.

Beijing Women's Federation. *Beijing funü baokan kao* [A study of Beijing women's newspapers and periodicals]. Beijing: Guangming ribao chubanshe, 1990.

"Bianji yulu" [Editor's words]. *Funü zazhi* [The ladies' journal] 7, no. 7 (1921): 116.

"Bianji yulu" [Editor's words]. *Funü zazhi* [The ladies' journal] 8, no 12 (1922): 124.

"Buke budu benbao" [One has to read this journal]. *Nübao* [The women's journal], no. 2 (1909).

C. K. "Funü wenti yu Zhongguo funü yundong" [Women problems and the Chinese women's movement]. *Funü zazhi* [The ladies' journal] 8, no. 11 (1922): 55–56.

Chen Bainian. "Yifuduoqi de xinhufu" [A new amulet of polygamy]. *Xiandai pinglun* [Modern reviews], no. 14 (1925): 6–8.

Chen Dongyuan. *Zhongguo funü shenghuoshi* [A history of the lives of Chinese women]. Shanghai: Commercial Press, 1928.

Chen Duxiu. "Funü wenti yu shehuizhuyi" [The woman problem and socialism]. 1921. *Guangdong qunbao* [Guangdong masses], January 21, 1921. In *Wusi shiqi funü wenti wenxuan* [Selected articles on women's problems in the May Fourth period], ed. All-China Women's Federation, 82–83. Beijing: Zhongguo funü chubanshe, 1981.

———. "Jinggao qingnian" [To the youth]. *Xin qingnian* [New youth] 1, no. 1 (1915): 1–6.

———. "Kongzi zhi dao yu xiandai shenghuo" [The way of Confucius and modern life]. *Xin qingnian* [New youth] 2, no. 4 (1916): 1–7.

———. "Yijiuyiliu" [1916]. *Xin qingnian* [New youth] 1, no 5 (1915): 1–4.

Chen Shizhen. "Shenfucong nüzhou zhiyi" [On the definitions of "woman"]. *Funü zazhi* [The ladies' journal] 2, no. 4 (1916): 12.

Chen Wangdao. "Zhongguo nüzi de juexing" [The awakening of Chinese women]. *Xinnüxing* [The new woman] 1, no. 9 (1926): 637–641.

Chen Wentao. "Tichang dulixingde nüzi zhiye" [Promoting independent women's careers]. *Funü zazhi* [The ladies' journal] 7, no. 8 (1921): 7–11.

Chen Yiyi. "Nanzhun nübei yu xianmu liangqi" [Men are superior, women are inferior and virtuous mothers and good wives]. *Nübao* [The women's journal], no. 2 (1909): 4–7.

Chen Zhongguang. "Minguo chuqi funü diwei de yanbian" [The changing status of women in the early republic]. Master's thesis, The History Research Institute, Chinese Culture College, Taiwan, 1972.

Chinese Department at Jinan University, ed. *Zhongguo lidai shige mingpian shangxi* [A selection of famous poems in Chinese history]. Changsha: Hunan renmin chubanshe, 1983.

Cihai Compiling Committee, ed. *Cihai* [The sea of words]. Shanghai: Cishu chubanshe, 1980.

"Cuxi tan Wusi" [A chat on the May Fourth]. *Dongfang* [The Orient], no. 2 (1995): 24–25.

Dai Xugong and Yao Weidou, eds. *Xiang Jingyu wenji* [Papers by Xiang Jingyu]. Changsha: Hunan renmin chubanshe, 1985.

Deng Yingchao. "Guanyu Zhonghua renmin gongheguo hunyinfa de baogao" [A report on the Marriage Law of the People's Republic of China]. In *Zhongguo funü yundong wenxian ziliao huibian* [Source material of Chinese women's movement], ed. Chinese Women Management Cadres College, 2: 49–64. Beijing: Zhongguo funü chubanshe, 1988.

———. "Jiemeimen, qiyao!" [Sisters, rise up!]. In *Deng Yingchao yu Tianjin zaoqi funü yundong* [Deng Yingchao and the early women's movement in Tianjin], ed. Tianjin Women's Federation, 274–276. Beijing: Zhongguo funü chubanshe, 1987.

———. "Wusi yundong de huiyi" [Recollections of the May Fourth movement].

In *Wusi shiqi funü wenti wenxuan* [Selected articles on women's problems in the May Fourth period], ed. All-China Women's Federation, 1–7. Beijing: Zhongguo funü chubanshe, 1981.

"Deng Yingchao zai Shanghai gejie funü lianhehui fabiao yanshuo" [Deng Yingchao made a speech to the Shanghai Women's Association]. *Minguo ribao* [Republic daily], July 20, 1925. In *Zhongguo funü yundong lishi ziliao* [Historical source materials of the Chinese women's movement], ed. All-China Women's Federation, 347. Beijing: Renmin chubanshe, 1986.

Ding Fengjia. "Nüjie zhenyan" [Admonishing women]. *Funü zazhi* [The ladies' journal] 4 (1918), no. 2: 5–6 and no. 3: 1–4.

Dong Zhujun. *Wode yige shiji* [My century]. Beijing: Sanlian shudian, 1997.

Du Fangqin. *Nüxing guannian de yianbian* [The transformation of views on women]. Zhengzhou: Henan renmin chubanshe, 1988.

"Duqianhao" [Comments on the previous issue]. *Funü zazhi* [The ladies' journal] 9, no. 6 (1923): 121–123.

"Duzhe julebu" [Readers club]. *Funü zazhi* [The ladies' journal] 7, no. 5 (1921): 104–106.

Fang Minyun, Zhang Youren, Zi Yaohua, Shang Yi, Lu Ziran, Zhang Youhe, Huang Heji, et. al. "Woguo muqian funü yundong yingqu de fangzhen" [Policies that the Chinese women's movement should adopt]. *Funü zazhi* [The ladies' journal] 9, no. 1 (1923): 87–127.

"Feikanci" [Abandoning the journal address]. *Xinnüxing* [The new woman] 4, no. 48 (1929).

"Funü xinwen" [Women's news]. *Funü zazhi* [The ladies' journal] 6, no. 3 (1920): 4.

"Funü xinwen" [Women's news]. *Funü zazhi* [The ladies' journal] 6, no. 3 (1920): 4.

"Funü xinxiaoxi" [Women's news]. *Funü zazhi* [The ladies' journal] 6, no. 4 (1920): 6.

"Funü xinxiaoxi" [Women's news]. *Funü zazhi* [The ladies' journal] 6, no. 5 (1920): 6.

"Funü xinxiaoxi" [Women's news]. *Funü zazhi* [The ladies' journal] 6, no. 6 (1920): 16.

"Funü xinxiaoxi" [Women's news]. *Funü zazhi* [The ladies' journal] 6, no. 7 (1920): 8.

"Funü xinxiaoxi" [Women's news]. *Funü zazhi* [The ladies' journal] 6, no. 8 (1920): 38

"Funü xinxiaoxi" [Women's news]. *Funü zazhi* [The ladies' journal] 6, no. 11 (1920): 10.

"Funü yaowen" [Women's important news]. *Funü zazhi* [The ladies' journal] 6, no. 11 (1920): 6, 10.

Gao Shan. "Jianglai de nüquan yundong" [The future feminist movement]. *Funü zazhi* [The ladies' journal] 9, no. 12 (1923): 14–15.

Harada Minoru. "Fuminieshimu gaishuo" [On feminism]. Trans. Wei Xin. *Funü zazhi* [The ladies' journal] 8, no. 5 (1922): 64–71.

He He. "Liuge nantongxue geiwodexing" [Letters from six male classmates]. *Funü zazhi* [The ladies' journal] 9, no. 7 (1923): 41–44.

He Huzhi. *Xiang Jingyu zhuan* [A biography of Xiang Jingyu]. Shanghai: Shanghai renmin chubanshe, 1990.

He Jueyu. "Funü yundong de cuolu yu zhenggui" [The right and wrong routes of the women's movement]. *Funü zazhi* [The ladies' journal] 10, no. 4 (1924): 591–593.

Hu Shengwu. *Cong Xinhai geming dao wusiyundong* [From the Xinhai Revolution to the May Fourth movement]. Changsha: Hunan renmin chubanshe, 1983.

Hu Shi. "Lun nüzi wei qiangbao suowu" [On women who are raped]. In *Hu Shi wencun* [An anthology of Hu Shi]. Vol. 1: 685–686. Taibei: Yuandong tushu gongsi, 1968.

———. "Lun zhencao wenti" [On chastity]. In *Hu Shi wencun* [An anthology of Hu Shi]. Vol. 1: 676–684. Taibei: Yuandong tushu gongsi, 1968.

———. "Meiguo de furen" [American women]. *Xin qingnian* [New youth] 5, no. 3 (1918): 213–224.

———. "Yibosheng zhuyi" [Ibsenism]. *Xin qingnian* [New youth] 4, no. 6 (1918): 489–507.

———. "Zhencao wenti" [The chastity problem]. *Xin qingnian* [New youth] 5, no. 1 (1918): 5–14.

Hu Shizhi (Hu Shi). "Nüzi wentide kaiduan" [The beginning of the women's problem], a speech recorded by Zhao Jingshen. *Funü zazhi* [The ladies' journal] 8, no. 10 (1922): 125–128.

Huang Heji. "Xinfunü yingyou de juewu" [The consciousness that the new women should have]. *Funü zazhi* [The ladies' journal] 6, no. 10 (1920): 18–20.

Huang Yi'nong. "Guomin zhi di" [The enemy of republican citizens]. *Funü zazhi* [The ladies' journal] 5, no. 9 (1919): 5–6.

"Hubeisheng diyici funü daibiao dahui xuanchuan wenti jueyi an" [The resolution on propaganda by the First Women's Conference in Hubei province]. March 18, 1927. In *Zhongguo funü yundong lishi ziliao* [Historical source materials of the Chinese women's movement], ed. All-China Women's Federation, 767. Beijing: Renmin chubanshe, 1986.

Ji Zhe. "Benzazhi jinhou zhi fangzhen" [The future policy of our journal]. *Funü zazhi* [The ladies' journal] 5, no. 12 (1919): 1–3.

Ji Zhe (Zhang Xichen). "Women jinhou de taidu" [Our views of the future]. *Funü zazhi* [The ladies' journal] 10, no. 1 (1924): 2–7.

Jiang Xuehui. "Nüquan pingyi" [On women's power]. *Funü zazhi* [The ladies' journal] 4, no. 8 (1918): 4–7.

Jin Feng. *Deng Yingchao zhuan* [A biography of Deng Yingchao]. Beijing: Renmin chubanshe, 1993.

Jin Yi. *Nüjie zhong* [The women's bell]. Shanghai: Datong shuju, 1903.

Jing Lingzi. *Shihai Gouxuan* [Exploring in the sea of history]. Beijing: Kunlun Press, 1989.

Jinian Xinhai geming qishi zhounian xueshu taolunhui lunwenji [Papers from the conference on the seventieth anniversary of the Xinhai Revolution]. Beijing: Zhonghua shuju, 1983.

"Jishumen" [Reporting column]. *Funü zazhi* [The ladies' journal] 2, no. 3 (1916): 1–16; 3, no. 3 (1917): 1–16; 3, no. 5 (1917): 1–20; 3, no. 10 (1917): 1–16; and 5, no. 5 (1919): 1–8.

Kang Youwei. *Datong shu* [The book of one world]. Shanghai: Zhonghua Shuju, 1935.

Lao Qiuying. "Duiyu disan jieji funü de xiwang" [Hopes for women of the "number three class"]. *Funü zazhi* [The ladies' journal] 7, no. 10 (1921): 110.

Lao Zeren. "Zhongguo funü yundong de jianglai" [The future of the Chinese women's movement]. *Funü zazhi* [The ladies' journal] 7, no. 9 (1921): 7–10.

Li Da. "Nüzi jiefanglun" [On women's emancipation]. *Jiefang Yu Gaizao* [Emancipation and reform] 1, no. 3 (October 1919). In *Wusi shiqi funü wenti wenxuan* [Selected articles on women's problems in the May Fourth period], ed. All-China Women's Federation, 35–48. Beijing: Zhongguo funü chubanshe, 1981.

Li Dazhao. "Funü jiefang yu democracy" [Women's emancipation and democracy]. *Shaonian Zhongguo* [The young China] 1, no. 4 (1919). In *Wusi shiqi funü wenti wenxuan* [Selected articles on women's problems in the May Fourth period], ed. All-China Women's Federation, 26–27. Beijing: Zhongguo funü chubanshe, 1981.

———. "Zhanhou zhi furen wenti" [Women's problems after the war]. *Xin qingnian* [New youth] 6, no. 2 (1919). In *Wusi shiqi funü wenti wenxuan* [Selected articles on women's problems in the May Fourth period], ed. All-China Women's Federation, 15–20. Beijing: Zhongguo funü chubanshe, 1981.

Li Peilan. "Jiefanghou de funü rengeguan" [The emancipated women's view of personhood]. *Funü zazhi* [The ladies' journal] 6, no. 5 (1920): 1–4.

Li Renjie. "Nannü jiefang" [Men's and women's emancipation]. In *Zhongguo funü wenti taolunji* [Collected essays on Chinese women's problems], ed. Mei Sheng, 1: 68–88. Shanghai: Xinwenhua chubanshe, 1929.

Li Xiaojiang. *Xiawa de tansuo* [The exploration of Eve]. Zhengzhou: Henan renmin chubanshe, 1988.

Li Yu-ning. "Nüjie zhong yu Zhonghua nüxing de xiandaihua" [The women's bell and the modernization of Chinese women]. In *Jinshi jiazu yu zhengzhi bijiaolishi lunwenji* [Family process and political process in modern Chinese history], ed. Zhongyang Yanjiuyuan jindaishi yanjiusuo, part 2, 1055–1082. Taibei: Zhongyang Yanjiuyuan jindaishi yanjiusuo, 1992.

Li Yu-ning and Zhang Yufa, eds. *Jindai Zhongguo nüquan yundong shiliao* [Historical source material on the modern Chinese feminist movement]. Taibei: Zhuanji wenxue chubanshe, 1975.

Lian Shi. "Funü de feiren shidai" [The inhuman age of women]. *Funü zazhi* [The ladies' journal] 9, no. 4 (1923): 44–46.

Liang Lingxian. "Jingshu wujia jiude wei funüzazhi shi" [Presenting my family morality to *The Ladies' Journal*]. *Funü zazhi* [The ladies' journal] 1, no. 1 (1915): 6–8.

Liang Qichao. "Bianfatongyi" [General ideas on reform]. In *Zhongguo funü shenghuoshi* [A history of the lives of Chinese women], by Chen Dongyuan, 321–324. Shanghai: Commercial Press, 1928.

———. "Changshe nüxuetang qi" [A suggestion to establish girls' schools]. *Shiwubao* 44 (1898). In *Jindai Zhongguo nüquan yundong shiliao* [Historical source material on the modern Chinese feminist movement], ed. Li Yu-ning and Zhang Yufa, 561–562. Taibei: Zhuanji wenxue chubanshe, 1975.

Liu Sheng. "Fakanci" [Opening remarks]. *Funü zazhi* [The ladies' journal] 1, no. 1 (1915): 2–4.

Liu-Wang Liming. *Zhongguo funü yundong* [The Chinese women's movement]. Shanghai: Commercial Press, 1933.

"Liu-Wang Liming zhuidaohui zaijing juxing" [Liu-Wang Liming's memorial service held in Beijing]. *Renmin ribao* [People's daily], March 19, 1981.

Lu Xun. "Bianwan xieqi" [Afterword]. In *Xin xingdaode taolun ji* [A collection of debate on the new sexual morality], ed. Zhang Xichen, 98–99. Shanghai: Kaiming shudian, 1929.

———. "Kuangren riji" [A madman's diary]. 1918. In *Lu Xun xuanji* [Selected works of Lu Xun], ed. Wenxue chubanshe, 53–63. Hong Kong: Wenxue chubanshe, 1956.

———. *Liangdishu* [Letters between two places]. Beijing: Renmin wenxue chubanshe, 1973.

———. "Zhufu" [The new year's sacrifice]. 1924. *Lu Xun xuanji* [Selected works of Lu Xun], ed. Wenxue chubanshe, 78–94. Hong Kong: Wenxue chubanshe, 1956.

Lü Yunzhang. *Funü wenti lunwenji* [A collection of papers on women's problems]. Shanghai: Nüzi shudian, 1933.

Lu Zhenquan. "Fu cong nüzhou shi" [Defining "woman"]. *Funü zazhi* [The ladies' journal] 2, no. 5 (1916): 2–3.

Luo Jialun. "Jinri Zhongguo zhi zazhijie" [Magazines in contemporary China]. In *Zhongguo xiandai chuban shiliao* [Historical materials on publishing in modern China], ed. Zhang Jinglu, 79–86. Beijing: Zhonghua shuju, 1954.

Luo Liuzhi. "Nüquan yundong lingxiu Tang Qunying" [Tang Qunying: A leader of the feminist movement]. *Funü* [Women] (Shenyang), no. 3 (1983): 25.

Luo Suwen. *Nüxing yu jindai Zhongguo shehui* [Women and modern Chinese society]. Shanghai: Shanghai renmin chubanshe, 1996.

———. "Zhongguo diyisuo ziban nüxiao" [The first girls' school established by the Chinese]. *Shehui Kexue* (Shanghai) 2 (1988): 144–146.

Luo Yijun, ed. *Ping xinrujia* [On New Confucians]. Shanghai: Shanghai renmin chubanshe, 1989.

M. Y. H. "Qingnian qiouai wenti" [The problem of courtship among youth]. *Funü zazhi* [The ladies' journal] 9, no. 9 (1923): 124–125.

Ma Renchang. "Ren bi ruhe er houneng duli lun" [On what one can do to achieve independence]. *Funü zazhi* [The ladies' journal] 4, no. 4 (1918): 2.

Mao Dun (Shen Yanbing). *Wo zouguo de daolu* [The journey I have made]. Hong Kong: Sanlian shudian, 1981.

Mei Sheng, ed. *Funü nianjian* [An almanac of women]. Shanghai: Wenhua shushe, 1924.

———, ed. *Nüxing wenti yanjiuji* [Collected studies of women's problems]. Shanghai: Wenhua shushe, 1928.

———, ed. *Zhongguo funü wenti taolunji* [Collected essays on Chinese women's problems]. Shanghai: Xinwenhua chubanshe, 1929.

Meng Yue and Dai Jinhua. *Fuchu lishi dibiao* [Emerging from history]. Zhengzhou: Henan renmin chubanshe, 1989.

Miao-Cheng Shuyi. "Xiang yu funü" [Scent and women]. *Funü zazhi* [The ladies' journal] 6, no. 3 (1920): 1–5.

"Ni'ai zuguo, zuguo geng'aini" [You love the country, the country loves you more]. *Xinmin Wanbao* [Shanghai evening news], February 14, 1995.

"Nüquan Yundong Tongmenghui xuanyan" [Declaration of the Feminist Movement Association]. *Funü zazhi* [The ladies' journal] 8, no. 9 (1922): 126–127.

Pei Wei (Shen Yanbing). "Funü jiefang wenti de jianshe fangmian" [Constructing women's emancipation]. *Funü zazhi* [The ladies' journal] 6, no. 1 (1920): 1–5.

———. "Jiefang de funü yu funu de jiefang" [Emancipated women and women's emancipation]. *Funü zazhi* [The ladies' journal] 5, no. 11 (1919): 1–6.

———. "Ping xinfunü" [On the new women]. *Funü zazhi* [The ladies' journal] 6, no. 2 (1920): 1–3.

Peng Ji'neng. "Jinri Zhongguo nüzi yingjuewu de yidian—zijide zeren" [A point today's Chinese women should be conscious of—self-responsibility]. *Funü zazhi* [The ladies' journal] 6, no. 6 (1920): 1–4.

Piao Ping Nüshi. "Lixiang zhi nüxuesheng" [The ideal female students]. *Funü zazhi* [The ladies' journal] 1, no. 3 (1915): 1–4.

Qi Wen. "Zhenshi de funü jiefang zai nazhong tiaojianxia caineng shixian?" [Under what conditions would a true women's emancipation be realized?]. *Zhongguo funü* [Chinese women], no. 2 (January 1926): 4–5.

Qian Liqun. *Zhou Zuoren lun* [On Zhou Zuoren]. Shanghai: Shanghai renmin chubanshe, 1991.

Qiu Jin. "Mian nüquan ge" [Promoting women's rights]. *Zhongguo nübao* [Chinese women's periodical], no. 2 (1907). In *Jindai Zhongguo nüquan yundong shilao* [Historical source material on the modern Chinese feminist movement], ed. Li Yu-ning and Zhang Yufa, 441. Taibei: Zhuanji wenxue chubanshe, 1975.

Russell, Madam (Dora Black). "Zhongguo de nüquanzhuyi yu nüxing gaizao yundong" [Chinese feminism and the female reform movement]. Trans. Yun He. *Funü zazhi* [The ladies' journal] 9, no. 1 (1923): 50–55.

Se Lu (Zhang Xichen). "Ailunkai nüshi yu qisixiang" [Madam Ellen Key and her ideas]. *Funü zazhi* [The ladies' journal] 7, no. 2 (1921): 21–27.

———. "Dao funü jiefang de tujing" [The way to women's emancipation]. *Funü zazhi* [The ladies' journal] 7, no. 1 (1921): 1–4.

———. "Funü yundong de xinqingxiang" [New tendencies of the women's movement]. *Funü zazhi* [The ladies' journal] 9, no. 1 (1923): 2–7.

———. "Guoji funü laodonghui yu Zhongguo Funü" [The international women's labor conference and Chinese women]. *Funü zazhi* [The ladies' journal] 7, no. 11 (1921): 1–5.

———. "Jindai sixiangjia de xingyuguan yu lian'aiguan" [An introduction to modern thinkers' concepts of sexuality and love]. *Funü zazhi* [The ladies' journal] 6, no. 10 (1920): 1–8.

———. "Zuijin shiniannei funüjie de huigu" [A review of women in the past ten years]. *Funü zazhi* [The ladies' journal] 10, no. 1 (1924): 16–22.

Shang Yi. "Funü yundong yu xinshehui de jianshe" [The women's movement and the construction of a new society]. *Funü zazhi* [The ladies' journal] 9, no. 1 (1923): 30–32.

Shanghai wenshi yanjiuguan guanyuan zhuanlue [Biographies and autobiographies of members of the Shanghai Wenshiguan]. Vols. 1–4. Shanghai: Shanghai Wenshiguan, 1990–1993.

Shanghai Women's Federation. *Shanghai funü yundong shi* [A history of the Shanghai women's movement]. Shanghai: Shanghai renmin chubanshe, 1990.

Shanxi Women's Federation. *Makesizhuyi funüguan gailun* [An introduction to the Marxist theory of women]. Beijing: Zhongguo funü chubanshe, 1991.

Shen Zhi. *Funü jiefangshi wenda* [Questions and answers on the history of women's liberation]. Hangzhou: Zhejiang renmin chubanshe, 1986.

———. "Xinhai geming qianhou de nüzi baokan" [Women's newspapers and periodicals before and during the Xinhai Revolution]. Paper presented at the conference on the Seventieth Anniversary of the Xinhai Revolution, Wuhan, 1981.

Shibao, October 14, 1919.

Shu Wu, ed. *Nüxing de faxian* [The discovery of women]. Beijing: Wenhua yishu chubanshe, 1990.

Su Ping. *Cai Chang zhuan* [The biography of Cai Chang]. Beijing: Zhongguo funü chubanshe, 1990.

Su Su. *Qianshi jinsheng* [The previous generation and life today]. Shanghai: Yuandong chubanshe, 1996.

"Suipei congling" [Miscellaneous news]. *Funü zazhi* [The ladies' journal] 6, no. 1 (1920): 4.

Sun Xiyu. "Nüxuesheng zhi zeren" [The duties of female students]. *Funü zazhi* [The ladies' journal] 4, no. 11 (1918): 3–4.

Tang Baolin and Lin Maoshen. *Chen Duxiu nianpu* [A chronicle of Chen Duxiu's life]. Shanghai: Shanghai renmin chubanshe, 1988.

Tang Jinggao. "Wosuo xiwangyu nüqingnian" [What I expect of young women]. *Funü zazhi* [The ladies' journal] 8, no. 2 (1922): 13–15.

Tang Si (Lu Xun). "Suiganlu sishi" [Informal essay, no. 40]. *Xin qingnian* [New youth] 6, no. 1 (1919). In *Wusi shiqi funü wenti wenxuan* [Selected articles on women's problems in the May Fourth period], ed. All-China Women's Federation, 200–201. Beijing: Zhongguo funü chubanshe, 1981.

———. "Wozhi jielieguan" [My views on *jielie*]. *Xin qingnian* [New youth] 5, no. 2 (1918). In *Wusi shiqi funü wenti wenxuan* [Selected articles on women's problems in the May Fourth period], ed. All-China Women's Federation, 115–123. Beijing: Zhongguo funü chubanshe, 1981.

Tao Lügong. "Nüzi wenti" [The woman problem]. *Xin qingnian* [New youth] 4, no. 1 (1918): 14–19.

Tian Han. "Disi jieji furen yundong" [The "number four class" women's movement]. *Shaonian Zhongguo* [The young China] 1, no. 4 (1919). In *Wusi shiqi funü wenti wenxuan* [Selected articles on women's problems in the May Fourth period], ed. All-China Women's Federation, 32–34. Beijing: Zhongguo funü chubanshe, 1981.

Tianjin Women's Federation. *Deng Yingchao yu Tianjin zaoqi funü yundong* [Deng Yingchao and the early women's movement in Tianjin]. Beijing: Zhongguo funü chubanshe, 1987.

Wang Chaozhu. *Gongchen yu zuiren* [The hero and criminal]. Shenzhen: Haitian Press, 1993.

Wang Hui. "Zhongguo de wusi jiyi" [China's May Fourth memory]. *Zhishi Fenzi* [The Chinese intellectual] (spring 1994): 42–56.

Wang Jiajian. "Minchu de nüzi canzheng yundong" [The women's suffrage movement in the early republic]. In *Zhongguo funüshi lunwenji* [Collection of essays on Chinese women's history], ed. Li Yu-ning and Zhang Yufa, vol. 2: 577–608. Taibei: Taiwan Commercial Press, 1988.

Wang Pingling. "Xinfunü de renge wenti" [The new women's problem of personhood]. *Funü zazhi* [The ladies' journal] 7, no. 10 (1921): 10–14.

Wang Shilun. "Qiu Jin chusheng niandai" [The year of Qiu Jin's birth]. *Lishi yanjiu* [Historical studies] 12 (1979): 64–65.

Wang Yiwei. *Wo yu Nüsheng* [*The Women's Voice* and I]. Shanghai: Daqian Shijie, 1987.

Wang Zheng. "'Nüxing yishi, shehui xingbie yishi bianyi" [An analysis of "female consciousness" and "gender consciousness"]. *Funü yanjiu luncong* [Collection of women's studies], no. 1 (1977): 14–20.

———. "Pingjie Ke Linqing zhu *Cong shehui xingbie jiaodu kan Zhongguo geming*" [A review of *Engendering the Chinese Revolution*]. *Jindai Zhongguo funüshi yanjiu* [Research on women in modern Chinese history], no. 4 (August 1996): 337–349.

Wang Zhuomin. "Lun wuguo daxue shangbuyi nannü tongxue" [On the inappropriateness of coeducation in China]. *Funü zazhi* [The ladies' journal] 4, no. 5 (1918): 1–8.

Wei Chuan. "Duiyu funüjie de xiwang" [Expectations of women]. *Funü zazhi* [The ladies' journal] 10, no. 1 (1924): 73–77.

Wu Yu. "Nüquan pingyi" [On women's rights]. In *Wusi shiqi funü wenti wenxuan* [Selected articles on women's problems in the May Fourth period], ed. All-China Women's Federation, 8–14. Beijing: Zhongguo funü chubanshe, 1981.

Wuhan Women's Federation. *Wuhan funü yundong dashiji* [A record of great events in the Wuhan women's movement]. Wuhan: Wuhan Women's Federation, 1981.

Xi Shen (Wang Yunzhang). "Tongxing wenda" [Correspondence with readers]. *Funü zazhi* [The ladies' journal] 3, no. 7 (1917): 14–17.

Xiang Jingyu. "Jinhou Zhongguo funü de guomin geming yundong" [The future Chinese women's national revolution movement]. *Funü zazhi* [The ladies' journal] 10, no. 1 (1924): 28–32.

———. "Nüguomin dahui de sanda yiyi" [Three significances of the assembly of women citizens]. In *Zhongguo funü yundong lishi ziliao* [Historical source materials of the Chinese women's movement], ed. All-China Women's Federation, 442–444. Beijing: Renmin chubanshe, 1986.

———. "Zhongguo zuijin funü yundong" [The recent Chinese women's movement]. 1923. In *Zhongguo funü yundong lishi ziliao* [Historical source materials of the Chinese women's movement], ed. All-China Women's Federation, 86–93. Beijing: Renmin chubanshe, 1986.

Xie Changfa. "Qingmo de liuri nüxuesheng jiqi huodong yu yingxiang" [Late Qing women students in Japan and their activities and influence]. *Jindai Zhongguo funüshi yanjiu* [Research on women in modern Chinese history], no. 4 (August 1996): 63–86.

Xie Dexian. *Zhou Jianren zhuan* [A biography of Zhou Jianren]. Chongqing: Chongqing chubanshe, 1991.

Xie Yuanding. "Cu funü chedi de juewu" [Stimulating women's thorough awakening]. *Funü zazhi* [The ladies' journal] 10, no. 1 (1924): 70–73.

Xin Zhu. "Wosuo xiwangyu nanzizhe" [My hopes for men]. *Funü zazhi* [The ladies' journal] 10, no. 10 (1924): 1518–1520.

Xiong Yuezhi. *Zhongguo jindai minzhu sixiangshi* [An intellectual history of democracy in modern China]. Shanghai: Shanghai renmin chubanshe, 1986.

Xu Shiheng. "Jinhou funü yingyou de jingshen" [The spirit women should have from now on]. *Funü zazhi* [The ladies' journal] 6, no. 8 (1920): 12–18.

Xu Yanzhi. "Beijing daxue nannü gongxiao ji" [A record of coeducation at Beijing University]. *Shaonian Shijie* 1, no. 7 (1920). In *Wusi shiqi funü wenti wenxuan* [Selected articles on women's problems in the May Fourth period], ed. All-China Women's Federation, 262–275. Beijing: Zhongguo funü chubanshe, 1981.

———. "Nannü jiaoji wenti zagan" [Thoughts on socializing between men and women]. *Chenbao*, May 4, 1919. In *Wusi shiqi funü wenti wenxuan* [Selected articles on women's problems in the May Fourth period], ed. All-China Women's Federation, 176–180. Beijing: Zhongguo funü chubanshe, 1981.

Xue Weiwei, ed. *Zhongguo funü mingren lu* [Chinese women's who's who]. Xi'an: Shaanxi renmin chubanshe, 1988.

Yan Shi. "Funü tuanti yundongli de weiruo" [The weakness of women's organized movement]. *Funü zazhi* [The ladies' journal] 9, no. 6 (1923): 17–18.

———. "Zuijin de nüquan yundong" [The recent feminist movement]. *Funü zazhi* [The ladies' journal] 8, no. 10 (1920): 61–63.

Yanbing (Shen Yanbing). "Du *Shaonian Zhongguo funühao*" [Reading *The*

Young China issue on women]. *Funü zazhi* [The ladies' journal] 6, no. 1 (1920): 1–4.

———. "Funü yundong de yiyi he yaoqiu" [The definition and demands of the women's movement]. *Funü zazhi* [The ladies' journal] 6, no. 8 (1920): 1–6.

———. "Women gaizenyang yubeile qutan funü jiefang wenti" [How should we be prepared to talk about women's emancipation?]. *Funü zazhi* [The ladies' journal] 6, no. 3 (1920): 1–5.

Yang Zhihua. *Funü yundong gailun* [A brief history of the women's movement]. Shanghai: Dongya tushuguan, 1927.

———. "Zhongguo funü yundong zuiyan" [Comments on the Chinese women's movement]. In *Zhongguo funü yundong lishi ziliao* [Historical source materials of the Chinese women's movement], ed. All-China Women's Federation, 555–561. Beijing: Renmin chubanshe, 1986.

Ye Shaojun. "Nüzi renge wenti" [On the problem of women's personhood]. *Xinchao* [New tide] 1, no. 2 (1919). In *Wusi shiqi funü wenti wenxuan* [Selected articles on women's problems in the May Fourth period], ed. All-China Women's Federation, 124–130. Beijing: Zhongguo funü chubanshe, 1981.

Yin Tongwei. "Nibenxiao xuesheng zizhihui zhengji huiyuanqi" [A notice calling for an autonomous student union in the school]. *Funü zazhi* [The ladies' journal] 4, no. 1 (1918): 2–3.

Yishibao. August 29, 1919.

———. October 4, 1919.

Yosano Akiko. "Zhencao Lun" [On chastity]. Trans. Zhou Zuoren. *Xin qingnian* [New youth] 4, no. 5 (1918): 386–394.

Yu Tiansui. "Yuzhi nüzi jiaoyuguan" [My view on women's education]. *Funü zazhi* [The ladies' journal] 1, no. 1 (1915): 1–2.

Yun Fang. "Gaizao shidai de funü yingjuyou shemo zige?" [What qualifications should women in the age of reform have?]. *Funü zazhi* [The ladies' journal] 6, no. 6 (1920): 1–5.

Zeng Changqiu and Zhou Jianchun. "Zhongguo diyige nü Gongchandangyuan Miao Boying" [The first female communist in China: Miao Boying]. *Renmin ribao* [People's daily], June 8, 1987.

Zeng Zhizhong. *Sanren xing* [A journey of the three]. Beijing: Zhongguo qingnian chubanshe, 1990.

Zhang Dengren. "Shuo nüzijiaoyu" [On women's education]. Translation and commentary by Song Guoshu. *Funü zazhi* [The ladies' journal] 5, no. 5 (1919): 4–8.

Zhang Jinglu, ed. *Zhongguo xiandai chuban shiliao* [Historical materials on publishing in modern China]. Beijing: Zhonghua shuju, 1954.

Zhang Ruomin. "Jixianfeng de nüzi" [Pioneering women]. In *Wusi shiqi funü wenti wenxuan* [Selected articles on women's problems in the May Fourth period], ed. All-China Women's Federation, 49–58. Beijing: Zhongguo funü chubanshe, 1981.

Zhang Xichen. "Lian'ai wenti de taolun" [Discussions on the love problem].

Funü zazhi [The ladies' journal] 8 (1922), no. 9: 121–123, and no. 10: 120–121.

———. Preface to *Funü wenti shijiang* [Ten lectures on the women's problem], by Hisao Honma, trans. Zhang Xichen. Vol. 1 in *Funü wenti congshu* [The series on women's problems], ed. The Women's Studies Association. Shanghai: The Women's Studies Association, 1924.

———. "Xin xingdaode shi shemo" [What is the new sexual morality?]. *Funü zazhi* [The ladies' journal] 11, no. 1 (1925): 2–7.

———, ed. *Xin xingdaode taolun ji* [A collection of debate on the new sexual morality]. Shanghai: Kaiming shudian, 1929.

———. "Zuijin funü yundong de shibai he jinhou yingqu de fangzhen" [The recent failure of the women's movement and policies we should adopt in the future]. *Funü zazhi* [The ladies' journal] 11, no. 7 (1925): 1120–1124.

Zhang Youluan. "Jinhou gengyao qieshixie" [Be more practical]. *Funü zazhi* [The ladies' journal] 8, no. 2 (1922): 28–29.

"Zhongguo Funü Xiehui chengli jiyao" [On the founding of the Chinese Women's Association]. In *Zhongguo funü yundong lishi ziliao* [Historical source materials of the Chinese women's movement], ed. All-China Women's Federation, 387–389. Beijing: Renmin chubanshe, 1986.

Zhongguo funü zazhishe. *Lieshi Xiang Jingyu* [Martyr Xiang Jingyu]. Beijing: Zhongguo funü zazhishe, 1958.

"Zhongguo Gongchandang disanci quanguo daibiao dahui guanyu funü yundong jueyi an" [The resolution on the women's movement by the Third National Congress of the CCP]. In *Zhongguo funü yundong lishi ziliao* [Historical source materials of the Chinese women's movement], ed. All-China Women's Federation, 68–69. Beijing: Renmin chubanshe, 1986.

"Zhongguo Gongchandang disanci zhongyang kuoda zhixing weiyuanhui guanyu funü yundong jueyi an" [The resolution on the women's movement by the third executive committee meeting of the central committee of the CCP]. In *Zhongguo funü yundong lishi ziliao* [Historical source materials of the Chinese women's movement], ed. All-China Women's Federation, 475–477. Beijing: Renmin chubanshe, 1986.

"Zhongguo Gongchandang disici quanguo daibiao dahui duiyu funü yundong zhi jueyi an" [The resolution on the women's movement by the Fourth National Congress of the CCP]. In *Zhongguo funü yundong lishi ziliao* [Historical source materials of the Chinese women's movement], ed. All-China Women's Federation, 279–281. Beijing: Renmin chubanshe, 1986.

"Zhongguo Gongchandang funübu guanyu Zhongguo funü yundong de baogao" [A report on the Chinese women's movement by the Women's Bureau of the CCP]. In *Zhongguo funü yundong lishi ziliao* [Historical source materials of the Chinese women's movement], ed. All-China Women's Federation, 168–186. Beijing: Renmin chubanshe, 1986.

"Zhongguo Guomindang dierci quanguo daibiao dahui funü yundong jueyi an" [The resolution on the women's movement by the Second National Congress of the GMD]. In *Zhongguo funü yundong lishi ziliao* [Historical source materials of the Chinese women's movement], ed. All-China Women's Federation, 505–507. Beijing: Renmin chubanshe, 1986.

Zhongguo renmin daxue shubao ziliao zhongxin. *Wenyi lilun* [Literary theories], nos. 7–12 (July–December 1995).

Zhou Jianren. "Erchong daode" [The double standard of morality]. *Xinnüxing* [The new woman] 1, no. 1 (1926): 1–11.

———. "Xingdaode zhi kexue de biaozhun" [The scientific standard of sexual morality]. *Funü zazhi* [The ladies' journal] 11, no. 1 (1925): 8–12.

Zhou Zuoren. "Beigouyan tongxin" [A correspondence from Beigouyan]. In *Nüxing de faxian* [The discovery of women], ed. Shu Wu, 11–16. Beijing: Wenhua yishu chubanshe, 1990.

———. "Ren de wenxue" [Human literature]. 1918. In *Nüxing de faxian* [The discovery of women], ed. Shu Wu, 3–10. Beijing: Wenhua yishu chubanshe, 1990.

———. *Zhitang huixianglu* [A memoir of Zhou Zuoren]. Hong Kong: Sanyu tushu wenju gongsi, 1974.

Zhu-Hu Binxia. "Meiguo jiating" [The American family]. *Funü zazhi* [The ladies' journal] 2, no. 2 (1916): 1–8.

WORKS IN ENGLISH

Anderson, Kathryn, Susan Armitage, Dana Jack, and Judith Wittner. "Beginning Where We Are: Feminist Methodology in Oral History." In *Feminist Research Methods*, ed. Joyce McCarl Nielsen, 94–112. Boulder: Westview Press, 1990.

Andors, Phyllis. *The Unfinished Liberation of Chinese Women*. Bloomington: Indiana University Press, 1983.

Barlow, Tani E. "Theorizing Woman: Funü, Guojia, Jiating." In *Body, Subject, and Power in China*, ed. Angela Zito and Tani E. Barlow, 253–289. Chicago: University of Chicago Press, 1994.

Bellamy, Edward. *Looking Backward*. New York: Penguin Books, 1986.

Bergere, Marie-Claire. *The Golden Age of the Chinese Bourgeoisie, 1911–1937*. Cambridge: Harvard University Press, 1989.

Butler, Judith. "Contingent Foundations." In *Feminists Theorize the Political*, ed. Judith Butler and Joan W. Scott. New York: Routledge, 1992.

Chan, Ching-kiu Stephen. "The Language of Despair: Ideological Representations of the 'New Women' by May Fourth Writers." *Modern Chinese Literature* 4, nos. 1 and 2 (1988): 19–38.

Chang, Pang-Wei Natasha. *Bound Feet and Western Dress*. New York: Anchor Books-Doubleday, 1996.

Chao, Buwei Yang. *Autobiography of a Chinese Woman*. New York: John Day Company, 1947.

Chow, Tse-tsung. *The May Fourth Movement: Intellectual Revolution in Modern China*. Stanford: Stanford University Press, 1960.

Cott, Nancy F. *The Bonds of Womanhood*. New Haven: Yale University Press, 1977.

——. *The Grounding of Modern Feminism*. New Haven: Yale University Press, 1987.

Croll, Elisabeth. *Feminism and Socialism in China*. London: Routledge and Kegan Paul, 1978.

Diamond, Irene, and Lee Quinby, eds. *Feminism and Foucault: Reflections on Resistance*. Boston: Northeastern University Press, 1988.

Duara, Prasenjit. *Rescuing History from the Nation: Questioning Narratives of Modern China*. Chicago: University of Chicago Press, 1995.

Fei, Xiaotong. *From the Soil: The Foundations of Chinese Society*. Trans. Gary G. Hamilton and Wang Zheng. Berkeley: University of California Press, 1992.

Feigon, Lee. *Chen Duxiu, Founder of the Chinese Communist Party*. Princeton: Princeton University Press, 1983.

Flax, Jane. *disputed subjects: essays on psychoanalysis, politics, and philosophy*. New York: Routledge, 1993.

Foucault, Michel. *The Archaeology of Knowledge*. New York: Pantheon Books, 1972.

Furth, Charlott, ed. *The Limits of Change: Essays on Conservative Alternatives in Republic China*. Cambridge: Harvard University Press, 1976.

Gilmartin, Christina Kelley. *Engendering the Chinese Revolution: Radical Women, Communist Politics, and Mass Movements in the 1920s*. Berkeley: University of California Press, 1995.

——. "Gender in the Formation of a Communist Body Politic." *Modern China* 19, no. 3 (1993): 299–329.

——. "Gender, Political Culture, and Women's Mobilization in the Chinese Nationalist Revolution, 1924–1927." In *Engendering China*, ed. Christina K. Gilmartin, Gail Hershatter, Lisa Rofel, and Tyrene White, 195–225. Cambridge: Harvard University Press, 1994.

Gluck, Sherna Berger, and Daphne Patai, eds. *Women's Words: The Feminist Practice of Oral History*. New York: Routledge, 1991.

Goodman, Dena. "Women and the Enlightenment." In *Becoming Visible: Women in European History*, ed. Renete Bridenthal, Susan Mosher Stuard, and Merry E. Wiesner. Boston: Houghton Mifflin Company, 1998.

Grieder, Jerome B. *Hu Shih and the Chinese Renaissance*. Cambridge: Harvard University Press, 1970.

Ho, Ping-ti. *The Ladder of Success in Imperial China*. New York: John Wiley and Sons, 1964

Hsieh, Ping-ying. *Autobiography of a Chinese Girl*. Boston: Pandora Press, 1986.

——. *Letters of a Chinese Amazon: And War-Time Essays*. Shanghai: Commercial Press, 1930.

Ip, Hung-yok. "More Than Ideological Beings." Ph.D. diss., University of California, Davis, 1994.

Irigaray, Luce. *This Sex Which Is Not One*. Ithaca: Cornell University Press, 1985.

Johnson, Kay Ann. *Women, the Family, and Peasant Revolution in China.* Chicago: University of Chicago Press, 1983.

Judge, Joan. "Knowledge for the Nation or of the Nation: Meiji Japan and the Changing Meaning of Female Literacy in the Late Qing." Paper delivered at a workshop on "New Perspectives on the Qing Dynasty" held at The Center for Chinese Studies, University of California, Los Angeles, October 4, 1997.

Kerber, Linda K., Alice Kessler-Harris, and Kathryn Kish Sklar, eds. *U.S. History as Women's History: New Feminist Essays.* Chapel Hill: University of North Carolina Press, 1995.

Kingston, Maxine Hong. *Woman Warrior.* New York: Knopf, 1976.

Kristeva, Julia. "Women's Time." *Signs* 7, no. 1 (summer 1981): 13–35.

Library of Congress. *Eminent Chinese of the Ch'ing Period (1644–1912).* Washington: GPO, 1943.

Liu, Lydia H. *Translingual Practice: Literature, National Culture, and Translated Modernity—China, 1900–1937.* Stanford: Stanford University Press, 1995.

Lo, Jung-pang. *Kang You-wei: A Biography and a Symposium.* Tucson: University of Arizona Press, 1967.

Mann, Susan. *Precious Records: Women in China's Long Eighteenth Century.* Stanford: Stanford University Press, 1997.

Mote, Frederick W. *Intellectual Foundations of China.* New York: McGraw-Hill, 1989.

Nivard, Jacqueline. "Women and the Women's Press." *Republican China* 10, no. 1b (November 1984): 37–55.

Offen, Karen. *European Feminism(s): 1700–1950.* Stanford: Stanford University Press, forthcoming.

Rabinow, Paul, ed. *The Foucault Reader.* New York: Pantheon Books, 1984.

Rosenberg, Rosalind. *Beyond Separate Spheres: Intellectual Roots of Modern Feminism.* New Haven: Yale University Press, 1982.

Russell, Dora. *The Tamarisk Tree: My Quest for Liberty and Love.* London: Elek-Pemberton, 1975.

Schreiber, Adele, and Margaret Mathieson. *Journey Towards Freedom: Written for the Golden Jubilee of the International Alliance of Women.* Copenhagen: International Alliance of Women, 1955.

Schwarcz, Vera. *The Chinese Enlightenment.* Berkeley: University of California Press, 1986.

———. *Time for Telling Truth Is Running Out.* New Haven: Yale University Press, 1992.

Schwartz, Benjamin. *Chinese Communism and the Rise of Mao.* Cambridge: Harvard University Press, 1951.

Scott, Joan W. "'Experience.'" In *Feminists Theorize the Political,* ed. Judith Butler and Joan W. Scott, 22–40. New York: Routledge, 1992.

Sievers, Sharon L. *Flowers in Salt: The Beginnings of Feminist Consciousness in Modern Japan.* Stanford: Stanford University Press, 1983.

Soloman, Barbara Miller. *In the Company of Educated Women*. New Haven: Yale University Press, 1985.

Spence, Jonathan D. *The Search for Modern China*. New York: W. W. Norton, 1990.

Stacey, Judith. *Patriarchy and Socialist Revolution in China*. Berkeley: University of California Press, 1983.

Stewart, Abigail J., and Joseph M. Healy, Jr., "Linking Individual Development and Social Changes." *American Psychologist* 44, no. 1 (1989): 30–42.

Tilly, Charles. *Big Structures, Large Processes, Huge Comparisons*. New York: Russell Sage Foundation, 1984.

Wang, Zheng. "Research on Women in Contemporary China." In *A Selected Guide to Women's Studies in China*, ed. Gail Hershatter, Emily Honig, Susan Mann, and Lisa Rofel, 1–42. Berkeley: Center for Chinese Studies, 1998.

Weedon, Chris. *Feminist Practice and Poststructuralist Theory*. Oxford: Blackwell Publishers, 1987.

Weisberg, D. Kelley. "Barred from the Bar: Women and Legal Education in the United States, 1870–1890." *Journal of Legal Education* 38 (1977): 485–507.

Witke, Roxane H. "Transformation of Attitudes towards Women during the May Fourth Era." Ph.D. diss., University of California, Berkeley, 1971.

Wolf, Arthur P. "Gods, Ghosts, and Ancestors." In *Religion in Chinese Society*, ed. A. P. Arthur, 150–152. Stanford: Stanford University Press, 1974.

Woloch, Nancy. *Women and the American Experience*. New York: McGraw-Hill, 1984.

Yosano Akiko. *Tangled Hair: Love Poems of Yosano Akiko*. Trans. Dennis Maloney and Hide Oshiro. Fredonia, N.Y.: White Pine Press, 1987.

Young, Marilyn B., ed. *Women in China*. Ann Arbor: Center for Chinese Studies at the University of Michigan, 1973.

Yow, Walerie Raleigh. *Recording Oral History: A Practical Guide for Social Scientists*. Thousand Oaks, Ca.: Sage, 1994.

Yue, Ming-bao. "Gendering the Origins of Modern Chinese Fiction." In *Gender and Sexuality in Twentieth-Century Chinese Literature and Society*, ed. Tonglin Lu, 47–65. Albany: State University of New York Press, 1993.

Zarrow, Peter. *Anarchism and Chinese Political Culture*. New York: Columbia University Press, 1990.

Zhang, Enqin, ed. *Chinese Qigong*. Volume in *A Practical English-Chinese Library of Traditional Chinese Medicine*. Shanghai: Publishing House of Shanghai College of Traditional Chinese Medicine, 1990.

Zhang, Naihua. "The All-China Women's Federation, Chinese Women, and the Women's Movement: 1949–1993." Ph.D. diss., Michigan State University, 1996.

Zhang, Naihua, with Wu Xu. "Discovering the Positive within the Negative: The Women's Movement in a Changing China." In *The Challenge of Local Feminisms: Women's Movements in Global Perspective*, ed. Amrita Basu, 25–57. Boulder: Westview Press, 1995.

Index

Composition: Integrated Composition Systems
Text: 10/13 Aldus
Display: Aldus
Printing and binding: Maple-Vail Book Manufacturing Group